# Swift Programming

## THE BIG NERD RANCH GUIDE

### Matthew Mathias & John Gallagher

Big Nerd
Ranch

# Swift Programming: The Big Nerd Ranch Guide

by Matthew Mathias and John Gallagher

Big Nerd Ranch, LLC
200 Arizona Ave NE
Atlanta, GA 30307
(770) 817-6373
http://www.bignerdranch.com/
book-comments@bignerdranch.com

The 10-gallon hat with propeller logo is a trademark of Big Nerd Ranch, LLC.

Exclusive worldwide distribution of the English edition of this book by

Pearson Technology Group
800 East 96th Street
Indianapolis, IN 46240 USA
http://www.informit.com

ISBN-10  0134398017
ISBN-13  978-0134398013

First edition, first printing, December 2015

# Dedication

*For my wife, who is smart, strong, and virtuous. And for my family, who has given me every opportunity to live a good life.*

— M.M.

*For my wife and best friend; you are "s'wonderful." And for my daughters, who bring me joy every day.*

— J.G.

# Acknowledgments

We received a lot of help in writing this book. Without it, this book would not be what it is, and it may have never even happened. Thanks are due.

First, we need to say thank you to our colleagues at Big Nerd Ranch. Thank you to Aaron Hillegass for providing us with the opportunity to write this book. It has been immensely gratifying to learn and teach Swift. Big Nerd Ranch provided us with the time and space to work on this project. We hope that this book lives up to the trust and the support that we have received.

Particular thanks are also due to our colleagues in the Cocoa Pod at Big Nerd Ranch. Your careful teaching revealed many bugs in the text, and your thoughtful recommendations led to many improvements in our approach. Those of you who are not instructors helped to review the materials, vetted our approach, and provided countless suggestions that we never thought of. It is truly wonderful to have colleagues such as you. Thank you Pouria Almassi, Matt Bezark, Nate Chandler, Step Christopher, Kynerd Coleman, Matthew Compton, Joseph Dixon, Robert Edwards, Sean Farrell, Brian Hardy, Florian Harr, Tom Harrington, Bolot Kerimbaev, Christian Keur, JJ Manton, Bill Monk, Chris Morris, Adam Preble, Scott Richie, Jeremy Sherman, Steve Sparks, Rod Strougo, TJ Usiyan, Zach Waldowski, Thomas Ward, and Mike Zornek.

Our colleagues in operations and sales are instrumental. Classes would literally never be scheduled without their work. Thank you Shannon Coburn, Nicole Rej, Heather Brown, Tasha Schroader, Mat Jackson, and Chris Kirksey for all of your hard work. We cannot do what you do.

Second, we need to acknowledge the many talented folks who worked on the book with us.

Elizabeth Holaday, our editor, helped refine the book, crystallize its strengths, and diminish its weaknesses.

Simone Payment, our copy-editor, found and corrected errors and ultimately made us look smarter than we are.

Ellie Volckhausen designed our cover; that skateboard looks pretty rad.

Chris Loper designed and produced the print book and the EPUB and Kindle versions.

Finally, thank you to our students. We learned with you and for you. Teaching is part of the greatest thing that we do, and it has been a pleasure working with you. We hope that the quality of this book matches your enthusiasm and determination.

# Table of Contents

# Introduction

## Learning Swift

Apple's World Wide Developers Conference is an annual landmark event for its developer community. It is a big deal every year, but 2014 was particularly special: Apple introduced an entirely new language called Swift for the development of iOS and OS X applications.

As a new language, Swift represents a fairly dramatic shift for Mac OS X and iOS developers. More experienced iOS developers have something new to learn, and new developers cannot rely on a venerable community for tried and true answers and patterns. Naturally, this shift creates some uncertainty.

But this is also an exciting time to be a Mac OS X and iOS developer. There is a lot to learn in a new language, and this is especially true for Swift. The language has evolved quite a bit since its beta release in the summer of 2014, and it continues to evolve.

We are all at the forefront of this language's development. As new features are added to Swift, its users can collaboratively determine its best practices. You can directly contribute to this conversation, and your work with this book will start you on your way to becoming a contributing member of the Swift community.

## Whither Objective-C?

So, what about Objective-C, Apple's previous *lingua franca* for its platforms? Do you still need to know that language? For the time being, we think that answer is an unequivocal "Yes." Apple's Cocoa library, which you will use extensively, is written in Objective-C, so debugging will be easier if you understand that language. Moreover, most learning materials and existing Mac and iOS apps are written in Objective-C. Indeed, Apple has made it easy, and sometimes preferable, to mix and match Objective-C with Swift in the same project. As an iOS or Mac developer, you are bound to encounter Objective-C, so it makes sense to be familiar with the language.

But do you need to know Objective-C to learn Swift? Not at all. Swift coexists and interoperates with Objective-C, but it is its own language. If you do not know Objective-C, it will not hinder you in learning Swift. (We will only use Objective-C directly in one chapter toward the end of this book, and even then it will not be important for you to understand the language.)

## Prerequisites

We have written this book for all types of iOS and Mac OS X developers, from platform experts to first-timers. For readers just starting software development, we will highlight and implement best practices for Swift and programming in general. Our strategy is to teach you the fundamentals of programming while learning Swift. For more experienced developers, we believe this book will serve as a helpful introduction to your platform's new language. So while having some development experience will be helpful, we do not believe that it is necessary in order to have a good experience with this book.

We have also written this book with numerous examples so that you can refer to it in the future. Instead of focusing on abstract concepts and theory, we have written in favor of the practical. Our approach favors using concrete examples to unpack the more difficult ideas and also to expose the best practices that make code more fun to write, more readable, and easier to maintain.

# How This Book Is Organized

This book is organized in six parts. Each is designed to accomplish a specific set of goals that build on each other. By the end of the book, you will have built your knowledge of Swift from that of a beginner to a more advanced developer.

| | |
|---|---|
| *Getting Started* | This part of the book focuses on the tools that you will need to write Swift code and introduces Swift's syntax. |
| *The Basics* | *The Basics* introduces the fundamental data types that you will use every day as a Swift developer. This part of the book also covers Swift's *control flow* features that will help you to control the order in which your code executes. |
| *Collections and Functions* | You will often want to gather related data in your application. Once you do, you will want to operate on that data. Swift offers *collections* and *functions* to help with these tasks. |
| *Enumerations, Structures, and Classes* | This part of the book covers how you will model your data in your own development. We cover the differences between these types and make some recommendations on when to use each. |
| *Advanced Swift* | As a modern language, Swift provides a number of more advanced features that enable you to write elegant, readable, and effective code. This part of the book discusses how to use these elements of Swift to write idiomatic code that will set you apart from more casual Swift developers. |
| *Event-Driven Applications* | This part of the book walks you through writing your first Mac OS X and iOS applications. For readers working with older Mac OS X or iOS applications, we conclude this part of the book by discussing how to interoperate between Objective-C and Swift. |

# How to Use This Book

Programming can be tough, and this book is here to make it easier. How can we help you with that? Follow these steps:

- Read the book. Really! Do not just browse it nightly before going to bed.

- Type out the examples as you read along. Part of learning is muscle memory. If your fingers know where to go and what to type without too much thought on your part, then you are on your way to becoming a more effective developer.

- Make mistakes! In our experience, the best way to learn how things work is to first figure out what makes them not work. Break our code examples and then make them work again.

- Experiment as your imagination sees fit. Whether that means tinkering with the code you find in the book or going off in your own direction, the sooner you start solving your own problems with Swift, the faster you will become a better developer.

- Do the challenges we have included in most chapters. As we mentioned, it is important to begin solving problems with Swift as soon as possible. Doing so will help you to start thinking like a developer.

More experienced developers may not need to go through some of the earlier parts of the book. *Getting Started* and *The Basics* may be very familiar to some developers.

One caveat: In *The Basics*, do not skip the chapter on Optionals as they are at the heart of Swift, and in many ways they define what is unique about the language.

Subsequent chapters like Arrays, Dictionaries, Functions, Enumerations, and Structs and Classes may seem like they will not present anything new to the practiced developer, but we feel that Swift's approach to these topics is unique enough that every reader should at least skim these chapters.

Last, remember that learning new things takes time. Dedicate some time to going through this book when you are able to avoid distractions. You will get more out of the text if you can.

# Challenges

Many of the chapters conclude with an exercise for you to work through on your own. These are an excellent opportunity for you to challenge yourself. In our experience, truly deep learning is accomplished when you solve problems in your own way.

# For the More Curious

Relatedly, we include sections entitled "For the More Curious" at the end of many chapters. These sections address questions that may have occurred to the curious reader working through the chapter. Sometimes, we discuss how a given language feature's underlying mechanics work, or we may explore a programming concept not quite related to the heart of the chapter.

# Typographical Conventions

You will be writing a lot of code as you work through this book. To make things easier, we use a couple of conventions to identify what text is old, what should be added, and what should be removed. For example, in the function implementation below, you are deleting the text `print("Hello")` and adding `print("Goodbye")`.

```
func talkToMe() {
    print("Hello")
    print("Goodbye")
}
```

## Necessary Hardware and Software

To build and run the applications in this book, you will need a Mac running OS X Yosemite (10.10) or newer. You will also need to install Xcode, Apple's *integrated development environment* (IDE), which is available on the App Store. Xcode includes the Swift compiler as well as other development tools you will use throughout the book.

Swift is still under rapid development. This book is written for Swift 2.0 and Xcode 7.0. Many of the examples will not work as written if you are using an older version of Xcode. If you are using a newer version of Xcode, it is possible there may have been changes in the language that will cause some examples to fail.

As this book is moving into the printing process, Xcode 7.1 Beta is available. The code samples in the book work with the latest beta version we have been able to use. If future versions of Xcode do cause problems, take heart – the vast majority of what you learn will continue to be applicable to future versions of Swift even though there may be changes in syntax or names. You can also check out our forums at http://forums.bignerdranch.com for help.

## Before We Begin

We hope to show you how much fun it can be to make applications for the Apple ecosystem. While writing code can be extremely frustrating, it can also be gratifying. There is something magical and exhilarating about solving a problem, not to mention the special joy that comes out of making an app that helps people and brings them happiness.

The best way to improve at anything is with practice. If you want to be a developer, then let's get started! If you find that you do not think you are very good at it, who cares? Keep at it and we are sure that you will surprise yourself. Your next steps lie ahead. Onward!

# Part I
## Getting Started

This part of the book introduces the toolchain for writing Swift code. It introduces Xcode as the Swift developer's primary development tool and uses playgrounds to provide a lightweight environment for trying out code. These initial chapters will also help you become familiar with some of Swift's most basic concepts, like constants and variables, which will set the stage for the rest of the book and a deeper understanding of the language.

# 1

# Getting Started

In this chapter, you will get your environment set up and take a small tour of some of the tools you will use every day as an iOS and Mac developer. Additionally, you will get your hands dirty with some code to get better acquainted with Swift and Xcode.

## Getting Started with Xcode

If you have not already done so, download and install Xcode, available in the App Store. Make sure to download Xcode 7 or higher.

Once you have Xcode installed, launch it. The welcome screen gives you several options, including Get started with a playground and Create a new Xcode project (Figure 1.1).

Figure 1.1 Starting with a playground

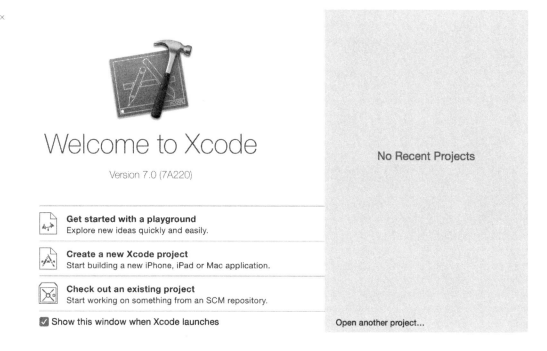

Playgrounds are a new feature released in Xcode 6. They are an interactive environment for rapidly developing and evaluating Swift code. A playground does not require that you compile and run a complete project. Instead, playgrounds evaluate your Swift code on the fly, so they are ideal for testing and experimenting with the Swift language in a lightweight environment. You will be using playgrounds frequently throughout this book to get quick feedback on your Swift code.

In addition to playgrounds, you will create native command-line tools. Why not just use playgrounds? You would miss out on a lot of Xcode's features and would not get as much exposure to the IDE. You will be spending a lot of time in Xcode, and it is good to get comfortable with it as soon as possible.

From the welcome screen, select Get started with a playground.

Next, name your playground `MyPlayground`. When asked to choose a platform (OS X or iOS), select OS X, even if you are an iOS developer (Figure 1.2). The Swift features you will be covering are common to both platforms. Click Next.

## Figure 1.2  Naming a playground

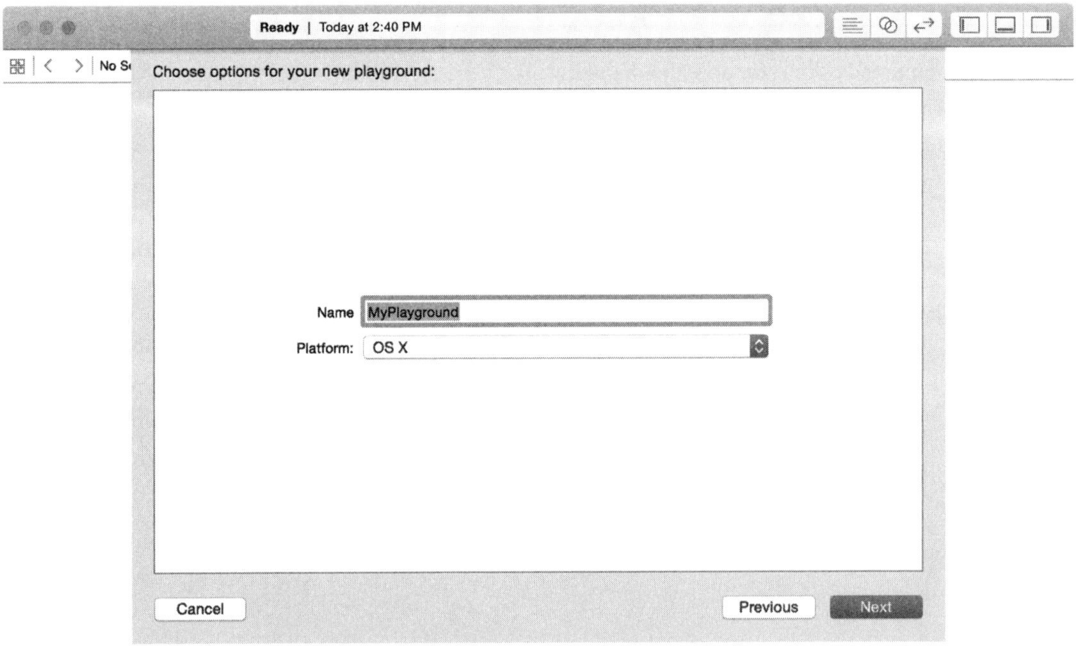

Finally, you are prompted to save your playground. As you work through this book, it is a good idea to put all of your work in one folder. Choose a location that works for you and click Create (Figure 1.3).

Figure 1.3  Saving a playground

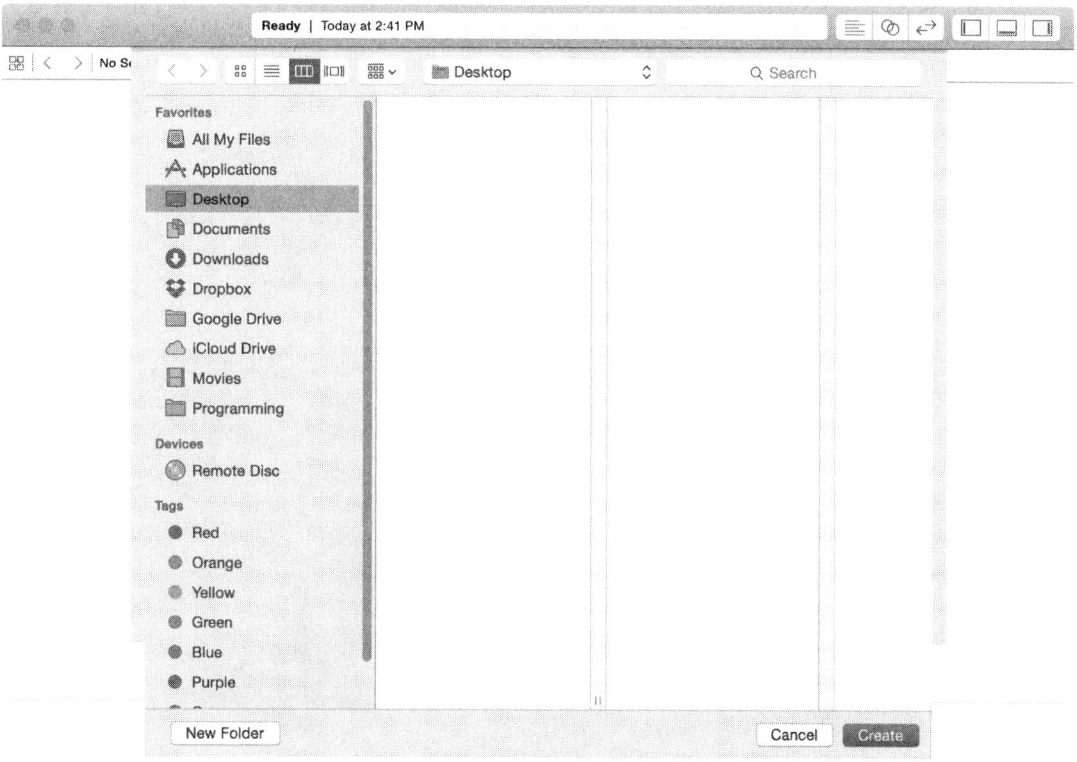

# Playing in a Playground

As you can see in Figure 1.4, a Swift playground opens with two sections. On the left, you have the Swift code editor. On the right, you have the results sidebar. The code in the editor is evaluated and run, if possible, every time the source changes. The results of the code are displayed in the results sidebar.

### Figure 1.4  Your new playground

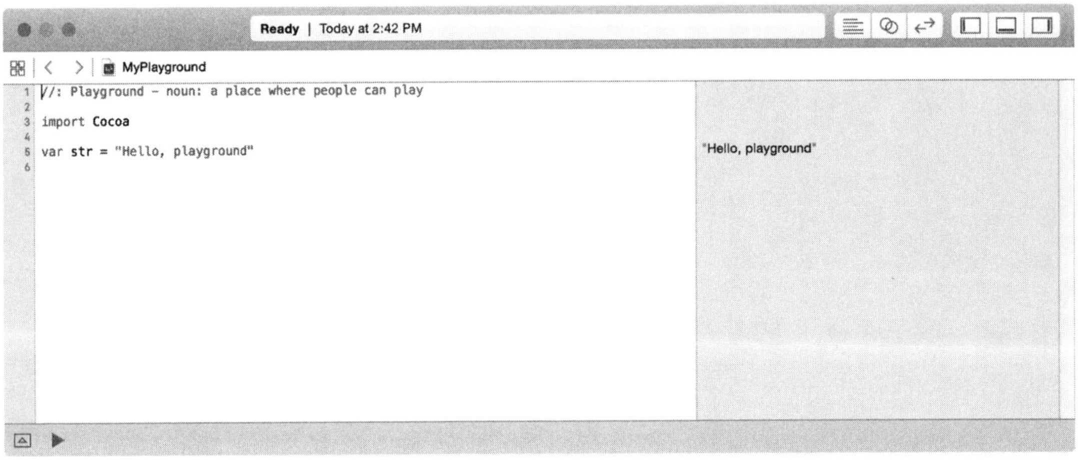

Let's take a look at your new playground. Notice that the first line of text is green and that it begins with two forward slashes: `//`. The slashes signify to the compiler that the line is a *comment*, and Xcode shows comments in green.

Developers use comments as inline documentation or for notes to help keep track of what happens where. Delete the forward slashes. The compiler will issue an error complaining that it cannot parse the expression. Add the slashes back by using the handy keyboard shortcut Command-/.

Just below the comment, the playground imports the Cocoa framework. This import statement means that your playground has complete access to all of the application programming interfaces (APIs) in the Cocoa framework. (An API is similar to a prescription – or set of definitions – for how a program can be written.)

Below the import statement is a line that reads: `var str = "Hello, playground"`. The text in quotes is copied on the right, in the results sidebar: "Hello, playground." Let's take a closer look at that line of code.

On the lefthand side of the equals sign, you have the text `var str`. Swift's keyword `var` is used to declare a variable. This is an important concept that you will see in greater detail in the next chapter. For now, a variable represents some value that you expect to change or vary.

On the righthand side of the equality, you have `"Hello, playground"`. In Swift, the quotation marks indicate a **String**, an ordered collection of characters. The template named this new variable `str`, but variables can be named almost anything. (There are limitations, of course. Try to change the name `str` to be `var`. What happens? Why do you think you cannot name your variable `var`? Be sure to change the name back to `str` before moving on.)

Now you can understand the text printed on the right in the results sidebar: it is the string value assigned to the variable `str`.

# Varying Variables and Printing to the Console

**String** is a *type*, and we say that the `str` variable is "an instance of the **String** type." Types describe a particular structure for representing data. Swift has many types, which you will meet throughout this book. Each type has specific abilities – what the type can do with that data – and limitations – what it cannot do with the data. For example, the `String` type is designed to work with an ordered collection of characters and defines a number of functions to work with that ordered collection of characters.

Recall that `str` is a *variable*. That means you can change the variable's value. Let's append an exclamation point to the end of the string to make it a well-punctuated sentence. (Whenever new code is added in this book, it will be shown in bold. Deletions will be struck through.)

## Listing 1.1  Proper punctuation

```
import Cocoa

var str = "Hello, playground"

str += "!"
```

To add the exclamation point, you are using the += *addition assignment operator*. The addition assignment operator combines the addition (+) and assignment (=) operations in a single operator. (You will see more details on operators in Chapter 3.)

Did you notice anything in the results sidebar on the right? You should see a new line of results representing `str`'s new value, complete with exclamation point (Figure 1.5).

## Figure 1.5  Varying `str`

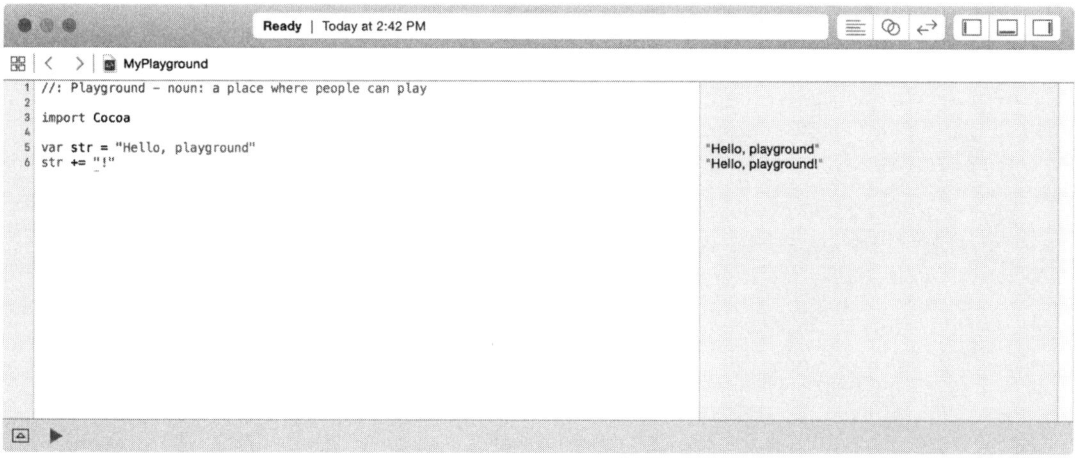

Next, add some code to print the value held by the variable str to the *console*. In Xcode, the console displays text messages that you create and want to log as things occur in your program. Xcode also uses the console to display warnings and errors as they occur.

To print to the console, you are going to use the function **print()**. *Functions* are groupings of related code that send instructions to the computer to complete a specific task. **print()** is a function used to print a value to the console followed by a line break. Unlike playgrounds, Xcode projects do not have a results sidebar, so you will use the **print()** function frequently when you are writing fully featured apps. The console is useful for checking the current value of some variable of interest.

## Listing 1.2  Printing to the console

```
import Cocoa

var str = "Hello, playground"

str += "!"
print(str)
```

Currently, the playground is not showing your console. You need to open the *Debug Area* to see it. Click on View → Debug Area → Show Debug Area (Figure 1.6). (Notice the keyboard shortcut next to this last step? You can also type Shift-Command-Y on your keyboard to open the Debug Area.)

## Figure 1.6  Showing the Debug Area

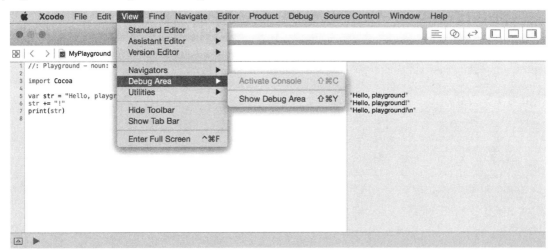

Now that you have your Debug Area open, you should see something like Figure 1.7.

## Figure 1.7  Your first Swift code

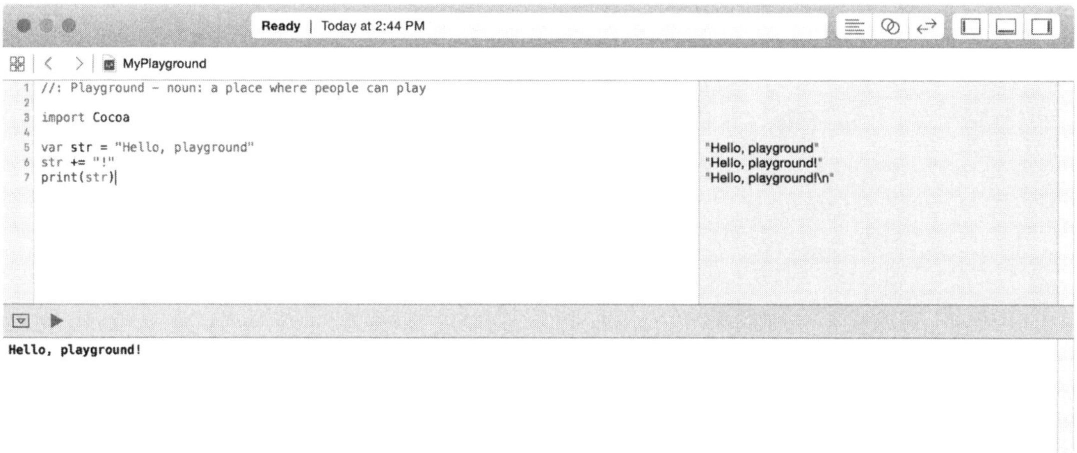

# You Are On Your Way!

Let's review what you have accomplished so far. You have:

- installed Xcode

- created and got acquainted with a playground

- used a variable and modified it

- learned about the **String** type

- used a function to print to the console

That is good! You will be making your own apps in no time. Until then, stick with it. As you continue, you will see that most everything in this book is merely a variation on the themes you have covered thus far.

# Bronze Challenge

Many of the chapters in this book end with one or more challenges. The challenges are for you to work through on your own to deepen your understanding of Swift and get a little extra experience. Your first challenge is below. Before you get started, create a new playground.

You learned about the **String** type and printing to the console using **print()**. Use your new playground to create a new instance of the **String** type. Set the value of this instance to be equal to your last name. Print its value to the console.

# 2

# Types, Constants, and Variables

This chapter will introduce you to constants, variables, and Swift's basic data types. These elements are the fundamental building blocks of any program. You will use constants and variables to store values and to pass data around in your applications. Types describe the nature of the data held by the constant or variable. There are important differences between constants and variables, as well as each of the data types, that shape their uses.

## Types

Variables and constants have a data type. The type describes the nature of the data and provides information to the compiler on how to handle the data. Based on the type of a constant or variable, the compiler knows how much memory to reserve and will also be able to help with *type checking*, a feature of Swift that helps to prevent you from assigning the wrong kind of data to a variable.

Let's see this in action. Create a new OS X playground. (From the welcome screen, choose Get started with a playground. From within Xcode, choose File → New → Playground... .) Name the playground **Variables**.

Suppose you want to model a small town in your code. You might want a variable for the number of stoplights in the town. Create a variable called numberOfStoplights and give it a value.

### Listing 2.1 Assigning a string to a variable

```
import Cocoa

var numberOfStoplights = "Four"
```

Here, you have assigned an instance of the **String** type to the variable called numberOfStoplights. Let's go piece by piece to see why this is so. The equality (=) assigns the value on its right side to whatever is on its left side. Swift uses *type inference* to determine the data type of your variable. In this case, the compiler knows the variable numberOfStoplights is of the **String** type because the value on the right side of the equality is an instance of **String**. Why is "Four" an instance of the **String** type? Because the quotation marks indicate that it is a **String** literal.

11

Now add the integer 2 to your variable, using += as you did in the last chapter.

## Listing 2.2  Adding "Four" and 2

```
import Cocoa

var numberOfStoplights = "Four"
numberOfStoplights += 2
```

The compiler gives you an error telling you that this operation does not make sense. You get this error because you are trying to add a number to a variable that is an instance of a different type: **String**. What does it mean to add the number 2 to a string? Does it double the string and give you "FourFour"? Does it put "2" on the end and give you "Four2"? Nobody knows. It just does not make sense to add a number to an instance of **String**.

If you are thinking that it does not make sense to have numberOfStoplights be of type **String** in the first place, you are right. Because this variable represents the number of stoplights in your theoretical town, it makes sense to use a numerical type. Swift provides an **Int** type that is perfect for your variable. Change your code to use **Int** instead. (Remember that code you are to delete is shown struck through.)

## Listing 2.3  Using a numerical type

```
import Cocoa

var numberOfStoplights = "Four"
var numberOfStoplights: Int = 4
numberOfStoplights += 2
```

Let's take a look at the changes here. Before, the compiler had to rely on type inference to determine the data type of the variable numberofStoplights. Now, you are explicitly declaring the variable to be of the **Int** type using Swift's *type annotation* syntax. The colon in the code above represents "… *of type* …," so the code could be read as: "Declare a variable called numberOfStoplights of type **Int** that starts out with a value of 4."

Note that type annotation does not mean that the compiler is no longer paying attention to what is on each side of the equality. If, for example, you tried to reassign your previous **String** instance of "Four" to be an integer using type annotation, the compiler would give you a warning telling you that it cannot convert a string to an integer.

Notice something else about the new code you have entered: your error has disappeared. It is perfectly fine to add 2 to the integer variable representing your town's number of stoplights. In fact, because you have declared this instance to be a variable, this operation is perfectly natural. You will return to this issue later on in the chapter.

Swift has a host of frequently used data types. You will learn more about strings, which contain textual data, in Chapter 7 and numbers in Chapter 4. Other commonly used types are the various *collection types*, which you will see later in the book.

# Constants vs. Variables

We said that types describe the nature of the data held by a constant or variable. What, then, are constants and variables? Up to now, you have only seen variables. Variables' values can vary, which means that you can assign them a new value. For example, you varied numberOfStoplights's value in this code: numberOfStoplights += 2.

Often, however, you will want to create instances whose values do not change. Use *constants* for these cases. As the name indicates, the value of a constant cannot be changed.

You made numberOfStoplights a variable, and you changed its value. But what if you did not want to vary the value of numberOfStoplights? In that case, making numberOfStoplights constant would be better. A good rule of thumb is to use variables for instances that must vary, and constants for instances that will not.

Swift has different syntax for declaring constants and variables. As you have seen, you declare a variable with var. You use the let keyword to declare that an instance is a constant.

Declare a constant in the current playground to fix the number of stoplights in your small town.

### Listing 2.4  Declaring a constant

```
import Cocoa

var numberOfStoplights: Int = 4
let numberOfStoplights: Int = 4
numberOfStoplights += 2
```

You declare numberOfStoplights to be a constant via the let keyword. This change makes sense, considering that the town you are modeling is small; it is not likely to get a new stoplight any time soon. Unfortunately, this change causes the compiler to issue an error. Why are you seeing this error?

You have just changed numberOfStoplights to be a constant, but you still have code that attempts to change its value: numberOfStoplights += 2. Since constants cannot change, the compiler gives you an error when you try to change it. Fix the problem by removing the addition and assignment code.

### Listing 2.5  Constants do not vary

```
import Cocoa

let numberOfStoplights: Int = 4
numberOfStoplights += 2
```

Now, add an **Int** to represent the town's population. (Do you think it should be a variable or a constant?)

### Listing 2.6  Declaring population

```
import Cocoa

let numberOfStoplights: Int = 4
var population: Int
```

Your town's population is likely to vary over time. Thus, you declared population with the var keyword to make this instance a variable. You also declared population to be an instance of type **Int**. You did so because a town's population is counted in terms of whole persons. But you did not *initialize* population with any value. It is therefore an *empty* **Int**.

(Initialization, which you will learn more about in Chapter 17, is the operation of setting up an instance of a type so that it is prepared and available to use.)

Use the assignment operator to give population its starting value.

### Listing 2.7  Giving population a value

```
import Cocoa

let numberOfStoplights: Int = 4
var population: Int
population = 5422
```

# String Interpolation

Every town needs a name. Your town is fairly stable, so it will not be changing its name any time soon. Make the town name a constant of type **String**.

### Listing 2.8  Giving the town a name

```
import Cocoa

let numberOfStoplights: Int = 4
var population: Int
population = 5422
let townName: String = "Knowhere"
```

It would be nice to have a short description of the town that the Tourism Council could use. The description is going to be a constant **String**, but you will be creating it a bit differently than the constants and variables you have created so far. The description will include all the data you have entered, and you are going to create it using a Swift feature called *string interpolation*.

String interpolation lets you combine constant and variable values into a new string. You can then assign the string to a new variable or constant, or just print it to the console. You are going to print the town description to the console.

### Listing 2.9  Crafting the town description

```
import Cocoa

let numberOfStoplights: Int = 4
var population: Int
population = 5422
let townName: String = "Knowhere"
let townDescription =
"\(townName) has a population of \(population) and \(numberOfStoplights) stoplights."
print(townDescription)
```

The \() syntax represents a placeholder in the **String** literal that accesses an instance's value and places it within the new **String**. For example, \(townName) accesses the constant townName's value and places it within the new **String** instance.

The result of the new code is shown in Figure 2.1.

### Figure 2.1  Knowhere's short description

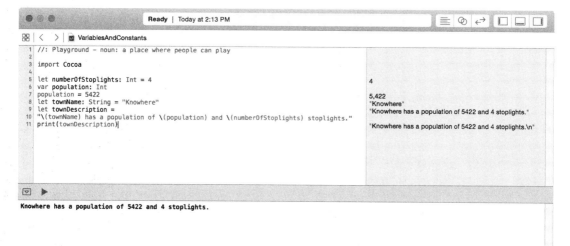

## Bronze Challenge

Add a new variable to your playground representing Knowhere's level of unemployment. Which data type should you use? Give this variable a value and update townDescription to use this new information.

# Part II
## The Basics

Programs execute code in a specific order. Writing software means having control over the order in which code executes. Programming languages provide *control flow statements* to help developers organize the execution of their code. This part of the book introduces the concepts of conditionals and loops to accomplish this task.

It will also show you how Swift represents numbers and text – often called strings – in code. These types of data are the building blocks of many applications. By the end of these chapters, you will have a good understanding of how numbers and strings work in Swift.

Last, this part of the book introduces the concept of *optionals* in Swift. Optionals play an important role in the language and provide a mechanism for the language to represent the concept of *nothing* safely. As you will see, how Swift deals with optionals highlights the language's approach to writing safe and reliable code.

# 3

# Conditionals

In previous chapters your code led a relatively simple life: you declared some simple constants and variables and then assigned them values. But of course, an application really comes to life – and programming becomes a bit more challenging – when the application makes decisions based on the contents of its variables. For example, a game may let players leap a tall building *if* they have eaten a power-up. You use conditional statements to help applications make these kind of decisions.

## if/else

if/else statements execute code based on a specific logical condition. You have a relatively simple either/or situation and depending on the result one branch of code or another (but not both) runs. Consider Knowhere, your small town from the previous chapter, and imagine that you need to buy stamps. Either Knowhere has a post office or it does not. If it has a post office, you will buy stamps there. If it does not have a post office, you will need to drive to the next town to buy stamps. Whether there is a post office is your logical condition. The different behaviors are "get stamps in town" and "get stamps out of town."

Some situations are more complex than a binary yes/no. You will see a more flexible mechanism called switch in Chapter 5. But for now, let's keep it simple.

Create a new OS X playground and name it **Conditionals**. Enter the code below, which shows the basic syntax for an if/else statement:

### Listing 3.1  Big or small?

```
import Cocoa

var population: Int = 5422
var message: String

if population < 10000 {
    message = "\(population) is a small town!"
} else {
    message = "\(population) is pretty big!"
}

print(message)
```

You first declare population as an instance of the **Int** type and then assign it a value of 5422. Next, you declare a variable called message that is of the **String** type. You leave this variable uninitialized at first, meaning that you do not assign it a value.

Next comes the conditional `if/else` statement. This is where `message` is assigned a value based on whether the "if" statement evaluates to true. (Notice that you use *string interpolation* to put the population into the `message` string.)

Figure 3.1 shows what your playground should look like. The console and the results sidebar show that `message` has been set to be equal to the string literal assigned when the conditional evaluates to true. How did this happen?

### Figure 3.1 Conditionally describing a town's population

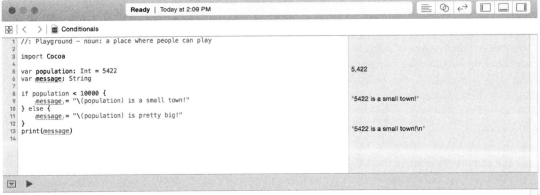

The condition in the `if/else` statement tests whether your town's population is less than 10,000 via the `<` comparison operator. If the condition evaluates to true, then `message` is set to be equal to the first string literal ("X is a small town!"). If the condition evaluates to false – if the population is 10,000 or greater – the `message` is set to be equal to the second string literal ("X is pretty big!"). In this case, the town's population is less than 10,000, so `message` is set to "5422 is a small town!"

Table 3.1 lists Swift's comparison operators.

### Table 3.1 Comparison operators

| Operator | Description |
|----------|-------------|
| < | Evaluates whether the number on the left is smaller than the number on the right. |
| <= | Evaluates whether the number on the left is smaller than or equal to the number on the right. |
| > | Evaluates whether the number on the left is greater than the number on the right. |
| >= | Evaluates whether the number on the left is greater than or equal to the number on the right. |
| == | Evaluates whether the number on the left is equal to the number on the right. |
| != | Evaluates whether the number on the left is not equal to the number on the right. |
| === | Evaluates whether the two instances point to the same reference. |
| !== | Evaluates whether the two instances do not point to the same reference. |

You do not need to understand all of the operators' descriptions right now. You will see many of them in action as you move through the book, and they will become clearer as you use them. Refer back to this table as a reference if you have questions.

Sometimes you only care about one aspect of the condition that is under evaluation. That is, you want to execute code if a certain condition is met and do nothing if it is not. Enter the code below. (Notice that new code, shown in bold, appears in two places.)

### Listing 3.2 Is there a post office?

```
import Cocoa

var population: Int = 5422
var message: String
var hasPostOffice: Bool = true

if population < 10000 {
    message = "\(population) is a small town!"
} else {
    message = "\(population) is pretty big!"
}

print(message)

if !hasPostOffice {
    print("Where do we buy stamps?")
}
```

Here, you add a new variable called `hasPostOffice`. This variable has the type **Bool**, short for "Boolean." Boolean types can take one of two values: `true` or `false`. In this case, the Boolean `hasPostOffice` variable keeps track of whether the town has a post office. You set it to `true`, meaning that it does.

The `!` is called a *logical operator*. This operator is known as "logical not." It tests whether `hasPostOffice` is false. You can think of `!` as inverting a **Boolean** value: true becomes false, and false becomes true.

The code above first sets `hasPostOffice` to true, then asks whether it is false. If `hasPostOffice` is false, you do not know where to buy stamps, so you ask. If `hasPostOffice` is true, you know where to buy stamps and do not have to ask, so nothing happens.

Because the town *does* have a post office (because `hasPostOffice` was initialized to `true`), the condition `!hasPostOffice` is false. That is, it is *not* the case that `hasPostOffice` is false. Therefore, the **print()** function never gets called.

Table 3.2 lists Swift's logical operators.

### Table 3.2 Logical operators

| Operator | Description |
|----------|-------------|
| && | Logical AND: true if and only if both are true (false otherwise) |
| \|\| | Logical OR: true if either is true (false only if both are false) |
| ! | Logical NOT: true becomes false, false becomes true |

# Ternary Operator

The *ternary operator* is very similar to an `if`/`else` statement, but has more concise syntax. The syntax looks likes this: a ? b : c. In English, the ternary operator reads something like, "If a is true, then do b. Otherwise, do c."

Let's rewrite the town population check that used `if`/`else` using the ternary operator instead.

### Listing 3.3  Using the ternary operator

```
...
if population < 10000 {
    message = "\(population) is a small town!"
} else {
    message = "\(population) is pretty big!"
}

message = population < 10000 ? "\(population) is a small town!" :
                    "\(population) is pretty big!"
...
```

The ternary operator can be a source of controversy: some programmers love it; some programmers loathe it. We come down somewhere in the middle. This particular usage is not very elegant. Your assignment to `message` requires more than a simple a ? b : c. The ternary operator is great for concise statements, but if your statement starts wrapping to the next line, we think you should use `if`/`else` instead.

Hit Command-Z to undo, removing the ternary operator and restoring your `if`/`else` statement.

### Listing 3.4  Restoring `if`/`else`

```
...
message = population < 10000 ? "\(population) is a small town!" :
                    "\(population) is pretty big!"
if population < 10000 {
    message = "\(population) is a small town!"
} else {
    message = "\(population) is pretty big!"
}
...
```

# Nested ifs

You can nest `if` statements for scenarios with more than two possibilities. You do this by writing an `if`/`else` statement inside the curly braces of another `if`/`else` statement. To see this, nest an `if`/`else` statement within the `else` block of your existing `if`/`else` statement.

Listing 3.5 Nesting conditionals

```
import Cocoa

var population: Int = 5422
var message: String
var hasPostOffice: Bool = true

if population < 10000 {
    message = "\(population) is a small town!"
} else {
    if population >= 10000 && population < 50000 {
        message = "\(population) is a medium town!"
    } else {
        message = "\(population) is pretty big!"
    }
}

print(message)

if !hasPostOffice {
    print("Where do we buy stamps?")
}
```

Your nested `if` clause makes use of the `>=` *comparator* (comparison operator) and the `&&` logical operator to check whether `population` is within the range of 10,000 to 50,000. Because your town's `population` does not fall within that range, your `message` is set to "5422 is a small town!" as before.

Try bumping up the population to exercise the other branches.

Nested `if`/`else` statements are common in programming. You will find them out in the wild, and you will be writing them as well. There is no limit to how deeply you can nest these statements. However, the danger of nesting them too deeply is that it makes the code harder to read. One or two levels are fine, but beyond that your code becomes less readable and maintainable.

There are ways to avoid nested statements. Next, you are going to *refactor* the code that you have just written to make it a little easier to follow. Refactoring means changing code so that it does the same work but in a different way. It may be more efficient, or may just look prettier or be easier to understand.

# else if

The else if conditional lets you chain multiple conditional statements together. else if allows you to check against multiple cases and conditionally executes code depending on which clause evaluates to true. You can have as many else if clauses as you want. Only one condition will match.

To make your code a little easier to read, extract the nested if/else statement to be a standalone clause that evaluates whether your town is of medium size.

### Listing 3.6 Using else if

```
import Cocoa

var population: Int = 5422
var message: String
var hasPostOffice: Bool = true

if population < 10000 {
    message = "\(population) is a small town!"
} else if population >= 10000 && population < 50000 {
    message = "\(population) is a medium town!"
} else {
    if population >= 10000 && population < 50000 {
        message = "\(population) is a medium town!"
    } else {
        message = "\(population) is pretty big!"
    }
    message = "\(population) is pretty big!"
}

print(message)

if !hasPostOffice {
    print("Where do we buy stamps?")
}
```

You are using one else if clause, but you could have chained many more. This block of code is an improvement over the nested if/else above. If you find yourself with lots of if/else statements, you may want to use another mechanism, such as switch described in Chapter 5. Stay tuned.

# Bronze Challenge

Add an additional else if statement to the town-sizing code to see if your town's population is very large. Choose your own population thresholds. Set the message variable accordingly.

# 4

# Numbers

Numbers are the fundamental language of computers. They are also a staple of software development. Numbers are used to keep track of temperature, determine how many letters are in a sentence, and count the zombies infesting a town. Numbers come in two basic flavors: integers and floating-point numbers.

## Integers

You have worked with integers already, but we have not yet defined them. An integer is a number that does not have a decimal point or fractional component – a whole number. Integers are frequently used to represent a count of "things," such as the number of pages in a book. A difference between integers used by computers and numbers you use elsewhere is that an integer type on a computer takes up a fixed amount of memory. Therefore, they cannot represent all possible whole numbers – they have a minimum and maximum value.

We could tell you those minimum and maximum values, but we are going to let Swift tell you instead. Create a new playground, name it `Numbers.playground`, and enter the following code:

Listing 4.1  Maximum and minimum values for **Int**

```
print("The maximum Int value is \(Int.max).")
print("The minimum Int value is \(Int.min).")
```

Open the Assistant Editor view for your playground by selecting View → Assistant Editor → Show Assistant Editor or by pressing Command-Option-Return. In playgrounds, the Assistant Editor defaults to showing you the timeline view. You should see the following output:

```
The maximum Int value is 9223372036854775807.
The minimum Int value is −9223372036854775808.
```

Why are those numbers the minimum and maximum **Int** values? Computers store integers in binary form with a fixed number of bits. A bit is a single 0 or 1. Each bit position represents a power of 2; to compute the value of a binary number, add up each of the powers of 2 whose bit is a 1. For example, the binary representations of 38 and -94 using an 8-bit signed integer are shown in Figure 4.1. (Note that the bit positions are read from right to left. *Signed* means that the integer can represent positive or negative values. More about signed integers in a moment.)

### Figure 4.1 Binary numbers

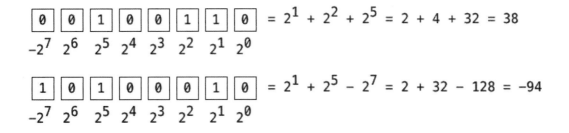

In OS X, **Int** is a 64-bit integer, which means it has $2^{64}$ possible values. Imagine Figure 4.1, only 64 bits wide instead of 8. The power of two represented by the top (left-most) bit would be $-2^{63}$ = -9,223,372,036,854,775,808 – exactly the value you see for Int.min in your playground. And, if you were to add up $2^0$, $2^1$, ..., $2^{62}$, you would arrive at 9,223,372,036,854,775,807 – the value you see for Int.max.

In iOS, **Int** is slightly more complicated. Apple introduced 64-bit devices starting with iPhone 5S, iPad Air, and iPad mini with Retina display. Earlier devices had a 32-bit architecture. If you write an iOS app for newer devices, which is called "targeting a 64-bit architecture," **Int** is a 64-bit integer just like in OS X. On the other hand, if you target a 32-bit architecture like iPhone 5 or iPad 2, **Int** is a 32-bit integer. The compiler determines the appropriate size for **Int** when it builds your program.

If you need to know the exact size of an integer, you can use one of Swift's explicitly sized integer types. For example, **Int32** is Swift's 32-bit signed integer type. Use **Int32** to see the minimum and maximum value for a 32-bit integer.

### Listing 4.2 Maximum and minimum values for **Int32**

```
print("The maximum Int value is \(Int.max).")
print("The minimum Int value is \(Int.min).")
print("The maximum value for a 32-bit integer is \(Int32.max).")
print("The minimum value for a 32-bit integer is \(Int32.min).")
```

Also available are **Int8**, **Int16**, and **Int64**, for 8-bit, 16-bit, and 64-bit signed integer types. You use the sized integer types when you need to know the size of the underlying integer, such as for some algorithms (common in cryptography) or to exchange integers with another computer (such as sending data across the Internet). You will not use these types much; good Swift style is to use an **Int** for most use cases.

All the integer types you have seen so far are signed, which means they can represent both positive and negative numbers. Swift also has unsigned integer types to represent whole numbers greater than or equal to 0. Every signed integer type (**Int**, **Int16**, etc.) has a corresponding unsigned integer type (**UInt**, **UInt16**, etc.). The difference between signed and unsigned integers at the binary level is that the power of two represented by the top-most bit ($2^7$ for 8-bit integers) is positive instead of negative. Test a couple of these.

## Listing 4.3 Maximum and minimum values for unsigned integers

```
print("The maximum Int value is \(Int.max).")
print("The minimum Int value is \(Int.min).")
print("The maximum value for a 32-bit integer is \(Int32.max).")
print("The minimum value for a 32-bit integer is \(Int32.min).")

print("The maximum UInt value is \(UInt.max).")
print("The minimum UInt value is \(UInt.min).")
print("The maximum value for a 32-bit unsigned integer is \(UInt32.max).")
print("The minimum value for a 32-bit unsigned integer is \(UInt32.min).")
```

Like **Int**, **UInt** is a 64-bit integer in OS X and may be 32-bit or 64-bit depending on the target for iOS. The minimum value for all unsigned types is 0. The maximum value for an N-bit unsigned type is $2^N$ - 1. For example, the maximum value for a 64-bit unsigned type is $2^{64}$ - 1, which equals 18,446,744,073,709,551,615.

There is a relationship between the minimum and maximum values of signed and unsigned types: the maximum value of **UInt64** is equal to the maximum value of **Int64** plus the absolute value of the minimum value of **Int64**. Both signed and unsigned types have $2^{64}$ possible values, but the signed version has to devote half of them to negative numbers.

Some quantities seem like they would naturally be represented by an unsigned integer. For example, it does not make sense for the count of a number of objects to ever be negative. However, Swift style is to prefer **Int** for all integer uses (including counts) unless an unsigned integer is required by the algorithm or code you are writing. The explanation for this involves topics we are going to cover later in this chapter, so we will return to the reasons behind consistently preferring **Int** soon.

# Creating Integer Instances

You created instances of **Int** in Chapter 2, where you learned that you can declare a type explicitly or implicitly.

## Listing 4.4 Declaring **Int** explicitly and implicitly

```
...
print("The maximum value for a 32-bit unsigned integer is \(UInt32.max).")
print("The minimum value for a 32-bit unsigned integer is \(UInt32.min).")

let numberOfPages: Int = 10 // Declares the type explicitly
let numberOfChapters = 3    // Also of type Int, but inferred by the compiler
```

Implicit declarations with integer values are always assumed to be **Int** by the compiler. However, you can create instances of the other integer types using explicit type declarations.

## Listing 4.5 Declaring other integer types explicitly

```
...
let numberOfPages: Int = 10 // Declares the type explicitly
let numberOfChapters = 3    // Also of type Int, but inferred by the compiler

let numberOfPeople: UInt = 40
let volumeAdjustment: Int32 = -1000
```

What happens if you try to create an instance with an invalid value? What if, for example, you try to create a **UInt** with a negative value or an **Int8** with a value greater than 127? Try it and find out.

### Listing 4.6  Declaring integer types with invalid values

```
...
let numberOfPeople: UInt = 40
let volumeAdjustment: Int32 = -1000

// Trouble ahead!
let firstBadValue: UInt = -1
let secondBadValue: Int8 = 200
```

You should see red exclamation marks in the left column of the playground. Click on the exclamation marks to see the errors (Figure 4.2).

### Figure 4.2  Integer overflow error

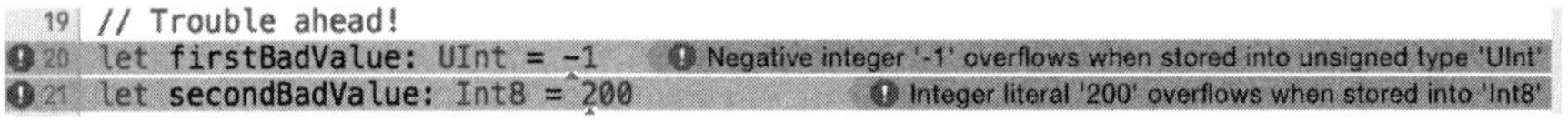

```
19  // Trouble ahead!
20  let firstBadValue: UInt = -1          ⓘ Negative integer '-1' overflows when stored into unsigned type 'UInt'
21  let secondBadValue: Int8 = 200        ⓘ Integer literal '200' overflows when stored into 'Int8'
```

The compiler reports that the two values you have typed in "overflow when stored into" constants of type **UInt** and **Int8**, respectively. "Overflows when stored into…" means that when the compiler tried to store your number into the type you specified, it did not fit in the type's allowed range of values. An **Int8** can hold values from -128 to 127; 200 is outside of that range, so trying to store 200 into an **Int8** overflows.

Remove the problematic code.

### Listing 4.7  No more bad values

```
...
// Trouble ahead!
let firstBadValue: UInt = -1
let secondBadValue: Int8 = 200
```

# Operations on Integers

Swift allows you to perform basic mathematical operations on integers using the familiar operators + (add), – (subtract), and * (multiply). Try printing the results of some arithmetic.

### Listing 4.8  Performing basic operations

```
...
let numberOfPeople: UInt = 40
let volumeAdjustment: Int32 = -1000

print(10 + 20)
print(30 - 5)
print(5 * 6)
```

The compiler respects the mathematical principles of *precedence* and *associativity*, which define the order of operations when there are multiple operators in a single expression. For example:

### Listing 4.9  Order of operations

```
...
print(10 + 20)
print(30 - 5)
print(5 * 6)

print(10 + 2 * 5) // 20, because 2 * 5 is evaluated first
print(30 - 5 - 5) // 20, because 30 - 5 is evaluated first
```

You could memorize the rules governing precedence and associativity. However, we recommend taking the easy route and using parentheses to make your intentions explicit, because parentheses are always evaluated first.

### Listing 4.10  Parentheses are your friends

```
...
print(10 + 2 * 5) // 20, because 2 * 5 is evaluated first
print(30 - 5 - 5) // 20, because 30 - 5 is evaluated first
print((10 + 2) * 5) // 60, because (10 + 2) is now evaluated first
print(30 - (5 - 5)) // 30, because (5 - 5) is now evaluated first
```

## Integer division

What is the value of the expression 11 / 3? You might (reasonably) expect 3.66666666667, but try it out.

### Listing 4.11  Integer division can give unexpected results

```
...
print((10 + 2) * 5)
print(30 - (5 - 5))

print(11 / 3) // Prints 3
```

The result of any operation between two integers is always another integer of the same type; 3.66666666667 is not a whole number and cannot be represented as an integer. Swift truncates the fractional part, leaving just 3. If the result is negative, such as –11 / 3, the fractional part is still truncated, giving a result of -3. Integer division, therefore, always rounds toward 0.

It is also occasionally useful to get the remainder of a division operation. The remainder operator, %, returns exactly that. (If you are familiar with the modulo operator in math and some other programming languages, be warned: the remainder operator is not the same, and using it on a negative integer may not return what you expect.)

### Listing 4.12  Remainders

```
...
print(11 / 3) // Prints 3
print(11 % 3) // Prints 2
print(-11 % 3) // Prints -2
```

## Operator shorthand

All the operators that you have seen so far return a new value. There are also versions of all of these operators that modify a variable in place. An extremely common operation in programming is to *increment* an integer (add 1 to it) or *decrement* an integer (subtract 1 from it). You can use the ++ operator and the -- operator to perform these operations.

### Listing 4.13  Incrementing and decrementing

```
...
print(-11 % 3) // Prints -2

var x = 10
x++
print("x has been incremented to \(x)")
x--
print("x has been decremented to \(x)")
```

What if you want to increase x by a number other than 1? You can use the += operator, which combines addition and assignment.

### Listing 4.14  Combining addition and assignment

```
...
x--
print("\(x) has been decremented")

x += 10 // Is equivalent to: x = x + 10
print("x has had 10 added to it and is now \(x)")
```

There are also shorthand operation-and-assignment combination operators for the other basic math operations: -=, *=, /=, and %=.

## Overflow operators

What do you think the value of z will be in the following code? (Think about it for a minute before you type it in to find out for sure.)

### Listing 4.15  Solve for z

```
...
let y: Int8 = 120
let z = y + 10
```

If you thought the value of z would be 130, you are not alone. But type it in, and you will find that instead Xcode is showing you an error. Click on it to see a more detailed message (Figure 4.3).

### Figure 4.3  Execution interrupted when adding to an **Int8**

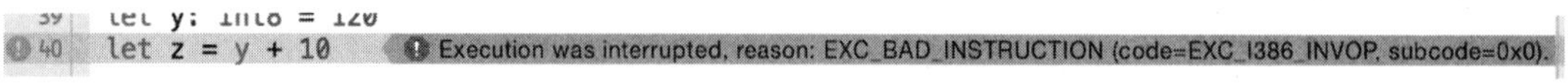

```
39   let y: Int8 = 120
40   let z = y + 10    ● Execution was interrupted, reason: EXC_BAD_INSTRUCTION (code=EXC_I386_INVOP, subcode=0x0).
```

What does "Execution was interrupted" mean? Let's break down what is happening:

1. y is an **Int8**, so the compiler assumes y + 10 must be an Int8, too.

2. Therefore, the compiler infers the type of z to be **Int8**.

3. When your playground runs, Swift adds 10 to y, resulting in 130.

4. Before storing the result back into z, Swift checks that 130 is a valid value for an **Int8**.

But **Int8** can only hold values from -128 to 127; 130 is too big! Your playground therefore hits a *trap*, which stops the program from running. We will discuss traps in more detail in Chapter 20. For now, know that a trap results in your program stopping immediately and noisily, which indicates a serious problem you need to examine.

Swift provides *overflow operators* that have different behavior when the value is too big (or too small). Instead of trapping the program, they "wrap around." To see what that means, try it now. The overflow addition operator is &+. Substitute it into your code.

## Listing 4.16  Using an overflow operator

```
...
let y: Int8 = 120
let z = y + 10
let z = y &+ 10
print("120 &+ 10 is \(z)")
```

The result of overflow-adding 120 + 10 and storing the result into an **Int8** is -126. Was that what you expected?

Probably not. (And that is OK!) To understand the logic of this result, think about incrementing y one at a time. Since y is an **Int8**, once you get to 127 you cannot go any higher. Instead, incrementing one more time wraps around to -128. So 120 + 8 = -128, 120 + 9 = -127, and 120 + 10 = -126.

There are also overflow versions of the subtraction and multiplication operators: &- and &*. It should be apparent why there is an overflow version of the multiplication operator, but what about subtraction? Subtraction clearly cannot overflow, but it can *underflow*. For example, trying to subtract 10 from an **Int8** currently holding -120 would result in a value too negative to be stored in an **Int8**. Using &- would cause this underflow to wrap back around and give you positive 126.

Integer operations overflowing or underflowing unexpectedly can be a source of serious and hard-to-find bugs. Swift is designed to prioritize safety and minimize these errors. Swift's default behavior of trapping on overflow calculations may come as a surprise to you if you have programmed in another language. Most other languages default to the "wrap-around" behavior that Swift's overflow operators provide. The philosophy of the Swift language is that it is better to trap (even though this may result in a program crashing) than potentially have a security hole. There are some use cases for wrapping arithmetic, so these special operators are available if you need them.

# Converting Between Integer Types

So far, all the operations you have seen have been between two values with exactly the same type. What happens if you try to operate on numbers with different types?

Listing 4.17  Adding values of different types

```
...
let a: Int16 = 200
let b: Int8 = 50
let c = a + b // Uh-oh!
```

This is a compile-time error. You cannot add a and b because they are not of the same type. Some languages will automatically convert types for you to perform operations like this. Swift does not. Instead, you have to manually convert types to get them to match.

In this case, you could either convert a to an **Int8** or convert b to an **Int16**. Actually, though, only one of these will succeed. (Why? Reread the previous section!)

Listing 4.18  Converting type to allow addition

```
...
let a: Int16 = 200
let b: Int8 = 50
let c = a + b // Uh-oh!
let c = a + Int16(b)
```

We can now return to the recommendation to stick with **Int** for almost all integer needs in Swift, even for values that might naturally only make sense as positive values (like a count of "things"). Swift's default type inference for literals is **Int**, and you cannot typically perform operations between different integer types without converting one of them. Using **Int** consistently throughout your code will greatly reduce the need for you to convert types, and it will allow you to use type inference for integers freely.

Requiring you, the programmer, to decide how to convert variables in order to do math between different types is another feature that distinguishes Swift from other languages. Again, this requirement is in favor of safety and correctness. The C programming language, for example, will convert numbers of different types in order to perform math between them, but the conversions it performs are sometimes "lossy" – you may lose information in the conversion. Swift code that requires math between numbers of different types will be more verbose, but it will be more clear about what conversions are taking place. The increase in verbosity will make it easier for you to reason about and maintain the code doing the math.

# Floating-Point Numbers

To represent a number that has a decimal point, like 3.2, you use a *floating-point number*. There are two things to bear in mind about floating-point numbers. First, in computers floating-point numbers are stored as a *mantissa* and an *exponent*, similar to how you write a number in scientific notation. For example, 123.45 could be stored similarly to $1.2345 \times 10^2$ or $12.345 \times 10^1$ (although the computer will use base 2 instead of base 10). Additionally, floating-point numbers are often imprecise: There are many numbers that cannot be stored with perfect accuracy in a floating-point number. The computer will store a very close approximation to the number you expect. (More on that in a moment.)

Swift has two basic floating-point number types: **Float**, which is a 32-bit floating-point number, and **Double**, which is a 64-bit floating-point number. The different bit sizes of **Float** and **Double** do not determine a simple minimum and maximum value range as they do for integers. Instead, the bit sizes determine how much precision the numbers have. **Double** has more precision than **Float**, which means it is able to store more accurate approximations.

The default inferred type for floating-point numbers in Swift is **Double**. As with different types of integers, you can also declare **Float**s and **Double**s explicitly.

### Listing 4.19  Declaring floating-point number types

```
...
let d1 = 1.1 // Implicitly Double
let d2: Double = 1.1
let f1: Float = 100.3
```

All the same numeric operators work on floating-point numbers, including the remainder operator.

### Listing 4.20  Operations on floating-point numbers

```
...
let d1 = 1.1 // Implicitly Double
let d2: Double = 1.1
let f1: Float = 100.3

print(10.0 + 11.4)
print(11.0 / 3.0)
print(12.4 % 5.0)
```

The fact that floating-point numbers are inherently imprecise is an important difference from integer numbers that you should keep in mind. Let's see an example. Recall the == operator from Chapter 3, which determines whether two values are equal to each other. As you might expect, you can also use it to compare floating-point numbers.

### Listing 4.21  Comparing two floating-point numbers

```
...
print(10.0 + 11.4)
print(11.0 / 3.0)
print(12.4 % 5.0)

if d1 == d2 {
    print("d1 and d2 are the same!")
}
```

d1 and d2 were both initialized with a value of 1.1. So far, so good. Now, let's add 0.1 to d1. You would expect that to result in 1.2, so compare the result to that value.

## Listing 4.22  Unexpected results

```
if d1 == d2 {
    print("d1 and d2 are the same!")
}

print("d1 + 0.1 is \(d1 + 0.1)")
if d1 + 0.1 == 1.2 {
    print("d1 + 0.1 is equal to 1.2")
}
```

The results you get may be very surprising! You should see the output d1 + 0.1 is 1.2 from your first print(), but the print() inside the if statement does not run. Why not? Isn't 1.2 equal to 1.2?

Well, sometimes it is and sometimes it is not.

As we said before, many numbers – including 1.2 – cannot be represented exactly in a floating-point number. Instead, the computer stores a very close approximation to 1.2. When you add 1.1 and 0.1, the result is really something like 1.2000000000000001. The value stored when you typed the literal 1.2 is really something like 1.1999999999999999. Swift will round both of those to 1.2 when you print them. But they are not technically equal, so the print() inside the if statement does not execute.

All the gory details behind floating-point arithmetic are outside the scope of this book. The moral of this story is to be aware that there are some potential pitfalls with floating-point numbers. One consequence is that you should never use floating-point numbers for values that must be exact (such as calculations dealing with money). There are other tools available for those purposes.

# Bronze Challenge

Set down your computer and grab a pencil and paper for this challenge. What is the binary representation of -1 using an 8-bit signed integer?

If you took that same bit pattern and interpreted it as an 8-bit unsigned integer, what would the value be?

# 5

# Switch

In an earlier chapter, you saw one sort of conditional statement: `if`/`else`. Along the way, we discussed that `if`/`else` can be somewhat inadequate in scenarios that have more than a few conditions. This chapter looks at the `switch` statement. Unlike `if`/`else`, `switch` is ideal for handling multiple conditions. As you will see, Swift's `switch` statement is an incredibly flexible and powerful feature of the language.

## What Is a Switch?

`if`/`else` statements execute code based on whether the condition under consideration evaluates to true. In contrast, `switch` statements consider a particular value and attempt to match it against a number of cases. If there is a match, the `switch` executes the code associated with that case. Here is the basic syntax of a `switch` statement.

```
switch aValue {
case someValueToCompare:
    // Do something to respond

case anotherValueToCompare:
    // Do something to respond

default:
    // Do something when there are no matches
}
```

In the example above, the `switch` only compares against two cases, but a `switch` statement can include any number of cases. If `aValue` matches any of the comparison cases, then the body of that case will be executed.

Notice the use of the `default:` case. It is executed when the comparison value does not match any of the cases. The `default` case is not mandatory. However, it *is* mandatory for `switch` statements to have a case for every value of the type being checked. So it is often efficient to use the `default` case rather than providing a specific case for every value in the type to be matched.

As you might guess, in order for the comparisons to be possible the type in each of the cases must match the type being compared against. In other words, `aValue`'s type must match the types of `someValueToCompare` and `anotherValueToCompare`.

This code shows the basic syntax of a `switch` statement, but it is not completely well formed. In fact, this `switch` statement would cause a compile-time error. Why? If you are curious, type it into a playground and see. Give aValue and all of the cases values. You should see an error for each of the cases, telling you "'case' label in a 'switch' should have at least one executable statement."

The problem is that every case must have at least one executable line of code associated with it. This is the purpose of a switch statement: for each case to represent a separate branch of execution. In the example, the cases only have comments under them. Because comments are not executable, the switch statement does not meet this requirement.

# Switch It Up

Create a new playground called **Switch** and set up a switch.

## Listing 5.1  Your first switch

```
import Cocoa

var statusCode: Int = 404
var errorString: String
switch statusCode {
case 400:
    errorString = "Bad request"

case 401:
    errorString = "Unauthorized"

case 403:
    errorString = "Forbidden"

case 404:
    errorString = "Not found"

default:
    errorString = "None"
}
```

The switch statement above compares an HTTP status code against four cases in order to match a **String** instance describing the error. Because case 404 matches statusCode, errorString is assigned to be equal to "Not found", as you can see in the sidebar (Figure 5.1). Try changing the value of statusCode to see the other results. When you are done, set it back to 404.

## Figure 5.1  Matching an error string to an status code

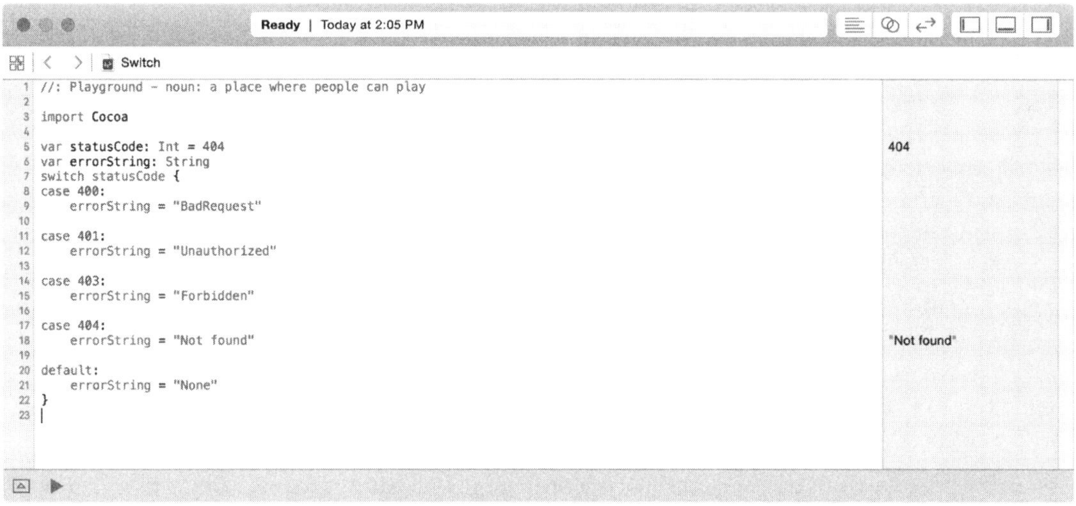

Suppose you want to use a switch statement to build up a meaningful error description. Update your code as shown.

## Listing 5.2  Switch cases can have multiple values

```
import Cocoa

var statusCode: Int = 404
var errorString: String = "The request failed with the error:"
switch statusCode {
case 400:
    errorString = "Bad request"

case 401:
    errorString = "Unauthorized"

case 403:
    errorString = "Forbidden"

case 404:
    errorString = "Not found"

default:
    errorString = "None"
case 400, 401, 403, 404:
    errorString = "There was something wrong with the request."
    fallthrough
default:
    errorString += " Please review the request and try again."
}
```

There is now only one case for all of the error status codes (which are listed and separated by commas). If the statusCode matches any of the values in the case, the text "There was something wrong with the request." is given to the errorString.

You have also added a *control transfer statement* called `fallthrough`. Control transfer statements allow you to modify the order of execution in some control flow. These statements *transfer* control from one chunk of code to another. You will see another way to use control transfer statements in Chapter 6 on looping.

Here, `fallthrough` tells the `switch` statement to "fall through" the bottom of a case to the next one. If a matching case has a `fallthrough` control transfer statement at the end of it, it will first execute its code, and then transfer control to the case immediately below. That case will execute its code – whether or not it matches the value being checked against. If it also has a `fallthrough` statement at the end, it will hand off control to the case below, and so on. `fallthrough` statements allow you to enter a case and execute its code without having to match against it.

In this example, the `fallthrough` statement means that even though the first case matches, the `switch` statement does not stop. It proceeds to the `default` case. Without the `fallthrough` keyword, the `switch` statement would have ended execution after the first match. The use of `fallthrough` in this example allows you to build up `errorString` without having to use strange logic that would guarantee that the comparison value matched all of the cases of interest.

The `default` case uses a compound-assignment operator (`+=`) to add a recommendation to review the request to the `errorString`. The end result of this `switch` statement is that `errorString` is set to: "There was something wrong with the request. Please review the request and try again." If the status code provided had not matched the values in the case, the end result would have been `errorString` being set to: "Please review the request and try again."

If you are familiar with other languages like C or Objective-C, you will see that Swift's `switch` statement works differently. `switch` statements in these languages automatically fall through their cases. These languages require a `break` control transfer statement at the end of the case's code to *break* out of the `switch`. Swift's `switch` works in the opposite manner. If you match on a case, then the case executes its code and the `switch` stops running.

# Ranges

You have seen `switch` statements where the cases have a single value to compare to the comparison value and others where the cases have multiple values. `switch` statements can also compare to a range of values using the syntax `valueX...valueY`. Update your code to see this in action.

## Listing 5.3 Switch cases can have single values, multiple values, or ranges of values

```
import Cocoa

var statusCode: Int = 404
var errorString: String
var errorString: String = "The request failed with the error:"
switch statusCode {
    case 400, 401, 403, 404:
        errorString += " There was something wrong with the request."
        fallthrough

    default:
        errorString += " Please review the request and try again."
}

switch statusCode {
case 100, 101:
    errorString += " Informational, 1xx."

case 204:
    errorString += " Successful but no content, 204."

case 300...307:
    errorString += " Redirection, 3xx."

case 400...417:
    errorString += " Client error, 4xx."

case 500...505:
    errorString += " Server error, 5xx."

default:
    errorString = "Unknown. Please review the request and try again."
}
```

The `switch` statement above takes advantage of the `...` syntax of *range matching* to create an inclusive range for categories of HTTP status codes. That is, `300...307` is a range that includes 300, 307, and everything in between.

You also have cases with a single HTTP status code (the second case) and with two codes explicitly listed and separated by a comma (the first case), as well as a default case. These are formed like the cases you saw before. All of the case syntax options can be combined in a `switch` statement.

The result of this `switch` statement is that `errorString` is set to equal "The request failed with the error: Client error, 4xx." Again, try changing the value of `statusCode` to see the other results. Be sure to set it back to `404` before continuing.

# Value binding

Suppose you want to include the actual numerical status codes in your errorString, whether the status code is recognized or not. You can build on your previous switch statement to include this information using Swift's *value binding* feature.

Value binding allows you to *bind* the matching value in a certain case to a local constant or variable. The constant or variable is thereafter available to use within only the matching case's body.

## Listing 5.4  Using value binding

```
...
switch statusCode {
case 100, 101:
    errorString += " Informational, 1xx."
    errorString += " Informational, \(statusCode)."

case 204:
    errorString += " Successful but no content, 204."

case 300...307:
    errorString += " Redirection, 3xx."
    errorString += " Redirection, \(statusCode)."

case 400...417:
    errorString += " Client error, 4xx."
    errorString += " Client error, \(statusCode)."

case 500...505:
    errorString += " Server error, 5xx."
    errorString += " Server error, \(statusCode)."

default:
    errorString = "Unknown. Please review the request and try again."

case let unknownCode:
    errorString = "\(unknownCode) is not a known error code."
}
```

Here you use *string interpolation* to pass statusCode into the errorString in each case.

Take a closer look at the last case. When the statusCode does not match any of the values provided in the cases above, you create a temporary constant, called unknownCode, binding it to the value of statusCode. For example, if the statusCode was set to be equal to 200, then your switch would set errorString to be equal to: "200 is not a known error code." Because unknownCode takes on the value of any status code that does not match the earlier cases, you no longer need an explicit default case.

Note that by using a constant, you fix the value of unknownCode. If you needed to do work on unknownCode, for whatever reason, you could have declared it with var instead of let. Doing so would mean, for example, that you could then modify unknownCode's value within the final case's body.

This example shows you the syntax of value binding, but does not really add much. The standard default case can produce the same result. Replace the final case with a standard default case.

## Listing 5.5  Reverting to the default case

```
...
switch statusCode {
case 100, 101:
    errorString += " Informational, \(statusCode)."

case 204:
    errorString += " Successful but no content, 204."

case 300...307:
    errorString += " Redirection, \(statusCode)."

case 400...417:
    errorString += " Client error, \(statusCode)."

case 500...505:
    errorString += " Server error, \(statusCode)."

case let unknownCode:
    errorString = "\(unknownCode) is not a known error code."

default:
    errorString = "\(statusCode) is not a known error code."
}
```

In the final case in Listing 5.4, you declared a constant whose value was bound to the status code. This meant that the final case by definition matched everything that had not already matched a case in the switch statement. The switch statement was, therefore, exhaustive.

Because your case for unknownCode now specifies a range of status codes, it is no longer exhaustive. So, you add a default case indicating an unknown error.

# where clauses

The code above is fine, as far as it goes. But it is not great. After all, a status code of 200 is not *really* an error – 200 represents success! Therefore, it would be nice if your switch statement did not catch these cases.

To fix this, use a where clause to make sure unknownCode is not a 2xx, success. where allows you to check for additional conditions within your switch statement. This feature creates a sort of dynamic filter within the switch.

## Listing 5.6  Using where to create a filter

```
import Cocoa

var statusCode: Int = 404
var statusCode: Int = 204
var errorString: String = "The request failed with the error:"
switch statusCode {
case 100, 101:
    errorString += " Informational, \(statusCode)."

case 204:
    errorString += " Successful but no content, 204."

case 300...307:
    errorString += " Redirection, \(statusCode)."

case 400...417:
    errorString += " Client error, \(statusCode)."

case 500...505:
    errorString += " Server error, \(statusCode)."

case let unknownCode where (unknownCode >= 200 && unknownCode < 300)
                           || unknownCode > 505:
    errorString = "\(unknownCode) is not a known error code."

default:
    errorString = "\(statusCode) is not a known error code."
    errorString = "Unexpected error encountered."
}
```

Without Swift's `fallthrough` feature, the `switch` statement will finish execution as soon as it finds a matching case and executes its body. When `statusCode` is equal to 204, the `switch` will match at the second case and the `errorString` will be set accordingly. So, even though 204 is within the range specified in the `where` clause, the `switch` statement never gets to that clause.

Change `statusCode` to exercise the `where` clause and confirm that it works as expected.

# Tuples and pattern matching

Now that you have your `statusCode` and `errorString`, it would be helpful to pair those two pieces. Though they are logically related, they are currently stored in independent variables. A *tuple* can be used to group the two.

A tuple is a finite grouping of two or more values that are deemed by the developer to be logically related. The different values are grouped as a single, compound value. The result of this grouping is an ordered list of elements.

Create your first Swift tuple that groups the `statusCode` and `errorString`.

## Listing 5.7  Creating a tuple

```
import Cocoa

var statusCode: Int = 204
var statusCode: Int = 418
var errorString: String = "The request failed with the error:"
switch statusCode {
case 100, 101:
    errorString += " Informational, \(statusCode)."

case 204:
    errorString += " Successful but no content, 204."

case 300...307:
    errorString += " Redirection, \(statusCode)."

case 400...417:
    errorString += " Client error, \(statusCode)."

case 500...505:
    errorString += " Server error, \(statusCode)."

case let unknownCode where (unknownCode >= 200 && unknownCode < 300)
                           || unknownCode > 505:
    errorString = "\(unknownCode) is not a known error code."

default:
    errorString = "Unknown error encountered."
}

let error = (statusCode, errorString)
```

You made a tuple by grouping statusCode and errorString within a pair of parentheses. The result was assigned to the constant error.

The elements of a tuple can be accessed by their index. Type in the following to access each element stored inside of the tuple.

## Listing 5.8  Accessing the elements of a tuple

```
...
let error = (statusCode, errorString)
error.0
error.1
```

You should see 418 and "Unknown error encountered." displayed in the results sidebar for error.0 (that is, the first element stored in the tuple) and error.1 (the second element stored in the tuple), respectively.

Swift's tuples can also have named elements. Naming a tuple's elements makes for more readable code. It is not very easy to keep track of what values are represented by error.0 and error.1. Named elements make error.code and error.error easier to parse.

Give your tuple's elements these more informative names.

## Listing 5.9 Naming the tuple's elements

```
...
let error = (statusCode, errorString)
error.0
error.1
let error = (code: statusCode, error: errorString)
error.code
error.error
```

Now you can access your tuple's elements by using their related names: code for statusCode and error for errorString. Your results sidebar should have the same information displayed.

## Pattern matching

You have already seen an example of pattern matching when you used ranges in the switch statement's cases. This form of pattern matching is called interval matching because each case attempts to match a given interval against the comparison value. Tuples are also helpful in matching patterns.

Imagine, for example, that you have an application that is making multiple web requests. You save the HTTP status code that comes back with the server's response each time. Later, you would like to see which requests, if any, failed with the status code 404 (the "requested resource not found" error). Using a tuple in the switch statement's cases enables you to match against very specific patterns.

Add the following code to switch on your new tuple.

## Listing 5.10 Pattern matching in tuples

```
...
let error = (code: statusCode, error: errorString)
error.code
error.error

let firstErrorCode = 404
let secondErrorCode = 200
let errorCodes = (firstErrorCode, secondErrorCode)

switch errorCodes {
case (404, 404):
    print("No items found.")
case (404, _):
    print("First item not found.")
case (_, 404):
    print("Second item not found.")
default:
    print("All items found.")
}
```

You first add a few new constants. firstErrorCode and secondErrorCode represent the HTTP status codes associated with two different web requests. errorCodes is a tuple that groups these codes.

The new switch statement matches against several cases to determine what combination of 404s the requests might have yielded. The underscore (_) in the second and third cases is a wildcard that matches anything, which allows these cases to focus on a specific request's error code. The first case will match only if both of the requests failed with error code 404. The second case will match only if the first request failed with 404. The third case will match only if the second request failed with 404. Finally, if we do not find a match, that means none of the requests failed with the status code 404.

Because `firstErrorCode` did have the status code 404, you should see `"First item not found."` in the results sidebar.

# switch vs. if/else

`switch` statements are primarily useful for comparing a value against a number of potentially matching cases. `if/else` statements, on the other hand, are better used for checking against a single condition. `switch`es also offer a number of powerful features that allow you to match against ranges, bind values to local constants or variables, and match patterns in tuples – to name just a few features covered in this chapter.

Sometimes you will be tempted to use a `switch` statement on a value that could potentially match against any number of cases, but you really only care about one of them. For example, imagine checking an age constant of type **Int** looking for a specific demographic: ages 18-35. You might think writing a `switch` statement with a single case is your best option:

Listing 5.11  Single case switch

```
...
let age = 25
switch age {
case 18...35:
    print("Cool demographic")
default:
    break
}
```

`age` is a constant set to be equal to 25. It is possible that `age` could take on any reasonable value between 0 and 100 or so, but you are only interested in a particular range. The `switch` checks to see whether `age` is in the range from 18 to 35. If it is, then `age` is in the desired demographic and some code is executed. Otherwise, `age` is not in the target demographic and the `default` case matches, which simply transfers the flow of execution to outside of the `switch` with the `break` control transfer statement.

Notice that you had to include a `default` case; `switch` statements have to be exhaustive. If this does not feel quite right to you, we agree. You do not really want to do anything here, which is why you used a `break`. It would be better to not have to write any code when you do not want anything to happen!

Swift provides a better way. In Chapter 3 you learned about `if/else` statements. Swift also provides an `if-case` statement that provides pattern matching similar to what a `switch` statement offers.

Listing 5.12  if-case

```
...
let age = 25
switch age {
case 18...35:
    print("Cool demographic")
default:
    break
}

if case 18...35 = age {
    print("Cool demographic")
}
```

This syntax is much more elegant. It simply checks to see if age is in the given range. You did not have to write a `default` case that you did not care about. Instead, the syntax of the `if-case` allows you to focus on the single case of interest: whether age is in the range of 18 to 35.

`if-cases` can also include `where` clauses, just like `switch` statements. Say, for example, you wanted to know if age was greater than or equal to 21.

## Listing 5.13  if-cases with where clauses

```
...
let age = 25

if case 18...35 = age {
    print("Cool demographic")
}
if case 18...35 = age where age >= 21 {
    print("In cool demographic and of drinking age")
}
```

The new code above does the same as before, but adds something new. It also checks to see if age is 21 or greater. In the United States, this means that the person in question is also old enough to drink.

`if-cases` provide an elegant substitute for `switch` statements with only one condition. They also enjoy all of the pattern matching power that make `switch` statements so wonderful. Use an `if-case` when you have only one case in mind for a `switch` and you do not care about the `default` case. Because `if-case` statements are just regular `if/else` statements with improved pattern matching, you can also write the usual `else` block – but doing so would mean that you are effectively writing the `default` case and would detract from some of the `if-case`'s allure.

# Bronze Challenge

Review the `switch` statement below. What will be logged to the console? After you have decided, enter the code in a playground to see if you were right.

```
let point = (x: 1, y: 4)

switch point {
case let q1 where (point.x > 0) && (point.y > 0):
    print("\(q1) is in quadrant 1")

case let q2 where (point.x < 0) && point.y > 0:
    print("\(q2) is in quadrant 2")

case let q3 where (point.x < 0) && point.y < 0:
    print("\(q3) is in quadrant 3")

case let q4 where (point.x > 0) && point.y < 0:
    print("\(q4) is in quadrant 4")

case (_, 0):
    print("\(point) sits on the x-axis")

case (0, _):
    print("\(point) sits on the y-axis")

default:
    print("Case not covered.")
}
```

# 6

# Loops

Loops help with tasks that are repetitive in nature. They execute a set of code repeatedly, either for a given number of iterations or as long as a defined condition is met. Loops can save you from writing tedious and repetitive code, so take note! You will be using them a lot in your development.

In this chapter, you will use two sorts of loops:

- the `for` loop

- the `while` loop

The `for` loop is ideal for iterating over the specific elements of an instance or collection of instances when the number of iterations to perform is either known or easy to derive. The `while` loop, on the other hand, is well suited for tasks that execute repeatedly as long as a certain condition is met. Each of these has variations. Let's start with a `for-in` loop, which performs a set of code for each item in a specific range, sequence, or collection.

## for-in Loops

Create a new `playground` called `Loops`. Create a loop as shown.

Listing 6.1 A `for-in` loop

```
import Cocoa

var myFirstInt: Int = 0

for i in 1...5 {
    ++myFirstInt
    print(myFirstInt)
}
```

First, you declare a variable called `myFirstInt` that is an instance of **Int** and is initialized to be equal to 0. Next, you create a `for-in` loop. Let's look at the components of the loop.

The `for` keyword signals that you are writing a loop. You next declare a constant called `i` that represents the current value of the *iterator*. This constant only exists inside the body of the loop. In the first iteration of the loop, its value is the first value in the range of the loop. Because you used `...` to create an inclusive range of 1 through 5, the first value of `i` is 1. In the second iteration, the value of `i` is 2, and so on. (To help keep track of where the loop is in its designated range, the value of this iterator is changed at each iteration of the loop.)

The code inside the braces ({}) is executed at each iteration of the loop. For each iteration, you increment myFirstInt by 1. You then log this value to the console. These two steps – incrementing and logging – continue until i reaches the end of the range: 5. This loop is represented in Figure 6.1.

Figure 6.1  Looping over a range

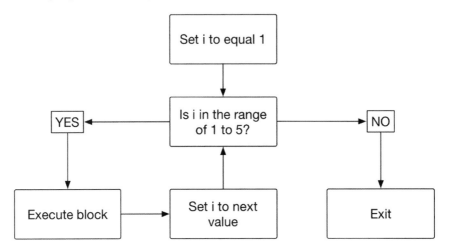

To see the results of your loop, find and click on the *results* button on the right edge of the results sidebar on the line with the code ++myFirstInt (Figure 6.2).

Figure 6.2  The results button

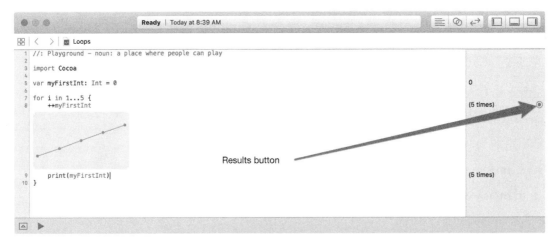

This opens a *results view* that displays the instance's value history inline with the code of the playground. You can grow or shrink the window of the graph by clicking and dragging its edges.

Move your mouse pointer into this new window and you will see that you can select individual points on this plot.

## Figure 6.3  Selecting a value on the plot

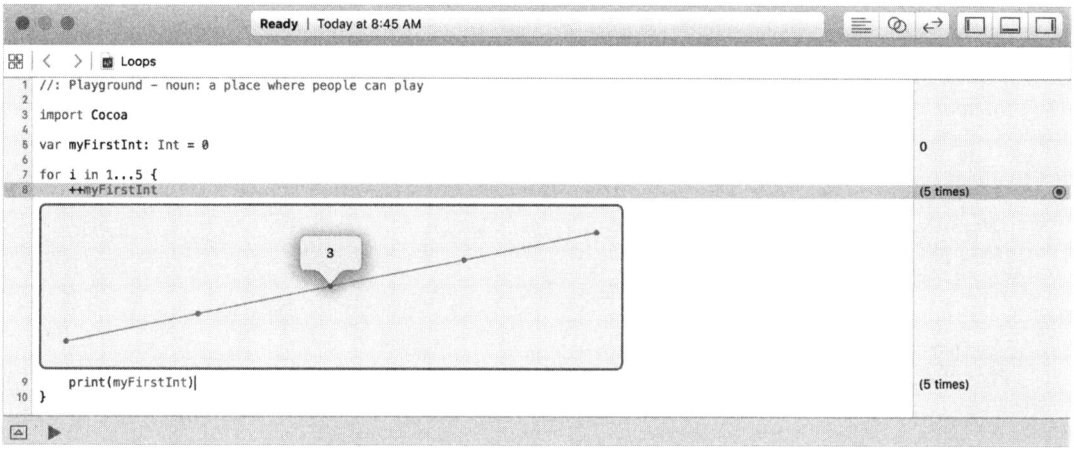

For example, if you click the middle point, the playground will tell you that the value of this point is 3.

Because you declared i to be the iterator in the for-in loop, you can access i inside of each iteration of the loop. Change your output to show the value of i at each iteration.

## Listing 6.2  Printing the changing value of i to the console

```
for i in 1...5 {
    ++myFirstInt
    print(myFirstInt)
    print("myFristInt equals \(myFirstInt) at iteration \(i)")
}
```

Instead of using an explicitly declared iterator, you can ignore it by using an _. Replace your named constant with this wildcard and return your print() statement to its earlier implementation.

## Listing 6.3  Replacing i with _

```
for i in 1...5 {
for _ in 1...5 {
    ++myFirstInt
    print("myFirstInt equals \(myFirstInt) at iteration \(i)")
    print(myFirstInt)
}
```

This implementation of the for-in loop ensures that a specific operation occurs a set number of times. It does not check and report the value of the iterator in each pass of the loop over its range. You would typically use the explicit iterator i if you wanted to refer to that iterator within your loop's code block.

# for case

Swift's `for-in` loop supports the use of `case` statements like the ones you saw in Chapter 5. Using a `case` allows for finer control over when the loop executes its code. Use a `case` with a `where` clause to provide a logical test that must be met in order to execute the loop's code. If the condition established by the `where` clause is not met, then the loop's code is not run.

For example, imagine that you want to write a loop that iterates over a range, but only executes its code when the loop encounters a value that is a multiple of 3.

### Listing 6.4  `for-in` loop with a `case`

```
for _ in 1...5 {
    ++myFirstInt
    print(myFirstInt)
}

for case let i in 1...100 where i % 3 == 0 {
    print(i)
}
```

The `case` lets you create a local constant `i` that you can then use in the `where` clause's condition. Each integer in the range of 1 to 100 is bound to `i`. The `where` clause then checks to see if `i` is divisible by 3. If the remainder is 0, the loop will execute its code. The result is that the loop will print out every multiple of 3 from 1 to 100.

Figure 6.4 demonstrates the flow of execution for this loop.

### Figure 6.4  `for case` diagram

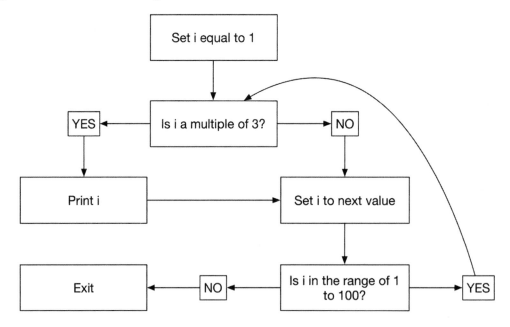

Imagine how you might accomplish this same result without the help of a `for case`.

```
for i in 1...100 {
    if i % 3 == 0 {
        print(i)
    }
}
```

The above code does the same work as the `for case` above, but it is less elegant. There are more lines of code and there is a nested conditional within the loop. Generally speaking, we prefer fewer lines of code, so long as it is not overly complex to read. Swift's `for case` pattern and `where` clauses are very readable, so we typically choose to use this more concise solution.

`for case` statements can be used in much more powerful ways. They are especially helpful with collections, as you will see in Chapter 9.

# A Quick Note on Type Inference

Take a look at this code that you entered earlier:

```
for i in 1...5 {
    ++myFirstInt
    print("myFirstInt equals \(myFirstInt) at iteration \(i)")
}
```

Notice that `i` is not declared to be of the **Int** type. It could be, as in: `for i: Int in 1...5` (the `let` portion of the declaration is assumed by the syntax for you). But it is not necessary. The type of `i` is inferred from its context. In this example, `i` is inferred to be of type **Int** because the specified range contains integers.

Type inference is handy. It lets you type less, which makes for fewer typos. However, there are a few cases where you need to specifically declare the type. We will highlight those when they come up. In general, however, we recommend that you take advantage of type inference whenever possible, and you will see many examples of it in this book.

# for Loops

Swift also supports the classic `for` loop:

```
for initialization; condition; increment {
    // Code to execute at each iteration
}
```

Semicolons separate the three parts of the `for` loop. Each part performs a specific function in the three steps of the loop's execution:

1. When the loop is entered, the *initialization* expression is evaluated to set up the iterator for the loop.

2. The *condition* expression is evaluated. If it is false, the loop is ended and execution of the code is transferred to after the loop. If it is true, then the code inside the loop's braces ({}) is executed.

3. After the code between the braces is executed, the *increment* expression is executed. Depending on the code, the incrementer can be increased or decreased. Once the incrementer is set, step 2 is repeated to determine whether the loop should continue iterating.

Refactor the implementation of the for-in loop from the beginning of this chapter to use the more traditional form.

Listing 6.5  A classic for loop

```
...
for var i = 1; i < 6; ++i {
    ++myFirstInt
    print(myFirstInt)
}
```

As you can see, the implementation is similar to the for-in loop and the result is exactly the same. Typically, you would choose this form over the for-in loop if you want to have specific control over the iterator's progress through the loop. For example, instead of incrementing i by 1 at each pass of the loop, you could instead increment by 3, or do something entirely different.

Figure 6.5 shows the flow of execution in this code.

Figure 6.5  for loop diagram

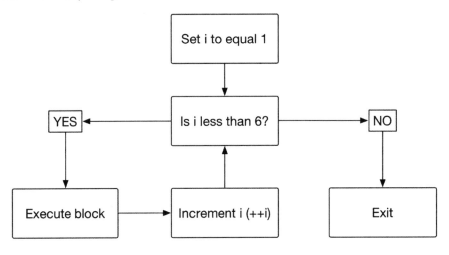

# while Loops

The classic for loop can also be expressed as a while loop.

Listing 6.6  A while loop

```
...
var i = 1
while i < 6 {
    ++myFirstInt
    print(myFirstInt)
    ++i
}
```

Like the `for` loop, this `while` loop initializes an incrementer (`var i = 1`), evaluates a condition (`i < 6`), executes code if the condition is valid (`++myFirstInt`, `print(myFirstInt)`, and increments the counter (`++i`)), and then returns to the top of the `while` loop to determine whether the loop should continue iterating.

`while` loops are best for circumstances in which the number of iterations the loop will pass through is unknown. For example, imagine a simple space shooter game with a spaceship that continuously fires its blasters so long as the spaceship has shields. Various external factors may lower or increase the ship's shields, so the exact number of iterations cannot be known. But if the shields have a value greater than 0, the blasters will keep shooting. The code snippet below illustrates a simplified implementation of this idea.

```
while shields > 0 {
    // Fire blasters!
    print("Fire blasters!")
}
```

# repeat-while Loops

Swift also supports a type of `while` loop called the `repeat-while` loop. The `repeat-while` loop is called a `do-while` loop in other languages. The difference between `while` and `repeat-while` loops is when they evaluate their condition. The `while` loop evaluates its condition before stepping into the loop. This means that the `while` loop may not ever execute, because its condition could be `false` when it is first evaluated. The `repeat-while` loop, on the other hand, executes its loop at least once, and *then* evaluates its condition. The syntax for the `repeat-while` loop demonstrates this difference.

```
repeat {
    // Fire blasters!
    print("Fire blasters!")
} while shields > 0
```

In this `repeat-while` version of the space shooter game, the code block that contains the line `print("Fire blasters!")` is executed first. Then the `repeat-while` loop's condition is evaluated to determine whether the loop should continue iterating. Thus, the `repeat-while` loop ensures that the spaceship fires its blasters at least one time.

The `repeat-while` loop avoids a somewhat depressing scenario: What if the spaceship is created and, by some freak accident, immediately loses all of its shields? Perhaps it spawns in front of an oncoming asteroid. It would not even get to fire a shot. That would be a pretty poor user experience. A `repeat-while` loop ensures that the blasters fire at least once to avoid this anticlimactic scenario.

# Control Transfer Statements, Redux

Let's revisit control transfer statements in the context of loops. Recall from Chapter 5 (where you used `fallthrough` and `break`) that control transfer statements change the typical order of execution. In the context of a loop, you can control whether execution iterates to the top of the loop or leaves the loop altogether.

Let's elaborate on the space shooter game to see how this works. You are going to use the `continue` control transfer statement to stop the loop where it is and begin again from the top.

## Listing 6.7  Using `continue`

```
var shields = 5
var blastersOverheating = false
var blasterFireCount = 0
while shields > 0 {

    if blastersOverheating {
        print("Blasters are overheated!  Cooldown initiated.")
        sleep(5)
        print("Blasters ready to fire")
        sleep(1)
        blastersOverheating = false
        blasterFireCount = 0
    }

    if blasterFireCount > 100 {
        blastersOverheating = true
        continue
    }
    // Fire blasters!
    print("Fire blasters!")

    ++blasterFireCount
}
```

You are adding a good bit of code, so let's break it down. First, you add some variables that keep track of the following information:

- `shields` is of type **Int**, keeps track of the shield strength, and is initialized to be equal to 5

- `blastersOverheating` is a **Boolean** initialized to `false` that keeps track of whether the blasters need time to cool down

- `blasterFireCount` is of type **Int** and keeps track of the number of shots the spaceship has fired (which determines whether the blasters are overheating)

After creating your variables, you wrote two `if` statements, both contained in a `while` loop with a condition of `shields > 0`. The first `if` statement checks whether the blasters are overheating, and the second checks the fire count. For the first, if the blasters are overheating, a number of code steps execute. You log information to the console and the **sleep()** function tells the system to wait for 5 seconds, which models the blasters' cooldown phase. You next log that the blasters are ready to fire again (after waiting for 1 more second, which you do simply because it makes it easier to see what logs to the console next), set `blastersOverheating` to be equal to `false`, and also reset `blasterFireCount` to 0.

With shields intact and blasters cooled down, the spaceship is ready to fire away.

The second `if` statement checks whether `blasterFireCount` is greater than 100. If this conditional evaluates to `true`, you set the **Boolean** for `blastersOverheating` to be `true`. At this point, the blasters are overheated, so you need a way to jump back up to the top of the loop so that the spaceship does not fire. You use `continue` to do this. Since the spaceship's blasters have overheated, the conditional in the first `if` statement will evaluate to `true`, and the blasters will shut down to cool off.

If the second conditional is evaluated to be `false`, you log to the console as before. Next, you increment the `blasterFireCount` by one. After you increment this variable, the loop will jump back up to the top, evaluate the condition, and either iterate again or hand off the flow of execution to the line immediately after the closing brace of the loop. Figure 6.6 shows this flow of execution.

Figure 6.6 `while` loop diagram

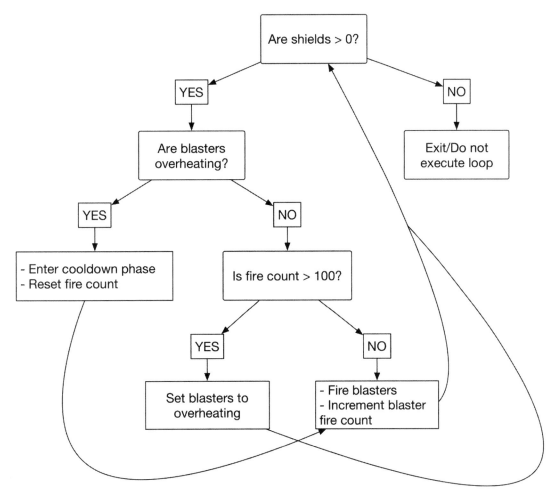

Note that this code will execute indefinitely. There is nothing to change the value of `shields`, so while `shields > 0` is always satisfied. If nothing changes, and your computer has enough power to run forever, this loop will continue to execute. This is what we call an *infinite loop*.

But all games must come to an end. Let's say that the game is over when the user has destroyed 500 space demons. To exit the loop, you will use the break control transfer statement.

## Listing 6.8  Using break

```
var shields = 5
var blastersOverheating = false
var blasterFireCount = 0
var spaceDemonsDestroyed = 0
while shields > 0 {

    if spaceDemonsDestroyed == 500 {
        print("You beat the game!")
        break
    }

    if blastersOverheating {
        print("Blasters are overheated!  Cooldown initiated.")
        sleep(5)
        print("Blasters ready to fire")
        sleep(1)
        blastersOverheating = false
        blasterFireCount = 0
        continue
    }

    if blasterFireCount > 100 {
        blastersOverheating = true
        continue
    }
    // Fire blasters!
    print("Fire blasters!")
    ++blasterFireCount
    ++spaceDemonsDestroyed
}
```

Here, you add a new variable called spaceDemonsDestroyed, which is incremented each time the blasters fire. (You are a pretty good shot, apparently.) Next, you add a new if statement that checks whether the spaceDemonsDestroyed variable is equal to 500. If it is, you log victory to the console.

Note the use of break. The break control transfer statement will exit the while loop, and execution will pick up on the line immediately after the closing brace of the loop. This makes sense: if the user has destroyed 500 space demons and the game is won, the blasters do not need to fire anymore.

# Bronze Challenge

Use a loop to count by 2 from 0 up to 100. Use another loop to make sure the first loop is run 5 times. Hint: one good way to do this is to use a nested loop.

# 7

# Strings

In programming, textual content is represented by strings. You have seen and used strings already. "Hello, playground", for example, is a string that appears at the top of every newly created playground. Like all strings, it can be thought of as an ordered collection of characters. In this chapter, you will see more of what strings can do.

## Working with Strings

In Swift, you create strings with the **String** type. Create a new playground called Strings.playground and add the following new instance of the **String** type.

Listing 7.1 Hello, playground

```
let playground = "Hello, playground"
```

You have created a **String** instance named playground using the string literal syntax, which encloses a sequence of text with quotation marks.

This instance was created with the let keyword, making it a constant. Recall that being a constant means that the instance cannot be changed. If you do try to change it, the compiler will give you an error.

Create a new string, but make this instance mutable.

Listing 7.2 Creating a mutable string

```
let playground = "Hello, playground"
var mutablePlayground = "Hello, mutable playground"
```

mutablePlayground is a mutable instance of the **String** type. In other words, you can change the contents of this string. Use the addition and assignment operator to add some final punctuation.

Listing 7.3 Adding to a mutable string

```
let playground = "Hello, playground"
var mutablePlayground = "Hello, mutable playground"
mutablePlayground += "!"
```

Take a look at the results sidebar on the righthand side of the playground. You should see that the instance has changed to "Hello, mutable playground!"

The characters that comprise Swift's strings are of the **Character** type. You use Swift's **Character** type to represent Unicode characters, and in combination **Character**s form a **String** instance.

Loop through the `mutablePlayground` string to see the **Character** type in action.

## Listing 7.4  `mutablePlayground`'s **Character**s

```
let playground = "Hello, playground"
var mutablePlayground = "Hello, mutable playground"
mutablePlayground += "!"
for c: Character in mutablePlayground.characters {
    print("\(c)")
}
```

This loop iterates through every **Character** c in `mutablePlayground`. In it, you access the `characters` property of the **String** `mutablePlayground`. Do not worry about what a property is right now; this topic will be covered in detail in Chapter 16. For now, all you need to know is that a property is a way a type holds on to data. In Swift, you access properties via *dot syntax*, as in `mutablePlayground.characters`.

The `characters` property represents the collection of characters that make up the instance. Each iteration of the loop logs one of the **String**'s characters to the console. Every character is logged to the console on its own line because **print()** prints a line break after logging its content.

Reveal the console. Your output should look like Figure 7.1.

## Figure 7.1  Logging characters in a string

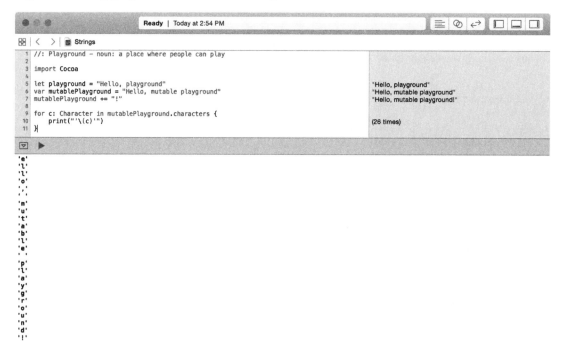

# Unicode

Unicode is an international standard that encodes characters so they can be seamlessly processed and represented regardless of the platform. Unicode represents human language (and other forms of communication like emoji) on computers. Every character in the standard is assigned a unique number.

Swift's **String** and **Character** types are built on top of Unicode and they do the majority of the heavy lifting. Nonetheless, it is good to have an understanding of how these types work with Unicode. Having this knowledge will likely save you some time and frustration in the future.

## Unicode scalars

At their heart, strings in Swift are composed of *Unicode scalars*. Unicode scalars are 21-bit numbers that represent a specific character in the Unicode standard. For example, U+0061 represents the Latin small letter 'a'. U+1F60E represents the smiley-faced emoji with sunglasses. The text U+1F60E is the standard way of writing a Unicode character. The 1F60E portion is a number written in hexadecimal, or base 16.

Create a constant to see how to use specific Unicode scalars in Swift and the playground.

Listing 7.5  Using a Unicode scalar

```
let playground = "Hello, playground"
var mutablePlayground = "Hello, mutable playground"
mutablePlayground += "!"

for c: Character in mutablePlayground.characters {
    print("'\(c)'")
}
let oneCoolDude = "\u{1F60E}"
```

This time, you used a new syntax to create a string. The quotation marks are familiar, but what is inside them is not a string literal, as you have seen before. It does not match the results in the sidebar (Figure 7.2).

Figure 7.2  Emoji in the sidebar

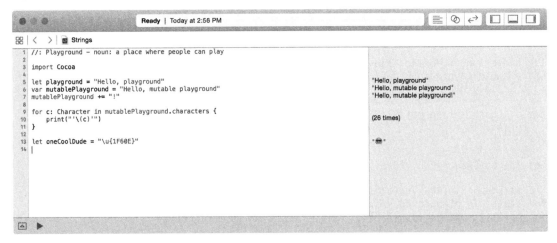

The \u{} syntax represents the Unicode scalar whose hexadecimal number appears between the braces. In this case, oneCoolDude is assigned to be equal to the character representing the sunglasses-wearing emoji.

How does this relate to more familiar strings? It turns out that every string in Swift is composed of Unicode scalars. So why do they look unfamiliar? To explain, we need to discuss a few more concepts.

Every character in Swift is built up from one or more Unicode scalars. One Unicode scalar maps onto one fundamental character in a given language. But we say that characters are built from "one or more" Unicode scalars because there are also *combining scalars*. For example, U+0301 represents the Unicode scalar for the combining acute accent: ´. This scalar is placed on top of – that is, combined with – the character that precedes it. You can use this scalar with the Latin small letter 'a' to create the character á.

## Listing 7.6  Using a combining scalar

```
let playground = "Hello, playground"
var mutablePlayground = "Hello, mutable playground"
mutablePlayground += "!"

for c: Character in mutablePlayground.characters {
    print("'\(c)'")
}

let oneCoolDude = "\u{1F60E}"
let aAcute = "\u{0061}\u{0301}"
```

You should see á, the combination of the letter 'a' and the acute accent, in the results sidebar.

Every character in Swift is an *extended grapheme cluster*. Extended grapheme clusters are sequences of one or more Unicode scalars that combine to produce a single human-readable character. Earlier, you decomposed the character á into its two constituent Unicode scalars: the letter and the accent. Making characters extended grapheme clusters gives Swift flexibility in dealing with complex script characters.

Swift also provides a mechanism to see all of the Unicode scalars in a string. For example, you can see all of the Unicode scalars that Swift uses to create the instance of **String** named playground that you created earlier using the unicodeScalars property, which holds all of the scalars that Swift uses to make the string. Add the following code to your playground to see playground's Unicode scalars.

## Listing 7.7  Revealing the Unicode scalars behind a string

```
let playground = "Hello, playground"
var mutablePlayground = "Hello, mutable playground"
mutablePlayground += "!"

for c: Character in mutablePlayground.characters {
    print("'\(c)'")
}

let oneCoolDude = "\u{1F60E}"

let aAcute = "\u{0061}\u{0301}"
for scalar in playground.unicodeScalars {
    print("\(scalar.value) ")
}
```

If it is not already open, open the assistant editor to view the console. You should see the following output: 72 101 108 108 111 44 32 112 108 97 121 103 114 111 117 110 100. What do all of these numbers mean?

Recall that the `unicodeScalars` property holds on to data representing all of the Unicode scalars used to create the string instance `playground`. Each number on the console corresponds to a Unicode scalar representing a single character in the string. But they are not the hexadecimal Unicode numbers. Instead, each is represented as an unsigned 32-bit integer. The first, 72, corresponds to the Unicode scalar value of U+0048, or an uppercase 'H'.

## Canonical equivalence

While there is a role for combining scalars, Unicode also provides already-combined forms for some common characters. For example, there is a specific scalar for á. You do not actually need to decompose it into its two parts: the letter and the accent. The scalar is U+00E1. Create a new constant string that uses this Unicode scalar.

### Listing 7.8  Using a precomposed character

```
...
let aAcute = "\u{0061}\u{0301}"

for scalar in playground.unicodeScalars {
    print("\(scalar.value) ")
}

let aAcutePrecomposed = "\u{00E1}"
```

As you can see, `aAcutePrecomposed` appears to have the same value as `aAcute`. Indeed, if you check to see if these two characters are the same, you will find that Swift answers "yes."

### Listing 7.9  Checking equivalence

```
let aAcute = "\u{0061}\u{0301}"

for scalar in playground.unicodeScalars {
    print("\(scalar.value) ")
}

let aAcutePrecomposed = "\u{00E1}"

let b = (aAcute == aAcutePrecomposed) // true
```

`aAcute` was created using two Unicode scalars, and `aAcutePrecomposed` only used one. Why does Swift say that they are equivalent? The answer is *canonical equivalence*.

Canonical equivalence refers to whether two sequences of Unicode scalars are the same *linguistically*. Two characters, or two strings, are considered equal if they have the same linguistic meaning and appearance, regardless of whether they are built from the same Unicode scalars. `aAcute` and `aAcutePrecomposed` are equal strings because both represent the Latin small letter 'a' with an acute accent. The fact that they were created with different Unicode scalars does not affect this.

## Counting elements

Canonical equivalence has implications for counting elements of a string. You might think that aAcute and aAcutePrecomposed would have different character counts. Write the following code to check.

### Listing 7.10  Counting characters

```
let aAcute = "\u{0061}\u{0301}"

for scalar in playground.unicodeScalars {
    print("\(scalar.value) ")
}

let aAcutePrecomposed = "\u{00E1}"
let b = (aAcute == aAcutePrecomposed)
print("aAcute: \(aAcute.characters.count);
        aAcuteDecomposed: \(AcutePrecomposed.characters.count)")
```

You use the count property on characters to determine the character count of these two strings. count iterates over a character of string's Unicode scalars to determine its length. The results sidebar reveals that the character counts are the same: both are 1 character long. Canonical equivalence means that whether you use a combining scalar or a precomposed scalar, the result is treated as a single character.

## Indices and ranges

Because strings can be thought of as ordered collections of characters, you might think that you can access a specific character on a string like so:

```
let index = playground[3] // 'l'???
```

The code playground[3] uses the subscript syntax. In general, the brackets ([]) indicate that you are using a subscript in Swift. Subscripts allow you to retrieve a specific value within a collection.

3 is an *index* that is used to find a particular element within a collection. The code above suggests that you are trying to select the fourth character from the collection of characters making up the playground string (the first index is 0). You will learn more about subscripts below, and will also see them in action in Chapter 9 and Chapter 10 on arrays and dictionaries.

If you tried to use a subscript like this, you would get an error: "'subscript' is unavailable: cannot subscript String with an Int." The Swift compiler will not let you access a specific character on a string via a subscript index. This limitation has to do with the way Swift strings and characters are stored. You cannot index a string with an integer because Swift does not know which Unicode scalar corresponds to a given index without stepping through every preceding character. This operation can be expensive. Therefore, Swift forces you to be more explicit.

Swift uses a type called **String.Index** to keep track of indices. Do not worry about the . in **String.Index**; it just means that **Index** is a type that is defined on **String** to help manage indices. To find the character at a particular index, you use the **String** type's startIndex property. This property yields the starting index of a string as a **String.Index**. You can then use this starting point in conjunction with the **advancedBy(_:)** function to move forward until you arrive at the position of your choosing.

Say you want to know the fifth character of the playground string that you created at the beginning of this chapter.

## Listing 7.11  Finding the fifth character

```
...
let fromStart = playground.startIndex
let toPosition = 4 // The first position is 0
let end = fromStart.advancedBy(toPosition)
let fifthCharacter = playground[end] // 'o'
```

You use the `startIndex` property on the string to get the first index of the string. This property yields an instance of type **String.Index**. Next, you create a constant to hold onto the position within the string to which you would like to advance. 4 represents the fifth character because the string is zero-indexed (i.e., 0 is the first index).

Next, you used the **advancedBy(_:)** function to advance from the starting point to your desired position. The result is a **String.Index** that you used to subscript your `playground` string instance, which resulted in the character 'o'. (`playground`, remember, is set to equal "Hello, playground".)

Ranges, like indices, depend upon the **String.Index** type. Imagine that you wanted to grab the first five characters of `playground`. You can use the same `fromStart` and `end` constants.

## Listing 7.12  Pulling out a range

```
...
let fromStart = playground.startIndex
let toPosition = 4
let end = fromStart.advancedBy(toPosition)
let fifthCharacter = playground[end] // 'o'
let range = fromStart...end
let firstFive = playground[range] // 'Hello'
```

The syntax `fromStart...end` creates a range of type **String.Index**, but it works similarly to the range you saw in Chapter 6 for the range `1...5`. You used this new range as a subscript on the `playground` string. This subscript grabbed the first five characters from `playground`. The result is that `firstFive` is a constant equal to "Hello".

# Silver Challenge

Replace the "Hello" string with an instance created out of its corresponding Unicode scalars. You can find the appropriate codes on the Internet.

# 8

# Optionals

Optionals are a special feature in Swift used to indicate that an instance may not have a value. When you see an optional, you know one of two things about that instance: either it has a value and it is ready for use, or it has no value. If an instance has no value associated with it, we say that it is *nil*.

You can use optionals with any type to signal that an instance is potentially nil. This feature distinguishes Swift from Objective-C, which only allows objects to be nil.

This chapter covers how to declare optional types, how to use *optional binding* to check whether an optional is nil and make use of its value if it has one, and how to use *optional chaining* to query a sequence of optional values.

## Optional Types

Optionals in Swift make the language safer. An instance that may potentially be nil should be declared to be an optional type. This means that if an instance is *not* declared as an optional type, this instance is guaranteed to *not* be nil. This way, the compiler knows whether an instance can be nil. This explicit declaration makes your code more expressive and safe.

Let's take a look at how to declare an optional type. Create a new playground and name it Optionals. Enter the code snippet below.

Listing 8.1 Declaring an optional type

```
import Cocoa

var errorCodeString: String?
errorCodeString = "404"
```

First, you make a variable named errorCodeString to hold on to error code information in a string format. Next, you explicitly declare the type of errorCodeString to be **String** – but in a slightly different way than what you have done before. This time you put a ? at the end of **String**. The ? makes errorCodeString an optional of the type **String**.

Now that you have declared an optional and given it a value, log the value of the optional to the console.

Listing 8.2 Logging the value of the optional to the console

```
import Cocoa

var errorCodeString: String?
errorCodeString = "404"
print(errorCodeString)
```

Because you have given errorCodeString a value of "404," logging its value to the console works as you have seen before. What would happen if you did not give errorCodeString a value? Try it! Comment out the line assigning a value to errorCodeString.

## Listing 8.3  Logging the nil value of the optional to the console

```
import Cocoa

var errorCodeString: String?
// errorCodeString = "404"
print(errorCodeString)
```

Checking the console, you will see that it has logged the value nil.

But logging nil to the console is not very helpful. Instead, you want to know when your variables are nil so that you can execute code based on whether there is a value. You can use a conditional to gain traction on a variable's value in these circumstances.

For example, let's say that if some operation generated an error, you would want to assign that error to a new variable and log it to the console. Add the following code to your playground.

## Listing 8.4  Adding a condition

```
import Cocoa

var errorCodeString: String?
// errorCodeString = "404"
print(errorCodeString)
if errorCodeString != nil {
    let theError = errorCodeString!
    print(theError)
}
```

Let's look at what you did here. You set up a conditional with code that executes if errorCodeString is not nil (remember that != means "is not equal to").

Next, you created a new constant called theError to hold the value of errorCodeString. To do this, you appended ! to errorCodeString. The exclamation mark here does what is called *forced unwrapping*.

Forced unwrapping accesses the underlying value of the optional, which allows you to grab "404" and assign it to the constant theError. This is called "forced" unwrapping because it tries to access the underlying value whether or not there is actually a value there at all. That is, the ! assumes there is a value; if there is no value, unwrapping the value in this way would lead to a runtime error.

There is some danger in forced unwrapping. If there is no value inside the optional, your program will crash at runtime. In this case, you checked to make sure that errorCodeString was not nil, so force-unwrapping it was not dangerous. Nonetheless, we suggest that you use force-unwrapping cautiously and sparingly.

Finally, you logged this new constant's value to the console.

What would have happened if you had not unwrapped errorCodeString's value but simply assigned the optional to the constant theError? The value of theError would still have been logged to the console correctly. So, why unwrap the optional's value and assign it to a constant? The answer requires a better understanding of the optional type.

If you had omitted the exclamation mark at the end of errorCodeString, you would have simply assigned the optional **String** to a constant instead of the actual **String** value for the error code. In fact, errorCodeString's type is **String?**. **String?** is not the same type as **String** – if you have a **String** variable, you cannot set it to the value of a **String?** without unwrapping the optional.

The optional errorCodeString was nil when it was first declared because it was given no value. In the next line, you assigned "404" to errorCodeString. You can compare an optional value to nil to determine whether it contains a value. In the code above, you first check whether errorCodeString has a value; if the value is not equal to nil, you know it is safe to unwrap errorCodeString.

Creating a constant inside the conditional is a little clunky. Fortunately, there is a better way to conditionally bind an optional's value to a constant. It is called *optional binding*.

# Optional Binding

Optional binding is a useful pattern to detect whether an optional contains a value. If there is a value, then you can assign it to a temporary constant or variable and make it available within a conditional's first branch of execution. This can make your code more concise while also retaining its expressive nature. Here is the basic syntax:

```
if let temporaryConstant = anOptional {
    // Do something with temporaryConstant
 } else {
    // There was no value in anOptional; i.e., anOptional is nil
}
```

With this syntax in hand, refactor the example above to make use of optional binding.

Listing 8.5  Optional binding

```
import Cocoa

var errorCodeString: String?
errorCodeString = "404"
if errorCodeString != nil {
    let theError = errorCodeString!
if let theError = errorCodeString {
    print(theError)
}
```

As you can see, the syntax for optional binding is more or less the same as the syntax using a constant created within the conditional. The constant theError moves from the body of the conditional to its first line. This makes theError a temporary constant that is available within the first branch of the conditional. In other words, if there is a value within the optional, then a temporary constant is made available for use in the block of code that is executed if the condition is evaluated as true.

Also, you no longer forcibly unwrap the optional. If the conversion is successful, then this operation is done for you and the optional's value is made available to you in the temporary constant you declared. Finally, note that you could have declared theError with the var keyword if you needed to manipulate the value inside the first branch of the conditional.

Imagine that you wanted to convert errorCodeString to its corresponding integer representation. You could accomplish this by nesting if let bindings.

## Listing 8.6  Nesting optional binding

```
import Cocoa

var errorCodeString: String?
errorCodeString = "404"
if let theError = errorCodeString {
    print(theError)
    if let errorCodeInteger = Int(theError) {
        print("\(theError): \(errorCodeInteger)")
    }
}
```

Notice that the second if let takes place within the first. Doing so makes theError available to use in the second optional binding. Here, you use a syntax that you saw in Chapter 4 to convert between integer types.

In the example above, you use Int(theError) to convert between the **String** instance in theError to its corresponding **Int**. This operation can fail; for example, the string "Error!" does not naturally translate to an integer. Therefore, Int(theError) returns an optional, in case a corresponding **Int** is not found for the given string.

The result of Int(theError) is unwrapped and assigned to errorCodeInteger in the second binding. Doing so makes the integer value available for use. You can then use both of these new constants in a call to **print()** to log them to the console.

Nesting optional binding can be convoluted. While it is not *too* bad with just a couple of optionals, you can imagine how complicated this strategy can get if you have several more optionals that need unwrapping. We call deeply nested optional bindings the "Pyramid of Doom," a reference to the many indentation levels. Thankfully, you can unwrap multiple optionals in a single if let binding. This feature helps to avoid the need for nesting multiple if let calls, avoiding nasty code like you saw above (and worse).

## Listing 8.7  Unwrapping multiple optionals

```
import Cocoa

var errorCodeString: String?
errorCodeString = "404"
if let theError = errorCodeString, errorCodeInteger = Int(theError) {
    if let errorCodeInteger = Int(theError) {
    print("\(theError): \(errorCodeInteger)")
    }
}
```

You now unwrap two optionals in a single line: if let theError = errorCodeString, errorCodeInteger = Int(theError). Next, errorCodeString is unwrapped, and its value is given to theError. You use Int(theError) to try to convert theError in an **Int**. Because this results in an optional, you next unwrap that optional and bind its value to errorCodeInteger. If either of these bindings return nil, then the success block of the conditional will not execute. In this case, errorCodeString has a value and the theError can be successfully unwrapped because theError can be converted into an integer.

Optional binding can even take a where clause that works very similarly to what you saw in Chapter 5. Imagine that you only care about an error code if the value is 404. A where clause can help you to focus on the values that you deem important.

### Listing 8.8  Optional binding and where clauses

```
import Cocoa

var errorCodeString: String?
errorCodeString = "404"
if let theError = errorCodeString, errorCodeInteger = Int(theError)
    where errorCodeInteger == 404 {
    print("\(theError): \(errorCodeInteger)")
}
```

Now, the conditional evaluates to true if errorCodeInteger is equal to 404. The where clause is only executed if both optionals are successfully unwrapped. Since theError is "404", and that string can be converted to the integer 404, all conditions are met and the value 404 is logged to the console.

# Implicitly Unwrapped Optionals

At this point it is worth mentioning *implicitly unwrapped optionals*, though you will not make much use of them until we discuss classes and class initialization later. Implicitly unwrapped optionals are like regular optional types, but with one important difference: you do not need to unwrap them. How is that the case? It has to do with how you declare them. Take a look at the code below, which refactors the example above to work with an implicitly unwrapped optional.

```
import Cocoa

var errorCodeString: String!
errorCodeString = "404"
print(errorCodeString)
```

Here, the optional is declared with the !, which signifies that it is an implicitly unwrapped optional. The conditional is removed because using an implicitly unwrapped optional signifies a great deal more confidence than its more humble counterpart. Indeed, much of the power and flexibility associated with the implicitly unwrapped optional is related to the idea that you do not need to unwrap it to access its value.

Note, however, that this power and flexibility comes with some danger: accessing the value of an implicitly unwrapped optional will result in a runtime error if it does not have a value. For this reason, we suggest that you do not use the implicitly unwrapped optional if you believe that the instance has any chance of becoming nil. Using implicitly unwrapped optionals is best limited to somewhat special cases. As we indicated, the primary case concerns class initialization, which we will discuss in detail in Chapter 17. For now, you know enough of the basics of implicitly unwrapped optionals to understand what is going on if you find them in the wild.

# Optional Chaining

Like optional binding, *optional chaining* provides a mechanism for querying an optional to determine whether it contains a value. One important difference between the two is that optional chaining allows the programmer to chain numerous queries into an optional's value. If each optional in the chain contains a value, then the call to each succeeds, and the entire query chain will return an optional of the expected type. If any optional in the query chain is `nil`, then the entire chain will return `nil`.

Let's begin with a concise example. Imagine that your app has a custom error code for some reason. If you encounter a 404, you actually want to use your customized error code instead. Afterward, you will want to add some more descriptive text to an error description you will display to the user. Add the following to your playground.

### Listing 8.9  Optional chaining

```
var errorCodeString: String?
errorCodeString = "404"
var errorDescription: String?
if let theError = errorCodeString, errorCodeInteger = Int(theError)
    where errorCodeInteger == 404 {
    print("\(theError): \(errorCodeInteger)")
    errorDescription = ("\(errorCodeInteger + 200):
                        the requested resource was not found.")
}

var upCaseErrorDescription = errorDescription?.uppercaseString
errorDescription
```

You added a new `var` named `errorDescription`. Inside of the `if-let` success block, you created a new interpolated string and assigned that instance to `errorDescription`. When you created the interpolated string (`\(errorCodeInteger + 200): `), you increased 404 to your custom error code value of 604 (this is arbitrary, and theoretically unique to your app). Last, you added some more informative text about the error.

Next, you used optional chaining to create a new instance of the error description to be in all uppercase text, perhaps to indicate its urgency. This instance is called `upCaseErrorDescription`. The question mark appended to the end of `errorDescription` signals that this line of code initiates the optional chaining process. If there is no value in `errorDescription`, then there is no string to uppercase. In that case, `upCaseErrorDescription` would be set to `nil`. This point demonstrates that optional chaining will return an optional.

Because `errorDescription` does have a value in it, you uppercased the description and reassigned that new value to `upCaseErrorDescription`. The results sidebar should display the updated value: "604: THE REQUESTED RESOURCE WAS NOT FOUND."

# Modifying an Optional in Place

You can modify an optional "in place." Add a call to **appendContentsOf(_:)** on upCaseErrorDescription.

## Listing 8.10  Modifying in place

```
...
upCaseErrorDescription?.appendContentsOf(" PLEASE TRY AGAIN.")
upCaseErrorDescription
```

Modifying an optional in place can be extremely helpful. In this case, all we wanted to do was update a string inside of an optional. We did not need anything returned. If there was a value inside of the optional, then we wanted to add some text to the string. If there was no value, then we did not want to do anything.

This is exactly what modifying an optional in place does. The ? at the end of upCaseErrorDescription works similarly to optional chaining insofar as it exposes the value of the optional to us if it exists. If upCaseErrorDescription were nil, then the optional would not have been modified because no value existed to update.

It is worth mentioning that you can also use the ! operator in the code above. This operation would forcibly unwrap the optional – which can be dangerous, as you have learned. If upCaseErrorDescription were nil, then upCaseErrorDescription!.appendContentsOf(" PLEASE TRY AGAIN.") would lead to a runtime crash.

As you have read above, it is best to use ? most of the time. The ! operator should be used when you know that the optional will not be nil or that the *only* reasonable action to take is to crash if the optional is nil.

# The Nil Coalescing Operator

A common operation when dealing with optionals is to either get the value (if the optional contains value) or to use some default value if the optional is nil. For example, when pulling out the error information inside of errorDescription, you might want to default to "No error" if the string does not contain an error. You could accomplish this with optional binding.

## Listing 8.11  Using optional binding to parse errorCodeString

```
...
let description: String
if let errorDescription = errorDescription {
    description = errorDescription
} else {
    description = "No error"
}
```

There is a problem with this technique. You had to write a lot of code for what should be a simple operation: get the value from the optional or use "No error" if the optional was nil. This can be solved via the *nil coalescing operator*: ??. Let's see what that looks like.

### Listing 8.12  Using the nil coalescing operator

```
...
let description: String
if let errorDescription = errorDescription {
    description = errorDescription
} else {
    description = "No error"
}
let description = errorDescription ?? "No error"
```

The lefthand side of ?? must be an optional – errorDescription in this case, which is an optional **String**. The righthand side must be a nonoptional of the same type – "No error" in your case, which is a **String**. If the lefthand side optional is nil, ?? returns the righthand side. If the lefthand side optional is not nil, ?? returns the value contained in the optional.

Try changing errorDescription so that it does not contain an error, and confirm that description gets the value "No error":

### Listing 8.13  Changing errorCodeString

```
...
errorDescription = nil
let description = errorDescription ?? "No error"
```

This chapter was fairly involved. You learned a lot of new material. Optionals are a new topic regardless of your level of experience in Mac or iOS development. They are also a powerful feature of Swift.

As a developer, you will often need to represent nil in an instance. Optionals help you keep track of whether instances are nil and provide a mechanism to respond appropriately.

If optionals do not quite feel comfortable yet, do not worry. You will be seeing them quite a bit in future chapters.

# Silver Challenge

Earlier in the chapter we told you that accessing an optional's value when it is nil will result in a runtime error. Make this mistake by force-unwrapping an optional when it is nil. Next, examine the error and understand what the error is telling you.

# Part III
## Collections and Functions

As a programmer, you will often have a *collection* of related values that you need to keep together. Collections in Swift help you do this, and this part of the book will introduce you to Swift's different collection options.

Swift provides functions to help developers transform data into something meaningful for the user or accomplish some other task. These chapters also describe how to use the system functions provided by the Swift language as well as how to create your own functions to accomplish your goals.

# 9

# Arrays

An important task in programming is to group together logically related values. For example, imagine your application keeps lists of a user's friends, favorite books, travel locations, and so on. It is often necessary to be able to keep those values together and pass them around your code. *Collections* make these operations convenient.

Swift has a number of collection types. The first we will cover is called an **Array**.

Arrays are an ordered collection of values. Each position in an array is identified by an index, and any value can appear multiple times in an array. Arrays are typically used when the order of the values is important or useful to know, but it is not a prerequisite that the order of the values be meaningful. Unlike in Objective-C, Swift's **Array** type can hold on to any sort of value – objects and nonobjects alike.

To get started, create a new Swift playground called `Arrays`.

## Creating an Array

In this chapter, you will create an array that represents your bucket list: the things that you would like to do in the future. Create `Arrays.playground` and declare an array.

Listing 9.1  Creating an array

```
import Cocoa

var bucketList: Array<String>
```

Here, you create a new variable called `bucketList` that is of the type **Array**. Much of that syntax should look familiar. For example, the `var` keyword means that `bucketList` is a variable. This means that `bucketList` is mutable, so the array can be changed. There are also immutable arrays, which we will discuss later in this chapter.

What is probably new in the syntax is `<String>`. This code tells `bucketList` what sort of instances it can accept. Here, your array will accept instances of the **String** type. Arrays can hold instances of any type. Because this array will hold information concerning your future goals, it makes sense that it takes instances of **String**.

There is an alternative syntax for declaring an array. Make the following change in your playground.

## Listing 9.2  Changing the syntax

```
import Cocoa

var bucketList: Array<String>
var bucketList: [String]
```

Here, the brackets identify bucketList as an instance of **Array**, and the **String** syntax tells bucketList what sort of values it can accept.

Your bucketList is only declared. It is not yet initialized. This means that it is not yet ready to accept instances of the **String** type. If you were to try to append an item to your bucketList, you would get an error saying that you are trying to add something before your bucketList is initialized.

Change your declaration of bucketList to initialize the array in the same line.

## Listing 9.3  Initializing the array

```
import Cocoa

var bucketList: [String] = ["Climb Mt. Everest"]
```

You use the assignment operator = in conjunction with the **Array** literal syntax ["Climb Mt. Everest"]. An **Array** literal is a shorthand syntax that initializes an array with whatever instances you include. In this case, you initialize bucketList with the bucket item to climb Mt. Everest.

As with other types, you can create an instance of **Array** by taking advantage of Swift's type inference capabilities. Remove the type declaration from your code to use type inference.

## Listing 9.4  Using type inference

```
import Cocoa

var bucketList: [String]= ["Climb Mt. Everest"]
```

Nothing has really changed. Your bucket list still contains the same item, and it still will only accept instances of the **String** type. The only difference is that it now infers this based on the type of the instance used to initialize it. If you were to try to add an integer to this array, you would see an error telling you that you cannot add an instance of **Int** to your array because it is expecting instances of the **String** type.

Now that you know how to create and initialize an array, it is time to learn how to access and modify your array's elements.

# Accessing and Modifying Arrays

So, you have a bucket list? Great! Sadly, you do not have all that many ambitions in there yet. But you are an interesting person with a zeal for life, so let's add some values to your bucketList. Update your list with another ambition.

### Listing 9.5  Hot air balloon adventure

```
import Cocoa

var bucketList = ["Climb Mt. Everest"]
bucketList.append("Fly hot air balloon to Fiji")
```

You are using **append(_:)** to add a value to bucketList. The **append(_:)** function takes an argument of whatever type an array accepts and makes it a new element in the array.

Your playground should look like Figure 9.1.

### Figure 9.1  Appending to your bucket list

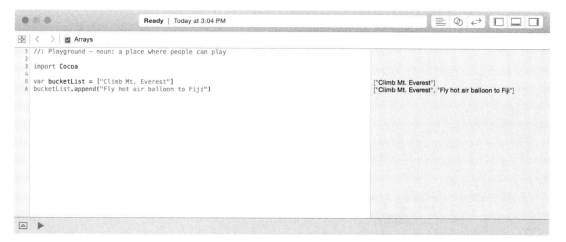

Add more future adventures to your bucket list using the **append(_:)** function.

### Listing 9.6  So many ambitions!

```
import Cocoa

var bucketList = ["Climb Mt. Everest"]
bucketList.append("Fly hot air balloon to Fiji")
bucketList.append("Watch the Lord of the Rings trilogy in one day")
bucketList.append("Go on a walkabout")
bucketList.append("Scuba dive in the Great Blue Hole")
bucketList.append("Find a triple rainbow")
```

Now you have six items in bucketList. But what if you have a change of heart? Or – thinking positively – what happens when you accomplish one of the items on your list?

Suppose last weekend you settled in and spent 10 hours watching the *Lord of the Rings* series. Now it is time to take that item off your list. Remove it with the function `removeAtIndex(_:)`.

### Listing 9.7  Removing an item from the array

```
import Cocoa

var bucketList = ["Climb Mt. Everest"]
bucketList.append("Fly hot air balloon to Fiji")
bucketList.append("Watch the Lord of the Rings trilogy in one day")
bucketList.append("Go on a walkabout")
bucketList.append("Scuba dive in the Great Blue Hole")
bucketList.append("Find a triple rainbow")
bucketList.removeAtIndex(2)
bucketList
```

To confirm that the value in the second index was removed from your `bucketList`, highlight the final line (`bucketList`) in the results sidebar and click the button that looks like an eye. This is called the *quick look* (Figure 9.2). The count of items in your array is now 5. The item formerly at the second index – your movie marathon – is gone. `"Go on a walkabout"` now occupies the second index.

(Why is the item at the second index not the hot air balloon voyage? Arrays are zero-indexed, so `bucketList[0]` is equal to `"Climb Mt. Everest"`.)

### Figure 9.2  Removing an item from your bucket list

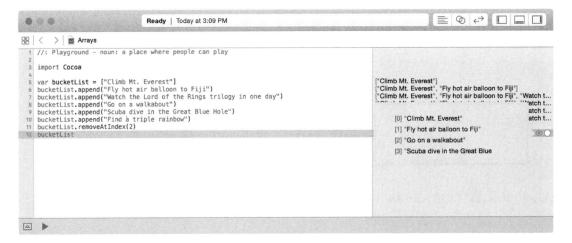

Having spent last weekend on a movie marathon, you decide to go out this weekend. You are at a party, and the topic of bucket lists comes up. As you begin to share your ambitious goals, the crowd's collective jaw starts to drop. "Just how many things do you want to do?" someone gasps.

No problem! It is easy to find the number of items in an array. Arrays keep track of the number of items in them via the `count` property. Use it to print the number of bucket list items you have to the console.

## Listing 9.8  Counting items in the array

```
import Cocoa

var bucketList = ["Climb Mt. Everest"]
bucketList.append("Fly hot air balloon to Fiji")
bucketList.append("Watch the Lord of the Rings trilogy in one day")
bucketList.append("Go on a walkabout")
bucketList.append("Scuba dive in the Great Blue Hole")
bucketList.append("Find a triple rainbow")
bucketList.removeAtIndex(2)
bucketList
print(bucketList.count)
```

"Five," the crowd gasps. "That is a lot of things to do!" Since the party is winding down, and everyone needs to go home and rethink their personal bucket lists, they beg you to tell them just your top three. You can easily do this using *subscripting*, which allows you to access specific indices in your array.

## Listing 9.9  Subscripting to find your top three items

```
import Cocoa

var bucketList = ["Climb Mt. Everest"]
bucketList.append("Fly hot air balloon to Fiji")
bucketList.append("Watch the Lord of the Rings trilogy in one day")
bucketList.append("Go on a walkabout")
bucketList.append("Scuba dive in the Great Blue Hole")
bucketList.append("Find a triple rainbow")
bucketList.removeAtIndex(2)
bucketList
print(bucketList.count)
print(bucketList[0...2])
```

The bracket syntax ([0...2]) is the subscripting syntax. Notice that your first three items print to the console. (You can also use the same basic syntax to log a single item, such as print(bucketList[2]).)

Subscripting is a powerful feature. Say that during your conversation someone asks, "Where do you want to do your walkabout?" The question makes you realize that you need some specifics. After all, you do not want to go on a walkabout just *anywhere*. Only a walkabout in Australia will do. You can use subscripting to change an item at a particular index (or range of indices).

## Listing 9.10  Using subscripting to append new information

```
import Cocoa

var bucketList = ["Climb Mt. Everest"]
bucketList.append("Fly hot air balloon to Fiji")
bucketList.append("Watch the Lord of the Rings trilogy in one day")
bucketList.append("Go on a walkabout")
bucketList.append("Scuba dive in the Great Blue Hole")
bucketList.append("Find a triple rainbow")
bucketList.removeAtIndex(2)
bucketList
print(bucketList.count)
print(bucketList[0...2])
bucketList[2] += " in Australia"
bucketList
```

You use the += addition and assignment operator to add some text to the item at index 2. This assignment works because the instance at index 2 is of the same type as the instance you added to it – "Go on a walkabout" and " in Australia" are both of the **String** type. Thus, you change the value at index 2 to be: "Go on a walkabout in Australia".

Thinking about all of these adventures has gotten you excited, and now you are having trouble sleeping. Since reading usually helps, you start to read up on climbing Mt. Everest. You discover that it is pretty dangerous, so you decide to update your top bucket item with a slightly less ambitious goal.

## Listing 9.11  Replacing an array item

```
import Cocoa

var bucketList = ["Climb Mt. Everest"]
bucketList.append("Fly hot air balloon to Fiji")
bucketList.append("Watch the Lord of the Rings trilogy in one day")
bucketList.append("Go on a walkabout")
bucketList.append("Scuba dive in the Great Blue Hole")
bucketList.append("Find a triple rainbow")
bucketList.removeAtIndex(2)
print(bucketList.count)
print(bucketList[0...2])
bucketList[2] += " in Australia"
bucketList[0] = "Climb Mt. Kilimanjaro"
bucketList
```

There! That is better. Now your top bucket list item is safer, but still quite adventurous.

While you are now happy with the content of your bucket list, you might not be all that happy that you had to type bucketList.append(_:) five times. You think to yourself, "There has to be a better way!"

And then you remember something: "I know how to use loops! What if I made an array of all the bucket list items I want to add? Then I could loop through that array and use **append(_:)** each time the loop iterates. I would only have to type bucketList.append(_:) one time!"

And this is exactly what you do.

## Listing 9.12  Using a loop to append items from one array to another

```
import Cocoa

var bucketList = ["Climb Mt. Everest"]
bucketList.append("Fly hot air balloon to Fiji")
bucketList.append("Watch the Lord of the Rings trilogy in one day")
bucketList.append("Go on a walkabout")
bucketList.append("Scuba dive in the Great Blue Hole")
bucketList.append("Find a triple rainbow")
var newItems = [
                "Fly hot air balloon to Fiji",
                "Watch the Lord of the Rings trilogy in one day",
                "Go on a walkabout",
                "Scuba dive in the Great Blue Hole",
                "Find a triple rainbow"
                ]

for item in newItems {
    bucketList.append(item)
}
bucketList.removeAtIndex(2)
print(bucketList.count)
print(bucketList[0...2])
bucketList[2] += " in Australia"
bucketList[0] = "Climb Mt. Kilimanjaro"
bucketList
```

You create an array for the bucket list items that you want to add, called newItems. Next, you make a for-in loop that iterates through each item in the array and appends it to your bucketList. You use the item variable in the local scope of the loop to append it to your bucket list array.

You are about to fall asleep, happy in how you have refactored your code to make it more concise and keep it just as expressive – but then a bolt of inspiration strikes.

"That is pretty good," you think. "But I think I can do better. Maybe I can use the addition and assignment operator!" Indeed you can. Just as you can use += to add one integer to another, you can use it to add one array to another.

## Listing 9.13 Refactoring with the addition and assignment operator

```
import Cocoa

var bucketList = ["Climb Mt. Everest"]
var newItems = [
                "Fly hot air balloon to Fiji",
                "Watch the Lord of the Rings trilogy in one day",
                "Go on a walkabout",
                "Scuba dive in the Great Blue Hole",
                "Find a triple rainbow"
                ]
for item in newItems {
    bucketList.append(item)
}
bucketList += newItems
bucketList
bucketList.removeAtIndex(2)
print(bucketList.count)
print(bucketList[0...2])
bucketList[2] += " in Australia"
bucketList[0] = "Climb Mt. Kilimanjaro"
bucketList
```

The += operator makes for an easy way to add your array of new items to your existing bucket list.

Finally, suppose you decide on a new goal – tobogganing across Alaska – that is more important than going on walkabout in Australia but less important than flying a hot air balloon to Fiji. Use the **insert(_:atIndex:)** function to add a new element to your array at a specified index.

## Listing 9.14 Inserting a new ambition

```
import Cocoa

var bucketList = ["Climb Mt. Everest"]
var newItems = [
                "Fly hot air balloon to Fiji",
                "Watch the Lord of the Rings trilogy in one day",
                "Go on a walkabout",
                "Scuba dive in the Great Blue Hole",
                "Find a triple rainbow"
                ]
bucketList += newItems
bucketList
bucketList.removeAtIndex(2)
print(bucketList.count)
print(bucketList[0...2])
bucketList[2] += " in Australia"
bucketList[0] = "Climb Mt. Kilimanjaro"
bucketList.insert("Toboggan across Alaska", atIndex: 2)
bucketList
```

The **insert(_:atIndex:)** function has two arguments. The first argument takes the instance to add to the array. (Recall that your array takes **String** instances.) The second argument takes the index for where you would like to add the new element in the array.

With your list fully formed, you lay your head down and dream of flying hot air balloons to mountain islands.

# Array Equality

The next morning you wake up and go to your neighborhood coffee shop. There, you meet a friend, named Myron, who had been at the party with you. Myron was inspired by your bucketList and decided to make his own bucket list modeled after yours. He went home after the party and wrote out all of your items, and now he wants to make sure that he got everything correct.

After updating Myron with the changes you made after the party, it is time to compare your arrays of bucket list items to ensure that they are the same. Use == to check for equality.

## Listing 9.15  Checking two arrays for equality

```
import Cocoa

var bucketList = ["Climb Mt. Everest"]
var newItems = [
                "Fly hot air balloon to Fiji",
                "Watch the Lord of the Rings trilogy in one day",
                "Go on a walkabout",
                "Scuba dive in the Great Blue Hole",
                "Find a triple rainbow"
                ]
bucketList += newItems
bucketList
bucketList.removeAtIndex(2)
print(bucketList.count)
print(bucketList[0...2])
bucketList[2] += " in Australia"
bucketList[0] = "Climb Mt. Kilimanjaro"
bucketList.insert("Toboggan across Alaska", atIndex: 2)
bucketList

var myronsList = [
                "Climb Mt. Kilimanjaro",
                "Fly hot air balloon to Fiji",
                "Toboggan across Alaska",
                "Go on a walkabout in Australia",
                "Find a triple rainbow",
                "Scuba dive in the Great Blue Hole"
                ]

let equal = (bucketList == myronsList)
```

Since the contents of both arrays are the same, you might expect equal to be set to true. Yet, equal was determined to be false. Why?

Remember that arrays are ordered. That means two arrays that have the same values are not equal if the ordering is different, and `myronsList` places "`Find a triple rainbow`" higher than your list does. Put this goal at the end of `myronsList` to make the two lists equal.

## Listing 9.16  Fixing `myronsList`

```
import Cocoa

var bucketList = ["Climb Mt. Everest"]
var newItems = [
                "Fly hot air balloon to Fiji",
                "Watch the Lord of the Rings trilogy in one day",
                "Go on a walkabout",
                "Scuba dive in the Great Blue Hole",
                "Find a triple rainbow"
                ]
bucketList += newItems
bucketList
bucketList.removeAtIndex(2)
print(bucketList.count)
print(bucketList[0...2])
bucketList[2] += " in Australia"
bucketList[0] = "Climb Mt. Kilimanjaro"
bucketList.insert("Toboggan across Alaska", atIndex: 2)
bucketList

var myronsList = [
                "Climb Mt. Kilimanjaro",
                "Fly hot air balloon to Fiji",
                "Toboggan across Alaska",
                "Go on a walkabout in Australia",
                "Find a triple rainbow",
                "Scuba dive in the Great Blue Hole",
                "Find a triple rainbow"
                ]

let equal = (bucketList == myronsList)
```

# Immutable Arrays

You have been doing a lot of tinkering with your bucket list array. But you can also create an array that cannot be changed. You use *immutable arrays* for these cases. Here is how.

Let's say you are making an application that allows users to keep track of the lunches they eat each week. Among other things, users will log what they ate and generate reports at a later time. You decide to put these meals in an immutable array to generate the reports. After all, it does not make sense to change last week's lunches after they have been eaten.

Create an immutable array and initialize it with a week's worth of lunches.

Listing 9.17  An immutable array

```
...
var myronsList = [
                "Climb Mt. Kilimanjaro",
                "Fly hot air balloon to Fiji",
                "Toboggan across Alaska",
                "Go on a walkabout in Australia",
                "Scuba dive in the Great Blue Hole",
                "Find a triple rainbow"
                ]

let equal = (bucketList == myronsList)
let lunches = [
                "Cheeseburger",
                "Veggie Pizza",
                "Chicken Caesar Salad",
                "Black Bean Burrito",
                "Falafel wrap"
                ]
```

You use the `let` keyword to create an immutable array. If you were to try to modify the array in any way, the compiler would issue an error stating that you cannot mutate an immutable array. If you even try to reassign a new array to `lunches`, you would get an error from the compiler telling you that you cannot reassign an instance to a constant created via the `let` keyword.

# Documentation

The documentation for any programming language is an indispensable resource, and Swift's is no exception.

Open the documentation that shipped with Xcode by clicking Help → Documentation and API Reference at the top. See Figure 9.3.

Figure 9.3  Help menu

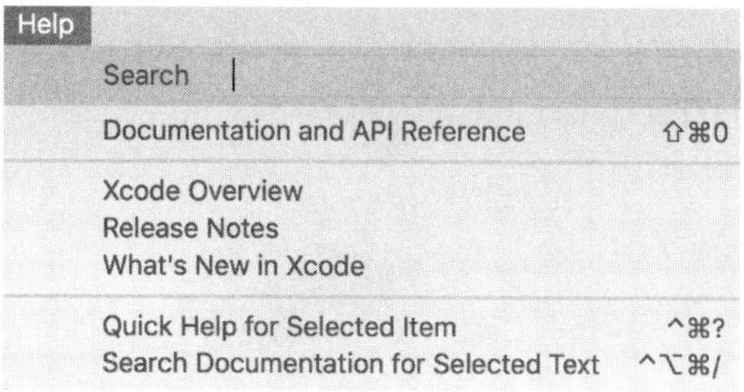

A new window will open. In the search bar at the top, type in "Array" and hit "Return" on your keyboard. This will open the documentation for Swift's **Array** type, as in Figure 9.4.

Figure 9.4  Opening the documentation

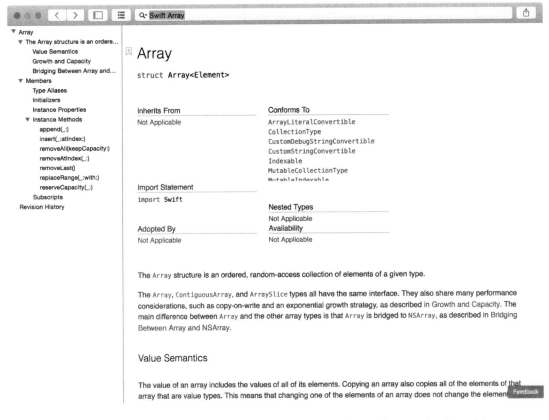

Take some time and explore the documentation for **Array**. Get to know the organization of the documentation, and you will save yourself a lot of time in the future. You will be visiting these pages regularly.

# Bronze Challenge

Look at the array below.

```
var toDoList = ["Take out garbage", "Pay bills", "Cross off finished items"]
```

Use the documentation to locate a var defined on the **Array** type that will tell you whether toDoList has any elements inside of it.

# Silver Challenge

Enter the array from the bronze challenge in your playground. Use a loop to reverse the order of the elements of this array. Log the results to the console. Finally, examine the documentation to see if there is a more convenient way to do this operation.

# 10
# Dictionaries

In the previous chapter, you became familiar with Swift's **Array** type. The **Array** type is a useful collection when the order of the elements in the collection is important.

But order is not always important. Sometimes you simply want to hold on to a set of information in a container and then retrieve the information as needed. That is what dictionaries are for.

A **Dictionary** is a collection type that organizes its content by *key-value* pairs. The keys in a dictionary map onto values. A key is like the ticket you give to the attendant at a coat check. You hand your ticket over, and the attendant uses it to find your coat. Similarly, you give a key to an instance of the **Dictionary** type, and it returns to you the value associated with that key.

The keys in a **Dictionary** must be unique. This requirement means that every key will uniquely map onto its value. To continue the coat check metaphor, a coat check might have several navy blue coats. So long as each coat has its own ticket, then you will be sure that the attendant will be able to find *your* navy blue coat when you return with your ticket. In short, you use a dictionary when you want to store and retrieve information with a specific key.

In this chapter, you will see how to:

- create and initialize a dictionary

- loop through dictionaries

- access and modify dictionaries via their keys

You will also learn more about keys and how they work, especially as they pertain to Swift. Last, you will see how to create arrays out of your dictionary's keys and values.

## Creating a Dictionary

The general syntax to create a Swift dictionary is as follows: `var dict: Dictionary<KeyType, ValueType>`. This code creates a mutable instance of the **Dictionary** type called `dict`. The declarations for what types the dictionary's keys and values accept are inside the angle brackets (<>), denoted here by `KeyType` and `ValueType`.

The only requirement for Swift's **Dictionary** type's keys is that the key must be *hashable*. That means that each `KeyType` must provide a mechanism that allows **Dictionary** to guarantee that any given key is unique. Swift's basic types, such as **String**, **Int**, **Float**, **Double**, and **Bool** are all hashable.

Before you begin typing code, let's take a look at the different ways you can get an instance of **Dictionary**.

```
var dict1: Dictionary<String, Double> = [:]
var dict2 = Dictionary<String, Double>()
var dict3: [String:Double] = [:]
var dict4 = [String:Double]()
```

Each of these four options yields the same result: a fully initialized instance of the **Dictionary** type with type information associated with its future keys and values. The KeyType is set to accept keys of the **String** type, and the ValueType is set to accept values of the **Double** type. In all four cases, the dictionary instance is empty: it has no keys and no values.

What is the difference between the [:] and the () syntax? They are essentially the same. They both create and prepare an instance of the **Dictionary** type. The [:] code uses the literal syntax to create an empty instance of the **Dictionary** type that will use the type information for its keys and values provided in its declaration. For example, dict1 specifies its type and then is initialized to be an empty dictionary. The () syntax uses the default initializer for the **Dictionary** type, which will prepare an empty dictionary instance. You will see more about initializers later in the book.

It is useful to take advantage of Swift's type inference capabilities. Type inference makes for more concise code that is just as expressive. Accordingly, you will stick with type inference in this chapter.

# Populating a Dictionary

To get started, create a new playground called Dictionary.playground. Declare a dictionary called movieRatings and use type inference to initialize it with some data.

### Listing 10.1  Creating a dictionary

```
import Cocoa

var movieRatings = ["Donnie Darko": 4, "Chungking Express": 5, "Dark City": 4]
```

You created a mutable dictionary using the **Dictionary** literal syntax. Your dictionary will hold movie ratings. Its keys are instances of the **String** type and represent individual movies. These keys map onto values that are instances of the **Int** type that represent individual ratings of the movies.

# Accessing and Modifying a Dictionary

Now that you have a mutable dictionary, how do you work with it? You will want to read from and modify the dictionary. Begin by using count to get some useful information about your dictionary.

### Listing 10.2  Using count

```
import Cocoa

var movieRatings = ["Donnie Darko": 4, "Chungking Express": 5, "Dark City": 4]
print("I have rated \(movieRatings.count) movies.")
```

count is a read-only property on the **Dictionary** type that keeps track of how many instances are held within the dictionary instance itself. We will discuss properties in detail in Chapter 16, but for now properties are variables on a type that store or compute some data about the type in which you are interested. In this case, you use count to log to the console: I have rated 3 movies.

Now let's read a value from the movieRatings dictionary.

## Listing 10.3  Reading a value from the dictionary

```
import Cocoa

var movieRatings = ["Donnie Darko": 4, "Chungking Express": 5, "Dark City": 4]
print("I have rated \(movieRatings.count) movies.")
let darkoRating = movieRatings["Donnie Darko"]
```

You access values from a dictionary by supplying the key associated with the value you would like to retrieve. In the example above, you supply the key "Donnie Darko" to the dictionary of movie ratings. darkoRating is now set to be equal to 4.

Option-click on the darkoRating instance. Its type is **Int?**, but movieRatings has type **[String: Int]**. Why the discrepancy? The **Dictionary** type needs a way to tell you that the value you asked for is not present. For example, you have not rated *Braveheart* yet, so this: let braveheartRating = movieRatings["Braveheart"] would result in braveheartRating having type **Int?** and being set to nil.

You subscripted movieRatings above using brackets: movieRatings["Donnie Darko"]. This syntax asks the dictionary for the value associated with the **String** key "Donnie Darko". Whenever you subscript a **Dictionary** instance for a given key, the dictionary will return an optional matching the type of the **Dictionary**'s values. In this case, subscripting movieRatings for a given key will return an **Int?** (an optional **Int**).

Next, you will modify a value in your dictionary of movie ratings.

## Listing 10.4  Modifying a value

```
import Cocoa

var movieRatings = ["Donnie Darko": 4, "Chungking Express": 5, "Dark City": 4]
print("I have rated \(movieRatings.count) movies.")
let darkoRating = movieRatings["Donnie Darko"]
movieRatings["Dark City"] = 5
movieRatings
```

As you can see, the value associated with the key "Dark City" is now equal to 5.

There is another useful way to update values associated with a dictionary's keys: the **updateValue(_:forKey:)** method. It takes two arguments: value: ValueType, forKey: KeyType. The first argument, value, takes the new value. The second argument, forKey, specifies the key whose value you would like to change.

This method is useful because it gives you a handle on the last value to which the key mapped. There is one small caveat: **updateValue(_:forKey:)** returns an optional. This return type is handy because the key may not exist in the dictionary. Therefore, it is helpful to assign the return of the **updateValue(_:forKey:)** method to an optional of the type that you are expecting and use optional binding to gain access to the key's old value. Let's see this in action.

## Listing 10.5  Updating a value

```
import Cocoa

var movieRatings = ["Donnie Darko": 4, "Chungking Express": 5, "Dark City": 4]
print("I have rated \(movieRatings.count) movies.")
let darkoRating = movieRatings["Donnie Darko"]
movieRatings["Dark City"] = 5
movieRatings
let oldRating: Int? = movieRatings.updateValue(5, forKey: "Donnie Darko")
if let lastRating = oldRating, currentRating = movieRatings["Donnie Darko"] {
    print("Old rating: \(lastRating); current rating: \(currentRating)")
}
```

Figure 10.1 shows the old and new values for *Donnie Darko*'s rating in the results sidebar.

## Figure 10.1  The updated value

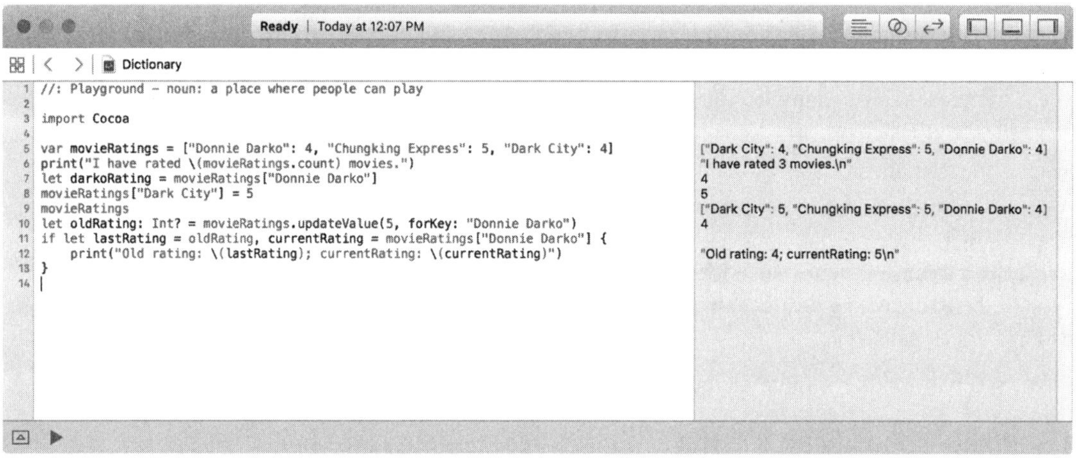

## Adding and Removing Values

Now that you have seen how to update a value, let's look at how you can update the key-value pairs in your dictionary by adding or removing a value. Begin by adding a value.

## Listing 10.6  Adding a value

```
import Cocoa

var movieRatings = ["Donnie Darko": 4, "Chungking Express": 5, "Dark City": 4]
print("I have rated \(movieRatings.count) movies.")
let darkoRating = movieRatings["Donnie Darko"]
movieRatings["Dark City"] = 5
movieRatings
let oldRating: Int? = movieRatings.updateValue(5, forKey: "Donnie Darko")
if let lastRating = oldRating {
    print(lastRating)
}
movieRatings["The Cabinet of Dr. Caligari"] = 5
```

Here, you add a new key-value pair to your dictionary using this syntax: `movieRatings["The Cabinet of Dr. Caligari"] = 5`. You use the assignment operator to associate a value (in this case, 5) with the new key ("The Cabinet of Dr. Caligari").

Next, remove the entry for *Dark City*.

## Listing 10.7  Removing a value

```
import Cocoa

var movieRatings = ["Donnie Darko": 4, "Chungking Express": 5, "Dark City": 4]
print("I have rated \(movieRatings.count) movies.")
let darkoRating = movieRatings["Donnie Darko"]
movieRatings["Dark City"] = 5
movieRatings
let oldRating: Int? = movieRatings.updateValue(5, forKey: "Donnie Darko")
if let lastRating = oldRating {
    print(lastRating)
}
movieRatings["The Cabinet of Dr. Caligari"] = 5
movieRatings.removeValueForKey("Dark City")
```

The method **removeValueForKey(_:)** takes a key as an argument and removes the key-value pair that matches what you provide. Now, `movieRatings` has no entry for *Dark City*.

Additionally, this method returns the value the key was associated with, if the key is found and removed successfully. However, you do not have to assign the return value of this method to anything. If the key is found in the dictionary, then the key-value pair is removed regardless of whether you assign the old value to anything.

In the example above, you could have typed: `let removedRating: Int? = movieRatings.removeValueForKey("Dark City")`. Because **removeValueForKey(_:)** returns an optional of the type that was removed, `removedRating` is an optional **Int**. Placing the old value in a variable or constant like this can be handy if you need to do something with the old value.

You can also remove a key-value pair by setting a key's value to `nil`.

## Listing 10.8  Setting the key's value to nil

```
import Cocoa

var movieRatings = ["Donnie Darko": 4, "Chungking Express": 5, "Dark City": 4]
print("I have rated \(movieRatings.count) movies.")
let darkoRating = movieRatings["Donnie Darko"]
movieRatings["Dark City"] = 5
movieRatings
let oldRating: Int? = movieRatings.updateValue(5, forKey: "Donnie Darko")
if let lastRating = oldRating {
    print(lastRating)
}
movieRatings["The Cabinet of Dr. Caligari"] = 5
movieRatings.removeValueForKey("Dark City")
movieRatings["Dark City"] = nil
```

The result is essentially the same, but this strategy does not return the removed key's value.

# Looping

You can use a `for-in` to loop through a dictionary. Swift's **Dictionary** type provides a convenient mechanism to loop through an instance's key-value pair for each entry. This mechanism breaks each entry into its constituent parts by providing temporary constants representing the key and the value. These constants are placed within a tuple that the `for-in` loop can access inside of its body.

### Listing 10.9  Looping through your dictionary

```
import Cocoa

var movieRatings = ["Donnie Darko": 4, "Chungking Express": 5, "Dark City": 4]
print("I have rated \(movieRatings.count) movies.")
let darkoRating = movieRatings["Donnie Darko"]
movieRatings["Dark City"] = 5
movieRatings
let oldRating: Int? = movieRatings.updateValue(5, forKey: "Donnie Darko")
if let lastRating = oldRating {
    print(lastRating)
}
movieRatings["The Cabinet of Dr. Caligari"] = 5
movieRatings["Dark City"] = nil
for (key, value) in movieRatings {
    print("The movie \(key) was rated \(value).")
}
```

Notice how you use string interpolation to combine the values of `key` and `value` into a single string. Open up the assistant editor to view the console. You should see that each movie and its rating was logged to the console.

You do not have to access both the key and the value of each entry. A **Dictionary** has properties for its `keys` and `values` that can be accessed separately if you only need the information from one.

### Listing 10.10  Just the keys, please

```
import Cocoa

var movieRatings = ["Donnie Darko": 4, "Chungking Express": 5, "Dark City": 4]
print("I have rated \(movieRatings.count) movies.")
let darkoRating = movieRatings["Donnie Darko"]
movieRatings["Dark City"] = 5
movieRatings
let oldRating: Int? = movieRatings.updateValue(5, forKey: "Donnie Darko")
if let lastRating = oldRating {
    print(lastRating)
}
movieRatings["The Cabinet of Dr. Caligari"] = 5
movieRatings["Dark City"] = nil
for (key, value) in movieRatings {
    print("The movie \(key) was rated: \(value).")
}
for movie in movieRatings.keys {
    print("User has rated \(movie).")
}
```

This new loop will iterate through `movieRatings`'s keys and log each movie the user has rated to the console.

# Immutable Dictionaries

Creating an immutable dictionary works much the same as creating an immutable array. You use the let keyword to tell the Swift compiler that you do not want your instance of **Dictionary** to change. Create an immutable dictionary that lists the track names of a short fictional album along with each track's length in seconds.

### Listing 10.11  Creating an immutable dictionary

```
...
let album = ["Diet Roast Beef": 268,
             "Dubba Dubbs Stubs His Toe": 467,
             "Smokey's Carpet Cleaning Service": 187,
             "Track 4": 221]
```

The track names are the keys and the track lengths are the values. If you try to change this dictionary, the compiler will give you an error and prevent the change. (Go ahead and try it!)

# Translating a Dictionary to an Array

Sometimes it is helpful to pull information out of a dictionary and put it into an array. Suppose, for example, that you want to list all of the movies that have been rated (without their ratings).

In this case, it makes sense to create an instance of the **Array** type with the keys from your dictionary.

### Listing 10.12  Sending keys to an array

```
import Cocoa

var movieRatings = ["Donnie Darko": 4, "Chungking Express": 5, "Dark City": 4]
print("I have rated \(movieRatings.count) movies.")
let darkoRating = movieRatings["Donnie Darko"]
movieRatings["Dark City"] = 5
movieRatings
let oldRating: Int? = movieRatings.updateValue(5, forKey: "Donnie Darko")
if let lastRating = oldRating {
    print(lastRating)
}
movieRatings["The Cabinet of Dr. Caligari"] = 5
movieRatings["Dark City"] = nil
for (key, value) in movieRatings {
    print("The movie \(key) was rated: \(value).")
}
for movie in movieRatings.keys {
    print("User has rated \(movie).")
}
let watchedMovies = Array(movieRatings.keys)
...
```

You use the Array() syntax to create a new **[String]** instance. Inside the (), you pass in the dictionary's keys. The result is that watchedMovies is a constant instance of the **Array** type representing all of the movies a user has in the movieRatings dictionary.

# Silver Challenge

It is not uncommon to place instances of the **Array** type inside of a dictionary. Create a dictionary that represents a state. Your dictionary's keys will refer to counties (to keep it short, only include three counties). Each key should map onto an array that holds five of the zip codes within that county. (You can make up the county names and zip codes.)

Finally, log only the dictionary's zip codes. Your result should look something like this:

```
Georgia has the following zip codes: [30306, 30307, 30308, 30309, 30310,
                                      30311, 30312, 30313, 30314, 30315,
                                      30301, 30302, 30303, 30304, 30305]
```

# 11

# Sets

Swift provides a third collection type called **Set**. **Set** is not frequently used, purely by convention, but we do not think that this should be the case. This chapter will introduce **Set** and show off some of its unique advantages.

## What Is a Set?

A **Set** is an unordered collection of distinct instances. This definition sets it apart from an **Array**, which is ordered and can accommodate repeated values. For example, an array could have the following content: [2,2,2,2], but a set cannot.

A **Set** has some strong similarities to a **Dictionary**, but is also a little different. Like **Dictionary**, a set's values are unordered within the collection. Similar to the requirement that a dictionary's keys must be unique, **Set** does not allow repeated values. In order to ensure that elements are unique, **Set** requires that its elements conform to the protocol **Hashable** just as a dictionary's keys do. However, while dictionary values are accessed via their corresponding key, a set only stores individual elements, not key-value pairs.

Table 11.1 summarizes this information.

Table 11.1  Comparing Swift's collections

| Collection Type | Ordered? | Unique? | Stores |
|---|---|---|---|
| Array | Yes | No | Elements |
| Dictionary | No | Keys | Key-value pairs |
| Set | No | Elements | Elements |

## Getting a Set

It is time to make an instance of **Set**. Create a new playground called Groceries.

Type in the following to get an instance of **Set**.

Listing 11.1  Creating a set

```
var groceryBag = Set<String>()
```

You made an instance of **Set** and declared that it will hold instances of the **String** type. It is a mutable **Set** called groceryBag and is currently empty. Let's fix that.

You can add groceries to your groceryBag by using the **insert(_:)** method.

## Listing 11.2  Adding to a set

```
var groceryBag = Set<String>()
groceryBag.insert("Apples")
groceryBag.insert("Oranges")
groceryBag.insert("Pineapple")
```

Now groceryBag has a few items inside of it. As with arrays and dictionaries, you can loop through a set to see its contents.

## Listing 11.3  Looping through a set

```
var groceryBag = Set<String>()
groceryBag.insert("Apples")
groceryBag.insert("Oranges")
groceryBag.insert("Pineapple")

for food in groceryBag {
    print(food)
}
```

If you open up the debug area, then you will see that each item in your groceryBag was logged to the console.

As of Swift 2.0, **Set** does not have its own literal syntax. Nonetheless, you can still create a **Set** with a more convenient syntax than what you saw above. Suppose that you already know the instances you would like to add to the **Set** instance when you create it.

## Listing 11.4  Creating a set, redux

```
var groceryBag = Set<String>(["Apples", "Oranges", "Pineapple"])
groceryBag.insert("Apples")
groceryBag.insert("Oranges")
groceryBag.insert("Pineapple")

for food in groceryBag {
    print(food)
}
```

You used an initializer on **Set** to create a **Set** instance from an **Array** instance (you will learn more about initializers in Chapter 17). Thus, you no longer need the three calls to the **insert(_:)** method.

**Set**s provide another convenient syntax to create an instance. This syntax combines declaring the instance to be of the **Set** type with the **Array**'s literal syntax. For example, you could replace the new code in Listing 11.4 with the example below.

```
var groceryBag = Set(["Apples", "Oranges", "Pineapple"])
var groceryBag: Set = ["Apples", "Oranges", "Pineapple"]

for food in groceryBag {
    print(food)
}
```

This code explicitly declares groceryBag to be of the **Set** type, which means that we can use the **Array** literal syntax to create an instance of **Set**.

# Working with Sets

Now that you have an instance of **Set**, you might be wondering how to work with the elements inside of it. For example, you might want to know if your groceryBag contains a particular item. The **Set** type provides a method called **contains(_:)** that looks inside of a set instance for a particular item.

### Listing 11.5  Has bananas?

```
var groceryBag: Set = ["Apples", "Oranges", "Pineapple"]

for food in groceryBag {
    print(food)
}

let hasBananas = groceryBag.contains("Bananas")
```

The value of hasBananas is false; your groceryBag does not have any bananas inside of it.

## Unions

Imagine that you are wandering around the grocery store and you bump into a friend. You get to talking, and your friend suggests that you do your shopping together. Taking a peek into her shopping cart, you see that she has a bunch of bananas. Since you were looking for bananas to complete the recipe for your famous fruit salad, you decide to combine your grocery bags.

### Listing 11.6  Combining sets

```
var groceryBag: Set = ["Apples", "Oranges", "Pineapple"]

for food in groceryBag {
    print(food)
}

let hasBananas = groceryBag.contains("Bananas")
let friendsGroceryBag = Set(["Bananas", "Cereal", "Milk", "Oranges"])
let commonGroceryBag = groceryBag.union(friendsGroceryBag)
```

You add a new constant **Set** instance representing your friend's grocery bag and use the **union(_:)** method to combine the two sets together. **union(_:)** is a method on the **Set** type that takes an argument that expects a **SequenceType** (which is a protocol that you will learn more about in

Chapter 22) and returns a new **Set** instance that includes the unique elements of both collections. In short, you can pass arrays and sets to **union(_:)** and get back a set with their combined elements, less any duplicates. Here, commonGroceryBag is a **Set** that contains the unique elements of both groceryBag and friendsGroceryBag.

Figure 11.1 demonstrates the union of the two sets graphically.

## Figure 11.1  Union of two sets

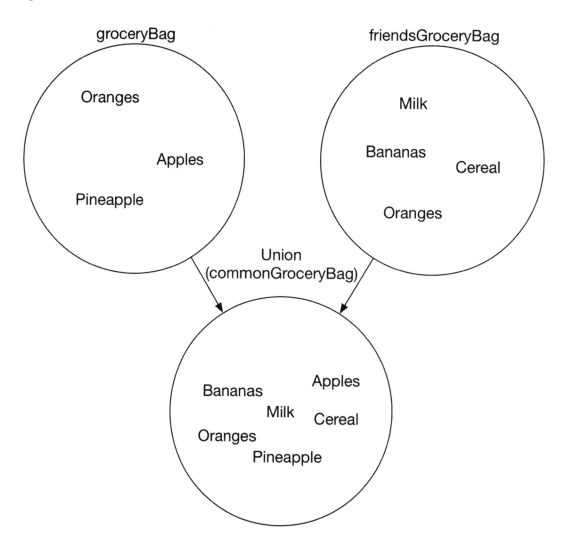

## Intersects

You and your friend finish grocery shopping and head to your house to make your famous fruit salad. When you get home, you find that your roommate also just got back from the grocery store. It turns out that your roommate also wants to make fruit salad, so you compare your grocery bags to figure out which items are duplicated and can be returned to the grocery store.

Listing 11.7  Intersecting sets

```
var groceryBag: Set = ["Apples", "Oranges", "Pineapple"]

for food in groceryBag {
    print(food)
}

let hasBananas = groceryBag.contains("Bananas")
let friendsGroceryBag = Set(["Bananas", "Cereal", "Milk", "Oranges"])
let commonGroceryBag = groceryBag.union(friendsGroceryBag)

let roommatesGroceryBag = Set(["Apples", "Bananas", "Cereal", "Toothpaste"])
let itemsToReturn = commonGroceryBag.intersect(roommatesGroceryBag)
```

**Set** provides a **intersect(_:)** that identifies the items that are present in both collections, and returns those duplicated items in a new **Set** instance. Figure 11.2 shows this relationship graphically as a Venn diagram. Your roommate's grocery bag duplicates several of your items – but not all of them.

Figure 11.2  Intersecting sets

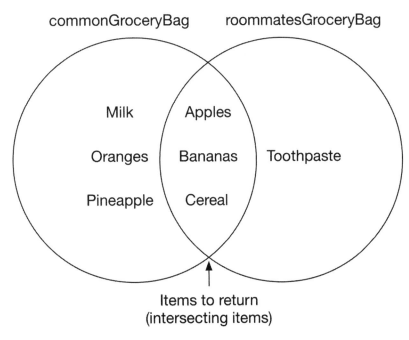

Items to return
(intersecting items)

# Disjoint

You have seen how to combine two sets into a new, all-inclusive set via the **union(_:)** method. You also used the **intersect(_:)** method to find the common elements of two sets and place them into a new set. What if you want to know if two sets contain any common elements?

Consider, for example, that you and your roommate realize that you both forgot several ingredients for your famous fruit salad. You leave your friend to start chopping, and you and your roommate go back to the store to pick up the final items (and return the duplicates). Your plan at the store is to split up and find different items to make the trip as fast as possible. Wouldn't it be nice if you could reconvene at the checkout and compare your carts quickly to make sure nothing is duplicated? Swift's **Set** type has a convenient method to help you with that.

### Listing 11.8  Detecting intersections in sets

```
var groceryBag: Set = ["Apples", "Oranges", "Pineapple"]

for food in groceryBag {
    print(food)
}

let hasBananas = groceryBag.contains("Bananas")
let friendsGroceryBag = Set(["Bananas", "Cereal", "Milk", "Oranges"])
let commonGroceryBag = groceryBag.union(friendsGroceryBag)

let roommatesGroceryBag = Set(["Apples", "Bananas", "Cereal", "Toothpaste"])
let itemsToReturn = commonGroceryBag.intersect(roommatesGroceryBag)

let yourSecondBag = Set(["Berries", "Yogurt"])
let roommatesSecondBag = Set(["Grapes", "Honey"])
let disjoint = yourSecondBag.isDisjointWith(roommatesSecondBag)
```

You decided to pick up the berries and yogurt, and your roommate got the grapes and honey. The two of you meet up at the register and check your carts to make sure nothing is repeated. **Set**'s **isDisjointWith(_:)** method returns true or false depending on whether any members of the set (e.g., yourSecondBag) are in the sequence provided to **isDisjointWith**'s argument (e.g., roommatesSecondBag).

In this case, disjoint will be true. The two sets, or grocery bags, do not share any items. You and your roommate are ready to check out and go home to make your fruit salad.

# Bronze Challenge

Consider the following code that models the cities two people have visited as sets.

```
let myCities = Set(["Atlanta", "Chicago",
                    "Jacksonville", "New York", "San Francisco"])
let yourCities = Set(["Chicago", "San Francisco", "Jacksonville"])
```

Find a method on **Set** that returns a **Bool** indicating whether or not myCities contains all of the cities contained by yourCities. (Hint: this relationship would make myCities a *superset* of yourCities.)

# Silver Challenge

In this chapter, you used methods like **union(_:)** and **intersect(_:)** to create new sets. Sometimes, however, you may not want to create new instances, but would rather modify the existing instances in place. Look through the documentation and find the appropriate methods on the **Set** type. Rework the examples in the chapter for **union(_:)** and **intersect(_:)** to use these methods.

# 12

# Functions

A function is a named set of code that is used to accomplish some specific task. The function's name describes the task the function performs. You have already used some functions, such as **print()**, which is a function provided to you by Swift. Other functions are created in code you write.

Functions execute code. Some functions define arguments that you can use to pass in data to help the function do its work. Some functions return something after they have completed their work. You might think of a function as a little machine. You turn it on and it chugs along, doing its work. You can feed it data and, if it is built to do so, it will return a new chunk of data that results from its work.

Functions are an extremely important part of programming. Indeed, a program is mostly a collection of related functions that combine to accomplish some sort of functionality. Accordingly, there is a lot to cover in this chapter. Take your time and make sure that you are comfortable before moving on.

Let's start with some examples.

## A Basic Function

Create a new playground called `Functions.playground`. Enter the code below.

Listing 12.1  Defining a function

```
import Cocoa

func printGreeting() {
    print("Hello, playground.")
}
printGreeting()
```

Here, you define a function with the `func` keyword followed by the name of the function: **printGreeting()**. The parentheses are empty because this function does not take any arguments. (More on arguments soon.)

The opening brace ({) denotes the beginning of the function's implementation. This is where you write the code that describes how the function will perform its work. When the function is called, the code inside the braces is executed. The **printGreeting()** function is fairly simple. You have one line of code that uses **print()** to log the string "Hello, playground." to the console.

Finally, you *call* the function to execute the code inside of it. To do this, you enter `printGreeting()` on the line following the definition of the function. Calling the function executes its code, and `Hello, playground.` is logged to the console.

Now that you have written and executed a simple function, it is time to graduate to more sophisticated varieties.

# Function Parameters

Functions begin to take on more life when they have *parameters*. You use parameters to give a function some inputs. We call these parts of a function "parameters" to indicate that they can change value depending upon the data the caller passes into the function. The function takes the data passed to its parameters to execute a task or produce a result.

Create a function that prints a more personal greeting by using a parameter.

## Listing 12.2  Using a parameter

```
import Cocoa

func printGreeting() {
    print("Hello, playground.")
}
printGreeting()
func printPersonalGreeting(name: String) {
    print("Hello \(name), welcome to your playground.")
}

printPersonalGreeting("Matt")
```

**printPersonalGreeting(_:)** takes a single argument, as indicated in the parentheses directly after the function name. An *argument* is the value a caller gives to a function's parameter. In this case, the function has a parameter called name that is an instance of the **String** type. You specify the type for name after the : that follows the parameter's name, just as you specify the types of variables and constants.

As a quick aside, although the terms *parameter* and *argument* technically have different meanings, they are used interchangeably by some. Also, you may be wondering why we wrote **printPersonalGreeting(_:)** with _: inside of the parentheses. This signifies that **printPersonalGreeting(_:)** has one parameter whose name is not used when calling the function: printPersonalGreeting("Matt"). While name is available for use within the function, it is not used when the function is called. You will learn more about external and internal parameter names below.

If the argument passed to the parameter name is an instance of **String**, it will be interpolated into the string that is logged to the console. Check it out. Your console should say something like: "Hello Matt, welcome to your playground."

If you happened to pass an argument that was not of the **String** type, the compiler would give you an error telling you that the type you passed in is incorrect. This behavior is useful; it lets you know what your inputs will look like when you are writing the implementations of your functions.

Functions can – and often do – take multiple arguments. Make a new function that does a little math.

## Listing 12.3  A function for division

```
...
func printPersonalGreeting(name: String) {
    print("Hello \(name), welcome to your playground.")
}
printPersonalGreeting("Matt")

func divisionDescription(num: Double, den: Double) {
    print("\(num) divided by \(den) equals \(num / den)")
}
divisionDescription(9.0, den: 3.0)
```

The function **divisionDescription(_:den:)** describes some basic division constructed from the instances of the **Double** type that you supply to the function's two parameters: num and den. Note that you did some math within the \() of the string printed to the console. You should see "9 divided by 3 equals 3" logged to the console.

# Parameter names

A function's parameters have names. For example, the function **divisionDescription(_:den:)** has two parameters with the parameter names num and den. You do not reference or see the first parameter name when you use **divisionDescription(_:den:)**, but you do use the second. By default, if you call a function with more than one parameter, the first parameter name is not used, but all others are. We use den when writing out the function (e.g., **divisionDescription(_:den:)**) because you use the second parameter name when you call the function.

Sometimes, however, it is useful to have all of a function's parameter names visible outside of your function's body.

Named parameters can make your functions more readable – provided the names are well chosen. At the moment, the only parameter name visible when you call **divisionDescription(_:den:)** is den, which is not very informative. This is fine within the function's body, because the function's implementation makes the role of these parameters clear. As you read the code inside the function's implementation, it is fairly simple to determine what num and den do.

However, if the function is going to be used in some other file in your application's code base, and the function's implementation is not immediately visible, it could be difficult to infer what values to give to the function's parameters. This would make the function less useful.

Change **divisionDescription(_:den:)**'s parameters to have external parameter names that are different from the function's internal parameter names to add some context to what values the function expects.

### Listing 12.4  Using explicit parameter names

```
...
func printPersonalGreeting(name: String) {
    print("Hello \(name), welcome to your playground.")
}
printPersonalGreeting("Matt")

func divisionDescription(num: Double, den: Double) {
    print("\(num) divided by \(den) equals \(num / den)")
}
divisionDescription(9.0, den: 3.0)
func divisionDescription(forNumerator num: Double, andDenominator den: Double) {
    print("\(num) divided by \(den) equals \(num / den)")
}
divisionDescription(forNumerator: 9.0, andDenominator: 3.0)
```

Now **divisionDescription(forNumerator:andDenominator:)** has two parameters with external names. When you call the function, you must use the external parameter names forNumerator and andDenominator. The num and den parameter names are still available for use within the function's implementation, but you cannot use them to call the function because they are only visible inside of the function's implementation. By creating explicit – and descriptive – names for these parameters, you have made the function more readable when you call it.

Naming functions and parameters can be tricky. In general, it is advisable to choose function and parameter names that are informative and simple to type. Another dimension to consider is that Swift style suggests that function and parameter names combine to form a readable phrase. For example, **divisionDescription(forNumerator:andDenominator:)**'s external parameter names forNumerator and andDenominator help make the function more readable. And while these external parameter names are useful for calling the function, shorter parameter names (num and den) are used inside the function to keep things simple.

## Variadic parameters

A *variadic* parameter takes zero or more input values for its argument. Functions can have only one variadic parameter, and it should typically be the final parameter in the list. The values provided to the argument are made available within the function's body as an array.

To make a variadic parameter, use three periods after the parameter's type: e.g., names: String.... In this example, names is available within the function's body and has the type **[String]**.

Update your **printPersonalGreeting(_:)** function to have a variadic parameter.

### Listing 12.5  Greeting a group

```
...
func printPersonalGreeting(name: String) {
    print("Hello \(name), welcome to your playground.")
}
printPersonalGreeting("Matt")

func printPersonalGreetings(names: String...) {
    for name in names {
        print("Hello \(name), welcome to the playground.")
    }
}
printPersonalGreetings("Alex","Chris","Drew","Pat")
...
```

Now, the **printPersonalGreeting(_:)** function is replaced with a plural version: **printPersonalGreetings(_:)**. Check the console. You should see that the function logged a personal greeting for each name that was supplied to the variadic parameter.

## Figure 12.1  Multiple greetings

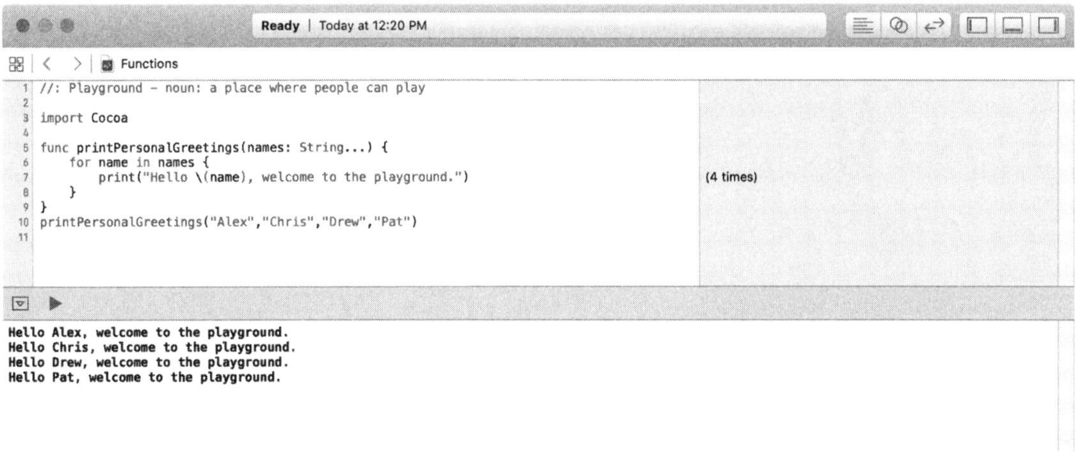

```
//: Playground - noun: a place where people can play

import Cocoa

func printPersonalGreetings(names: String...) {
    for name in names {
        print("Hello \(name), welcome to the playground.")
    }
}
printPersonalGreetings("Alex","Chris","Drew","Pat")
```

```
Hello Alex, welcome to the playground.
Hello Chris, welcome to the playground.
Hello Drew, welcome to the playground.
Hello Pat, welcome to the playground.
```

# Default parameter values

Swift's parameters can take default values. Default values should be placed at the end of the function's parameter list. If a parameter has a default value you can omit that argument when calling the function. (In which case, as you might expect, the function will use the parameter's default value.)

Let's see a default parameter value in action in your division function.

## Listing 12.6  Adding a default parameter value

```
...
func divisionDescription(forNumerator num: Double, andDenominator den: Double) {
    print("\(num) divided by \(den) equals \(num / den)")
}
divisionDescription(forNumerator: 9.0, andDenominator: 3.0)
func divisionDescription(forNumerator num: Double,
                         andDenominator den: Double,
                         withPunctuation punctuation: String = ".") {
    print("\(num) divided by \(den) equals
          \(num / den)\(punctuation)")
}
divisionDescription(forNumerator: 9.0, andDenominator: 3.0)
divisionDescription(forNumerator: 9.0, andDenominator: 3.0, withPunctuation: "!")
```

Now, the function takes three parameters:
`divisionDescription(forNumerator:andDenominator:withPunctuation:)`. Notice the new code: `punctuation: String = "."`. You add a new parameter for punctuation, add its expected type, and give it a default value via the `= "."` syntax. This means that the string created by the function will conclude with a period by default.

Your two function calls illustrate how the default value works. To use the default, as in your first function call, you can simply omit the final parameter. Or, as in your second function call, you can substitute the default value for a new punctuation mark by passing in a new argument. The first call of the **divisionDescription(forNumerator:andDenominator:withPunctuation:)** function logs the description with a period, and the second logs the description with an exclamation point.

## Figure 12.2  Default and explicit punctuation

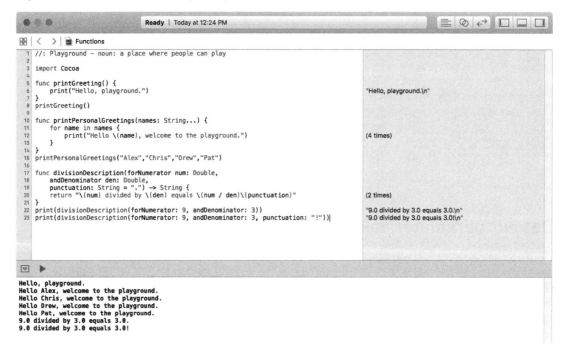

## In-out parameters

Sometimes there is reason to have a function modify the value of an argument. *In-out parameters* allow a function's impact on a variable to live beyond the function's body. There are a couple of caveats: First, in-out parameters cannot have default values. Second, variadic parameters cannot be marked with inout.

Say you have a function that will take an error message as an argument and will append some information based on certain conditions. Consider the example below.

## Listing 12.7  An in-out parameter

```
...
var error = "The request failed:"
func appendErrorCode(code: Int, inout toErrorString errorString: String) {
    if code == 400 {
        errorString += " bad request."
    }
}
appendErrorCode(400, toErrorString: &error)
error
```

The function **appendErrorCode(_:toErrorString:)** has two parameters. The first is the error code that the function will compare against, which expects an instance of **Int**. Notice that this parameter is not given an external name. Its name is added at the end of the function name. The second is an `inout` parameter – denoted by the `inout` keyword before its name – named `toErrorString`, which expects an instance of **String**. `toErrorString` is an external parameter name used when calling the function, while `errorString` is an internal parameter name used within the function.

When you use the function, the variable you pass into the `inout` parameter is preceded by an ampersand (&). This indicates that the variable will be modified by the function. Here, the `errorString` is modified to read: "The request failed: bad request," which you should see displayed in the results sidebar.

In-out parameters are not the same as a function returning a value. If you want your function to produce something, there is a more elegant way to handle this scenario.

# Returning from a Function

Functions can give you information after they finish executing the code inside of their implementation. This information is called the *return* of the function. It is often the case that you write a function to do some work and return you some data. Make your **divisionDescription(forNumerator:andDenominator:withPunctuation:)** function return an instance of the **String** type.

Listing 12.8  Returning a string

```
...
func divisionDescription(forNumerator num: Double,
                         andDenominator den: Double,
                         withPunctuation punctuation: String = ".") {
    print("\(num) divided by \(den) equals
           \(num / den)\(punctuation)")
}
divisionDescription(forNumerator: 9.0, andDenominator: 3.0)
divisionDescription(forNumerator: 9.0, andDenominator: 3.0, withPunctuation: "!")
func divisionDescription(forNumerator num: Double,
                         andDenominator den: Double,
                         withPunctuation punctuation: String = ".") -> String {
    return "\(num) divided by \(den) equals
            \(num / den)\(punctuation)"
}
print(divisionDescription(forNumerator: 9.0,
      andDenominator: 3.0,
      withPunctuation: "!"))
...
```

The behavior of this new function is very similar to your earlier implementation with an important twist: this new implementation returns a value. This return value is denoted by the **-> String** syntax, which indicates that the function will return an instance of the specified type. Since you want to log a string to the console, your function returns an instance of the **String** type. The details of the string to be returned are inside the body of the function.

Since **divisionDescription(forNumerator:andDenominator:withPunctuation:)** returns a **String** and **print()** expects to take a **String** argument, you can call **divisionDescription(forNumerator:andDenominator:withPunctuation:)** within a call to **print()** to log the string instance to the console.

# Nested Functions and Scope

Swift's function definitions can be nested. Nested functions are declared and implemented within the definition of another function. The nested function is not available outside of the enclosing function. This feature is useful when you need a function to do some work, but only within another function. Let's look at an example.

### Listing 12.9  Nested functions

```
...
func areaOfTriangle(withBase base: Double, andHeight height: Double) -> Double {
    let numerator = base * height
    func divide() -> Double {
        return numerator / 2
    }
    return divide()
}
areaOfTriangle(withBase: 3.0, andHeight: 5.0)
```

The function **areaOfTriangle(withBase:andHeight:)** takes two arguments of type **Double**: a base and a height. **areaOfTriangle(withBase:andHeight:)** also returns a **Double**. Inside of this function's implementation, you declare and implement another function called **divide()**. This function takes no arguments and returns a **Double**. The **areaOfTriangle(withBase:andHeight:)** function calls the **divide()** function and returns the result.

The **divide()** function above makes use of a constant called numerator that is defined in **areaOfTriangle(withBase:andHeight:)**. Why does this work?

The constant is defined within the **divide()** function's enclosing *scope*. Anything within a function's braces ({}) is said to be enclosed by that function's scope. In this case, both the numerator constant and the **divide()** function are enclosed by the scope of **areaOfTriangle(withBase:andHeight:)**.

A function's scope describes the visibility an instance or function will have. It is a sort of horizon. Anything defined within a function's scope will be visible to that function; anything that is not is past that function's field of vision. numerator is visible to the **divide()** function because they share the same enclosing scope.

On the other hand, because the **divide()** function is defined within **areaOfTriangle(withBase:andHeight:)** function's scope, it is not visible outside of it. The compiler will give you an error if you try to call the **divide()** function outside of **areaOfTriangle(withBase:andHeight:)**. Give it a try to see the error.

**divide()** is a very simple function. Indeed, **areaOfTriangle(withBase:andHeight:)** could achieve the same result without it: return (base * height) / 2. The important lesson to focus on here is how scope works. You will see a more sophisticated example of nested functions in Chapter 13. Stay tuned!

# Multiple Returns

Functions can return more than one value. To do this, Swift uses the tuple data type, which you learned about in Chapter 5. Recall that a tuple is an ordered list of related values. To better understand how to use tuples, you are going to make a function that takes an array of integers and sorts them into arrays for even and odd integers.

## Listing 12.10  Sorting evens and odds

```
...
func sortEvenOdd(numbers: [Int]) -> (evens: [Int], odds: [Int]) {
    var evens = [Int]()
    var odds = [Int]()
    for number in numbers {
        if number % 2 == 0 {
            evens.append(number)
        } else {
            odds.append(number)
        }
    }
    return (evens, odds)
}
```

Here, you first declare a function called **sortEvenOdd(_:)**. You specify this function to take an array of integers as its only argument. The function returns what is called a *named tuple*. You can tell that the tuple is named because its constituent parts are named: evens will be an array of integers, and odds will also be an array of integers.

Next, inside the implementation of the function, you initialize the evens and odds arrays to prepare them to store their respective integers. You then loop through the array of integers provided to the function's parameter, numbers. At each iteration through the loop, you use the % operator to see if number is even. If the result is even, then you append it to the evens array. If the result is not even, this integer is added to the odds array.

Now that your function is set up, call it and pass it an array of integers.

## Listing 12.11  Calling **sortEvenOdd(_:)**

```
...
func sortEvenOdd(numbers: [Int]) -> (evens: [Int], odds: [Int]) {
    var evens = [Int]()
    var odds = [Int]()
    for number in numbers {
        if number % 2 == 0 {
            evens.append(number)
        } else {
            odds.append(number)
        }
    }
    return (evens, odds)
}

let aBunchOfNumbers = [10,1,4,3,57,43,84,27,156,111]
let theSortedNumbers = sortEvenOdd(aBunchOfNumbers)
print("The even numbers are: \(theSortedNumbers.evens);
        the odd numbers are: \(theSortedNumbers.odds)")
```

First, you create an instance of the **Array** type to house a number of integers. Second, you give that array to the **sortEvenOdd(_:)** function and assign the return value to a constant called theSortedNumbers. Because the return value is specified above as (evens: [Int], odds: [Int]), this is the type the compiler infers for your newly created constant. Finally, you log the result to the console.

Notice that you use string interpolation in combination with a tuple. You can access a tuple's members by name if they are defined. For example, theSortedNumbers.evens inserts the contents of the evens array into the string logged to the console. Your console output should be The even numbers are: [10, 4, 84, 156]; the odd numbers are: [1, 3, 57, 43, 27, 111].

# Optional Return Types

Sometimes you want a function to return an optional. When there is a chance that a function will sometimes need to return nil but will have a value to return at other times, Swift allows you to use an optional return.

Imagine, for example, that you need a method that looks at a person's full name and pulls out and returns that person's middle name. Not all people have a middle name, so your function will need a mechanism to return the person's middle name if there is one and return nil otherwise. Use an optional to do just that.

### Listing 12.12  Using an optional return

```
...
func grabMiddleName(name: (String, String?, String)) -> String? {
    return name.1
}

let middleName = grabMiddleName(("Matt",nil,"Mathias"))
if let theName = middleName {
    print(theName)
}
```

Here, you create a function called **grabMiddleName(_:)**. This function looks a little different than what you have seen before. This function takes one argument: a tuple of type (String, String?, String). The tuple's three **String** instances are for the first, middle, and last names, and the instance for the middle name is declared as an optional type.

The **grabMiddleName(_:)** function's one parameter is called name. You access this parameter inside the implementation of the function using the index of the name that you want to return. Because the tuple is zero-indexed, you use 1 to access the middle name provided to the argument. And because the middle name might be nil, the return type of the function is optional.

You then call **grabMiddleName(_:)** and provide it a first, middle, and last name (feel free to change the names). Since you declared the middle name component of the tuple to be of type **String?**, you can pass nil to that portion of the tuple. You cannot do this for the first or last name portion of the tuple.

Nothing is logged to the console. Because the middle name provided is nil, the Boolean used in the optional binding does not evaluate to true and **print()** is not executed.

Try giving the middle name a valid **String** instance and note the result.

# Exiting Early from a Function

You already learned about Swift's conditional statements in Chapter 3, but there is one more to introduce: guard statements. Just like if/else statements, guard statements execute code depending on a Boolean value resulting from some expression. But guard statements are different from what you have seen before. A guard statement is used to exit early from a function if some condition is not met, hence the name *guard*. Think of guard statements as a way to protect your code from running under improper conditions.

Following the example above, consider an example in which you want to write a function that greets a person by their middle name if they have one. If they do not have a middle name, you would rather use something more generic.

## Listing 12.13  Early exits with guard statements

```
...
func greetByMiddleName(name: (first: String, middle: String?, last: String)) {
    guard let middleName = name.middle else {
        print("Hey there!")
        return
    }
    print("Hey \(middleName)")
}
greetByMiddleName(("Matt","Danger","Mathias"))
```

**greetByMiddleName(_:)** is similar to **grabMiddleName(_:)** in that it takes the same argument, but it differs in that it has no return value. Another difference is that the elements in the tuple name are named to match specific components of a person's name. As you can see, these element names are available inside of the function.

The code guard let middleName = name.middle binds the value in middle to a constant called middleName. If there is no value in the optional, then the code in the guard statement's body is executed. This would result in a generic greeting being logged to the console that omits the middle name: "Hey there!". After this, you must explicitly return from the function, which represents that the condition established by the guard statement was not met and the function needs to return early.

You can think of guard as protecting you from embarrassingly addressing somebody as "mumble-mumble" when you do not know his middle name. But if the tuple did get passed to the function with a middle name, then its value is bound to middleName and is available after the guard statement. This means that middleName is visible in the parent scope that encompasses the guard statement.

You pass in a middle name to the tuple name to **greetByMiddleName(_:)** when you call the function. That means "Hey Danger!" will be logged to the console. If nil were passed to the middle name element, then "Hey there!" would have been logged to the console. (Go ahead and try it!)

# Function Types

Each function you have been working with in this chapter has a specific type. In fact, all functions do. *Function types* are made up of the function's parameter and return types. Consider the **sortEvenOdd(_:)** function. This function takes an array of integers as an argument and returns a tuple with two arrays of integers. Thus, the function type for **sortEvenOdd(_:)** is expressed as: ([Int]) -> ([Int], [Int]).

The function's parameters are listed inside the left parentheses, and the return type comes after the ->. You can read this function type as: "A function with one parameter that takes an array of integers and returns a tuple with two arrays containing integers." For comparison, a function with no arguments and no return has the following type: () -> ().

Function types are useful because you can assign them to variables. This feature will become particularly handy in the next chapter when you see that you can use functions in the arguments and returns of other functions. For now, let's just take a look at how you can assign a function type to a constant:

```
let evenOddFunction: ([Int]) -> ([Int], [Int]) = sortEvenOdd
```

This code creates a constant named evenOddFunction whose value is the function type of the **sortEvenOdd(_:)** function. Pretty cool, right? Now you can pass this constant around just like any other. You can even use this constant to call the function: evenOddFunction([1,2,3]) will sort the numbers in the array supplied to the function's sole argument into a tuple of two arrays – one for even and odd integers.

You accomplished a lot in this chapter. There was a lot of material here, and it may make sense to go through it all a second time. Be sure to type out all of the code in this chapter. In fact, try to extend the examples to different cases. Try to break the examples and then fix them.

If you are still a little fuzzy on functions, do not worry. They are also a major focus in the next chapter, so you will get lots more practice.

# Bronze Challenge

guard statements support the use of where clauses. Using a where clause with a guard statement gives you further control over the statement's condition. Refactor the **greetByMiddleName(_:)** function to have a where clause in its guard statement. This where clause should check to see if the middle name is fewer than 4 characters. If it is, then greet that person by their middle name. If it is not, then use the generic greeting.

# Silver Challenge

Write a function called **beanSifter(_:)** that takes a grocery list (as an array of strings) and "sifts out" the beans from the other groceries. The function should take one argument that has an external parameter name called groceryList, and it should return a named tuple of the type (beans: [String], otherGroceries: [String]).

Here is an example of how you should be able to call your function and what the result should be:

```
let result = beanSifter(groceryList: ["green beans",
                                      "milk",
                                      "black beans",
                                      "pinto beans",
                                      "apples"])

result.beans == ["green beans", "black beans", "pinto beans"]
result.otherGroceries == ["milk", "apples"]
```

Hint: you may need to make use of a function on the **String** type called **hasSuffix(_:)**.

# 13
# Closures

*Closures* are discrete bundles of functionality that can be used in your application to accomplish specific tasks. Functions, which you learned about in the last chapter, are a special case of closures. You can think of a function as a named closure.

In Chapter 12, you worked primarily with global and nested functions. Closures differ from functions in that they have a more compact and lightweight syntax. They allow you to write a "function-like" construct without having to give it a name and a full function declaration. This makes closures easy to pass around in function arguments and returns.

Let's get started. Create a new playground called `Closures.playground`.

## Closure Syntax

Imagine that you are a community organizer managing a number of organizations. You want to keep track of how many volunteers there are for each organization, and have created an instance of the `Array` type for this task.

### Listing 13.1  Starting with an array

```
import Cocoa

var volunteerCounts = [1,3,40,32,2,53,77,13]
```

You entered the number of volunteers for each organization as they were provided to you. This means that the array is completely disorganized. It would be better if your array of volunteers was sorted from lowest to highest number. Good news: Swift provides a *method* called `sort(_:)` that allows you to specify how an instance of `Array` will be sorted. (We call a function a method when it is defined on a type, like the `Array` type. More on this topic in Chapter 15.)

`sort(_:)` takes one argument: a closure that describes how the sorting should be done. The closure takes two arguments, whose types must match the type of the elements in the array, and returns a `Bool`. The two arguments are compared to produce this return value, which represents whether the instance in the first argument should be sorted before the instance in the second argument. Use < in the return if you would like argument one to be sorted before argument two. Doing so will sort the array in an *ascending* fashion – that is, from smallest to largest. Use > in the return if you would like argument two to come before argument one. This will sort the array in a *descending* fashion – that is, from largest to smallest.

Because your array of volunteer-counts is filled with integers, the function type for **sort(_:)** will look like this in your code: ((Int, Int) -> Bool) -> [Int]. In words, "**sort(_:)** is a method that takes a closure that takes two integers to compare and returns a Boolean value specifying which integer should come first. **sort(_:)** returns a new array of integers that have been ordered according to how the closure organizes them."

Add the following code to sort your array.

## Listing 13.2  Sorting the array

```
import Cocoa

var volunteerCounts = [1,3,40,32,2,53,77,13]

func sortAscending(i: Int, j: Int) -> Bool {
    return i < j
}
let volunteersSorted = volunteerCounts.sort(sortAscending)
```

First, you create a function called **sortAscending(_:j:)** that has the required type. It compares two integers and returns a Boolean that indicates whether **Int** i should be placed before **Int** j. In particular, **sortAscending(_:j:)** will return true if i should be placed before j. As this global function is a named closure (remember, all functions are closures), you can provide this function as the value of the argument in **sort(_:)**.

Next, you call **sort(_:)**, passing in **sortAscending(_:j:)** for the second argument. Because **sort(_:)** returns a new array, you assign that result to a new constant array called volunteersSorted. This instance will serve as your new record for the organizations' volunteer counts, correctly sorted.

Look in the results sidebar of your playground. You should see that the values inside volunteersSorted are sorted from lowest to highest.

## Figure 13.1  Sorting volunteer counts

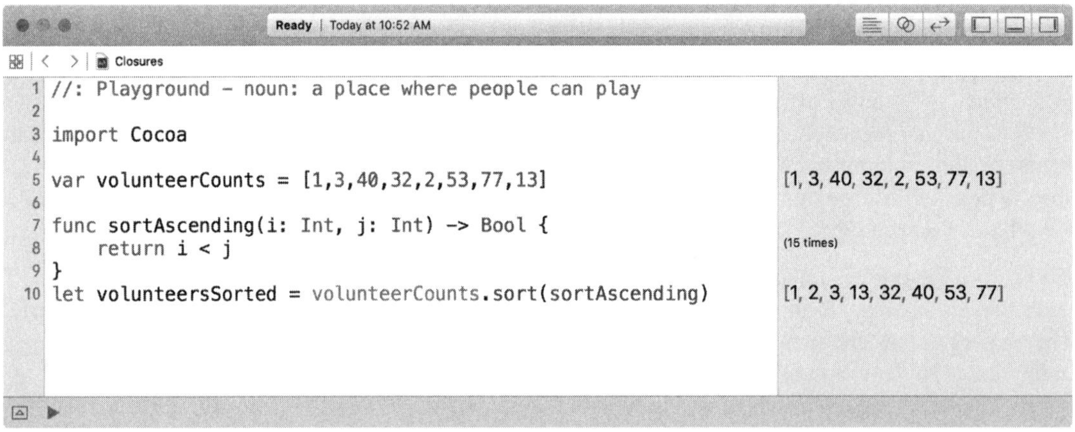

# Closure Expression Syntax

This works, but you can clean up your code. Closure syntax follows this general form:

```
{(parameters) -> return type in
    // Code
}
```

You write a closure expression inside of the braces ({}). The closure's parameters are listed inside of the parentheses immediately after the opening brace. Its return type comes after the parameters and uses the regular syntax. The keyword in is used to separate the closure's parameters and return type from the statements inside of its body.

Refactor your code to use a closure expression: create a closure inline instead of defining a separate function outside of the **sort(_:)** function.

## Listing 13.3  Refactoring your sorting code

```
import Cocoa

var volunteerCounts = [1,3,40,32,2,53,77,13]

func sortAscending(i: Int, j: Int) -> Bool {
    return i < j
}
let volunteersSorted = volunteerCounts.sort(volunteerCounts, sortAscending)

let volunteersSorted = volunteerCounts.sort({
    (i: Int, j: Int) -> Bool in
    return i < j
    })
```

This code is a bit cleaner and more elegant than the first version. Instead of providing a function defined elsewhere in the playground, you implement a closure inline in the **sort(_:)** function's second argument. You define the parameters and their type (**Int**) inside of the closure's parentheses and also specify its return type. Next, you implement the closure's body by providing the logical test (is i less than j?) that will inform the closure's return.

The result is just as before: the sorted array is assigned to volunteersSorted.

This refactoring is a step in the right direction, but it is still a little verbose. Closures can take advantage of Swift's type inference system, so you can clean up your closure even more by trimming out the type information.

## Listing 13.4  Taking advantage of type inference

```
import Cocoa

var volunteerCounts = [1,3,40,32,2,53,77,13]

let volunteersSorted = volunteerCounts.sort({
    (i: Int, j: Int) -> Bool in
    return i < j
    })

let volunteersSorted = volunteerCounts.sort({ i, j in i < j })
```

There are three new developments here. First, you remove the type information for both the parameters and the return. You can remove the return type because the compiler knows that checking if i < j will return true or false, that is a **Bool** value. Second, you move the entire closure expression to be one line.

Third, you remove the keyword return. Not all closure statements can omit the return keyword. This one can because it only has one expression (i < j). If more expressions were needed, an explicit return would be needed.

Notice that the result in the sidebar is the same.

Your closure is getting fairly compact, but it can become even more so. Swift provides shorthand argument names that you can refer to in inline closure expressions. These shorthand argument names behave similarly to the explicitly declared arguments you have been using: they have the same types and values. The compiler's type inference capabilities help it to know the number and types of arguments your closure takes, which means it is not necessary to name them.

For example, the compiler knows that **sort(_:)** takes a closure. That closure itself takes two parameters that are of the same type as the items in the array you pass into the **sort(_:)** function's argument. Because the closure has two arguments, whose values are compared to determine their order, you can refer to the values of the arguments using $0 for the first and $1 for the second.

Adjust your code to take advantage of the shorthand syntax.

## Listing 13.5  Using shorthand syntax for arguments

```
import Cocoa

var volunteerCounts = [1,3,40,32,2,53,77,13]

let volunteersSorted = volunteersCounts.sort({ i, j in i < j })

let volunteersSorted = volunteersCounts.sort({ $0 < $1 })
```

Now that your inline closure expression makes use of the shorthand argument syntax, you do not need to explicitly declare the parameters as you did for i and j. The compiler knows that the values in the closure's arguments are of the correct type and knows what to infer based on the < operator.

Incidentally, for a closure with more than two arguments you can use $2, $3, and so on.

Before you think this closure could not possibly get any slimmer, just wait, there is more! If a closure is a passed to a function's final argument, it can be written inline, outside of and after the function's parentheses. Since **sort(_:)** only takes one argument, this means you do not need any parentheses at all. Make this change.

## Listing 13.6  Inline closure as the function's final argument

```
import Cocoa

var volunteerCounts = [1,3,40,32,2,53,77,13]

let volunteersSorted = volunteerCounts.sort({ $0 < $1 })

let volunteersSorted = volunteerCounts.sort { $0 < $1 }
```

116

This "trailing closure syntax" is especially helpful if the closure's body is long. Here, the trailing closure makes for only a little less typing.

Truly, "Brevity is the soul of wit." The code above works just as well in this terse form as the earlier, much more verbose version. After all, there is really only one thing that you care about (is one integer less than another?), and that can be easily expressed. However, do not go too crazy with these tricks. It is always more important to make sure that your code is readable and maintainable.

# Functions as Return Types

Now that you have more experience with functions and closures, recall from Chapter 12 that every function has a *function type*. A function type defines a function's or closure's parameter and return types. For example, a function that takes a **String** argument and returns an **Int** has the function type of (String) -> Int. Function types are frequently used to determine what sort of closure you need to satisfy a given parameter's type or what sort of function needs to be returned.

In Swift, functions are *first-class objects*. One implication of this is that functions can return other functions as their return type. Remember your little town of Knowhere? It is time to make a function to improve your town. You are going to build some roads.

## Listing 13.7  Return to Knowhere

```
import Cocoa

var volunteerCounts = [1,3,40,32,2,53,77,13]

let volunteersSorted = volunteerCounts.sort { $0 < $1 }

func makeTownGrand() -> (Int, Int) -> Int {
    func buildRoads(lightsToAdd: Int, toLights: Int) -> Int {
        return toLights + lightsToAdd
    }
    return buildRoads
}
```

The function **makeTownGrand()** takes no arguments – it is like your grandfather. It does, however, return a function. This function takes two arguments, both integers, and returns an integer. Inside the **makeTownGrand()** function's body, you implement the function you return. In terms of implementation details, the function you return is a nested function called **buildRoads(_:toLights:)**. Its arguments and return type match what was declared in **makeTownGrand()**.

Exercise your new function and build some roads.

## Listing 13.8 The roads to Knowhere

```
import Cocoa

var volunteerCounts = [1,3,40,32,2,53,77,13]

let volunteersSorted = volunteerCounts.sort { $0 < $1 }

func makeTownGrand() -> (Int, Int) -> Int {
    func buildRoads(lightsToAdd: Int, toLights: Int) -> Int {
        return toLights + lightsToAdd
    }
    return buildRoads
}
var stoplights = 4
let townPlan = makeTownGrand()
stoplights = townPlan(4, stoplights)
print("Knowhere has \(stoplights) stoplights.")
```

First, you set up a variable called stoplights. This instance is declared as a variable because you are going to build some roads that will add to the town's number of stoplights. Next, you declare a constant called townPlan that refers to the function that is created by the **makeTownGrand()** function. Then you call that function and pass into it the number of lights to add (the first argument) and the current number of stoplights (the second argument). The result of this function, an instance of type **Int** is reassigned to the stoplights variable. Last, you print this new value to the console.

Check your console. It should read, "Knowhere has 8 stoplights."

# Functions as Arguments

Functions can serve as arguments to other functions. Recall, for example, that you initially gave **sort(_:)** the **sortAscending(_:j:)** function as an argument.

Practicality suggests that your town can only build roads when it has a suitable budget. Adjust your previous **makeTownGrand()** function to take a budget parameter and a condition parameter. The budget parameter will serve as your town's budget, and the condition parameter will evaluate whether this budget is suitable to build the new roads.

## Listing 13.9 Adding budget considerations

```
import Cocoa

var volunteerCounts = [1,3,40,32,2,53,77,13]

let volunteersSorted = volunteerCounts.sort { $0 < $1 }

func makeTownGrand() -> (Int, Int) -> Int {
    func buildRoads(lightsToAdd: Int, toLights: Int) -> Int {
        return toLights + lightsToAdd
    }
    return buildRoads
}

var stoplights = 4
let townPlan = makeTownGrand()
stoplights = townPlan(4, stoplights)

func makeTownGrand(budget: Int, condition: Int -> Bool) -> ((Int, Int) -> Int)? {
    if condition(budget) {
        func buildRoads(lightsToAdd: Int, toLights: Int) -> Int {
            return toLights + lightsToAdd
        }
        return buildRoads
    } else {
        return nil
    }
}
func evaluateBudget(budget: Int) -> Bool {
    return budget > 10000
}

var stoplights = 4

if let townPlan = makeTownGrand(1000, condition: evaluateBudget) {
    stoplights = townPlan(4, stoplights)
}
print("Knowhere has \(stoplights) stoplights.")
```

Let's go over the changes here.

One change is the new **makeTownGrand(_:condition:)** function, which takes two arguments. The first is an instance of the **Int** type representing the town's budget. The second is called condition and takes a function. This function determines whether the town's budget is sufficient. Thus, it will take an **Int** and return a **Bool**. If the integer budget is high enough, then this function will return true. If the budget is not high enough, then the function will return false.

Did you notice that the **makeTownGrand(_:condition:)** function has a different return type? The return type is now ((Int, Int) -> Int)?. The previous implementation of **makeTownGrand(_:)** returned a function that took two integers and returned an integer. In this revised version, **makeTownGrand(_:condition:)** returns the same thing, but in an optional incarnation. Why? Consider the budget requirement. If the town has the appropriate budget, then the **buildRoads(_:toLights:)** function will be created and returned. If, on the other hand, the budget is not sufficient, the **buildRoads(_:toLights:)** will not be created and nil will be returned. An optional is needed to handle the possibility of a nil return.

The implementation of **makeTownGrand(_:condition:)** runs the function passed into the condition parameter. If it evaluates to true, then the **buildRoads(_:toLights:)** function is created and returned. If condition evaluates to false, then nil is returned.

Also, you create the **evaluateBudget(_:)** function. This function takes an integer and returns a Boolean. Its implementation evaluates the integer to see whether it is greater than a threshold (arbitrarily set at 10,000).

Finally, you use optional binding to conditionally set townPlan. If the budget provided to the **makeTownGrand(_:condition:)** function is sufficiently large, then the **buildRoads(_:toLights:)** function will be created, returned, and assigned to townPlan. In this case, your town's number of stoplights will be increased by 4. If, however, the budget is not large enough, then **makeTownGrand(_:condition:)** will return nil. In this case, your town's number of stoplights will not be increased.

Check your console. Unfortunately, your town's budget is too small. A budget of 1,000 is certainly less than the requisite 10,000. Thus, **makeTownGrand(_:condition:)** returned nil and **buildRoads(_:toLights:)** was never executed. Your town will have to keep saving before it can build any new roads...

OK, enough time for saving. Your town now has enough money to build some roads. Update the code with a higher budget to see the effect.

## Listing 13.10 Building more roads

```
import Cocoa

var volunteerCounts = [1,3,40,32,2,53,77,13]

let volunteersSorted = volunteerCounts.sort { $0 < $1 }

func makeTownGrand(budget: Int, condition: Int -> Bool) -> ((Int, Int) -> Int)? {
    if condition(budget) {
        func buildRoads(lightsToAdd: Int, toLights: Int) -> Int {
            return toLights + lightsToAdd
        }
        return buildRoads
    } else {
        return nil
    }
}
func evaluateBudget(budget: Int) -> Bool {
    return budget > 10000
}

var stoplights = 4

if let townPlan = makeTownGrand(1000, evaluateBudget) {
    stoplights = townPlan(4, stoplights)
}
if let newTownPlan = makeTownGrand(10500, condition: evaluateBudget) {
    stoplights = newTownPlan(4, stoplights)
}
print("Knowhere has \(stoplights) stoplights.")
```

The budget of 10,500 exceeds the minimum necessary to build roads. You should see in the sidebar and on the console that your town now has a whopping 8 stoplights!

# Closures Capture Values

Closures and functions can keep track of internal information encapsulated by a variable defined in their enclosing scope. To see an example of this, imagine that Knowhere is booming. As growth can be erratic, you create a function that will allow you to update the town's population data based on recent growth. Your town planner will update the town's census data every time the population grows by 500 people.

Listing 13.11  Tracking growth

```
...
print("Knowhere has \(stoplights) stoplights.")

func makeGrowthTracker(forGrowth growth: Int) -> () -> Int {
    var totalGrowth = 0
    func growthTracker() -> Int {
        totalGrowth += growth
        return totalGrowth
    }
    return growthTracker
}
var currentPopulation = 5422
let growBy500 = makeGrowthTracker(forGrowth: 500)
```

The function **makeGrowthTracker(forGrowth:)** builds a **growthTracker()** function. **makeGrowthTracker(forGrowth:)** takes one argument, an integer representing the growth to track, and returns a function that takes no arguments and returns an integer. This integer is a running total of the growth your town is experiencing, totalGrowth. The **growthTracker()** function captures the value of the totalGrowth variable from its enclosing scope. After **growthTracker()** is created, the totalGrowth variable will be incremented by the amount specified in the argument passed to the **makeGrowthTracker(forGrowth:)** function.

Exercise and test this function by calling it a few times.

Listing 13.12  The population is booming

```
...
print("Knowhere has \(stoplights) stoplights.")

func makeGrowthTracker(forGrowth growth: Int) -> () -> Int {
    var totalGrowth = 0
    func growthTracker() -> Int {
        totalGrowth += growth
        return totalGrowth
    }
    return growthTracker
}
var currentPopulation = 5422
let growBy500 = makeGrowthTracker(forGrowth: 500)
growBy500()
growBy500()
growBy500()
currentPopulation += growBy500() // currentPopulation is now 7422
```

You call **growBy500()** four times to model a growth of 2,000 people for your town. Notice that the first three calls to **growBy500()** do not assign its result to any constant or variable. This is fine because the

121

function is keeping an internal running total of your town's growth. All you have to do to update your town's population is assign the result of the function to your `currentPopulation` variable when your town planner is ready.

# Closures Are Reference Types

Closures are *reference types*. This means that when you assign a function to a constant or variable you are actually setting that constant or variable to *point to* the function. You are not creating a distinct copy of that function. One important consequence of this fact is that any information captured by the function's scope will be changed if you call the function via a new constant or variable.

To see this, create a new constant and set it equal to your **growBy500()** function.

## Listing 13.13  Duplicate growth

```
...
func makeGrowthTracker(forGrowth growth: Int) -> () -> Int {
    var totalGrowth = 0
    func growthTracker() -> Int {
        totalGrowth += growth
        return totalGrowth
    }
    return growthTracker
}
var currentPopulation = 5422
let growBy500 = makeGrowthTracker(forGrowth: 500)
growBy500()
growBy500()
growBy500()
currentPopulation += growBy500() // currentPopulation is now 7422
let anotherGrowBy500 = growBy500
anotherGrowBy500() // totalGrowth now equal to 2500
```

`anotherGrowBy500` now points to the same function to which `growBy500` points, so when you call **anotherGrowBy500()**, the variable `totalGrowth` is incremented by 500. Thus, `totalGrowth`'s value is increased to 2,500 in this code. But remember that `currentPopulation` is unchanged because we do not increment its value by the return value of **anotherGrowBy500()**!

For comparison, suppose a large neighboring city has fallen in love with your town planner's function. The city wants its own growth-tracker function to update its population data every time the population grows by 10,000. Create the city's population and use the **makeGrowthTracker(forGrowth:)** function to create another growth-tracker function for the larger city.

## Listing 13.14  Another population to track

```
...
let anotherGrowBy500 = growBy500
anotherGrowBy500() // totalGrowth now equal to 2500
var someOtherPopulation = 4061981
let growBy10000 = makeGrowthTracker(forGrowth: 10000)
someOtherPopulation += growBy10000()
currentPopulation
```

You now have another population that you are keeping track of, and you have a new growth-tracker function called **growBy10000()** to help. You use **growBy10000()** to grow the city's population:

`someOtherPopulation += growBy10000()`. This is analogous to your use of **growBy500()**. The city's population is increased to 4,071,981 after this line. Notice that small-town Knowhere's population, represented by `currentPopulation`, does not change. It is still 7,422. This is because you used the **makeGrowthTracker(forGrowth:)** function to create a new growth-tracker function. This new growth-tracker function is separate and distinct from **growBy500()**.

# Functional Programming

Swift adopts some patterns from the *functional programming* paradigm. It is difficult to provide a concrete definition of functional programming because people use the phrase with different meanings and intentions, but typically it is understood to include:

- *First-class functions* – functions can be passed as arguments to other functions, can be stored in variables, etc.; they are just like any other type.

- *Pure functions* – functions have no side effects; functions, given the same input, always return the same output, and do not modify other states elsewhere in the program. Most math functions like sin, cos, fibonacci, and factorial are pure.

- *Immutability* – mutability is de-emphasized as it is more difficult to reason about data whose values can change.

- *Strong typing* – a strong type system increases the runtime safety of the code because the guarantees of the language's type system are checked at compile time.

Swift supports all of these approaches.

Functional programming can make your code more concise and expressive. By emphasizing immutability and strong compile time type checking, your code can also be safer at runtime. These hallmarks of functional programming can also make code easier to reason about and maintain.

Swift's `let` keyword allows you to declare immutable instances in your code. Its strong type system helps you to catch errors at compile time instead of at runtime. Swift also provides several *higher-order functions* that are well known to developers fond of functional programming: **map(_:)**, **filter(_:)**, and **reduce(_:combine:)**. These functions emphasize that Swift's functions are indeed first-class citizens.

Let's look at what these functions add to Swift's toolkit.

## Higher-order functions

*Higher-order functions* take at least one function as an input. You have already worked with higher-order functions in this chapter (for example, recall the use of **sort(_:)** above). Let's take a look at three more: **map(_:)**, **filter(_:)**, and **reduce(_:combine:)**.

## map(_:)

map(_:) is a function that you can use to transform an array's contents. You *map* an array's contents from one value to another and put these new values into a new array. Because map(_:) is a higher-order function, you provide it with another function that tells it how to transform the array's contents.

The Swift standard library provides an implementation of map(_:) on the **Array** type. Suppose your town, Knowhere, has three precincts, each with its own population. Hold these values in an array named precinctPopulations.

### Listing 13.15  Setting populations by precinct

```
...
let anotherGrowBy500 = growBy500
anotherGrowBy500() // totalGrowth now equal to 2500

var someOtherPopulation = 4061981
let growBy10000 = makeGrowthTracker(forGrowth: 10000)
someOtherPopulation += growBy10000()
currentPopulation

let precinctPopulations = [1244, 2021, 2157]
```

As before, Knowhere is a town on the move. Given Knowhere's growth, the town's city planner needs to make projections for each precinct's population. The city planner could use map(_:) in conjunction with the precinctPopulations array to do some estimating.

### Listing 13.16  Using map(_:) to estimate population

```
...
let anotherGrowBy500 = growBy500
anotherGrowBy500() // totalGrowth now equal to 2500

var someOtherPopulation = 4061981
let growBy10000 = makeGrowthTracker(forGrowth: 10000)
someOtherPopulation += growBy10000()
currentPopulation

let precinctPopulations = [1244, 2021, 2157]
let projectedPopulations = precinctPopulations.map {
    (population: Int) -> Int in
    return population * 2
}
projectedPopulations
```

Here, you use map(_:) to apply an estimate to each value of precinctPopulations. (Notice that you use the trailing closure syntax.) Next, you declare a parameter named population of type **Int** and specify that the closure will return an **Int**. map(_:) will apply this function to the value at each index in precinctPopulations. The estimate increases each precinct's population by 200% and results in a new array called projectedPopulations, which has the values 2488, 4042, and 4314.

## filter(_:)

filter(_:), like map(_:), can be called on an instance of the **Array** type. It also takes a closure expression as an argument. Its purpose is to *filter* an array based upon some criteria. The resulting array will contain the values of the original array that passed the test.

After applying her estimate, your city planner wants to know which precincts have projected populations greater than 4,000 people. filter(_:) is an ideal choice for this operation.

### Listing 13.17 Filtering an array

```
...

let precinctPopulations = [1244, 2021, 2157]
let projectedPopulations = precinctPopulations.map {
    (population: Int) -> Int in
    return population * 2
}
projectedPopulations

let bigProjections = projectedPopulations.filter {
    (projection: Int) -> Bool in
    return projection > 4000
}
bigProjections
```

As above, you use the trailing closure syntax. The closure takes a population projection of type **Int** as its argument and returns a **Bool** indicating whether the projection passed the test. Inside of this closure, you check to see whether the projection's value is greater than 4,000 and return the result. The values that pass this test are given to the bigProjections array. Only two projections pass the test, so bigProjections contains 4,042 and 4,314.

## reduce(_:combine:)

Imagine that Knowhere's mayor asked the city planner to provide an estimate of the town's projected population. With the data spread out in an array, how could the city planner figure this out? **reduce(_:combine:)** provides a great way to accomplish this task. You can call **reduce(_:combine:)** on an instance of the array type. Its job is to *reduce* the values in the collection to a single value that is returned from the function.

### Listing 13.18  Reducing an array to a single value

```
...

let bigProjections = projectedPopulations.filter {
    (projection: Int) -> Bool in
    return projection > 4000
}
bigProjections

let totalProjection = projectedPopulations.reduce(0) {
    (accumulatedProjection: Int, precinctProjection: Int) -> Int in
    return accumulatedProjection + precinctProjection
}
totalProjection
```

**reduce(_:combine:)**'s first argument refers to an initial amount (or some other value) that can be added at the outset. The second argument is a closure that defines how the values inside the collection should be combined. (Notice that you used the trailing closure syntax once again.) Here, all you need is to add up the projections in the projectedPopulations array, so the initial value you give is 0. Next, the closure has two arguments, accumulatedProjection and precinctProjection, both of type **Int**, that are combined as the **reduce(_:combine:)** traverses the array. When the function is done, totalProjection is set to be equal to 10844.

# Gold Challenge

Use what you have learned in this chapter to clean up the implementation of **reduce(_:combine:)** presented above. The implementation can be shortened quite significantly: your solution should be expressed in one line. When you are done, take a look at the sample code for the other higher-order functions and practice with them.

# Part IV
# Enumerations, Structures, and Classes

You will be learning about a lot of new tools and concepts in the chapters included in this part of the book. You will be adding features to projects that you will change in later projects. This will simulate the act of writing code in a real way: sometimes you start developing an application with one solution in mind and then have to modify your code when you learn a better pattern or a feature has changed. That does not mean the first code or tools were bad – just that they would be better for other circumstances. Projects often evolve and develop, and decisions that are ideal at one stage may become inadequate as requirements change. Learning to be flexible in the face of these changes is part of the trade.

# 14

# Enumerations

As you have worked through the book up to this point, you have been using all the built-in types that Swift provides, like integers, strings, arrays, and dictionaries. The next couple of chapters will show the capabilities the language provides to create your own types. The focus of this chapter is *enumerations* (or enums), which allow you to create instances that are one of a predefined list of cases. If you have used enumerations in other languages, much of this chapter will be familiar. But Swift's enums also have some advanced features that make them unique.

## Basic Enumerations

Create a new playground called `Enumerations.playground`. Define an enumeration of possible text alignments:

Listing 14.1 Defining an enumeration

```
enum TextAlignment {
    case Left
    case Right
    case Center
}
```

You define an enumeration with the enum keyword followed by the name of the enumeration. The opening brace ({) opens the body of the enum, and it must contain at least one case statement that declares the possible values for the enum. Here, you include three. The name of the enumeration (**TextAlignment** in this case) is now usable as a type, just like **Int** or **String** or the various other types you have used so far.

Types (and, therefore, enums) are named with a capital first letter by convention. If multiple words are needed, use camel-casing: **UpperCamelCasedType**. Variables and functions begin with a lowercase first letter, and also use camel-casing as needed.

Because the enumeration declares a new type, you can now create instances of that type.

Listing 14.2 Creating an instance of **TextAlignment**

```
enum TextAlignment {
    case Left
    case Right
    case Center
}

var alignment: TextAlignment = TextAlignment.Left
```

Although **TextAlignment** is a type that you have defined, the compiler can still infer the type for alignment. Therefore, you can omit the explicit type of the alignment variable:

## Listing 14.3  Taking advantage of type inference

```
...
var alignment: TextAlignment = TextAlignment.Left
```

The compiler's ability to infer the type of enumerations is not limited to variable declarations. If you have a variable known to be of a particular enum type, you can omit the type from the case statement when assigning a new value to the variable.

## Listing 14.4  Inferring the enum type

```
...
var alignment = TextAlignment.Left
alignment = .Right
```

Notice that you had to specify the enum's type and value when initially creating the alignment variable, because that line gives alignment both its type and its value. In the next line, you can omit the type and simply reassign alignment to be equal to a different value within its type. You can also omit the enum type when passing its values to functions or comparing them.

## Listing 14.5  Type inference when comparing values

```
...
alignment = .Right

if alignment == .Right {
    print("we should right-align the text!")
}
```

While enum values can be compared in if statements, switch statements are typically used to handle enum values. Use switch to print the alignment in a human-readable way.

## Listing 14.6  Switching to switch

```
...
alignment = .Right

if alignment == .Right {
    print("we should right-align the text!")
}
switch alignment {
case .Left:
    print("left aligned")

case .Right:
    print("right aligned")

case .Center:
    print("center aligned")
}
```

Recall from Chapter 5 that all switch statements must be exhaustive. In that chapter, you wrote `switch` statements that included a `default` case. When switching on enumeration values, that is not necessary: The compiler knows all possible values the enumeration can check. If you have included a case for each one, the switch is exhaustive.

You *could* include a `default` case when switching on an enum type.

### Listing 14.7  Making center the default case

```
...
switch alignment {
case .Left:
    print("left aligned")

case .Right:
    print("right aligned")

case .Center:
default:
    print("center aligned")
}
```

This code works, but we recommend avoiding `default` clauses when switching on enum types, because using a default is not as "future proof." Suppose you later want to add another alignment option for justified text.

### Listing 14.8  Adding a case

```
enum TextAlignment {
    case Left
    case Right
    case Center
    case Justify
}

var alignment = TextAlignment.LeftJustify
alignment = .Right
...
```

Notice that your program still runs, but it now prints the wrong value. The `alignment` variable is set to `Justify`, but the `switch` statement prints "center aligned." This is what we mean when we say that using a default is not future proof: it adds complication to modifying your code in the future.

Change your `switch` back to listing each case explicitly.

### Listing 14.9  Returning to explicit cases

```
...
switch alignment {
case .Left:
    print("left aligned")

case .Right:
    print("right aligned")

default:
case .Center:
    print("center aligned")
}
```

Now, instead of your program running and printing the wrong answer, you have a compile-time error that your `switch` statement is not exhaustive. It may seem odd to say that a compiler error is desirable, but that is exactly the situation here.

If you use a `default` clause when switching on an enum, your `switch` statement will always be exhaustive and satisfy the compiler. If you add a new case to the enum without updating the `switch`, the `switch` statement will fall to the `default` when it encounters the new case. Your code will compile, but it will not do what you intended, as you saw in Listing 14.8.

By listing each enum case in the `switch`, you ensure that the compiler will help you find all of the places in your code that need to be updated if you add cases to your enum. That is what is happening here: the compiler is telling you that your `switch` statement does not include all of the cases defined in your enum.

Let's fix that.

### Listing 14.10  Including all cases

```
...
switch alignment {
case .Left:
    print("left aligned")

case .Right:
    print("right aligned")

case .Center:
    print("center aligned")

case .Justify:
    print("justified")
}
```

# Raw Value Enumerations

If you have used enumerations in a language like C or C++, you may be surprised to learn that Swift enums do not have an underlying integer type. You can, however, choose to get the same behavior by using what Swift refers to as a *raw value*. To use **Int** raw values for your text alignment enumeration, change the declaration of the enum.

### Listing 14.11  Using raw values

```
enum TextAlignment: Int {
    case Left
    case Right
    case Center
    case Justify
}
...
```

Specifying a raw value type for **TextAlignment** gives a distinct raw value of that type (**Int**) to each case. The default behavior for integral raw values is that the first case gets raw value 0, the next case gets raw value 1, and so on. Confirm this by printing some interpolated strings.

## Listing 14.12  Confirming the raw values

```
...
var alignment = TextAlignment.Justify

print("Left has raw value \(TextAlignment.Left.rawValue)")
print("Right has raw value \(TextAlignment.Right.rawValue)")
print("Center has raw value \(TextAlignment.Center.rawValue)")
print("Justify has raw value \(TextAlignment.Justify.rawValue)")
print("The alignment variable has raw value \(alignment.rawValue)")
...
```

You are not limited to the default behavior for raw values. If you prefer, you can specify the raw value for each case.

## Listing 14.13  Specifying raw values

```
enum TextAlignment: Int {
    case Left    = 20
    case Right   = 30
    case Center  = 40
    case Justify = 50
}
...
```

When is a raw value enumeration useful? The most common reason for using a raw value is to store or transmit the enum. Instead of writing functions to transform a variable holding an enum, you can use rawValue to convert the variable to its raw value.

This brings up another question: if you have a raw value, how do you convert it back to the enum type? Every enum type with a raw value can be created with a rawValue: argument, which returns an optional enum.

## Listing 14.14  Converting raw values to enum types

```
...
print("Justify has raw value \(TextAlignment.Justify.rawValue)")
print("The alignment variable has raw value \(alignment.rawValue)")

// Create a raw value.
let myRawValue = 20

// Try to convert the raw value into a TextAlignment
if let myAlignment = TextAlignment(rawValue: myRawValue) {
    // Conversion succeeded!
    print("successfully converted \(myRawValue) into a TextAlignment")
} else {
    // Conversion failed.
    print("\(myRawValue) has no corresponding TextAlignment case")
}
...
```

What is going on here? You start with myRawValue, a variable of type **Int**. Then you try to convert that raw value into a TextAlignment case using TextAlignment(rawValue:). Because TextAlignment(rawValue:) has a return type of TextAlignment?, you use optional binding to determine whether you get a TextAlignment value or nil back.

The raw value you used here corresponds to `TextAlignment.Left`, so the conversion succeeds. Try changing it to a raw value that does not exist to see the message that conversion is not possible.

## Listing 14.15  Trying a bad value

```
...
let myRawValue = 20 100
...
```

Figure 14.1 shows the `else` block being executed:

## Figure 14.1  Result of failed **TextAlignment** conversion

```
} else {
    // Conversion failed
    println("\(myRawValue) has no corresponding TextAlignment case")
}
```
"100 has no corresponding TextAlignment case"

So far, you have been using **Int** as the type for your raw values. Swift allows a variety of types to be used, including all the built-in numeric types and **String**. Create a new enum that uses **String** as its raw value type.

## Listing 14.16  Creating an enum with strings

```
...
enum ProgrammingLanguage: String {
    case Swift     = "Swift"
    case ObjectiveC = "Objective-C"
    case C         = "C"
    case Cpp       = "C++"
    case Java      = "Java"
}

let myFavoriteLanguage = ProgrammingLanguage.Swift
print("My favorite programming language is \(myFavoriteLanguage.rawValue)")
```

You did not have to specify values when you first used a raw value of type **Int** – the compiler automatically set the first case to 0, the second case to 1, and so on. Here, you specified the corresponding raw **String** value for each case. This is not necessary: if you omit the raw value, Swift will use the name of the case itself! Modify **ProgrammingLanguage** to take out the raw values that match their case names.

## Listing 14.17  Using default string raw values

```
...
enum ProgrammingLanguage: String {
    case Swift     = "Swift"
    case ObjectiveC = "Objective-C"
    case C         = "C"
    case Cpp       = "C++"
    case Java      = "Java"
}

let myFavoriteLanguage = ProgrammingLanguage.Swift
print("My favorite programming language is \(myFavoriteLanguage.rawValue)")
```

Your declaration of devotion to Swift does not change.

# Methods

A method is a function that is associated with a type. In some languages, methods can only be associated with classes (which we will discuss in Chapter 15). In Swift, methods can also be associated with enums. Create a new enum that represents the state of a lightbulb.

### Listing 14.18 Lightbulbs can be on or off

```
...
enum Lightbulb {
    case On
    case Off
}
```

One of the things you might want to know is the temperature of the lightbulb. (For simplicity, assume that the bulb heats up immediately when it is turned on and cools off to the ambient temperature immediately when it is turned off.) Add a method for computing the surface temperature.

### Listing 14.19 Establishing temperature behaviors

```
...
enum Lightbulb {
    case On
    case Off

    func surfaceTemperatureForAmbientTemperature(ambient: Double) -> Double {
        switch self {
        case .On:
            return ambient + 150.0

        case .Off:
            return ambient
        }
    }
}
```

Here, you add a function inside the definition of the **Lightbulb** enumeration. Because of the location of the definition of this function, it is now a method associated with the **Lightbulb** type. We would call it "a method on **Lightbulb**." The function appears to take a single argument (ambient), but because it is a method, it also takes an implicit argument named self of type **Lightbulb**. All Swift methods have a self argument, which is used to access the instance on which the method is called – in this case, the instance of **Lightbulb**.

Create a variable to represent a lightbulb and call your new method.

## Listing 14.20 Turning on the light

```
...
enum Lightbulb {
    case On
    case Off

    func surfaceTemperatureForAmbientTemperature(ambient: Double) -> Double {
        switch self {
        case .On:
            return ambient + 150.0

        case .Off:
            return ambient
        }
    }
}

var bulb = Lightbulb.On
let ambientTemperature = 77.0

var bulbTemperature = bulb.surfaceTemperatureForAmbientTemperature(ambientTemperature)
print("the bulb's temperature is \(bulbTemperature)")
```

First you create bulb, an instance of the **Lightbulb** type. When you have an instance of the type, you can call methods on that instance using the syntax instance.methodName(parameters). You do exactly that here when you call bulb.surfaceTemperatureForAmbientTemperature(ambientTemperature). The bulb variable is an instance of **Lightbulb**, surfaceTemperatureForAmbientTemperature is the name of the method you are calling, and ambientTemperature is a parameter you pass in to the method. You store the result of the method call, a **Double**, in the bulbTemperature variable. Finally, you print a string with the bulb's temperature to the console.

Another method that seems like it might be useful is one that would toggle the lightbulb. To toggle the lightbulb, you need to modify `self` to change it from `On` to `Off` or `Off` to `On`. Try to add a **`toggle()`** method that takes no arguments and does not return anything.

## Listing 14.21  Trying to toggle

```
...
enum Lightbulb {
    case On
    case Off

    func surfaceTemperatureForAmbientTemperature(ambient: Double) -> Double {
        switch self {
        case .On:
            return ambient + 150.0

        case .Off:
            return ambient
        }
    }

    func toggle() {
        switch self {
        case .On:
            self = .Off

        case .Off:
            self = .On
        }
    }
}
...
```

After typing this, you will get a compiler error that states that you cannot assign to `self` inside a method. In Swift, an enumeration is a *value type*, and methods on value types are not allowed to make changes to `self` (there will be more discussion of value types in Chapter 15). If you want to allow a method to change `self`, you need to mark it as a *mutating* method. Add this to your code.

## Listing 14.22  Making **toggle** a mutating method

```
...
    mutating func toggle() {
        switch self {
        case .On:
            self = .Off

        case .Off:
            self = .On
        }
    }
...
```

Now you can toggle your lightbulb and see what the temperature is when the bulb is off.

### Listing 14.23  Turning off the light

```
...
var bulbTemperature = bulb.surfaceTemperatureForAmbientTemperature(ambientTemperature)
print("the bulb's temperature is \(bulbTemperature)")

bulb.toggle()
bulbTemperature = bulb.surfaceTemperatureForAmbientTemperature(ambientTemperature)
print("the bulb's temperature is \(bulbTemperature)")
```

# Associated Values

Everything you have done so far with enumerations falls into the same general category of defining static cases that enumerate possible values or states. Swift also offers a much more powerful flavor of enumeration: cases with associated values. Associated values allow you to attach data to instances of an enumeration, and different cases can have different types of associated values.

Create an enumeration that allows for tracking the dimensions of a couple of basic shapes. Each kind of shape has different types of properties. To represent a square, you need a single value (the length of one side). To represent a rectangle, you need two values: a width and a height.

### Listing 14.24  Setting up **ShapeDimensions**

```
...
enum ShapeDimensions {
    // Square's associated value is the length of one side
    case Square(Double)

    // Rectangle's associated value defines its width and height
    case Rectangle(width: Double, height: Double)
}
```

You have defined a new enumeration type, **ShapeDimensions**, with two cases. The Square case has an associated value of type **Double**. The Rectangle case has an associated value with the type **(width:Double, height:Double)**, a named tuple (first seen in Chapter 12).

To create instances of **ShapeDimensions**, you must specify both the case and an appropriate associated value for the case.

### Listing 14.25  Creating shapes

```
...
enum ShapeDimensions {
    // Square's associated value is the length of one side
    case Square(Double)

    // Rectangle's associated value defines its width and height
    case Rectangle(width: Double, height: Double)
}

var squareShape = ShapeDimensions.Square(10.0)
var rectShape = ShapeDimensions.Rectangle(width: 5.0, height: 10.0)
```

Here, you create a square with sides 10 units long and a rectangle that is 5 units by 10 units.

You can use a `switch` statement to unpack an associated value and make use of it. Add a method to **ShapeDimensions** that computes the area of a shape.

### Listing 14.26  Using associated values to compute area

```
...
enum ShapeDimensions {
    // Square's associated value is the length of one side
    case Square(Double)

    // Rectangle's associated value defines its width and height
    case Rectangle(width: Double, height: Double)

    func area() -> Double {
        switch self {
        case let .Square(side):
            return side * side

        case let .Rectangle(width: w, height: h):
            return w * h
        }
    }
}
...
```

In your implementation of **area()**, you `switch` on `self` just as you did earlier in the chapter. Here, the `switch` cases use Swift's *pattern matching* to bind `self`'s associated value with a new variable (or variables).

Call the **area()** method on the instances you created earlier to see it in action.

### Listing 14.27  Computing areas

```
...
var squareShape = ShapeDimensions.Square(10.0)
var rectShape = ShapeDimensions.Rectangle(width: 5.0, height: 10.0)

print("square's area = \(squareShape.area())")
print("rectangle's area = \(rectShape.area())")
```

Not all enum cases have to have associated values. For example, you could add a **Point** case. Geometric points do not have any dimensions. To add a **Point**, leave off the associated value type.

Add a **Point** and update the **area()** method to include its area.

## Listing 14.28 Setting up a **Point**

```
...
enum ShapeDimensions {
    // Point has no associated value - it is dimensionless
    case Point

    // Square's associated value is the length of one side
    case Square(Double)

    // Rectangle's associated value defines its width and height
    case Rectangle(width: Double, height: Double)

    func area() -> Double {
        switch self {
        case .Point:
            return 0

        case let .Square(side):
            return side * side

        case let .Rectangle(width: w, height: h):
            return w * h
        }
    }
}
...
```

Now, create an instance of a point and confirm that **area()** works as expected.

## Listing 14.29 What is the area of a point?

```
...
var squareShape = ShapeDimensions.Square(10.0)
var rectShape = ShapeDimensions.Rectangle(width: 5.0, height: 10.0)
var pointShape = ShapeDimensions.Point

print("square's area = \(squareShape.area())")
print("rectangle's area = \(rectShape.area())")
print("point's area = \(pointShape.area())")
```

# Recursive Enumerations

You now know how to attach associated values to enum cases. This brings up a curious question. Can you attach an associated value of an enum's own type to one of its cases? (Perhaps this question brings up another: why would you want to?)

A data structure that comes up frequently in computer science is a tree. Most hierarchical data can naturally be represented as a tree. Think of a family tree: it contains people (the "nodes" of the tree) and ancestral relationships (the "edges" of the tree). The family tree branching stops when you reach an ancestor you do not know, as in Figure 14.2.

Figure 14.2  A family tree

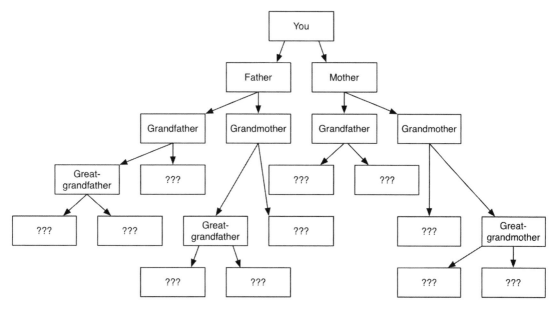

Modeling a family tree can be difficult because for any given person, you may know zero, one, or both of their parents. If you know one or both parents, you would like to keep track of their ancestors as well. Try to create an enum that will let you build up as much of your family tree as you know.

Listing 14.30  Incorrect attempt at **FamilyTree**

```
...
enum FamilyTree {
    case NoKnownParents
    case OneKnownParent(name: String, ancestors: FamilyTree)
    case TwoKnownParents(fatherName: String, fatherAncestors: FamilyTree,
                         motherName: String, motherAncestors: FamilyTree)
}
```

Once you have typed this in, Xcode gives you an error that contains a suggested fix: "Recursive enum 'FamilyTree' is not marked 'indirect'." **FamilyTree** is "recursive" because its cases have an associated value that is also of type **FamilyTree**. Why does the language care if an enum is recursive, though?

The answer to that question requires a little bit of understanding of how enumerations work under the hood. The Swift compiler has to know how much memory every instance of every type in your program will occupy. You do not (usually) have to worry about this, as the compiler figures it all out for you when it builds your program. Enumerations, however, are a little tricky.

The compiler knows that any instance of an enum will only ever be in one case at a time, although it may change cases as your program runs. Therefore, when the compiler is deciding how much memory an instance of enum requires, it will look at each case and figure out which case requires the most memory. The enum will require that much memory (plus a little bit more that the compiler will use to keep track of which case is currently assigned).

Look back at your **ShapeDimensions** enum. The .Point case has no associated data, so it requires no extra memory. The .Square case has an associated **Double**, so it requires one **Double**'s worth of memory (8 bytes). The .Rectangle case has two associated **Double**s, so it requires 16 bytes of memory. The actual size of an instance of **ShapeDimensions** is 17 bytes: enough room to store .**Rectangle**, if necessary, plus one byte to keep track of which case the instance actually is.

Now consider your **FamilyTree** enum. How much memory is required for the .OneKnownParent case? Enough memory for a **String** plus enough memory for an instance of **FamilyTree**. See the problem? The compiler cannot determine how big a **FamilyTree** is without knowing how big a **FamilyTree** is. Looking at it another way, **FamilyTree** would require an infinite amount of memory!

To solve this issue, Swift can introduce a layer of indirection. Instead of deciding how much memory .OneKnownParent will require (which would lead back into infinite recursion), you can use the keyword indirect to instruct the compiler to instead store the enum's data behind a pointer. We do not discuss pointers much in this book because Swift does not make you deal with them. Even in this case, you do not have to do anything except opt in to making **FamilyTree** use pointers under the hood. Do that now, and you are well on your way to modeling a family tree.

## Listing 14.31  Correct **FamilyTree**

```
...
indirect enum FamilyTree {
    case NoKnownParents
    case OneKnownParent(name: String, ancestors: FamilyTree)
    case TwoKnownParents(fatherName: String, fatherAncestors: FamilyTree,
                         motherName: String, motherAncestors: FamilyTree)
}
```

How does using a pointer solve the "infinite memory" problem? The compiler now knows to store a pointer to the associated data, putting the data somewhere else in memory rather than making the instance of **FamilyTree** big enough to hold the data. The size of an instance of **FamilyTree** is now 8 bytes on a 64-bit architecture – the size of one pointer.

It is worth noting that you do not have to mark the entire enumeration as indirect: you can also mark the individual recursive cases as indirect. Make that change now.

### Listing 14.32 **FamilyTree** indirect cases

```
...
indirect enum FamilyTree {
    case NoKnownParents
    indirect case OneKnownParent(name: String, ancestors: FamilyTree)
    indirect case TwoKnownParents(fatherName: String, fatherAncestors: FamilyTree,
                                  motherName: String, motherAncestors: FamilyTree)
}
```

Now that **FamilyTree** is accepted by the compiler, create an instance to model Fred's family tree. Fred does not know many of his ancestors, which is nice for you because typing out an instance of **FamilyTree** is a little onerous!

He knows both of his parents, so you need to use the **.TwoKnownParents** case. He only knows one of his father's parents, so you need to use the **.OneKnownParent** case for his father's ancestors. He does not know either of his mother's parents or either of his great-grandparents on his father's side, so you need to use the **.NoKnownParents** case for both of those ancestor values.

### Listing 14.33 Creating a **FamilyTree**

```
...
let fredAncestors = FamilyTree.TwoKnownParents(
    fatherName: "Fred Sr.",
    fatherAncestors: .OneKnownParent(name: "Beth", ancestors: .NoKnownParents),
    motherName: "Marsha",
    motherAncestors: .NoKnownParents)
```

### Figure 14.3 Fred's family tree

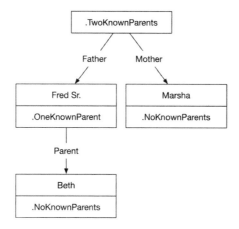

The new code above is described graphically by Figure 14.3. fredAncestors is a recursive enumeration that represents Fred's known family tree, with each node in the tree representing an instance of the same enumeration. As you can see, this sort of enumeration models nested information quite well.

# Bronze Challenge

Add a `perimeter()` method to the **ShapeDimensions** enum. This method should compute the perimeter of a shape (the sum of the length of all its edges). Make sure you handle all the cases!

# Silver Challenge

Add another case to the **ShapeDimensions** enum for a right triangle. You can ignore the orientation of the triangle. Just keep track of the lengths of its three sides. Adding a new case will cause your playground to give you an error in the **area()** method. Fix the error.

# 15

# Structs and Classes

Structures (commonly referred to as structs) and classes are the pillars on which you build your applications. They provide important mechanisms to model the things you wish to represent in your code.

You are going to transition from the playground and create a *command-line tool*, which you will work in for the next several chapters. Your command-line tool project will represent a town undergoing a serious monster infestation. You will use both structs and classes to model these entities and will give them properties to store data and functions so that these entities can do some work.

As you will see, structs and classes have similarities and differences. Which to use for any particular situation is an important decision. This chapter will get you started with understanding their strengths, and in Chapter 18 you will learn more about when to use each.

## A New Project

Create a new project by clicking on your Xcode icon. The first screen that you see is the Welcome screen (Figure 15.1). Click Create a new Xcode project.

Figure 15.1  Welcome window

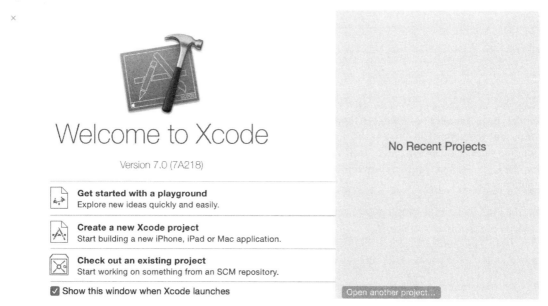

Next, you will see a screen for selecting a project template. A template formats your project with a number of presets and configurations common to a given style of application. On the lefthand side of the window, notice that there are two sections: iOS and OS X. Select Application from within the OS X section. Then, in the main area of the window, choose the Command Line Tool template option and click Next (Figure 15.2). This template will create a very basic project file.

Figure 15.2  Choosing a template

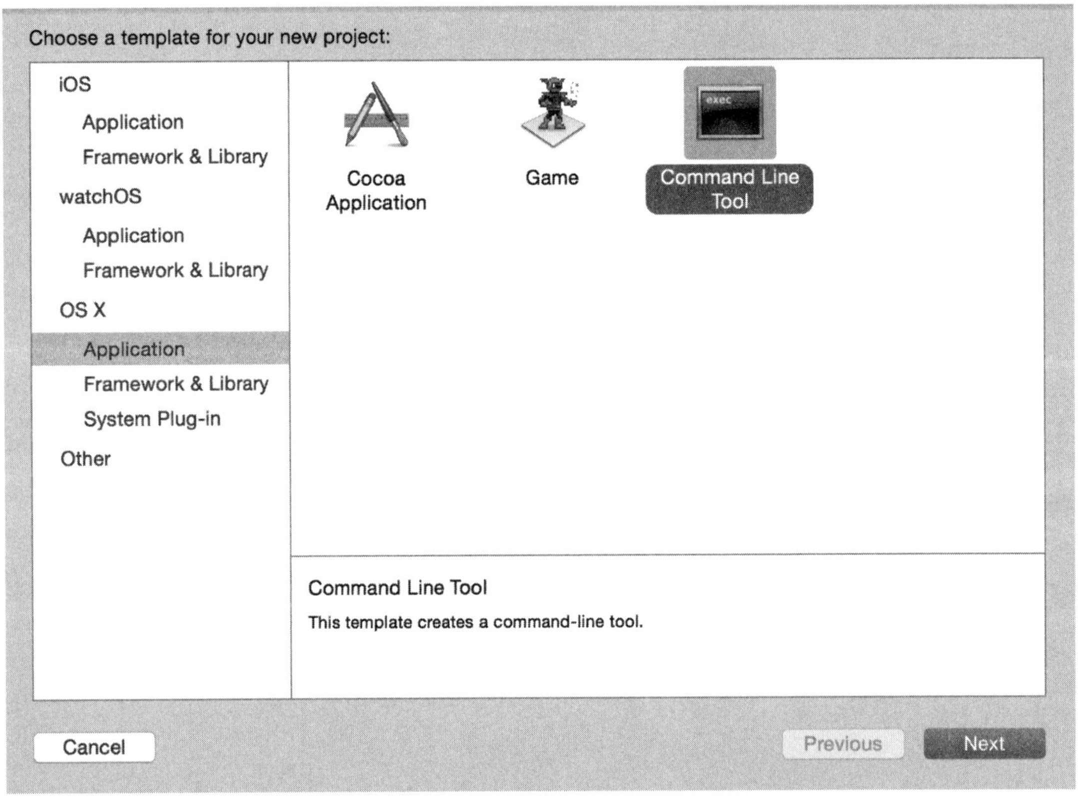

Now you will choose options for your project, including a name (Figure 15.3). In the Product Name field, type in **MonsterTown**. Enter **BigNerdRanch** (or whatever you would like) for the project's Organization Name. The Organization Identifier fills in for you using *reverse Domain Name Service* notation ("reverse DNS"), and is used with the product name to create the Bundle Identifier. The bundle ID is used to identify your application on iTunes Connect when you are ready to distribute your application.

Select Swift for the Language option and click Next.

## Figure 15.3  Naming your project

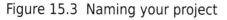

Choose options for your new project:

Product Name:         MonsterTown

Organization Name:    BigNerdRanch

Organization Identifier:  com.bignerdranch

Bundle Identifier:    com.bignerdranch.MonsterTown

Language:             Swift

Cancel                                    Previous    Next

Last, Xcode asks you where to save the project. Select a good location and click Create.

Your project opens in Xcode with the main.swift file selected, as in Figure 15.4. (If you see any other screen, click main.swift in the lefthand panel.)

## Figure 15.4  main.swift

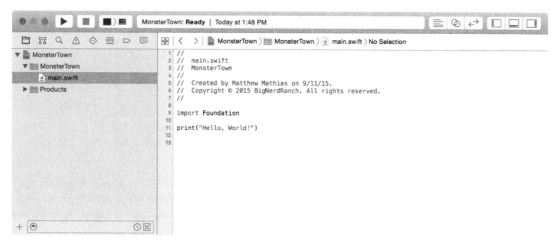

Let's take a moment to look at the organization of the Xcode application window. Figure 15.5 provides a high-level overview of the most prominent sections.

## Figure 15.5  Organization of Xcode

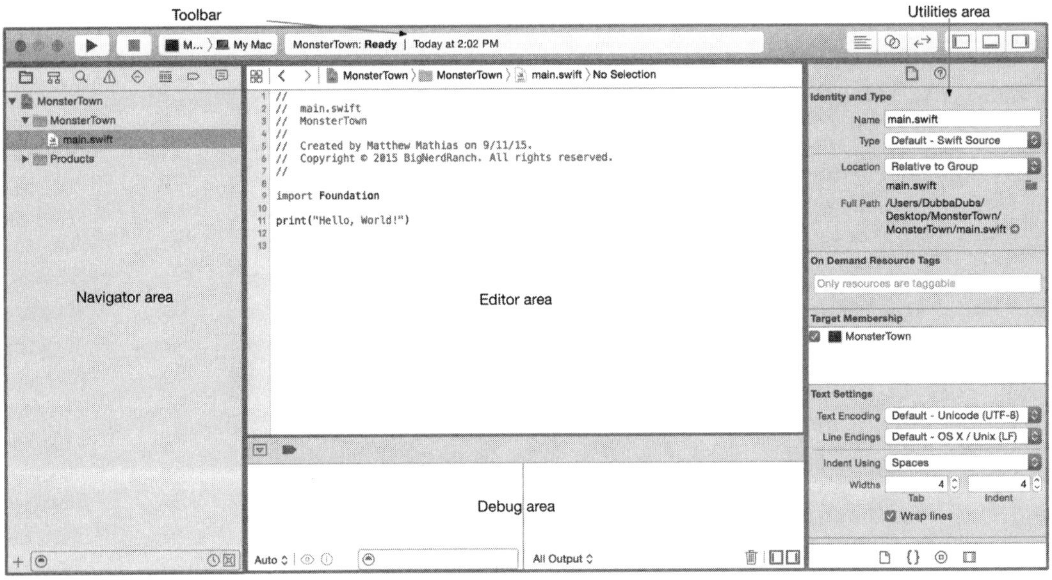

The pane on the far left is the *navigator area*. It provides several views that encapsulate how your project is organized. The view that opens by default is the *project navigator*. In the project navigator, you see a listing of your files, which at the moment only includes main.swift.

Moving one section to the right, you see the *editor area*. This is where you will add, view, and edit the code in a selected file.

On the far right is the *utilities area*. The utilities area provides several inspectors that allow you to get more information, such as the *file inspector* that gives information about a file's location, name, and so on.

At the bottom of the Xcode window is the debug area. You will use this area to debug your code when there are problems.

At the top of the window is the toolbar, which has Play and Stop buttons you will use to run and stop your programs. The toolbar also has three buttons on the far right to display and hide the navigator, utilities, and debug areas.

In a command-line tool, main.swift represents the entry point of your program. main.swift typically contains "top-level" code, or code that is not contained within the implementation of any function or defined on a specific type (like a struct or a class). The execution of the code in this file is order-dependent: it executes from the top to the bottom.

Because main.swift is where your program starts running, the code in this file typically does set-up work. As you will see, you will define types in other files and create instances of them in main.swift. For example, you will create a Town.swift file to hold a definition of a struct called **Town**. Then you will create an instance of **Town** in main.swift.

Types are frequently defined in their own files to help organize an application's source code. This strategy makes it easier to find and debug code.

Notice that the `main.swift` file already has the following code:

```
import Foundation

print("Hello, World!")
```

The `import Foundation` code brings the `Foundation` *framework* into the `main.swift` file. This framework consists of a number of classes primarily designed to do work in and with Objective-C. In the future, we will ignore this line of code unless you need it for context in the code listing or for using one of the types it provides. The `print("Hello, World!")` code should look familiar. It logs the string `"Hello, World!"` to the console.

Build and run your program. You can do this several ways:

- click Product in the toolbar at the top of your screen (see Figure 15.6), then select Run

- press Command-R on your keyboard

- click the triangular play button in the upper lefthand corner

## Figure 15.6 Xcode toolbar

| **Xcode** | File | Edit | View | Find | Navigate | Editor | Product | Debug | Source Control | Window | Help |

After you run your program, `"Hello, World!"` is logged to the console. That is great, but you have seen this behavior before. Let's make your program more interesting by creating custom structs and classes. Before you move on, make sure to delete the `print("Hello, World!")` because you will not need it.

## Listing 15.1 Removing "Hello, World!" (`main.swift`)

```
import Foundation

print("Hello, World!")
```

# Structures

A struct is a type that groups a set of related chunks of data together in memory. You use structs when you would like to group data together under a common type. For example, you will create a struct called **Town** in MonsterTown to model a town with a monster problem.

Making **Town** a struct encapsulates its data within a single type, and placing its definition in its own file provides a convenient location to find its implementation. In previous chapters, you modeled a town in a playground. Because the example was relatively small, this was not all that limiting. But it is better to encapsulate the definition of the town within its own type. A playground is great for rapidly prototyping some code, but it does not really match the sort of projects that you will be working with in real app development.

Add a new file to your project by clicking File → New → File.... You can also type Command-N on your keyboard. A new window, like the one shown in Figure 15.7, prompts you to select a template for your new file. Select Source in the OS X section on the left, then choose Swift File and click Next.

Figure 15.7  Adding a Swift file

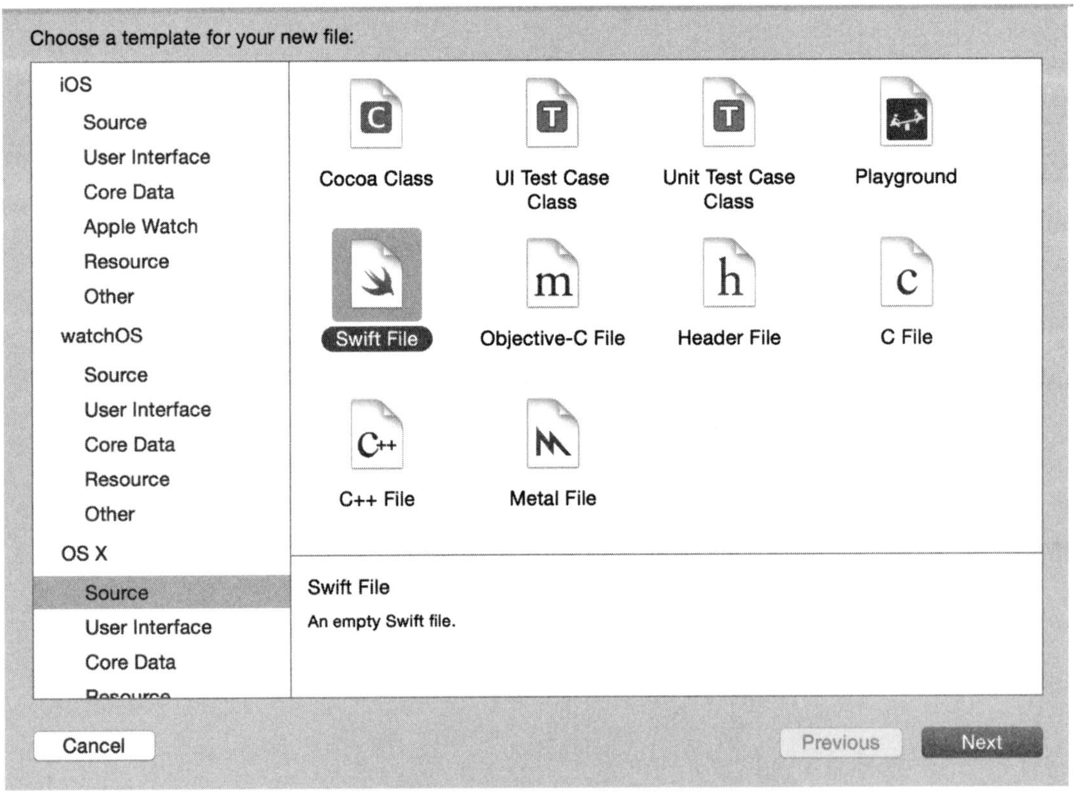

Next you are asked to name the new file and set its location. Call this file Town and make sure the box is checked to add it to the MonsterTown target (Figure 15.8). Click **Create**.

Figure 15.8 Town.swift

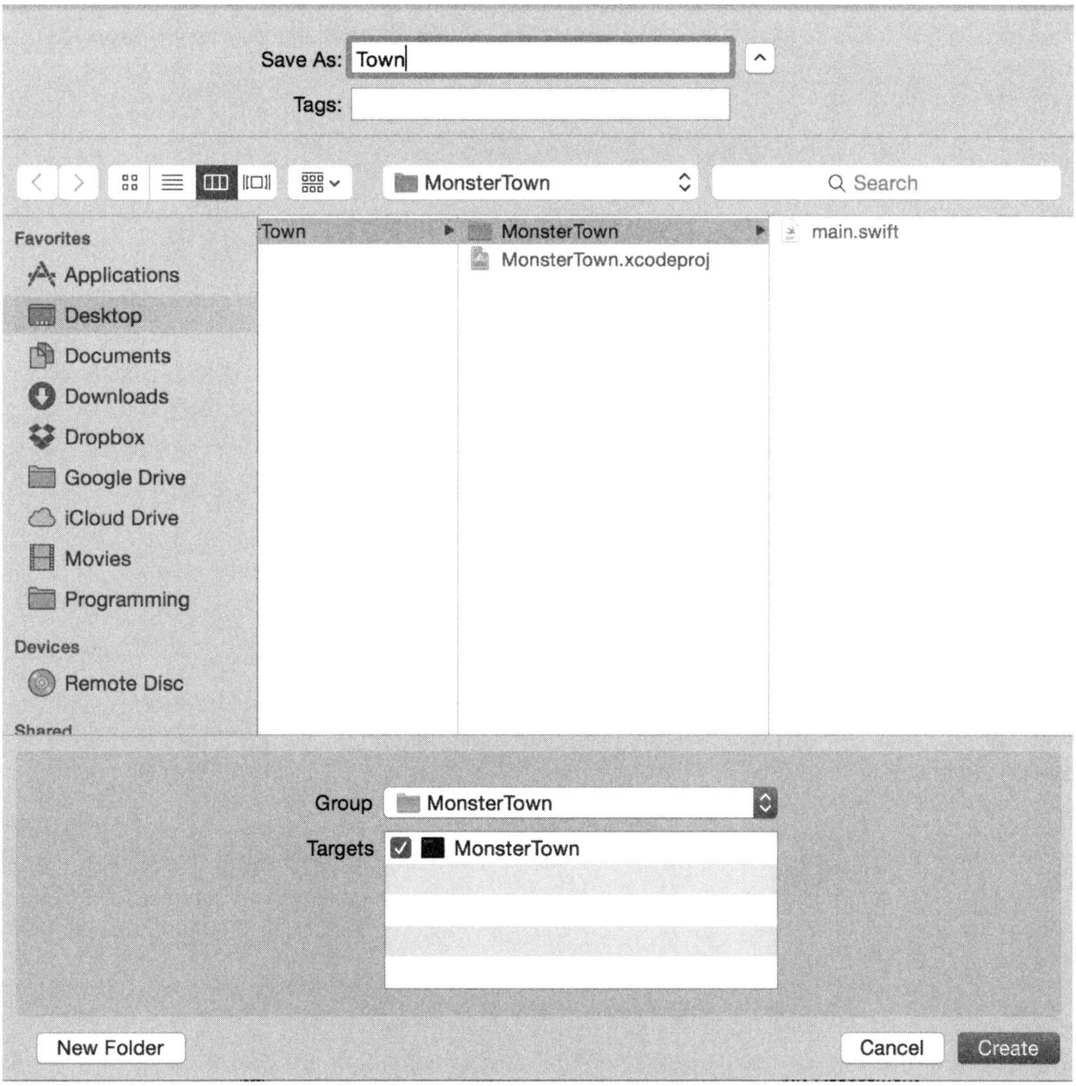

Select Town.swift in the navigator area. When the file opens, you will find that it is nearly blank, except for the comments at the top and the import Foundation line.

Start by declaring your Town struct.

Listing 15.2  Declaring a struct (Town.swift)

```
import Foundation

struct Town {

}
```

The keyword `struct` signals that you are declaring a struct, in this case named **Town**. You will add code between the braces ({}) to define the behavior of this struct. For example, you are about to add variables to your new struct so that it can hold on to some data that will help to model the characteristics of your town.

Technically, these variables are called *properties*, which is the subject of the next chapter. Properties can be variable or constant, as you have seen before using the `var` and `let` keywords. Add some properties to your struct.

## Listing 15.3 Adding properties (Town.`swift`)

```
struct Town {
    var population = 5422
    var numberOfStoplights = 4
}
```

Here, you add two properties to **Town**: `population` and `numberOfStoplights`. Both of these properties are mutable – this makes sense, because a town's population and number of stoplights are likely to change over time. These properties also have default values for the sake of simplicity. When a new instance of the **Town** struct is made, it will default to having a population of 5422 and 4 stoplights.

Switch to your `main.swift` file and create a new instance of **Town** to see your struct in action.

## Listing 15.4 Creating an instance of **Town** (`main.swift`)

```
var myTown = Town()
print("Population: \(myTown.population),
        number of stoplights: \(myTown.numberOfStoplights)")
```

(Note that the code in the **print()** call above is split into two lines due to page-size limitations. If you enter the code exactly as it is shown above, you will see an error. Avoid this by writing the **print()** call on one line, like so: print("Population: \(myTown.population), number of stoplights: \(myTown.numberOfStoplights)").)

You accomplish three things with this code.

First, you create an instance of the **Town** type. You do this by entering the name of the type (here, **Town**) followed by empty parentheses (). Including the empty parentheses calls the default initializer for **Town** (more on initialization in Chapter 17).

Second, you set this new instance equal to a variable you call `myTown`.

Third, you use string interpolation to print the values of the **Town** struct's two properties to the console. Notice that you use dot syntax to access the properties' values. For example, the syntax `myTown.population` retrieves the population of the `myTown` instance.

Run your program. The output reads `Population: 5422, number of stoplights: 4` (Figure 15.9).

Figure 15.9  Describing myTown

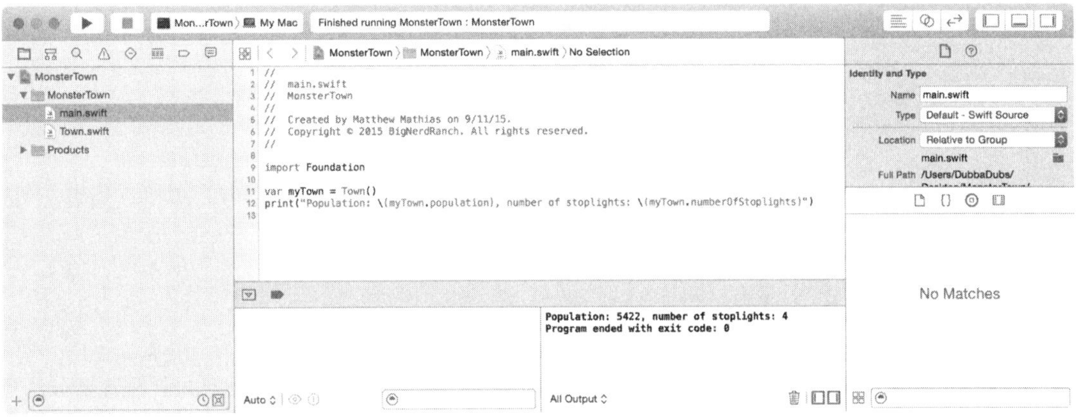

# Instance Methods

The `print()` function above is a fine way to print a description of myTown. But a town should know how to describe itself. Create a function on the struct **Town** that prints the values of its properties to the console. Navigate to your Town.swift file and add the following function definition.

Listing 15.5  Letting **Town** describe itself (Town.swift)

```
struct Town {
    var population = 5422
    var numberOfStoplights = 4

    func printTownDescription() {
        print("Population: \(population);
            number of stoplights: \(numberOfStoplights)")
    }
}
```

`printTownDescription()` is a method because it is a function that is associated with a particular type. (Recall from Chapter 14 that this is the definition of a method.) Thus far, you have mainly worked with what are called *global functions*. Global functions are not defined on any specific type, and for this reason they are also called *free functions*.

`printTownDescription()` takes no arguments and returns nothing. Its purpose is to log a description of a town's properties to the console. That makes `printTownDescription()` an *instance method*, because it is called on a specific instance of **Town**.

To make use of your new instance method, you need to call it on an instance of **Town**. Navigate back to main.swift and replace the **print()** function with your new instance method.

Listing 15.6  Calling your new instance method (main.swift)

```
var myTown = Town()
print("Population: \(myTown.population),
        number of stoplights: \(myTown.numberOfStoplights)")
myTown.printTownDescription()
```

You use dot syntax to call a function on an instance: myTown.printTownDescription().

Run your program. The console output is the same as before.

# Mutating methods

Your **printTownDescription()** method is great for displaying your town's current information. But what if you need a function that *changes* your town's information? If an instance method on a struct changes any of the struct's properties, it must be marked as mutating. In Town.swift, add a mutating method to the **Town** type to increase a town instance's population.

Listing 15.7  A mutating method to increase population (Town.swift)

```
struct Town {
    var population = 5422
    var numberOfStoplights = 4

    func printTownDescription() {
        print("Population: \(population);
                number of stoplights: \(numberOfStoplights)")
    }

    mutating func changePopulation(amount: Int) {
        population += amount
    }
}
```

Note that you mark the instance method **changePopulation()** with the mutating keyword. As in Chapter 14, this means that the method can change the values in the struct. Both structures and enumerations are value types (which you will read more about later in the chapter) and require the mutating keyword on methods that change the value of an instance's properties.

The method has one parameter, amount, that is of the **Int** type. This parameter is used to increase the town's population: population += amount. Switch over to main.swift to exercise this function.

Listing 15.8  Increasing the population (main.swift)

```
var myTown = Town()
myTown.changePopulation(500)
myTown.printTownDescription()
```

As before, you use dot syntax to call the function on your town. If you build and run the program you will see that myTown's population has been increased by 500: Population: 5922; number of stoplights: 4.

# Classes

Like structs, classes are used to model related data under a common type. Classes differ from structs in a few very important ways, and this section will be careful to highlight those differences. You will use classes in MonsterTown to model various types of monsters that will be terrorizing your town.

## A monster class

Now that you have a struct representing a town, it is time to make things a little more interesting. Your town is, unfortunately, infested with monsters. This is not good for property values.

Create a new Swift file called `Monster`. As before, click File → New → File... or press Command-N. Select Source in the OS X section and the Swift File template.

This file will contain the definition for a **Monster** class that will be used to model a monster's properties and town-terrorizing activities. Start by creating a new class.

Listing 15.9  Monster setup (`Monster.swift`)

```
import Foundation

class Monster {

}
```

The syntax to define a new class instance is nearly identical to the syntax used to define a new struct instance. You begin with the keyword `class`, followed by the name you are assigning to your new class. And, as before, the definition of the class takes place between the braces: {}.

For reasons relating to inheritance (discussed in the next section), the class **Monster** is defined in very general terms. This means that the **Monster** class will describe the general behavior of a monster. Later you will create different kinds of monsters that will have specific behaviors.

Listing 15.10  Defining the **Monster** class (`Monster.swift`)

```
class Monster {
    var town: Town?
    var name = "Monster"

    func terrorizeTown() {
        if town != nil {
            print("\(name) is terrorizing a town!")
        } else {
            print("\(name) hasn't found a town to terrorize yet...")
        }
    }
}
```

It is well known that monsters do one thing very well: they terrorize towns. The **Monster** class has an optional property for the town that a given monster is terrorizing. Recall that optionals are used when an instance may become `nil`. Because the monster may or may not have found a town to terrorize yet, the town property is an optional (**Town?**), and starts out `nil`. You also create a property for the **Monster**'s name and give it a generic default value.

Next, define a basic stub for a method called **terrorizeTown()**. This method will be called on an instance of **Monster** to represent the monster terrorizing a town.

Notice that you check whether the instance has a town: if town != nil. If it does, then
**terrorizeTown()** will log to the console the name of the monster wreaking havoc. If the instance does
not have a town yet, then the method will log that information.

As each sort of monster will terrorize a town differently, *subclasses* will provide their own
implementation of this function. You will learn about subclasses in the next section.

Switch to main.swift to exercise the **Monster** class. Add an instance of this type, give it a town, and
call the **terrorizeTown()** function on it.

## Listing 15.11  Setting a generic monster loose (main.swift)

```
var myTown = Town()
myTown.changePopulation(500)
myTown.printTownDescription()
let gm = Monster()
gm.town = myTown
gm.terrorizeTown()
```

First, you create an instance of the **Monster** type called gm (for "generic monster"). This instance is
declared as a constant because there is no need for it to be mutable. Next, you assign myTown to gm's
town property. Finally, you call the **terrorizeTown()** function on the **Monster** instance. Run the
program, and Monster is terrorizing a town! logs to the console.

# Inheritance

One of the main features of classes that structures do not have is *inheritance*. Inheritance is a
relationship in which one class, a *subclass*, is defined in terms of another, a *superclass*. The subclass
*inherits* the properties and methods of its superclass. In a sense, inheritance defines the genealogy of
class types.

The fact that classes can take advantage of inheritance is the primary reason you made the **Monster**
type a class. You are going to create subclasses of **Monster** class to represent different kinds of
monsters. Let's start with a **Zombie** subclass to see this relationship in practical terms.

## A zombie subclass

Create a new Swift file called Zombie, following the same steps as you did to create Town.swift and
Monster.swift.

This file will hold the definition of a new class describing a zombie. The **Zombie** class will inherit from
the **Monster** class. Add the following class declaration to see how.

## Listing 15.12  Zombie creation (Zombie.swift)

```
import Foundation

class Zombie: Monster {
    var walksWithLimp = true

    override func terrorizeTown() {
        town?.changePopulation(-10)
        super.terrorizeTown()
    }
}
```

Your new class defines a type called **Zombie**. It inherits from the **Monster** type, which is indicated by the colon (:) after Zombie. Inheriting from **Monster** means that **Zombie** has all of **Monster**'s properties and methods, like the town property and the **terrorizeTown()** function used here.

**Zombie** also adds a new property. The property is called walksWithLimp and is of type **Bool**. This type is inferred from the property's default value: true.

Finally, **Zombie** *overrides* the **terrorizeTown()** function. Overriding a method means that a subclass provides its own definition of a method that is defined on its superclass. Note the use of the override keyword. Failing to use this keyword when overriding a method will result in a compiler error.

Figure 15.10 shows **Zombie**'s relationship to **Monster**.

## Figure 15.10 **Zombie** inheritance

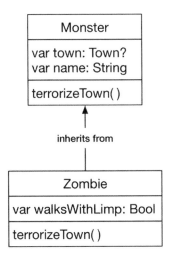

**Zombie** inherits the properties town and name from the **Monster** class. It also inherits the **terrorizeTown()** method, but provides an override, which is why it is listed in both areas in the figure. Last, **Zombie** adds a property of its own: walksWithLimp.

Notice the line super.terrorizeTown() in Listing 15.12. super is a prefix used to access a superclass's implementation of a method. In this case, you use super to call the **Monster** class's implementation of **terrorizeTown()**.

Because super is predicated on the idea of inheritance, it is not available to value types like enums or structs. It is invoked to borrow or override functionality from a superclass.

Recall that **Zombie**'s town property, inherited from the **Monster** class, is an optional of type **Town?**. The fact that town is an optional means that it can potentially be nil. You need to make sure that an instance of **Zombie** has a town to terrorize before calling any methods on the town. How can you check this?

One possible solution is to use optional binding. You may be tempted to try something like this:

```
if let terrorTown = town {
    // Do something to terrorTown
}
```

In the code above, if the **Zombie** instance has a town, then the value in the optional is unwrapped and put into the constant terrorTown. After that, this value is ready to be terrorized, but with an important caveat: the value semantics of structs means that the terrorTown instance will not be the same as the town instance. Why? Because value types, including structs, are always copied when you pass them around in your code.

The problem with this is that any changes made on terrorTown will not be reflected in the **Zombie** instance's town property. In addition to this limitation, this code could also be more concise. In short, this is not an ideal solution.

As you saw in Chapter 8, optional chaining allows a check like this to be done on a single line. It is just as expressive and is also more concise. Furthermore, the copy problem described above is avoided because the **Town** instance of interest is changed directly.

You have already used optional chaining in MonsterTown. Look back at Listing 15.12. The code town?.changePopulation(-10) makes sure it is safe to call a function on the town instance. If the optional town has a value, then the method **changePopulation()** is called on that instance, and the population is decreased by 10 people. In a moment, you will use optional chaining like this to call **printTownDescription()** on a zombie's town.

## Preventing overriding

Sometimes you want to prevent subclasses from being able to override methods or properties. The need to do this is rare in practice, but it does come up occasionally. In these cases, you use the final keyword to prevent a method or property from being overridden.

Imagine, for example, that you specifically do not want subclasses of the **Zombie** type to provide their own implementation of the **terrorizeTown()** function. In other words, all subclasses of **Zombie** should terrorize their towns in the exact same way. Add the final keyword to this function's declaration.

### Listing 15.13  Preventing overriding of **terrorizeTown()** (Zombie.swift)

```
class Zombie: Monster {
    var walksWithLimp = true

    final override func terrorizeTown() {
        town?.changePopulation(-10)
        super.terrorizeTown()
    }
}
```

Now, subclasses of the **Zombie** class will not be able to override the **terrorizeTown()** function. Go ahead and create a new subclass of **Zombie** (in a new Swift file, as before) and name it **ZombieBoss**. Try to override the **terrorizeTown()** function.

## Listing 15.14 Zombie bosses causing trouble (ZombieBoss.swift)

```
import Foundation

class ZombieBoss: Zombie {
    override func terrorizeTown() {
        print("terrorizing town...")
    }
}
```

You should see the following error on the line where you try to override the **terrorizeTown()** method: `Instance method overrides a 'final' instance method`. The error is telling you that you cannot override **terrorizeTown()** because it is marked as `final` in the superclass.

Go ahead and delete the `ZombieBoss.swift` file. You will not be using it again. Select the file in the project navigator and press Delete on your keyboard. Choose Move to Trash in the pop-up.

### Your town has a zombie problem

Now is a good time to exercise the **Zombie** type. Choose the `main.swift` file from the project navigator. Create an instance of the **Zombie** class. (Note that you delete the code that prints the town's description to free the console from clutter. You also delete the code that created a generic instance of the **Monster** type as you no longer need it.)

## Listing 15.15 Who's afraid of fredTheZombie? (main.swift)

```
var myTown = Town()
myTown.changePopulation(500)
myTown.printTownDescription()
let gm = Monster()
gm.town = myTown
gm.terrorizeTown()
let fredTheZombie = Zombie()
fredTheZombie.town = myTown
fredTheZombie.terrorizeTown()
fredTheZombie.town?.printTownDescription()
```

You first create a new instance of the **Zombie** type named `fredTheZombie`. Next, you assign your preexisting instance of the **Town** type, `myTown`, to the **Zombie** type's property `town`. At this point, `fredTheZombie` is free to terrorize `myTown`, which he will do with alacrity. (Or, at least, as much alacrity as a zombie can muster.)

After `fredTheZombie` has terrorized the townsfolk, you check the results with the **printTownDescription()**. As discussed earlier, because `fredTheZombie`'s town property is an optional of type **Town?**, you have to unwrap it before you can call the **printTownDescription()** function on it. You do this with optional chaining: `fredTheZombie.town?`. This code ensures that `fredTheZombie` has a town before you try to use **printTownDescription()**.

After `fredTheZombie` is done terrorizing its town, the console output should read: `"Population: 5912; number of stoplights: 4"`.

# Method Parameter Names

Recall from Chapter 12 that the first parameter name is by default not used when calling a function or method. This convention impacts both how we name functions and how we name parameters.

To see this in action, open `Zombie.swift` and add a new method to change the name and limp status of an instance of the **Zombie** class.

Listing 15.16 **changeName(_:walksWithLimp:)** (`Zombie.swift`)

```swift
class Zombie: Monster {
    var walksWithLimp = true

    final override func terrorizeTown() {
        town?.changePopulation(-10)
        super.terrorizeTown()
    }

    func changeName(name: String, walksWithLimp: Bool) {
        self.name = name
        self.walksWithLimp = walksWithLimp
    }
}
```

**changeName(_:walksWithLimp:)** is a simple method that allows a developer to change a **Zombie**'s name and `walksWithLimp` properties. Because `name` is not used when calling the method, it is stylish in Swift to place the name of the first parameter at the end of the method name. This convention is a common pattern in naming methods in iOS and Mac OS X frameworks, and helps to identify all of the method's parameters.

Switch to `main.swift` to exercise this function and see how it is called.

Listing 15.17  Fred the Zombie (`main.swift`)

```swift
...
fredTheZombie.changeName("Fred the Zombie", walksWithLimp: false)
```

Here, you call **changeName(_:walksWithLimp:)** on `fredTheZombie`. Notice that the name of the first parameter is omitted in the call (but it is the last word in the method's name), and the name of the second parameter is used. The result of this line is that `fredTheZombie`'s name property is assigned the string `"Fred the Zombie"` and its `walksWithLimp` property is set to `false`.

# What Should I Use?

The question of when to use a struct or a class is a difficult one. The answer involves understanding the differences between value types and reference types. We discuss the nuances of each in Chapter 18 and provide guidance on when to use both properly.

# Bronze Challenge

There is currently a bug in the **Zombie** type. If an instance of **Zombie** terrorizes a town with a population of 0, then its population will decrement to -10. This result does not make sense. Fix this bug by changing the `terrorizeTown()` function on the **Zombie** type to only decrement the town's population if its population is greater than 0. Also, make sure that the town's population is set to 0 if the amount to decrement is greater than the current population.

# Silver Challenge

Create another subclass of the **Monster** type. Call this one **Vampire**. Override the `terrorizeTown()` function so that every time an instance of the **Vampire** type terrorizes a town, it adds a new vampire thrall to an array of vampires on the **Vampire** type. This array of vampire thralls should be empty by default. Terrorizing a town should also decrement the town's population by one. Last, exercise this **Vampire** type in `main.swift`.

# For the More Curious: Type Methods

In this chapter, you defined some instance methods that were called on instances of a type. For example, **terrorizeTown()** is an instance method that you can call on instances of the **Monster** type. You can additionally define methods that are called on the type itself. These are called type methods. Type methods are useful for working with type-level information.

Imagine a struct named **Square**:

```
struct Square {
    static func numberOfSides() -> Int {
        return 4
    }
}
```

For value types, you indicate that you are defining a type method with the `static` keyword. The method **numberOfSides()** simply returns the number of sides a **Square** can have.

In distinction, type methods on classes use the `class` keyword. Here is a type method on the **Zombie** class that represents the universal zombie catchphrase.

```
class Zombie: Monster {
    class func makeSpookyNoise() -> String {
        return "Brains..."
    }

    var walksWithLimp = true

    override func terrorizeTown() {
        town?.changePopulation(-10)
    }
}
```

To use type methods, you simply call them on the type itself:

```
let sides = Square.numberOfSides() // sides is 4
let spookyNoise = Zombie.makeSpookyNoise() // spookyNoise is "Brains..."
```

Type methods can work with type-level information on a given type. This means that type methods can call other type methods and can even work with type properties, which we will discuss in Chapter 16. Note, however, that type methods cannot call instance methods or work with any instance properties. The reason for this limitation is that an instance is not available for use at the type level.

# For the More Curious: Function Currying

After working through this chapter, you might be wondering about the `mutating` keyword. Why is it needed to allow you to modify a struct or enum? The concept of *function currying* helps to explain the answer.

Create a new playground called `Curry.playground`.

Function currying allows you to rewrite an existing function that takes multiple parameters as a new function that takes one parameter and returns another function. The function you return takes the original function's remaining parameters and returns what the original function returns. This process of nesting functions, each with the remaining number of parameters, continues until there are no remaining parameters.

The rewritten function is called a *curried function*. A curried function partially applies an existing function. That is, a curried function allows you to bind values to a function's arguments before you call it. This feature of curried functions is similar to supplying default values to a function's parameters, but is far more dynamic.

Add a simple function to your playground that returns a **String** greeting.

## Listing 15.18  A simple greeting function

```
func greetName(name: String, withGreeting greeting: String) -> String {
    return "\(greeting) \(name)"
}
```

The **greetName(_:withGreeting:)** function takes two arguments: a `name` and a `greeting`. It constructs and returns a greeting based on these two arguments. This function is straightforward to use.

## Listing 15.19  Using **greetName(_:withGreeting:)**

```
func greetName(name: String, withGreeting greeting: String) -> String {
    return "\(greeting) \(name)"
}

let personalGreeting = greetName("Matt", withGreeting: "Hello,")
print(personalGreeting)
```

Now, rewrite **greetName(_:withGreeting:)** to be a curried function.

## Listing 15.20  Curried **greetingForName(_:)**

```
func greetName(name: String, withGreeting greeting: String) -> String {
    return "\(greeting) \(name)"
}

let personalGreeting = greetName("Matt", withGreeting: "Hello,")
print(personalGreeting)

func greetingForName(name: String) -> (String) -> String {
    func greeting(greeting: String) -> String {
        return "\(greeting) \(name)"
    }
    return greeting
}
```

The function **greetingForName(_:)** takes one argument, the **String** name, and returns a function. This returned function itself takes a **String**, representing the greeting, and returns a **String** with a greeting for the given name.

You define a nested function called **greeting(_:)** inside of the implementation of **greetingForName(_:)**. **greeting(_:)**'s function type matches the type specified by **greetingForName(_:)**: it takes a **String** and returns a **String**. Notice that you combine the greeting parameter with the name parameter from the two functions to construct the personalized greeting.

Finally, you return the **greeting(_:)** function.

Add the following code to exercise the curried function.

## Listing 15.21  Using the curried function

```
func greetName(name: String, withGreeting greeting: String) -> String {
    return "\(greeting) \(name)"
}

let personalGreeting = greetName("Matt", withGreeting: "Hello,")
print(personalGreeting)

func greetingForName(name: String) -> (String) -> String {
    func greeting(greeting: String) -> String {
        return "\(greeting) \(name)"
    }
    return greeting
}

let greeterFunction = greetingForName("Matt")
let theGreeting = greeterFunction("Hello,")
print(theGreeting)
```

You call the **greetingForName(_:)** function and pass in the desired name to greet ("Matt"). The result is assigned to a constant named greeterFunction. greeterFunction holds a function that matches the return type of **greetingForName(_:)**: It takes a **String** and returns a **String**. The specific name, "Matt", is passed along in the enclosing scope of the **greeting(_:)** function that is returned by **greetingForName(_:)**.

To make a personalized greeting for a specific name, you call the **greeterFunction(_:)** function and pass in a greeting (here, "Hello,") to its only parameter. The result of this function is assigned to theGreeting, which you log to the console. You should see the same result log to the console.

Thankfully, Swift supplies a more convenient syntax for writing curried functions. The example below is equivalent to what you have just written.

## Listing 15.22  A more concise curried function

```
func greetName(name: String, withGreeting greeting: String) -> String {
    return "\(greeting) \(name)"
}

let personalGreeting = greetName("Matt", withGreeting: "Hello,")
print(personalGreeting)

func greetingForName(name: String) -> (String) -> String {
    func greeting(greeting: String) -> String {
        return "\(greeting) \(name)"
    }
    return greeting
}

let greeterFunction = greetingForName("Matt")
let theGreeting = greeterFunction("Hello,")
print(theGreeting)

func greeting(greeting: String)(name: String) -> String {
    return "\(greeting) \(name)"
}

let friendlyGreeting = greeting("Hello,")
let newGreeting = friendlyGreeting(name: "Matt")
print(newGreeting)
```

The **greeting(_:name:)** function's syntax looks a little different from what you just saw. This time, you separate each argument by enclosing each parameter within its own parentheses. Notice that this syntax is more concise, but it gives the same result.

Calling this curried function works very much like your earlier implementation. You call **greeting(_:name:)** and pass in a **String** greeting to its first argument. The resulting function is assigned to a constant called friendlyGreeting. Next, you call the function in friendlyGreeting and pass in a name to greet. Note that the second argument, name, was automatically given an external name that you had to use.

Check the console. The results should be the same.

Now that you understand how function currying works, let's return to the `mutating` keyword. Create a new struct called **Person**.

## Listing 15.23  Creating a **Person**

```
...

let friendlyGreeting = greeting("Hello,")
let newGreeting = friendlyGreeting(name: "Matt")
print(newGreeting)

struct Person {
    var firstName = "Matt"
    var lastName = "Mathias"

    mutating func changeName(fn: String, ln: String) {
        firstName = fn
        lastName = ln
    }
}
```

There is nothing very special or unfamiliar taking place here. The **Person** struct has properties for a person's first and last names. It also defines a mutating function to change these properties.

Create a new instance of the **Person**.

## Listing 15.24  Creating a new instance of **Person**

```
...

let friendlyGreeting = greeting("Hello,")
let newGreeting = friendlyGreeting(name: "Matt")
print(newGreeting)

struct Person {
    var firstName = "Matt"
    var lastName = "Mathias"

    mutating func changeName(fn: String, ln: String) {
        firstName = fn
        lastName = ln
    }
}
var p = Person()
```

There is nothing new here either, but here is where things start to get interesting. It turns out that Swift's instance methods, the very ones that you learned about in this chapter, are actually curried functions. Type in the following code to see this in action.

## Listing 15.25 Instance methods are curried functions

```
...

let friendlyGreeting = greeting("Hello,")
let newGreeting = friendlyGreeting(name: "Matt")
print(newGreeting)

struct Person {
    var firstName = "Matt"
    var lastName = "Mathias"

    mutating func changeName(fn: String, ln: String) {
        firstName = fn
        lastName = ln
    }
}

var p = Person()
let changer = Person.changeName
```

You can access the **changeName()** function on the **Person** struct. Notice that you are not calling the **changeName()** function (i.e., you omit the () after **changeName**). Instead, you are assigning it to a constant called changer.

Just what is changer? To find out, hold down the Option key and click on the word changer. You should see something like Figure 15.11. (Incidentally, you should also see the same function signature in the playground's result sidebar.)

## Figure 15.11 A curried function signature

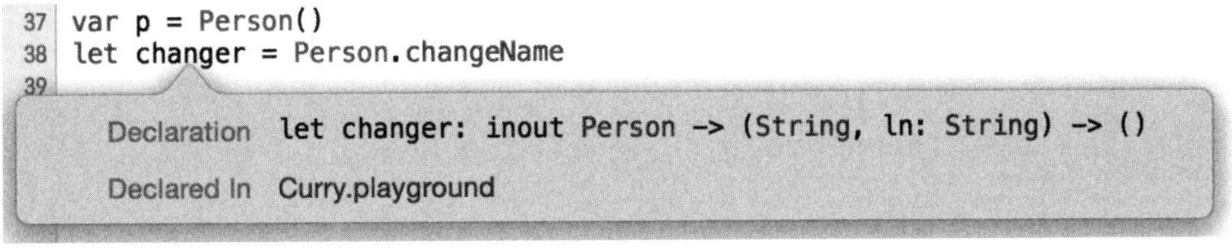

```
37  var p = Person()
38  let changer = Person.changeName
39
```

    Declaration   let changer: inout Person -> (String, ln: String) -> ()

    Declared In   Curry.playground

What does that signature mean? In short, it tells you that changer is a curried function. More specifically, changer holds a function whose only argument is an instance of the **Person** struct passed in as an inout parameter. This function returns a function that takes two arguments, a **String** for the new first name and a **String** for the new last name. The resulting function returns nothing.

Recall from Chapter 12 that an inout parameter allows a function to modify the value passed into that parameter. The changes on the inout parameter made within the function also persist outside of the function after it is called. In other words, the modifications replace the parameter's original value.

Putting all of this information together, a mutating function is simply a curried function whose first argument is self, passed in as an inout parameter. Because value types are copied when they are passed, for nonmutating methods self is actually a copy of the value. In order to make changes, self needs to be declared as inout, and mutating is the way Swift allows you to accomplish that.

Type in the following to demonstrate this point and to see `changer` in action.

## Listing 15.26  `changer` in action

```
...

let friendlyGreeting = greeting("Hello,")
let newGreeting = friendlyGreeting(name: "Matt")
print(newGreeting)

struct Person {
    var firstName = "Matt"
    var lastName = "Mathias"

    mutating func changeName(fn: String, ln: String) {
        firstName = fn
        lastName = ln
    }
}

var p = Person()
let changer = Person.changeName
changer(&p)("John", ln: "Gallagher")
p.firstName // John
```

You call `changer`'s function, passing in the instance of **Person** that you want to modify. Remember that you need to prefix `inout` parameters with an & to ensure that you pass in the instance's reference to the function. Next, you give two strings ("John" and "Gallagher") to the curried function's final two parameters, one each for the first and last names. These strings are used to modify the **Person** instance's values for those properties. Last, you print out the result of the function call to confirm that p's first name has been changed to John.

The point of this section was to show what the keyword `mutating` does. In practice, you will likely not want to use function currying to mutate a struct. Go ahead and remove the function currying code, and make use of a name-changing function more directly. The result will be the same.

## Listing 15.27  Using **changeName(_:ln:)** instead of `changer`

```
...

let friendlyGreeting = greeting("Hello,")
let newGreeting = friendlyGreeting(name: "Matt")
print(newGreeting)

struct Person {
    var firstName = "Matt"
    var lastName = "Mathias"

    mutating func changeName(fn: String, ln: String) {
        firstName = fn
        lastName = ln
    }
}

var p = Person()
let changer = Person.changeName
changer(&p)("John", ln: "Gallagher")
p.changeName("John", ln: "Gallagher")
p.firstName // John
```

# 16
# Properties

Chapter 15 introduced properties in a limited way. Its focus was on structures and classes, but you also gave your types some basic stored properties so that they had data to represent. This chapter discusses properties in detail and will deepen your understanding of how to use them with your custom types.

Properties model the characteristics of the entity that a type represents. They do this by associating values with the type. The values properties can take may be constant or variable values. Classes, structures, and enumerations can all have properties.

Properties can be of two varieties: *stored* and *computed*. Stored properties can be given default values, and computed properties can return the result of some calculation based on available information. You can observe properties for changes and can execute specific code when the property is set to a new value. You can even establish rules that determine properties' visibility to other files in your application.

In short, properties have a lot of power and flexibility. Let's see what they can do.

## Basic Stored Properties

Stored properties are properties in their most basic form. To see how they work, you will be expanding the behavior of the types you developed in Chapter 15. Start by making a copy of your MonsterTown project. Find and click on the folder called `MonsterTown` in your filesystem. Press Command-C on your keyboard, then press Command-V to create the copy. Open the new folder and double-click `MonsterTown.xcodeproj` to launch Xcode and open your copied project.

Open `Town.swift`. Take a look at the declaration of your `population` property: `var population = 5422`. This code signifies three important items.

- `var` marks this property as variable, which means that it can be mutated.

- `population` has a default value of 5422.

- `population` is a stored property whose value can be read and set.

How can you tell that `population` is a stored property? Because it holds on to a piece of information – the town's population. That is what stored properties do: they store data.

`population` is a *read/write* property. You can both read the property's value *and* set the property's value. You can also make stored properties *read-only*, so that their values cannot be changed. Read-only properties are known by their more familiar name: constants.

Use let to create a read-only property storing information about what region the town you are modeling is in. After all, towns cannot move, so they are always in the same region.

**Listing 16.1  Adding a region constant (Town.swift)**

```
struct Town {
    let region = "South"
    var population = 5422
    var numberOfStoplights = 4

    func printTownDescription() {
        print("Population: \(population);
                number of stoplights: \(numberOfStoplights)")
    }

    mutating func changePopulation(amount: Int) {
        population += amount
    }
}
```

This implementation of region is fine for now, but it has a flaw. We will explain the problem and show you a better solution later in the chapter.

# Nested Types

Nested types are types that are defined within another enclosing type. They are often used to support the functionality of a type and are not intended to be used separately from that type. You have seen nested functions already, which are similar.

Enumerations are frequently nested. In Town.swift, create a new enumeration called **Size**. You will be using this enumeration, in coordination with another new property to be added later, to calculate whether the town can be designated as small, medium, or large. Make sure that you define the enum within the definition for the **Town** struct.

**Listing 16.2  Setting up the Size enum (Town.swift)**

```
struct Town {
    let region = "South"
    var population = 5422
    var numberOfStoplights = 4

    enum Size {
        case Small
        case Medium
        case Large
    }

    func printTownDescription() {
        print("Population: \(population);
                number of stoplights: \(numberOfStoplights)")
    }

    mutating func changePopulation(amount: Int) {
        population += amount
    }
}
```

Because **Size** is defined within the braces ({}) of the **Town** struct's definition, it will not (and cannot) be used outside of Town.

Size will determine what size of town an instance of the **Town** type is. The instance of **Town** will need a value in its population property before this nested type is used. All of the properties you have worked with so far have calculated the property's value when the instance was created. The next section introduces a new sort of property that delays the computation of its value until the necessary information is available.

# Lazy Stored Properties

Sometimes a stored property's value cannot be assigned immediately. The necessary information may be available but computing the values of a property immediately would be costly in terms of memory or time. Or, perhaps a property depends on factors external to the type that will be unknown until after the instance is created. These circumstances call for *lazy loading*.

In terms of properties, lazy loading means that the calculation of the property's value will not occur until the first time it is needed. This delay defers computation of the property's value until after the instance is initialized. This means that lazy properties must be declared with var, because their values will change.

Create a new lazy property called townSize. Make it of type **Size**, because its value will be an instance of the **Size** enum. Again, make sure to define this new property inside of the **Town** type.

Listing 16.3 Setting up townSize (Town.swift)

```
struct Town {
    ...
    enum Size {
        case Small
        case Medium
        case Large
    }
    lazy var townSize: Size = {
        switch self.population {
        case 0...10000:
            return Size.Small

        case 10001...100000:
            return Size.Medium

        default:
            return Size.Large
        }
    }()
    func printTownDescription() {
        print("Population: \(population);
            number of stoplights: \(numberOfStoplights)")
    }
    ...
}
```

townSize looks different than the properties that you have written before. Let's go through this code step by step.

First, you mark `townSize` as `lazy`. This means that `townSize`'s value will only be calculated when it is first accessed. The need for this will become clear in a moment.

Next, you declare the type of the property as **Size**. You will not be setting the value of this property directly, as you have done with other properties. For example, you will not be writing code like this: `myTown.townSize = Size.Small`. Instead, you will take advantage of the nested enum **Size** in coordination with a closure to calculate the town's size given its population.

`townSize` sets a default property value, the town's size, with the result returned by a closure (notice the opening brace: `lazy var townSize: Size = {`). Recall that functions and closures are first-class types and that properties can reference functions and closures.

A closure works well here because the value of the town's `population` is needed in order to determine the town's size. The closure uses a `switch` statement to determine the size of the town. Put another way, the closure "switches over" the instance's `population` (`self.population`). The `self` reference in this line is important and we will return to it in a moment.

Inside of the `switch` statement, you specify three cases. A town with a population of `0...10000` is a small town and `10001...100000` is a medium-sized town. The third case is a `default` case that captures any `population` larger than 100,000 and describes it as a large town. The case bodies return an instance of the enum **Size** that matches the given population.

Notice that the closure for `townSize` ends with empty parentheses after the final brace `}()`. These parentheses, combined with the lazy marking, ensure that Swift will call the closure and assign the result it returns to `townSize` when the property is accessed for the first time. If you had omitted the parentheses, you would simply be assigning a closure to the `townSize` property. With the parentheses, the closure will be executed the first time you access the `townSize` property.

Finally, let's return to the importance of the `self` reference in `self.population` and the need for `townSize` to be lazy. If a closure works with an instance's properties, then the compiler requires that the closure use `self` when accessing any property on that instance. The requirement to use `self` explicitly inside of a closure is a reminder to developers that the closure is capturing a reference to the instance in order to access its properties. This capture may cause a memory leak if the closure is stored in a property, and so they need to be careful. (Do not worry about memory management issues right now; they will be discussed in Chapter 24.)

Because the closure needs to reference `self` in order to gain access to the instance's `population` property, the property `townSize` needs to be marked as `lazy` in order to ensure that the instance (what `self` references) is fully prepared to do work.

Switch to `main.swift` to exercise this `lazy` property.

### Listing 16.4  Using the lazy `townSize` property (`main.swift`)

```
var myTown = Town()
let ts = myTown.townSize
print(ts)
myTown.changePopulation(500)
let fredTheZombie = Zombie()
fredTheZombie.town = myTown
fredTheZombie.terrorizeTown()
fredTheZombie.town?.printTownDescription()
fredTheZombie.changeName("Fred the Zombie", walksWithLimp: false)
```

Here, you create a constant named ts to hold myTown's size information. This line accesses the lazy property townSize and causes its closure to execute. After the closure switches over myTown's population, an instance of the **Size** enum is assigned to ts. Next, you print the value of the ts constant. As a result, when you run the program Small logs to the console.

It is important to note that properties marked with lazy are calculated only one time. This feature of lazy means that changing the value of myTown's population will never cause myTown's townSize to be recalculated. To see this, increase myTown's population by 1,000,000 and then check myTown's size by logging it to the console. Include myTown's population to compare against what is reported for townSize.

(Note that from here on we will be showing small changes within a line of code inline, rather than showing the entire line deleted and re-entered with the change. In the first change shown below, for example, (500) is replaced with (1000000).)

## Listing 16.5 Changing myTown's population does not change townSize (main.swift)

```
var myTown = Town()

let ts = myTown.townSize
print(ts)

myTown.changePopulation(500)(1000000)
print("Size: \(myTown.townSize); population: \(myTown.population)")
let fredTheZombie = Zombie()
fredTheZombie.town = myTown
fredTheZombie.terrorizeTown()
fredTheZombie.town?.printTownDescription()
fredTheZombie.changeName("Fred the Zombie", walksWithLimp: false)
```

Run the program, and you will see the following line in the console: Size: Small; population: 1005422. myTown's size has not changed, even though its population increased dramatically. This discrepancy is due to townSize's lazy nature. The property is only calculated when it is first accessed and is not recalculated thereafter.

This kind of discrepancy between myTown's population and townSize is undesirable. It seems that townSize should not be marked lazy, if lazy means that myTown will not be able to recalibrate its townSize to reflect population changes.

In the right circumstances, lazy loading is a powerful tool. You will use it again in Chapter 27. But, in this case, it is not the best tool for the job. A *computed property* is a better option.

# Computed Properties

You can use computed properties with any class, struct, or enum that you define. Computed properties do not store values like the properties that you have been working with thus far. Instead, a computed property provides a *getter* and optional *setter* to retrieve or set the property's value. This difference allows the value of a computed property to change, unlike the value of a lazy stored property.

Replace your definition of the townSize property on the **Town** type with a computed read-only property.

Listing 16.6  Using a computed property (Town.swift)

```
...
lazy var townSize: Size = {
var townSize: Size {
    get {
        switch self.population {
        case 0...10000:
            return Size.Small

        case 10001...100000:
            return Size.Medium

        default:
            return Size.Large
        }
    }
}()
...
```

The changes here may look small. You delete lazy and the = in the first line, add a new second line with a get statement (and its ending brace, after the switch statement), and delete the parentheses in the final line. That is all. But those small changes have a big impact.

townSize is now defined as a computed property declared, like all computed properties, with the var keyword. It provides a custom getter that uses the same switch statement that you used before. Notice that you explicitly declare the type of the computed property to be **Size**. You must provide computed properties with their type information. This information helps the compiler know what the property's getter should return.

You access this property via dot syntax: myTown.townSize, so the code you already added to main.Swift does not need to be changed. Accessing the property executes the getter for townSize, which results in using myTown's population to calculate the townSize. Run your program again. You will see Size: Large; population: 1005422 logged to the console.

townSize is now a read-only computed property. In other words, townSize cannot be set directly. It can only retrieve and return a value based upon the calculation you defined in the getter. A read-only property is perfect in this case because you want myTown to calculate its townSize based upon the instance's population, which may change at runtime.

# A getter and a setter

Computed properties can also be declared with both a getter and a setter. A getter allows you to *read* data from a property. A setter allows you to *write* data to the property. Properties with both a getter and a setter are called read/write. Open your `Monster.swift` file and add a computed property to the declaration for the `Monster`.

Listing 16.7  Creating a computed `victimPool` property with a getter and a setter (`Monster.swift`)

```
class Monster {
    var town: Town?
    var name = "Monster"
    var victimPool: Int {
        get {
            return town?.population ?? 0
        }
        set(newVictimPool) {
            town?.population = newVictimPool
        }
    }
    func terrorizeTown() {
        if town != nil {
            print("\(name) is terrorizing a town!")
        } else {
            print("\(name) hasn't found a town to terrorize yet...")
        }
    }
}
```

Imagine that you need each instance of **Monster** to keep track of its potential pool of victims. This number will match the `population` of the town that the monster is terrorizing. Accordingly, `victimPool` is a new computed property with both a getter and a setter. As before, you declare it as a var and give it specific type information. In this case, `victimPool` is an **Int**.

In the property's definition, you define a getter for the property via the same `get` that you use for `townSize`. The getter uses the `nil` coalescing operator to check whether the **Monster** instance has a town that it is currently terrorizing. If it does, then it returns the value of that town's population. If the instance has not yet found a town to terrorize, it simply returns 0.

The setter for the computed property is written within the `set` block. Notice the new syntax: `set(newVictimPool)`. Specifying `newVictimPool` within the parentheses means that you are supplying an explicitly named new value. You can refer to this variable within the setter's implementation. For example, you use optional chaining to ensure that the **Monster** instance has found a town, and then set that town's population to match `newVictimPool`. If you had not explicitly named the new value, Swift would have provided a variable for you called `newValue` to hold on to the same information.

Switch back to `main.swift` to use this new computed property. Add the code below to the bottom of the file.

Listing 16.8  Using `victimPool` (`main.swift`)

```
...
print("Victim pool: \(fredTheZombie.victimPool)")
fredTheZombie.victimPool = 500
print("Victim pool: \(fredTheZombie.victimPool);
    population: \(fredTheZombie.town?.population)")
```

The first new line exercises the getter for the computed property. Run the program and `Victim pool:` `1005412` logs to the console. The next new line uses the setter to change `fredTheZombie`'s `victimPool`: `fredTheZombie.victimPool = 500`. Last, you once again log the `victimPool` to the console via the property's getter. In the console, the `victimPool` should be updated to be 500, and the town's population should match this change.

Notice that the output for the town's population is listed as `Optional(500)`. This looks different from the output for `victimPool`, and this is because `fredTheZombie`'s `town` property is optional. If you are curious about what is causing this difference, Chapter 22 discusses how optionals are put together.

# Property Observers

Swift provides an interesting feature called *property observation*. Property observers watch for and respond to changes in a given property. Property observation is available to any stored property that you define and is also available to any property that you inherit. You cannot use property observers with computed properties that you define. (But you have full control over the definition of a computed property's setter and getter, and can respond to changes there.)

Imagine that the citizens of your beleaguered town are getting restless. They demand that the mayor do something to protect them from the monstrous pox patrolling the countryside. The mayor's first action is to track the attacks on the townspeople. Property observers are perfect for this task.

You can observe changes to a property in one of two ways:

- when a property is about to change, via `willSet`

- when a property did change, via `didSet`

In order to keep track of how many attacks the town is suffering, the mayor decides to pay close attention to when the `population` of the town changes. Use a `didSet` observer to be notified right after the property receives a new value.

### Listing 16.9  Observing population changes (`Town.swift`)

```
struct Town {
...
    var population = 5422 {
        didSet(oldPopulation) {
            print("The population has changed to \(population)
                    from \(oldPopulation).")
        }
    }
    ...
}
```

The syntax for property observers looks similar to computed properties' getters and setters. The response to the change is defined within the braces. In the example above, you create a custom parameter name for the old population: `oldPopulation`. The `didSet` observer gives you a handle on the property's old value. (In distinction, the `willSet` observer gives you a handle on the new value of the property.) If you had not specified a new name, Swift would have given you the parameter `oldValue` automatically. (For a `willSet` observer, Swift generates a `newValue` parameter.)

This property observer logs the town's `population` information to the console every time it changes. This means that you should see a log for the population change after `fredTheZombie` terrorizes the town. Run the program and take a look at the console. It should look like the output shown below, with a log for every time the `population` changes.

```
Small
The population has changed to 1005422 from 5422.
Size: Large; population: 1005422
The population has changed to 1005412 from 1005422.
Monster is terrorizing a town!
Population: 1005412; number of stoplights: 4
Victim pool: 1005412
The population has changed to 500 from 1005412.
Victim pool: 500; population: Optional(500)
```

Because you are logging changes to `population` with a property observer, you no longer need to log the population change in `main.swift` after you update the `victimPool`. Remove that code from the call to **print()** at the bottom of `main.swift`.

### Listing 16.10  Removing population from **print()** (main.swift)

```
...
print("Victim pool: \(fredTheZombie.victimPool)")
fredTheZombie.victimPool = 500
print("Victim pool: \(fredTheZombie.victimPool)+
     population: \(fredTheZombie.town?.population)")
```

# Type Properties

Up to now, you have been working with instance properties. Whenever you create a new instance of a type, that instance gets its own properties that are distinct from other instances of that type. Instance properties are useful for storing and computing values on an instance of a type, but what about values that belong to the type itself?

You can also define *type properties*. These are properties that are universal to the type – the values in these properties will be shared across all of the type's instances. These properties store information that will be the same across all instances. For example, all instances of a **Square** type will have exactly four sides, so the number of sides for **Square** might be stored in a type property.

Value types (i.e., structures and enumerations) can take both stored and computed type properties. As with type methods, type properties on value types begin with the `static` keyword.

Recall that earlier in the chapter you created a constant read-only property on the **Town** type for the town's `region`. This use of a constant instance property made every instance of **Town** be in the same region: the South. That means all instances of **Town** will share this information. A type property works better for the `region` property because you are modeling the region "South" as universal to the type. Change **Town** to reflect this revision.

### Listing 16.11  Making `region` a stored type property (Town.swift)

```
struct Town {
    static let region = "South"
    ...
}
```

Stored type properties have to be given a default value. This requirement makes sense because types do not have initializers (which are the topic of Chapter 17). This means that the stored type property has to have all the information it needs in order to vend its value to any caller. Here, region is given the value South.

Classes can also have stored and computed type properties, which use the same static syntax as structs. Subclasses cannot override a type property from their superclass. If you want a subclass to be able to provide its own implementation of the property, you use the class keyword instead.

In a For the More Curious section in Chapter 15, we showed you a type method on the **Zombie** type to make a spooky noise:

```
class Zombie: Monster {
    class func makeSpookyNoise() -> String {
        return "Brains..."
    }
}
```

Notice that **makeSpookyNoise()** does not take any arguments. This makes it a great candidate for being a computed type property and not a method. Open Zombie.swift and add a computed type property for a zombie's catchphrase.

### Listing 16.12  Creating the spookyNoise computed type property (Zombie.swift)

```
class Zombie: Monster {
    class var spookyNoise: String {
        return "Brains..."
    }

    var walksWithLimp = true
    ...
}
```

The definition of a computed property is very similar to a type method's. The main differences are that you use the var keyword, rather than func, and you do not use the parentheses.

One new element in the code above is that you use shorthand getter syntax. If you are not providing a setter for a computed property, you can omit the get block of the computed property's definition and simply return the computed value as needed.

Switch to main.swift. Add a line at the bottom of the file to print the **Zombie** type's spookyNoise property to the console.

### Listing 16.13  "Brains..." (main.swift)

```
...
print("Victim pool: \(fredTheZombie.victimPool)")
fredTheZombie.victimPool = 500
print("Victim pool: \(fredTheZombie.victimPool)")
print(Zombie.spookyNoise)
```

Run the program. Spooky.

To see that `class` type properties can be overridden by subclasses, add a `spookyNoise` computed type property to **Monster**.

### Listing 16.14  Generic **Monster** noise (`Monster.swift`)

```
class Monster {
    class var spookyNoise: String {
        return "Grrr"
    }
    var town: Town?
    var name = "Monster"
    ...
}
```

Switch back to `Zombie.swift` and you will notice that the compiler is now giving you an error. If you click the red exclamation mark on the lefthand side of the editor area, the error will display (see Figure 16.1).

### Figure 16.1  Override error

**Zombie** is now overriding a computed type property from its superclass. Because you used the `class` keyword for this type property, it is perfectly fine for subclasses to provide their own definition of `spookyNoise`. You just need to add the keyword `override` to **Zombie**'s definition of `spookyNoise`.

Make this change and the compiler error disappears.

### Listing 16.15  Override `spookyNoise` (`Zombie.swift`)

```
class Zombie {
    override class var spookyNoise: String {
        return "Brains..."
    }
    var walksWithLimp = true
    ...
}
```

Build and run your program, and everything should work as it did before.

We mentioned above that classes can have static properties at the type level. These properties work a bit differently than class properties on a type.

A defining characteristic of all monsters is that they are terrifying. Add a static property to the **Monster** class to represent this fact.

### Listing 16.16  All **Monster**s are terrifying (`Monster.swift`)

```
class Monster {
    static let isTerrifying = true
    class var spookyNoise: String {
        return "Grrr"
    }
    ...
}
```

You add a new `static` property on **Monster** to represent the fact that all monsters are terrifying by definition. Because you added this property to **Zombie**'s superclass **Monster**, it is also available on **Zombie**. Add the following to `main.swift` to see this in action.

### Listing 16.17 Run away from **Zombie** (`main.swift`)

```
...
print(Zombie.spookyNoise)
if Zombie.isTerrifying {
    print("Run away!")
}
```

As you can see, you access the `isTerrifying` property on the **Zombie** via dot syntax. If the **Zombie** is terrifying, you run away.

Build and run your program. The console warns you to `Run away!`

One of the major differences between static and class type properties is that static properties cannot be overridden by a subclass. Making this type property a static constant is very definitive: monsters are terrifying, and subclasses cannot change that.

## Access Control

You do not always want elements of your program's code to be visible to all other elements. In fact, you will frequently want to have much more granular control over your code's access. You can grant components of your code specific levels of access to other components of your code. This is called *access control*.

For example, you might want to hide or expose a method on a class. Suppose you have a property that is used only within a class's definition. It could be problematic if another, external type modified that property by mistake. With access control, you can manage the visibility of that property to hide it from other parts of the program. Doing so will encapsulate the property's data and prevent external code from meddling with it.

Access control is organized around two important and related concepts: *modules* and *source files*. In terms of your project's files and organization, these are the central building blocks of your application.

A module is a unit of code that is distributed together. You may recall seeing `import UIKit` or `import Cocoa` at the top of your playgrounds. These are frameworks, which bundle together a number of related types that perform a series of related tasks. For example, UIKit is a framework designed to facilitate the development of user interfaces. Modules are brought into another module using Swift's `import` keyword, as suggested by the above examples.

Source files, on the other hand, are more discrete units. They represent a single file and live within a specific module. It is good practice to define a single type within a source file. This is not a requirement, but doing so helps keep your project organized.

Swift provides a choice of three levels of access (Table 16.1).

## Table 16.1  Swift access control

| Access Level | Description |
|---|---|
| Public | Public access makes entities visible to all files in the module or those that import the module. |
| Internal | Internal access (the default) makes entities visible to all files in the same module. |
| Private | Private access makes entities visible only within their defining source file. |

public access is the least restrictive and private access is the most restrictive level of access control. In general, a type's access level needs to be consistent with the access levels of its properties and methods. A property cannot have a less restrictive level of access control than its type. For example, a property with an access control level of internal cannot be declared on a type with private access. Likewise, the access control of a function cannot be less restrictive than the access control listed for its parameters. If you violate these requirements, then the compiler will issue an error to help you correct the mistake.

Swift specifies internal as the default level of access control for your app. Having a default level of access means that you do not need to specifically declare access controls for every type, property, and method in your code. You only need to declare a level of access control when you need to specify public or private access.

Let's see the private level of access in action. Create an isFallingApart **Boolean** property defined on the **Zombie** type. Give it a default value of false. This property will keep track of an instance's physical integrity (zombies, after all, sometimes lose bits). This property really does not need to be exposed to the rest of the program because it is an implementation detail of the **Zombie** class. Therefore, set it to private.

## Listing 16.18  Falling apart is a private matter (Zombie.swift)

```
class Zombie: Monster {
    override class var spookyNoise: String {
        return "Brains..."
    }

    var walksWithLimp = true
    private var isFallingApart = false

    final override func terrorizeTown() {
        if !isFallingApart {
            town?.changePopulation(-10)
        }
        super.terrorizeTown()
    }

    func changeName(name: String, walksWithLimp: Bool) {
        self.name = name
        self.walksWithLimp = walksWithLimp
    }
}
```

After you create the property, you make use of it in the **terrorizeTown()** function. You check to see whether isFallingApart is false. If it is false, then the instance is free to terrorize its town. If the instance is falling apart, then it will not be able to terrorize its town.

## Controlling getter and setter visibility

If a property has both a getter and a setter, you can control the visibility of the two independently. But by default, the getter and setter have the same visibility. Here, isFallingApart has a private getter and a private setter.

However, you probably want other files in your project to be able to tell whether a **Zombie** is falling apart. You just do not want them to change its falling-apart-ness. Change the isFallingApart property to have an internal getter and a private setter.

Listing 16.19  Making the getter internal and the setter private (Zombie.swift)

```
class Zombie: Monster {
    ...
    ~~private~~ internal private(set) var isFallingApart = false
    ...
}
```

You use the syntax internal private(set) to specify that the getter should be internal and the setter should be private. You could use public, internal, or private for either, with one restriction: the setter cannot be more visible than the getter. That means, for example, that if you make the getter internal, you cannot use public(set), because public is more visible than internal. Furthermore, the **Zombie** class is defaulting to internal because you do not specify any level of access yourself. That means marking isFallingApart's getter or setter with public will prompt the compiler to remind you with a warning that its defining class has internal visibility.

You can clean this code up a little. If you leave off a modifier for the getter, the access control defaults to internal, which is what you want here. Refactor **Zombie** to use the default visibility for the getter (internal) and private visibility for the setter.

Listing 16.20  Using default getter visibility (Zombie.swift)

```
class Zombie: Monster {
    ...
    ~~internal~~ private(set) var isFallingApart = false
    ...
}
```

Using the default does not change anything except the amount of typing you have to do. The getter for isFallingApart is still visible to the other files in your project, and the setter is now visible only within Zombie.swift.

This chapter introduced a lot of material. Take some time to let all of the ideas sink in. You learned about:

- property syntax
- stored vs. computed properties
- read-only and read/write properties
- lazy loading and lazy properties
- property observers
- type properties
- access control

Properties are a central concept in Swift programming. It is a good idea to get comfortable with all of these ideas. The challenges below will help you master the important concepts.

# Bronze Challenge

Your town's mayor is busy. Every birth and relocation does not require the mayor's attention. After all, the town is in crisis! Only log changes to the town's population if the new population is less than the old value.

# Silver Challenge

Make a new type called **Mayor**. It should be a struct. The **Town** type should have a property called `mayor` that holds an instance of the **Mayor** type.

Have your town inform the `mayor` every time the property for `population` changes. If the town's `population` decreases, have the instance of the **Mayor** log this statement to the console: `"I'm deeply saddened to hear about this latest tragedy. I promise that my office is looking into the nature of this rash of violence."` If the population increases, then the `mayor` should do nothing.

(Hint: You should define a new instance method on the **Mayor** type to complete this challenge.)

# Gold Challenge

Mayors are people too. An instance of the **Mayor** type will naturally get nervous whenever its town loses some `population` due to a **Zombie** attack. Create a stored instance property on the **Mayor** type called `anxietyLevel`. It should be of type **Int**, and should start out with a default value of 0.

Increment the `anxietyLevel` property every time a **Mayor** instance is notified of a **Zombie** attack. Last, as a mayor will not want to outwardly display anxiety, mark this property as `private`. Verify that this property is not accessible in `main.swift`.

# 17
# Initialization

Initialization is the operation of setting up an instance of a type. It entails giving each stored property an initial value and may involve other preparatory work. After this process, the instance is prepared and available to use.

The types that you have been creating up to this point have all been created in more or less the same way. The values for the properties were either given default stored values or were computed on demand. Initialization was not customized, and it was not particularly considered.

It is very common to want control over how an instance of a type is created. For example, it would be ideal for the instance to have all of the correct values in its properties immediately. Previously, you have given default values to an instance's stored properties and changed these properties' values after you created the instance. This strategy is inelegant. *Initializers* help you create an instance with the appropriate values.

## Initializer Syntax

Structures and classes are required to have initial values for their stored properties by the time initialization completes. This requirement explains why you have been giving all of your stored properties default values. If you had not given these stored properties default values, the compiler would have given you errors saying that the type's properties were not ready to use. Defining an initializer on the type is another way to ensure that properties have values when the instance is created.

The syntax for writing an initializer is a little different from what you have already seen. Initializers are written with the init keyword. Even though they are methods on a type, initializers are not preceded with the func keyword. Initializer syntax looks like this:

```
struct CustomType {
    init(someValue: SomeType) {
        // Initialization code here...
    }
}
```

This general syntax does not differ among structures, enumerations, and classes. In the example above, the initializer has one parameter called someValue of type **SomeType**. While initializers typically have one or more parameters, they can also have zero parameters (in which case there is a set of empty parentheses after the init keyword).

The initializer's implementation is defined within the braces, just as you have been doing with regular functions and methods throughout this book. But unlike other methods, initializers do not return values. Instead, initializers are tasked with giving values to a type's stored properties.

# Struct Initialization

Structures can have both default and custom initializers. When working with structs, you will typically want to take advantage of the default initializer provided, but there are some circumstances in which you will want to customize the initialization process.

## Default initializers for structs

Remember how you have been getting instances of your **Town** type? You gave the type's stored properties default values. What you did not know is that you were taking advantage of an *empty initializer* (an initializer without parameters) provided to you by the Swift compiler automatically. When you entered code like var myTown = Town(), that syntax called the empty initializer and set the new instance's properties to the default values you specified.

Another form of default initializer is the *memberwise initializer*. A memberwise initializer has a parameter for each stored property on the type. In this case, you do not ask the compiler to fill in the values of the new instance's properties based on default values you specified elsewhere. Instead, the free memberwise initializer includes arguments for all of the stored properties that need values. (We call it "free" because it is provided by the Swift compiler automatically – you do not need to define it.)

Remember, one of the principal goals of initialization is to give all of the type's stored properties values so that the new instance is ready to use. The compiler will enforce the requirement that your new instance has values in its stored properties. If you do not provide an initializer for your custom struct, you must provide the necessary values through default values or memberwise initialization.

Make a copy of the MonsterTown project, as you did in the previous chapter. Open the copy and navigate to main.swift.

In main.swift, replace your use of the empty initializer on the **Town** type with a call to the free memberwise initializer. Add a call to **printTownDescription()**, too, but do not run the program to see what is logged to the console just yet.

### Listing 17.1  Using a memberwise initializer (main.swift)

```
...
var myTown = Town()(population: 10000, numberOfStoplights: 6)
myTown.printTownDescription()
...
```

Next, visit the Town.swift file. Notice that its properties for population and numberOfStoplights have default values. These default values differ from the arguments you have provided to **Town**'s memberwise initializer.

Now run your program. Is the output what you expected? myTown's description reads Population: 10000; number of stoplights: 6 in the console. Those are not the default values you gave to the **Town** type's stored properties. How did these properties' values change from the default values?

The instance myTown is now created with the free memberwise initializer. The **Town** type's stored properties are listed in the initializer, which allows you to specify new values for the instance's properties. As the console reveals, the values you gave to the initializer replace the default values.

Notice that the **Town**'s property names are used as external parameter names in the call to this initializer. Swift provides default external parameter names to every initializer automatically, one for each parameter given by the initializer. This convention is important because Swift's initializers all have the same name: `init`. Therefore, the function name cannot be used to identify which specific initializer should be called. The parameter names, and their types, help the compiler to differentiate between initializers so that it knows which initializer to call.

Default memberwise initializers on structs are helpful because Swift provides them to you automatically. You get them for free. This benefit of structs makes them particularly attractive. Nonetheless, it is common that you will want to customize the initialization of your type. That is where custom initializers come in.

# Custom initializers for structs

It is time to write your own initializer for the `Town` type. Custom initializers are powerful, and with great power comes great responsibility. When you write your own initializer, Swift will not give you any free initializers (say good-bye to the default memberwise initializer!). You are responsible for ensuring that instances' properties are all given their appropriate values.

First you need to do some housecleaning. You are going to remove all of default values for the properties. These were helpful before you knew about initializers, as they ensured that the properties for instances of your type had values when an instance was created. Now, however, they do not really add much value to the `Town` struct. Additionally, you will change `region` back to an instance property – the monster infestation is starting to spread outside the South. Last, you will add the town's `region` to the description that is logged by **printTownDescription** because a town's `region` can now vary from instance to instance.

Open the `Town.swift` file and make these changes.

### Listing 17.2  Cleaning house (`Town.swift`)

```
struct Town {
    static let region = "South"

    var population: Int = 5422 {
        didSet(oldPopulation) {
            print("The population has changed to \(population)
                    from \(oldPopulation).")
        }
    }
    var numberOfStoplights = 4

    enum Size {
        case Small
        case Medium
        case Large
    }

    func printTownDescription() {
        print("Population: \(population); number of stop lights:
                \(numberOfStoplights); region: \(region)")
    }
...
```

After deleting the default values for these types, you may have noticed that the compiler issued an error in two places, both indicating `Type annotation missing in pattern`. Previously, you took advantage of type inference for these properties, which worked well with the default values you gave them. Without the default values, the compiler does not know what type information to give to the properties. You need to explicitly declare their types.

## Listing 17.3  Declaring types (Town.swift)

```
struct Town {
    let region: String
    var population: Int {
        didSet(oldPopulation) {
            print("The population has changed to \(population)
                    from \(oldPopulation).")
        }
    }
    var numberOfStoplights: Int

    enum Size {
        case Small
        case Medium
        case Large
    }
...
```

Now it is time to create your custom initializer. Later, you will call this initializer from another initializer defined within this same type. For now, add the following initializer to your **Town** type.

## Listing 17.4  Adding a memberwise initializer (Town.swift)

```
...
var numberOfStoplights: Int
init(region: String, population: Int, stoplights: Int) {
    self.region = region
    self.population = population
    numberOfStoplights = stoplights
}
enum Size {
    case Small
    case Medium
    case Large
}
...
```

The **init(region:population:stoplights:)** method here takes three arguments, one for each of the stored properties on the **Town** type. You take the values given to the arguments of the initializer and pass them to the actual properties of the type. For example, the value passed to the region argument of the initializer is set as the value for the region property. Because the parameter name in the initializer is the same as the property name, you need to explicitly access the property via self. The numberOfStoplights property does not have this problem, so you simply set the value of the initializer's argument for stoplights to the numberOfStoplights property.

Notice that you set the value for the region property even though it was declared as a constant. The Swift compiler allows you to initialize a constant property at one point during initialization. Remember, the goal of initialization is to ensure that a type's properties have values after initialization completes.

At this point, you may be noticing that there is an icon in Xcode's toolbar informing you that there is an error (see Figure 17.1).

## Figure 17.1 Toolbar error

Click the red icon and Xcode will open the issue navigator in the project navigator's pane on the left. You will see that the error is located in `main.swift` and relates to the initializer that the compiler was giving you by default (see Figure 17.2).

## Figure 17.2 Error in issue navigator

Switch to `main.swift` to fix the error there.

The memberwise initializer that the compiler previously gave you used the actual property name for `numberOfStoplights` for the argument name in the initializer. In **Town**'s initializer, you shortened this parameter name to be `stoplights`. Change the parameter name in `main.swift`. While you are there, add the `region` parameter.

## Listing 17.5 Making sure the parameters align (`main.swift`)

```
var myTown = Town(region: "West", population: 10000, numberOfStoplights stoplights: 6)
```

Build and run the program. The error should disappear, and you should see the same console log output.

## Initializer delegation

You can define initializers to call other initializers on the same type. This procedure is called *initializer delegation*. It is typically used to provide multiple paths for creating an instance of a type.

In value types (i.e., enumerations and structures), initializer delegation is relatively straightforward. Because value types do not support inheritance, initializer delegation only involves calling another initializer defined on the type. It is somewhat more complicated for classes, as you will soon see.

Switch to Town.swift to write a new initializer on this type that makes use of initializer delegation.

### Listing 17.6  Using initializer delegation (Town.swift)

```
...
init(region: String, population: Int, stoplights: Int) {
    self.region = region
    self.population = population
    numberOfStoplights = stoplights
}
init(population: Int, stoplights: Int) {
    self.init(region: "N/A", population: population, stoplights: stoplights)
}
enum Size {
    case Small
    case Medium
    case Large
}
...
```

Here, you define a new initializer on the **Town** type. This initializer, however, is different from the previous one that you created. It only takes two arguments: population and stoplights.

What about the region property? How is that getting set?

Look at this new initializer's implementation. You call **Town**'s other initializer on self: self.init(region: "N/A", population: population, stoplights: stoplights). Notice that you pass in the supplied arguments for population and stoplights. Because you do not have an argument for region, you have to supply your own value. In this case, you specify the string "N/A" to signify that there was no region information given to the initializer.

Initializer delegation helps to avoid duplication of code. Instead of retyping the same code to assign the values passed in to the initializer's arguments to the type's properties, you can simply call across to another initializer on the type. Avoiding duplication of code does more than save you from typing the same thing twice. It can also help avoid bugs. When you have the same code in two places, you have to remember to change both places any time you make a change.

This is why we say that initializer delegation "defines a path" by which a type creates an instance. One initializer calls across to another on a given type to provide specific pieces that are needed to create an instance. Eventually, initializer delegation ends up inside an initializer that has all it needs to fully prepare an instance for use.

Because you defined your own memberwise initializer, the compiler will give you no free initializers. This is not all that limiting; it can even be a benefit. For example, you might want to use this new initializer if there is no region information available for a given town that you would like to create. In that case, you would use your handy new initializer with arguments for population and stoplights to set the corresponding properties while also giving region a placeholder value.

Make use of this new initializer in `main.swift`.

## Listing 17.7 Using the new initializer (`main.swift`)

```
...
var myTown = Town(region: "West", population: 10000, stoplights: 6)
myTown.printTownDescription()
...
```

If you build and run your application, the result is the same, but with one key difference. You are no longer setting the instance's `region` to anything specific, and will see that N/A is logged to the console for `region`'s value.

# Class Initialization

The general syntax for initialization in classes looks very similar to initialization in value types. Nonetheless, there are some different rules for classes that must be observed. These additional rules are mainly due to the fact that classes can inherit from other classes, which necessarily adds some complexity to initialization.

In particular, classes add the concepts of *designated* and *convenience* initializers. An initializer on a class is either one or the other. Designated initializers are responsible for making sure that an instance's properties all have values before initialization completes, thus making the instance ready to use. Convenience initializers are auxiliary to designated initializers. They supplement designated initializers by calling across a class to its designated initializer. The role of convenience initializers is typically to create an instance of a class for a very specific use case.

## Default initializers for classes

You have already seen examples of using a class's default initializer. Classes get a default, empty initializer if you provide default values to all properties and do not write your own initializer. Classes do not get a free memberwise initializer like structs. This explains why you gave your classes default values before: it allowed you to take advantage of the free empty initializer. Thus, you were able to get an instance of the **Zombie** class like so: `let fredTheZombie = Zombie()`, with the empty parentheses indicating that you were using the default initializer.

# Initialization and class inheritance

Open `Monster.swift` and modify the class to give it an initializer. Also, remove the default value of "Monster" from the name property.

## Listing 17.8  Initializing **Monster** (Monster.swift)

```
class Monster {
    ...
    var town: Town?
    var name = "Monster"
    var name: String

    var victimPool: Int {
        get {
            return town?.population ?? 0
        }
        set(newVictimPool) {
            town?.population = newVictimPool
        }
    }
    init(town: Town?, monsterName: String) {
        self.town = town
        name = monsterName
    }
    func terrorizeTown() {
        if town != nil {
            print("\(name) is terrorizing a town!")
        } else {
            print("\(name) hasn't found a town to terrorize yet...")
        }
    }
}
```

This initializer has two arguments: one for an optional instance of the **Town** type, and another for the name of the monster. The values for these arguments are assigned to the class's properties within the initializer's implementation. Once again, note that the argument for the town in the initializer matches the property name on the class, so you have to set the property's value by accessing it through `self`. But you do not have to access name through `self` because the initializer's parameter has a different name.

Now that you have added this initializer, you may notice that the toolbar is indicating that there are two compiler errors. Click on the red icon and you will find that they are in `main.swift`. Switch to this file to examine the errors.

You should see that your previous use of `Zombie()` to get an instance of this class is no longer satisfying the compiler. Why not? The error states: `Missing argument for parameter 'town' in call`.

The error signifies that the compiler is expecting **Zombie**'s initializer to include a parameter for town. This expectation may seem strange because you did not provide an initializer to the **Zombie** class that required town. In fact, you have provided no initializer to this class whatsoever. Instead you have been relying on the empty initializer the compiler gives you for free when your properties have default values.

That is the source of the error: **Zombie** no longer gets the free empty initializer that you were making use of earlier. Why not? *Automatic initializer inheritance.*

## Automatic initializer inheritance

Classes do not typically inherit their superclass's initializers. This feature of Swift is intended to prevent subclasses from inadvertently providing initializers that do not set values on all the properties of the subclass type, because subclasses frequently add additional properties that do not exist in the superclass. Requiring subclasses to have their own initializers helps prevent types from being partially initialized with incomplete initializers.

Nonetheless, there are circumstances in which a class *does* automatically inherit its superclass's initializers. If your subclass provides default values for all new properties it adds, then there are two scenarios in which it will inherit its superclass's initializers.

- If the subclass does not define any designated initializers, it will inherit its superclass's designated initializers.

- If the subclass implements all of its superclass's designated initializers – either explicitly or via inheritance, it will inherit all of its superclass's convenience initializers.

Your **Zombie** type falls within the first of these two scenarios. It is inheriting the **Monster** type's sole designated initializer because it provides default values for all new properties it adds and it does not define its own designated initializer. The signature for this initializer is: init(town:monsterName:). And, because the **Zombie** type is inheriting an initializer, the compiler is no longer providing the free initializer you were using before.

Thus, from the compiler's point of view, the **Zombie** class does not have an empty initializer available to use. And, QED, the **Zombie** class's initializer lacks a parameter for town.

You need to update fredTheZombie's initialization to remove the error. Update his parameters to remove the compiler errors.

### Listing 17.9 Updating fredTheZombie's initialization (main.swift)

```
...
let fredTheZombie = Zombie()Zombie(town: myTown, monsterName: "Fred")
fredTheZombie.town = myTown
fredTheZombie.terrorizeTown()
fredTheZombie.town?.printTownDescription()
fredTheZombie.changeName("Fred the Zombie", walksWithLimp: false)
...
```

Now, when you create an instance of the **Monster** or **Zombie** type, you give the instance a value for its town and name properties. Build and run the application. The errors should be gone, and the results are the same.

## Designated initializers for classes

Classes use designated initializers as their primary initializers. As part of this role, designated initializers are responsible for ensuring that the class's properties are all given values before initialization is ended. If a class has a superclass, then its designated initializer must also call its superclass's designated initializer.

You have already written a designated initializer for the **Monster** class. Recall:

```
init(town: Town?, monsterName: String) {
    self.town = town
    name = monsterName
}
```

Designated initializers are *unadorned*, meaning that designated initializers are denoted by no special keywords placed before **init**. This syntax distinguishes designated initializers from convenience initializers, which use the keyword `convenience`.

The **Monster** class's initializer ensures that all of its properties are given values before initialization completes. Currently, the **Zombie** type gives default values to all of its properties (except for the ones inherited from **Monster**). Thus, the initializer you defined for **Monster** works fine for the **Zombie**. Nonetheless, it would be better if **Zombie** defined its own initializer so that you can customize its initialization.

Start by removing the default values for **Zombie**'s properties.

### Listing 17.10  Removing default values (Zombie.swift)

```
class Zombie: Monster {
    override class var spookyNoise: String {
        return "Brains..."
    }

    var walksWithLimp = false
    var walksWithLimp: Bool
    private(set) var isFallingApart = false
    private(set) var isFallingApart: Bool

    final override func terrorizeTown() {
        if !isFallingApart {
            town?.changePopulation(-10)
        }
        super.terrorizeTown()
    }
    ...
}
```

Removing these default values triggers a compiler error: `Class 'Zombie' has no initializers`. With no default values assigned, the **Zombie** class needs an initializer to give its properties values before initialization completes.

Add a new initializer to the **Zombie** class to solve this problem.

## Listing 17.11  Adding a zombie initializer (`Zombie.swift`)

```
class Zombie: Monster {
    override class var spookyNoise: String {
        return "Brains..."
    }

    var walksWithLimp: Bool
    private(set) var isFallingApart: Bool
    init(limp: Bool, fallingApart: Bool, town: Town?, monsterName: String) {
        walksWithLimp = limp
        isFallingApart = fallingApart
        super.init(town: town, monsterName: monsterName)
    }
    final override func terrorizeTown() {
        if !isFallingApart {
            town?.changePopulation(-10)
        }
    super.terrorizeTown()
    }
}
```

Your new initializer takes care of the error because you are now ensuring that the **Zombie**'s properties have values by the end of initialization. There are two parts to what you have added here. First, the new initializer sets the values of the `walksWithLimp` and `isFallingApart` properties via the `limp` and `fallingApart` arguments. These properties are specific to the **Zombie** class, so the designated initializer initializes them with appropriate values.

Second, you call the designated initializer of **Zombie**'s superclass. As you saw in Chapter 15, `super` points to a subclass's superclass. Thus, the syntax `super.init(town: town, monsterName: monsterName)` passes the values of the parameters `town` and `monsterName` from the initializer on the **Zombie** class to the designated initializer on the **Monster** class. Doing so calls this initializer on **Monster**, which will ensure that the **Zombie**'s properties for `town` and `name` will be set. Figure 17.3 shows this relationship graphically.

Figure 17.3  Calling **super.init**

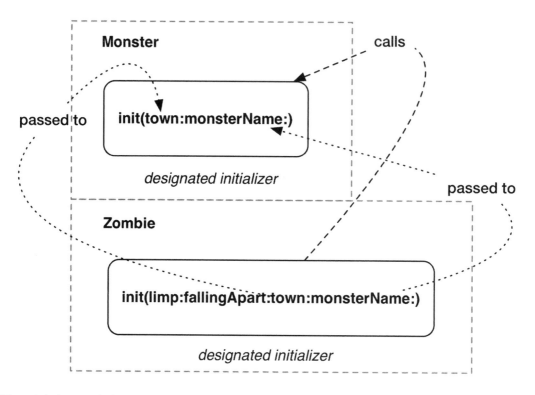

You might be wondering why you called the superclass's initializer last. Because **Zombie**'s initializer is the designated initializer on the **Zombie** class, it is responsible for initializing all of the properties it introduced. After these properties have been given values, the designated initializer of a subclass is responsible for calling its superclass's initializer so that it can initialize *its* properties.

There is still one more error to fix. The **Zombie** class is not getting initialized correctly in main.swift. Switch to this file, and you will see that there is an error from the compiler telling you that the initializer for **Zombie** is missing an argument. Fix this by updating fredTheZombie's initializer to include all the arguments from **Zombie**.

Listing 17.12  Does Fred walk with a limp? Is he falling apart? (main.swift)

```
...
let fredTheZombie = Zombie(town: myTown, monsterName: "Fred")
let fredTheZombie = Zombie(
    limp: false, fallingApart: false, town: myTown, monsterName: "Fred")
...
```

fredTheZombie is now getting initialized with all of the information that it needs in order to be ready for use.

## Convenience initializers for classes

Unlike designated initializers, convenience initializers are not responsible for making sure all of a class's properties have a value. Instead, they do the work that they are defined to do and then hand off that information to either another convenience initializer or a designated initializer. All convenience initializers call across to another initializer on the same class. Eventually, a convenience initializer must call through to its class's designated initializer. The relationship between convenience and designated initializers on a given class defines a path by which a class's stored properties receive initial values.

Make a convenience initializer on the Zombie type. This initializer will provide arguments for whether the **Zombie** instance walks with a limp and whether the instance is falling apart. It will omit parameters for town and monsterName, meaning that callers of this initializer will only need to be responsible for providing arguments to this initializer's parameters.

Listing 17.13  Using a convenience initializer (`Zombie.swift`)

```
...
init(limp: Bool, fallingApart: Bool, town: Town?, monsterName: String) {
    walksWithLimp = limp
    isFallingApart = fallingApart
    super.init(town: town, monsterName: monsterName)
}
convenience init(limp: Bool, fallingApart: Bool) {
    self.init(limp: limp, fallingApart: fallingApart, town: nil, monsterName: "Fred")
    if walksWithLimp {
        print("This zombie has a bad knee.")
    }
}
final override func terrorizeTown() {
    if !isFallingApart {
        town?.changePopulation(-10)
    }
}
...
```

You mark an initializer as a convenience initializer with the `convenience` keyword. This keyword tells the compiler that the initializer will need to delegate to another initializer on the class, eventually calling to a designated initializer. After this call, an instance of the class is ready for use.

Here, the convenience initializer calls the designated initializer on the **Zombie** class. It passes in the values for the parameters it received: `limp` and `fallingApart`. For the parameters that the convenience initializer did not receive values for, town and monsterName, you pass `nil` and "Fred" to **Zombie**'s designated initializer.

Once the convenience initializer calls the designated initializer, the instance is fully prepared for use. Thus, you can check the value of the `walksWithLimp` property on the instance. If you had tried to do this check before calling across to the **Zombie**'s designated initializer, the compiler would have issued an error: `Use of 'self' in delegating initializer before self.init is called`. This error tells you that the delegating initializer is trying to use `self`, which is needed to access the `walksWithLimp` property, before it is ready for use.

Figure 17.4 shows the relationships between the convenience and designated initializers.

## Figure 17.4  Initializer delegation

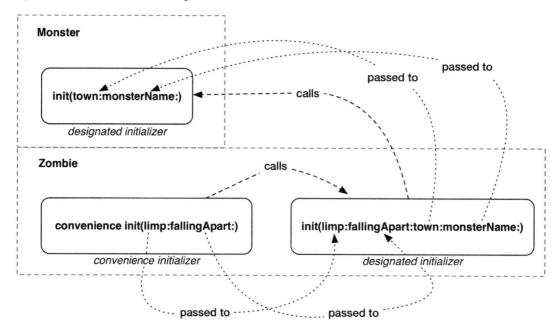

You can now create instances of the **Zombie** type with this convenience initializer. Switch to main.swift and use it to create an instance. Remember, however, that instances of **Zombie** created with this convenience initializer will have nil for the town property and "Fred" for the name property.

## Listing 17.14  Creating a convenient zombie (main.swift)

```
...
let fredTheZombie = Zombie(
    limp: false, fallingApart: false, town: myTown, monsterName: "Fred")
fredTheZombie.terrorizeTown()
fredTheZombie.town?.printTownDescription()
fredTheZombie.changeName("Fred the Zombie", walksWithLimp: false)

var convenientZombie = Zombie(limp: true, fallingApart: false)
...
```

Build and run your program, and you will see that convenientZombie has a bad knee.

# Required initializers for classes

A class can require its subclasses to provide a specific initializer. For example, suppose you want all subclasses of the **Monster** class to provide values for the monster's name and the town it is terrorizing (or nil, if the monster has not yet found a town). To do so, you mark the initializer with the keyword required to indicate that all subclasses of this type must provide the given initializer.

Switch to Monster.swift to make this change.

### Listing 17.15 Making town and monsterName required (Monster.swift)

```
class Monster {
    ...

    var victimPool: Int {
        ...
    }
    required init(town: Town?, monsterName: String) {
        self.town = town
        name = monsterName
    }

    func terrorizeTown() {
        ...
    }
}
```

The sole designated initializer on the **Monster** class is now required. Subclasses must implement this initializer.

Unfortunately, the change triggers a compiler error, as revealed by Xcode's toolbar. Select the red icon to display the Issue navigator to see what is wrong: 'required' initializer 'init(town:monsterName:)' must be provided by subclass of 'Monster'. The error is telling you that you are not yet implementing this newly required initializer on the **Zombie** class. Navigate to Zombie.swift to implement the initializer.

### Listing 17.16 Adding the required initializer (Zombie.swift)

```
...
convenience init(limp: Bool, fallingApart: Bool) {
    self.init(limp: limp, fallingApart: fallingApart, town: nil, monsterName: "Fred")
    if walksWithLimp {
        print("This zombie has a bad knee.")
    }
}
required init(town: Town?, monsterName: String) {
    walksWithLimp = false
    isFallingApart = false
    super.init(town: town, monsterName: monsterName)
}
final override func terrorizeTown() {
    if !isFallingApart {
        town?.changePopulation(-10)
    }
    super.terrorizeTown()
}
...
```

To implement a superclass's required initializer, you prefix the subclass's implementation of the initializer with the `required` keyword. Unlike other functions that you must override if you inherit them from your superclass, you do not mark `required` initializers with the `override` keyword. It is implied by marking the initializer with `required`.

Your implementation of this `required` initializer makes it a designated initializer for the **Zombie** class. Why, you ask? Good question.

Recall that designated initializers are responsible for initializing the type's properties and for delegating up to the superclass's initializer. This implementation does exactly those two things. You can therefore use this initializer to instantiate the **Zombie** class.

At this point, you might be wondering, "How many designated initializers does **Zombie** have?" The answer is two: **init(limp:fallingApart:town:monsterName:)** and **init(town:monsterName:)**. Having more than one designated initializer is completely fine, and is not uncommon.

# Deinitialization

*Deinitialization* is part of the process of removing instances of a class from memory when they are no longer needed. Conceptually, it is the opposite of initialization. Deinitialization is limited to reference types. It is not available for use by value types because they are removed from memory when they are removed from scope.

In Swift, a deinitializer is called immediately prior to when the instance is removed from memory. It provides an opportunity to do any final maintenance before the instance is deallocated.

The details of memory management are covered in greater detail in Chapter 24, but it makes sense to introduce the idea of deinitialization while we are discussing initialization.

A class may only have one deinitializer. Deinitializers are written with **deinit** and take no arguments. Let's see a deinitializer in action in the **Zombie** class.

Listing 17.17 One less zombie (Zombie.`swift`)

```
...
required init(town: Town?, monsterName: String) {
    walksWithLimp = false
    isFallingApart = false
    super.init(town: town, monsterName: monsterName)
}

...

func changeName(name: String, walksWithLimp: Bool) {
    ...
}

deinit {
    print("Zombie named \(name) is no longer with us.")
}
...
```

Your new deinitializer simply logs a farewell to the **Zombie** instance that is about to be deallocated from memory. Notice that the deinitializer accesses the **Zombie**'s name. Deinitializers have full access to a instance's properties and methods.

Open `main.swift` to trigger the **Zombie**'s **deinit** method. You will set `fredTheZombie` to be `nil` at the end of the file. Doing so will trigger the process of removing this instance from memory.

Only optional types can be or become `nil` in Swift. Therefore, you have to declare `fredTheZombie` as an optional – **Zombie?** – before you can make it `nil`. This change also means that you have to use optional chaining to unwrap the optional's value. Finally, you also need to declare `fredTheZombie` with `var` instead of `let` so that the instance can optionally change to become `nil`.

### Listing 17.18 Fred, we hardly knew ye (`main.swift`)

```
...
let var fredTheZombie: Zombie? = Zombie(
    limp: false, fallingApart: false, town: myTown, monsterName: "Fred")
fredTheZombiefredTheZombie?.terrorizeTown()
fredTheZombiefredTheZombie?.town?.printTownDescription()
fredTheZombiefredTheZombie?.changeName("Fred the Zombie", walksWithLimp: false)

var convenientZombie = Zombie(limp: false, fallingApart: false)

print("Victim pool: \(fredTheZombiefredTheZombie?.victimPool)")
fredTheZombiefredTheZombie?.victimPool = 500
print("Victim pool: \(fredTheZombiefredTheZombie?.victimPool)")

print(Zombie.spookyNoise)
if Zombie.isTerrifying {
    print("Run away!")
}
fredTheZombie = nil
```

Build and run the program now. You will see that you bid `fredTheZombie` farewell when the instance is deallocated.

# Failable Initializers

Sometimes it is useful to define a type whose initialization can fail. In these cases, you need a way to report to the caller that you were not able to initialize the instance. You use *failable initializers* to handle these scenarios.

There are a number of reasons why you might want initialization to fail. A type's initializer may be given invalid parameters. For example, you might want to have an initializer fail if someone tries to initialize an instance of **Town** with a negative population. Or perhaps a type's initialization depends on an external resource that is not available, as in `let image = UIImage(named: "non-existing-image")`. This code would fail to create a **UIImage** instance because the image resource does not exist. When this happens, **UIImage**'s failable initializer would return `nil` to indicate that initialization has failed.

## A failable Town initializer

Failable initializers return an optional instance of the type. You append a question mark after the keyword `init` to indicate that an initializer is failable (i.e., init?). You can also use an exclamation point after `init` to create a failable initializer that returns an implicitly unwrapped optional (i.e., `init!`). Returning an implicitly unwrapped optional would mean that you can avoid all of the optional unwrapping syntax that Swift provides to make optionals safe to use. For this reason, while returning an implicitly unwrapped optional is a bit easier to use, it is markedly less safe, and should be used with caution.

Switch to `Town.swift` to give the **Town** struct a failable initializer. If an instance of **Town** is being created with a population of 0, then initialization will fail. This result makes sense, because you cannot have a town without a population.

**Town** has two initializers. Remember that you delegated from the **init(population:stoplights:)** initializer to the **init(region:population:stoplights:)** initializer in this type. For now, just make the **init(region:population:stoplights:)** failable.

### Listing 17.19  Using a failable initializer (`Town.swift`)

```
struct Town {
    ...
    ~~init~~init?(region: String, population: Int, stoplights: Int) {
        if population <= 0 {
            return nil
        }
        self.region = region
        self.population = population
        numberOfStoplights = stoplights
    }
    ...
}
```

Notice that you now use the failable initializer syntax: **init?(region:population:stoplights:)**. After this declaration, you check to see whether the given value for population is less than or equal to 0. If population is less than or equal to 0, then you return nil. The initializer fails in this case. In the context of failable initializers, "fail" means that the initializer will create an optional instance of the **Town** type with a value of nil. This is good. It is preferable to have an instance set to nil rather than an instance with bad data in its properties.

Open `main.swift` to see your new failable initializer in action. Initialize an instance of **Town** with a value of 0 for its population parameter.

### Listing 17.20  myTown, population zero (`main.swift`)

```
var myTown = Town(region: "West", population: ~~100000~~, stoplights: 6)
myTown.printTownDescription()
...
```

At this point, you should notice a few errors in your program. Take a moment to consider what is going on before you build and run the program.

The initializer **init(population:stoplights:)** currently delegates to a failable initializer. This suggests that **init(population:stoplights:)** may get nil back from the designated initializer. Receiving nil back from the designated initializer will be unexpected, because **init(population:stoplights:)** is not failable itself.

Fix this problem by also making **init(population:stoplights:)** a failable initializer.

### Listing 17.21  Making both **Town** initializers failable (Town.swift)

```
struct Town {
...
    init?(region: String, population: Int, stoplights: Int) {
        if population <= 0 {
            return nil
        }
        self.region = region
        self.population = population
        numberOfStoplights = stoplights
    }


    initinit?(population: Int, stoplights: Int) {
        self.init(region: "N/A", population: population, stoplights: stoplights)
    }
...
}
```

Run the program. You will see that there are still a number of errors that you have to fix. You can find these errors in the main.swift file.

The line of code myTown.printTownDescription() has an error that reads: Value of optional type 'Town?' not unwrapped; did you mean to use '!' or '?'? Remember that changing the initializers on the **Town** struct to be failable means that they now return optionals. The initializers now return **Town?** and not **Town**. That means you have to unwrap the optionals before using them.

Use optional chaining to fix the errors in main.swift.

### Listing 17.22  Using optional chaining (main.swift)

```
var myTown = Town(region: "West", population: 0, stoplights: 6)
myTownmyTown?.printTownDescription()

let ts = myTownmyTown?.townSize
print(tsts)

myTownmyTown?.changePopulation(1000000)
print("Size: \(myTownmyTown?.townSize);
               population: \(myTownmyTown?.population)")
...
```

As you can see, representing nil in Swift tends to have a fairly extensive impact on your code. These changes can add complexity and more code to your project. Both increase the chances of making a troublesome mistake.

We recommend that you minimize your use of optionals to those cases in which you absolutely need them.

Build and run the program now. You removed the errors, so the project runs fine. It is time to say farewell to MonsterTown. You will be moving on to a new project – free of zombies – in the next chapter.

# Failable initializers in classes

Failable initializers work a bit differently in classes than in value types (like enumerations and structures). In value types, a failable initializer can fail at any point, and you return `nil` at that time. Failable initializers in classes have to assign initial values in all of the class's properties before failing.

This requirement means that you cannot write the following code:

```
class MyClass {
    let myProperty: String
    init?(myProperty: String) {
        if myProperty.isEmpty {
            return nil
        }
        self.myProperty = myProperty
    }
}
```

Code like the above will trigger an error from the compiler telling you that all stored properties of a class must be initialized before returning nil. `myProperty` does not receive an initial value before the initializer fails. How can you avoid this error? One possibility is to use an implicitly unwrapped optional:

```
class MyClass {
    let myProperty: String!
    init?(myProperty: String) {
        if myProperty.isEmpty {
            self.myProperty = nil
            return nil
        }
        self.myProperty = myProperty
    }
}
```

The code above makes `myProperty` an implicitly unwrapped optional. Since `myProperty` is declared as a constant, it can only be assigned to once. That means `myProperty` does not default to `nil`. If it did, then that would count as its only allowed assignment. You have to assign `myProperty` to `nil` before returning from the initializer. Therefore, the initializer can fail before giving `myProperty` a non-nil value.

Because `myProperty` is a constant, you will not be able to assign `nil` to it after initialization. For example, assuming an instance of **MyClass** called `mc`, this code would trigger an error: `mc?.myProperty = nil`. Thus, you can be sure that `myProperty` has a valid value if initialization succeeds. Moreover, the implicitly unwrapped optional syntax means that you can access `myProperty`'s value without having to use optional binding or chaining.

Nonetheless, the usual guidance about force-unwrapping optionals is still important to keep in mind. If **MyClass** is initialized with a **String** instance that causes the initializer to fail (e.g., an empty **String**), then force-unwrapping the resulting optional instance will cause a runtime crash. For example, this hypothetical code is unsafe and should be avoided: `mc!.myProperty`.

# Initialization Going Forward

"How am I going to remember all this?" We hear you. Initialization in Swift is a very defined process with a lot of rules. Thankfully, the compiler will remind you of what you need to do in order to comply and write a valid initializer. Rather than memorizing all of the rules to initialization, it is useful to think of Swift initialization in terms of value types and classes.

For value types, such as structs, initialization is principally responsible for ensuring that all of the instance's stored properties have been initialized and given appropriate values. This statement is true for classes as well, but initialization is a bit more complicated in this case.

Initialization for classes can be thought of as unfolding in two sequential phases.

In the first phase, a class's designated initializer is eventually called (either directly or by delegation from a convenience initializer). At this point, all of the properties declared on the class are initialized with appropriate values inside of the designated initializer's definition. Next, a designated initializer delegates up to its superclass's designated initializer. The designated initializer on the superclass then ensures that all of its own stored properties are initialized with appropriate values, which is a process that continues until the class at the top of the inheritance chain is reached. The first phase is now completed.

The second phase begins, providing an opportunity for a class to further customize the values held by its stored properties. For example, a designated initializer can modify properties on self after it calls to the superclass's designated initializer. Designated initializers can also call instance methods on self. It is finally at this point that initialization reenters the convenience initializer, providing it with an opportunity to perform any customization on the instance.

The instance is fully initialized after these two phases, and all of its properties and methods are available for use.

The goal of this very definite initialization process is to guarantee the successful initialization of a class. The compiler secures this procedure and will issue errors if you do not adhere to any step in the process. In the end, it is not important that you remember each step in the process so long as you follow the compiler's guidance. Over time, the details of initialization will become more secure in your mind.

## Silver Challenge

Currently, the required initializer on the **Monster** class is implemented as a designated initializer on the **Zombie** subclass. Make this initializer a convenience initializer on the **Zombie** class instead. This change will involve delegating across the **Zombie** class to its designated initializer.

## Gold Challenge

The **Monster** class can be initialized with any **String** instance for the monsterName parameter, even an empty **String**. Doing so would lead to an instance of **Monster** with no name. Even though Frankenstein's monster had no name, you want all of yours to be individually identified. Fix this problem in the **Monster** class by ensuring that monsterName cannot be empty.

Your solution will involve giving **Monster** a failable initializer. Also note that this change will have an impact on initialization in the **Zombie** subclass. Make the necessary adjustments in this class as well.

# For the More Curious: Initializer Parameters

Like functions and methods, initializers can provide explicit external parameter names. External parameter names distinguish between the parameter names available to callers and the local parameter names used in the initializer's implementation. Because initializers follow different naming conventions than functions (i.e., initializer names are always **init**), the parameters' names and types help to determine which initializer should be called. Thus, Swift provides external parameter names for all of the initializer's arguments by default.

You can provide your own external parameter names as needed. For example, imagine a **WeightRecordInLBS** struct that should be able to be initialized with kilograms.

```
struct WeightRecordInLBS {
    let weight: Double

    init(weightInKilos kilos: Double) {
        weight = kilos * 2.20462
    }
}
```

This initializer supplies `weightInKilos` as an explicit external parameter, and gives `kilos` as a local parameter. In its implementation, you simply convert `kilos` to pounds by multiplying with the correct conversion. You would then use this initializer like so: `let wr = WeightRecordInLBS(weightInKilos: 84)`.

You can even use `_` as an explicit external parameter name if you do not want to expose a parameter name. For example, our fictitious **WeightRecordInLBS** struct obviously defines a weight record in terms of pounds. Thus, it would make sense for the initializer to default to taking pounds in its argument.

```
struct WeightRecordInLBS {
    let weight: Double

    init(_ pounds: Double) {
        weight = pounds
    }

    init(weightInKilos kilos: Double) {
        weight = kilos * 2.20462
    }
}
```

The new initializer above can be used in the following manner: `let wr = WeightRecordInLBS(185)`. Because this type rather explicitly represents a weight record in pounds, there is no need for a named parameter in the argument list. Using `_` can make your code more concise, which is convenient when it is quite explicit what will be passed into the argument.

# 18

# Value vs. Reference Types

This chapter builds on the lessons you have been learning about value types and references types. You will explore the differences between the two by comparing and contrasting their differing behaviors in a variety of scenarios. At the end of this chapter, you should have a good understanding of when to use a value type (e.g., a struct) or a reference type (e.g., a class).

## Value Semantics

Create a new playground called `ValueVsRef` and save it in a good place. Your playground should have the same code below:

```
import Cocoa

var str = "Hello, playground"
```

You have seen this code many times before: you have a mutable instance of type **String** set to the value of `"Hello, playground"`. Make a new string by giving the value of `str` to another instance.

### Listing 18.1  Making a new string

```
import Cocoa

var str = "Hello, playground"
var playgroundGreeting = str
```

`playgroundGreeting` has the same value as `str`. They both hold the string `"Hello, playground"`, which you can verify in the results sidebar. But what happens when you change the value of `playgroundGreeting`? Will it also change the value of `str`? Change `playgroundGreeting` to find out.

### Listing 18.2  Updating `playgroundGreeting`

```
import Cocoa

var str = "Hello, playground"
var playgroundGreeting = str
playgroundGreeting += "! How are you today?"
str
```

As you can see, even though `playgroundGreeting`'s value has been updated, `str`'s value has not changed. Why not? The answer has to do with *value semantics*.

To better understand the meaning of value semantics, hold down the Option key and click on playgroundGreeting. You should see the window shown in Figure 18.1 pop up:

Figure 18.1  playgroundGreeting information

This window shows some useful information. For example, playgroundGreeting is of type **String**. Click on the word "String" in this window and it will reveal the documentation for the **String** type (see Figure 18.2).

Figure 18.2  **String** documentation

You will see at the top of this document that **String** is listed as a struct. This means that **String** is implemented as a struct in Swift's standard library. Furthermore, this means that **String** is a *value type*.

"What are value types?" you may be asking. Value types are always *copied* when they are assigned to an instance or passed as an argument to a function. This should remind you of what you just saw above.

When you assigned str to playgroundGreeting, you gave a copy of str's value to playgroundGreeting. They do not point to the same underlying instance. Thus, when you changed playgroundGreeting's value, it had no impact on str's value. They are distinct from each other. Figure 18.3 shows this relationship graphically.

Figure 18.3 Value semantics and copy behavior

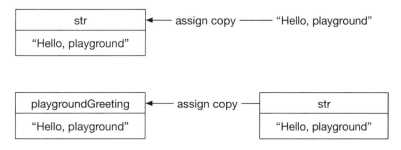

Swift's basic types – **Array**, **Dictionary**, **Int**, **String**, and so on – are all implemented as structs, as value types. This design choice made at the level of the standard library should indicate to you how important value types are to Swift. You should always consider modeling your data with a struct first, and then move on to using a class if needed.

Let's look at how *reference semantics* work to get a better understanding of when it is appropriate to make use of them.

# Reference Semantics

Reference semantics work differently than value semantics. With value types, you get a copy of the instance when you assign it to a new constant or variable. The same is true when you pass an instance of a value type as the argument to a function. An instance of a reference type, however, behaves differently in that these two actions actually create an additional *reference* to the same underlying instance.

Let's add a new class to model a Greek god to the playground to see just what this means.

### Listing 18.3  Adding a Greek god class

```
import Cocoa

var str = "Hello, playground"
var playgroundGreeting = str
playgroundGreeting += "! How are you today?"
str

class GreekGod {
    var name: String
    init(name: String) {
        self.name = name
    }
}
```

The class **GreekGod** is small – it supplies a single stored property to hold on to a god or goddess's name. Make a new instance of this class.

### Listing 18.4  Making a Greek god

```
...

class GreekGod {
    var name: String
    init(name: String) {
        self.name = name
    }
}

let hecate = GreekGod(name: "Hecate")
```

You now have a new instance of **GreekGod** with the name "Hecate," goddess of the crossroads. Make a new constant called anotherHecate and assign hecate to it.

### Listing 18.5  Getting a reference to a Greek god

```
...

class GreekGod {
    var name: String
    init(name: String) {
        self.name = name
    }
}
let hecate = GreekGod(name: "Hecate")
let anotherHecate = hecate
```

At this point, you have two constants – but they both point to the same instance of the **GreekGod** class. Change anotherHecate's name to illustrate this point.

## Listing 18.6 Changing a Greek god's name

```
...

class GreekGod {
    var name: String
    init(name: String) {
        self.name = name
    }
}
let hecate = GreekGod(name: "Hecate")
let anotherHecate = hecate

anotherHecate.name = "AnotherHecate"
anotherHecate.name
hecate.name
```

The code in Listing 18.6 changes the name of only `anotherHecate` and leaves `hecate`'s name alone. But the `name` property for both of the gods has changed to "AnotherHecate" in the results sidebar. What happened?

The code `GreekGod(name: "Hecate")` created an instance of the **GreekGod** class. When you assign an instance of a class to a constant or variable, as you did with `hecate`, that constant or variable gets a reference to the instance. And as you can see, a reference works differently than a copy.

With a reference, the constant or variable *refers* to an instance of some class in memory. Therefore, both `hecate` and `anotherHecate` refer to the *same* instance of the **GreekGod** class. Figure 18.4 shows this relationship.

## Figure 18.4 Reference semantics

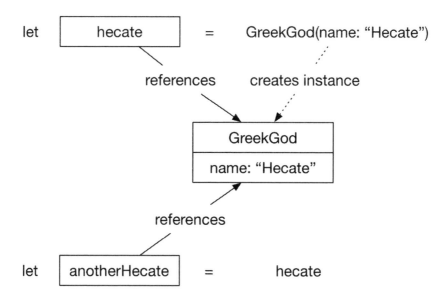

Because `hecate` and `anotherHecate` refer to the same instance of **GreekGod**, a change in one will be reflected in the other.

# Constant Value and Reference Types

Value and reference types behave differently when they are constants. Create a new struct called **Pantheon** so that you have a value type of your own to work with.

## Listing 18.7  Making the Greek **Pantheon**

```
...
class GreekGod {
    var name: String
    init(name: String) {
        self.name = name
    }
}
let hecate = GreekGod(name: "Hecate")
let anotherHecate = hecate

anotherHecate.name = "AnotherHecate"
anotherHecate.name
hecate.name

struct Pantheon {
    var chiefGod: GreekGod
}
```

The new struct above represents the Greek pantheon. It has one stored property to reflect the foremost god in the pantheon. Greek gods are always squabbling, so you made this property mutable with var.

Make a new instance of **Pantheon** with hecate as the chiefGod.

## Listing 18.8  Hecate's **Pantheon**

```
...
class GreekGod {
    var name: String
    init(name: String) {
        self.name = name
    }
}
let hecate = GreekGod(name: "Hecate")
let anotherHecate = hecate

anotherHecate.name = "AnotherHecate"
anotherHecate.name
hecate.name

struct Pantheon {
    var chiefGod: GreekGod
}

let pantheon = Pantheon(chiefGod: hecate)
```

You now have an instance of **Pantheon** with hecate at its head. Note that this instance is created with let, so it is a constant. Try to change pantheon's chiefGod property.

### Listing 18.9  A new chief god

```
...
struct Pantheon {
    var chiefGod: GreekGod
}

let pantheon = Pantheon(chiefGod: hecate)
let zeus = GreekGod(name: "Zeus")
pantheon.chiefGod = zeus
```

First, you create a new instance of **GreekGod** named zeus. Second, you assign that new instance to the chiefGod property on pantheon. You should see a compiler error on that line: Cannot assign to property: 'pantheon' is a 'let' constant.

This error is telling you that pantheon is an immutable instance, which means you cannot change it. Value types that are declared as constants cannot have their properties changed, even if these properties are declared with var in the type's implementation. You can think of the instances of a value type as representing a single whole value, like an integer. If you declare an integer as a constant, then you cannot change some part of it later on.

Remove this assignment to the chiefGod property to silence the compiler error. Leave zeus alone; you will be using him in the next example.

### Listing 18.10  Demoting Zeus

```
...
struct Pantheon {
    var chiefGod: GreekGod
}

let pantheon = Pantheon(chiefGod: hecate)
let zeus = GreekGod(name: "Zeus")
pantheon.chiefGod = zeus
```

This works differently for reference types. Try to change the name property on zeus.

### Listing 18.11  Changing Zeus's name

```
...
struct Pantheon {
    var chiefGod: GreekGod
}

let pantheon = Pantheon(chiefGod: hecate)
let zeus = GreekGod(name: "Zeus")
zeus.name = "Zeus Jr."
zeus.name
```

This is not *that* Zeus; this is one of his many sons. You need to update his name with the requisite "Jr." Despite zeus being declared with let, you will see that the compiler is absolutely fine with this name change.

Why can we not change the value of a property on a constant that is an instance of a value type, but we *can* change the value of a property on a constant that is an instance of a reference type?

Because zeus is an instance of a reference type, it refers to the instance of **GreekGod** that was made via this code: GreekGod(name: "Zeus"). When you change the value that the name property stores, you are not actually changing what zeus really is, which is a *reference* to a **GreekGod**. Because you made name a mutable stored property when you defined the **GreekGod** class (via its var declaration), you are free to change it however much you like. No matter how many times you change zeus's name, zeus still refers to the same instance.

# Using Value and Reference Types Together

This chapter may have made you wonder, "Can I put a value type inside of a reference type? Can I put a reference type inside of a value type?" The answer to both of these questions is "Yes," and you did the latter by adding a property of the class **GreekGod** to **Pantheon**. But you must be very careful about using a reference type inside of a value type. Consider the following example that changes the name of hecate.

## Listing 18.12  The Romans are coming

```
...
struct Pantheon {
    var chiefGod: GreekGod
}

let pantheon = Pantheon(chiefGod: hecate)
let zeus = GreekGod(name: "Zeus")
zeus.name = "Zeus Jr."
zeus.name

pantheon.chiefGod.name // "AnotherHecate"
let greekPantheon = pantheon
hecate.name = "Trivia"
greekPantheon.chiefGod.name // ???
```

When you log the value of pantheon.chiefGod.name, the results sidebar bar lists AnotherHecate. You next assign a copy of pantheon to a new constant named greekPantheon. Remember that **Pantheon** is a value type, and so you should expect greekPantheon to receive a copy of pantheon. Afterward, you change the name of hecate to "Trivia." The Greeks have given way to the Romans, and so all of the names are changing. Last, you check the name of the pantheon's chiefGod and are met with a surprise.

The chiefGod's name is now "Trivia," which is surprising because we would expect greekPantheon to have a copy of pantheon. How did this happen?

Remember that the chiefGod property is of type **GreekGod**. **GreekGod** is a class, and is therefore a reference type. When you created the pantheon with hecate as the chiefGod (Pantheon(chiefGod: hecate)), you gave the pantheon's chiefGod a reference to the same instance of **GreekGod** to which hecate refers. Consequently, modifying the name of hecate will also change the name of the pantheon's chiefGod.

This example demonstrates the complications of placing a reference type within a value type. You should expect instances of value types to be copied when assigned to a new variable or constant or passed into a function. Somewhat confusingly, however, a value type with a reference type in a property will pass along that same reference to the new variable or constant. That reference will still point to the same instance as the original reference, and changes to any of them will be reflected in all of them.

## Immutable reference types

The previous section underscores the lesson that you have to be careful if you make a reference type property within a value type. To avoid the confusion described above, we urge you to avoid using reference type properties inside of value types in almost all cases.

If you find yourself needing a reference type property in your struct, however, then it is best to use an immutable instance. For example, imagine that you need a `dateCreated` property on **Pantheon**. Use the `Foundation` class **NSDate** to encapsulate this date information.

### Listing 18.13  Adding a date to **Pantheon**

```
...
struct Pantheon {
    ~~var~~let chiefGod: GreekGod
    let dateCreated = NSDate()
}
...
greekPantheon.chiefGod.name
greekPantheon.dateCreated
```

`NSDate()` will get the current date and time. The code above will store this information in the `dateCreated` property. Now, whenever you create an instance of **Pantheon**, that instance will have an immutable property with the date that instance was created.

This property is immutable for two reasons. First, you declare the property with a `let`, which means that you cannot reassign to the property. Second, **NSDate** itself is an immutable class. You cannot change the instance once you have it. (Remember that you could change `hecate`'s `name` property even though you made that instance with `let`? **NSDate** is not like that because the date an instance represents cannot be changed; the **NSDate** class does not have any mutable properties or mutating methods that can modify the instance.)

Go ahead and try to change `dateCreated`. You will not be able to reassign to this property. Moreover, you will find that there is no property on this **NSDate** instance that you can modify. You are stuck with what you received when you made an instance.

Using reference types within value types can be confusing, but it is not uncommon to have the need. In these cases, be sure to make these properties immutable. Taking advantage of immutability will help to protect instances of value types from having properties whose data can change unexpectedly.

# Copying

The concept of making copies has been lurking behind nearly every topic covered in this chapter. Developers often want to know if copying an instance yields a *shallow* or a *deep* copy. Swift does not provide any language-level support for making a deep copy, which means copies in Swift are shallow.

Let's look at an example to get a better sense of what these concepts mean. Create a new instance of **GreekGod** and put that and the existing instances into an array.

### Listing 18.14  Adding some gods

```
...
let athena = GreekGod(name: "Athena")
let gods = [athena, hecate, zeus]
```

You created a new Greek god named `athena` and added that instance, `hecate`, and `zeus` to a new array. You should see these gods contained within the new array listed in the results sidebar.

Make a copy of the array `gods`. You will also change the name of `zeus`, and compare `gods` to its copy.

### Listing 18.15  Copying gods

```
...
let athena = GreekGod(name: "Athena")
let gods = [athena, hecate, zeus]
let godsCopy = gods
gods.last?.name = "Jupiter"
gods
godsCopy
```

`last` refers to the last element an array. It is an optional because the array may be empty. Your results sidebar should look like Figure 18.5.

### Figure 18.5  Comparing `gods` and `godsCopy`

```
let athena = GreekGod(name: "Athena")          GreekGod

let gods = [athena, hecate, zeus]              [{name "Athena"}, {name "Trivia"}, {name "Zeus Jr."}]
let godsCopy = gods                            [{name "Athena"}, {name "Trivia"}, {name "Zeus Jr."}]
gods.last?.name = "Jupiter"                    ()
gods                                           [{name "Athena"}, {name "Trivia"}, {name "Jupiter"}]
godsCopy                                       [{name "Athena"}, {name "Trivia"}, {name "Jupiter"}]
```

Notice that both `gods` and its copy have the same contents after you change zeus's `name` property (via `gods.last?.name = "Jupiter"`). Why did changing the name of the last god in the `gods` array change the name of the last god in `godsCopy`? After all, arrays are structs, which means that they are value types. The expectation for value types is that `godsCopy` is a distinct copy of `gods`. Yet a change to an item in one is reflected in the other; why?

Remember that gods contains instances of **GreekGod**. **GreekGod** is a class, and that means it is a reference type. That means that `godsCopy` shares the same references to **GreekGod** instances that gods has. You have seen something very similar above with `pantheon` and `greekPantheon`.

Pulling it all together, `last` will get the last element in the gods array, which is zeus. So, when you change the name on this instance, you are changing it for the instance of **GreekGod** to which zeus refers. Thus, a change to zeus here will be reflected in both arrays.

This form of copying is referred to as *shallow copying*. Shallow copying does not create a distinct copy of an instance; instead, it provides a duplicate of the instance's reference. Figure 18.6 is a graphical visualization of this.

Figure 18.6  Shallow copy of an array of gods

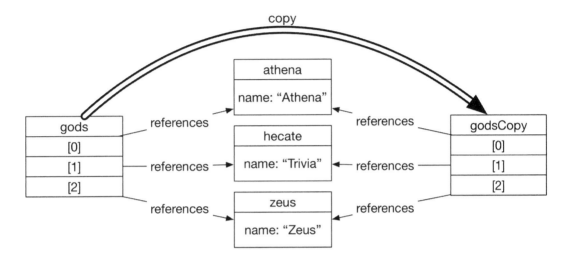

A *deep copy*, on the other hand, would duplicate the instance at the destination of a reference. That would mean that godsCopy's indices would not reference the same instances of **GreekGod**. Instead, a deep copy of gods would create a new array with references to its own instances of **GreekGod**. That form of copying would look something like Figure 18.7.

Figure 18.7  Deep copy of an array of gods

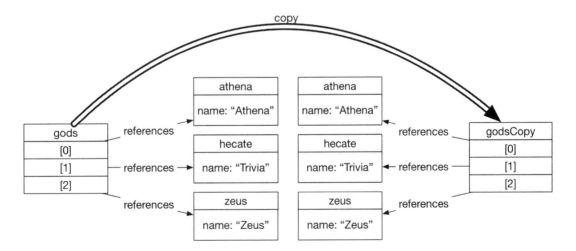

Swift does not supply any means to perform a deep copy. If you would like this behavior, then you will need to make it yourself.

# Identity vs. Equality

Now that you understand the difference between value and reference types, you are ready to learn about equality and identity. *Equality* refers to two instances having the same values for their observable characteristics, such as two instances of the **String** type that have the same text. *Identity*, on the other hand, refers to whether two variables or constants point to the same instance in memory. Take a look at this sample code.

```
let x = 1
let y = 1
x == y // True
```

Two constants, x and y, are created. They are both of type **Int** and hold on to the same value, 1. Not surprisingly, the equality check, done via ==, evaluates to true. This makes sense because x and y hold on to exactly the same value.

This is exactly what we want to know from an equality check: do two instances have the same values? All of Swift's basic data types (**String**, **Int**, **Float**, **Double**, **Array**, and **Dictionary**) can be checked for equality.

athena and hecate are both reference types because they point to an instance of the **GreekGod** class. Thus, you can check for identity on these two constants using the identity operator: ===. Here is what that would look like:

```
athena === hecate // False
```

This identity check fails because athena and hecate do not point to the same location in memory where an instance of the **GreekGod** class lives.

What if you want to check for identity on x and y? You might think you could use the identity operator: x === y. But this code will generate an error from the compiler. Why? The reason for the error is that value types are passed by value. Because the **Int** type is implemented in Swift as a struct, both x and y are value types. Therefore, you cannot compare these two constants based upon their location in memory.

What if you tried to check for equality on athena and hecate, like: athena == hecate? You would see a compiler error. The compiler is telling you that it does not know how to call the == function on the **GreekGod** class. If you want to check for equality on classes that you make, you have to teach your classes how by implementing the == function. Doing so entails conforming to a protocol called **Equatable**, which you will read about in Chapter 22.

As a final note, it is important to realize that two constants or variables may be equal (i.e., they have the same values), but they may not be identical (i.e., they may point to distinct instances of a given type). But it does not work the other way around: if two variables or constants point to the same instance in memory, then they will be equal as well.

# What Should I Use?

Structures and classes are well suited for defining many custom types. Before Swift, structs were so distinct from classes in Mac OS X and iOS development that the use-cases for both types were obvious. In Swift, however, the functionality added to structs makes their behavior more similar to that of classes. This similarity makes the decision of which to use somewhat more complicated.

But do not despair. There are important differences between structs and classes that give some guidance on which to use when. Strict rules are hard to define because there are many factors to consider, but here are some general guidelines.

1. If you want a type to be passed by value, use a struct. Doing so will ensure that the type is copied when assigned or passed into a function's argument.

2. If the type does not need to support subclasses inheriting from it, then use a struct. Structs do not support inheritance, and so they cannot be subclassed.

3. If the behavior you would like to represent in a type is relatively straightforward and encompasses a few simple values, consider starting out with a struct. You can always change the type to be a class later.

4. Use a class in all other cases.

Structs are commonly used when modeling shapes (e.g., rectangles have a width and a height), ranges (e.g., a race has start and an end), and points in a coordinate system (e.g., a point in a two-dimensional space has an X and Y value). They are also great for defining data structures: the **String**, **Array**, and **Dictionary** types are all defined as structs in Swift's standard library.

There are some other cases in which you might want to use a class instead of a struct, but they will be somewhat less common than the above. For example, if you want to take advantage of passing a reference around, but do not want a class to be subclassed, you might ask yourself whether or not you should use a struct (to avoid inheritance) or a class (to have reference semantics). The answer here is to use a `final class { ... }`. Marking a class as `final` will prevent the class from being subclassed, and will also offer you the desired reference semantics for instances of the class.

In general, we suggest starting out with a struct unless you absolutely know you need the benefits of a reference type. Value types are easier to reason about because you do not need to worry about what happens to an instance when you change values on a copy.

# Part V
# Advanced Swift

Swift provides advanced language features that give developers more sophisticated tools to control their applications. This part of the book introduces concepts that will be essential to the more experienced Swift developer. *Protocols*, *extensions*, and *generics* provide mechanisms for developing idiomatic code that leverages the strengths of Swift.

# 19

# Protocols

In Chapter 16, you learned about using access controls to hide information. Hiding information is a form of *encapsulation*, which allows you to design your software in such a way that you can change one part without affecting the rest. Swift also supports another form of encapsulation: a *protocol*, which allows you to specify and work with the *interface* of a type without knowing the type itself. An interface is a set of properties and methods that a type provides.

Protocols are a more abstract concept than many of the topics you have learned about so far. To get a handle on protocols and how they work, you will create a function that formats data into a table that looks like a simple spreadsheet. Next, you will use a protocol to make that function flexible enough to handle different *data sources*. Mac and iOS apps commonly separate the presentation of data from the source that provides the data. This separation is an extremely useful pattern that allows Apple to provide classes that handle presentation while leaving it up to you to determine how data should be stored.

## Formatting a Table of Data

Create a new playground called `Protocols.playground`. Begin with a function that takes an array whose individual elements are themselves arrays – an array of arrays, in other words – and prints the numbers in a table. Each element of the `data` array is an array of integers that represent the columns of a single row, so the total number of rows is `data.count`.

## Listing 19.1  Setting up a table

```
func printTable(data: [[Int]]) {
    for row in data {
        // Create an empty string
        var out = ""

        // Append each item in this row to our string
        for item in row {
            out += " \(item) |"
        }

        // Done - print it!
        print(out)
    }
}

let data = [
    [30, 6],
    [40, 18],
    [50, 20],
]

printTable(data)
```

Open up the debug area to see a simple table displaying the data:

```
30 | 6 |
40 | 18 |
50 | 20 |
```

Next, you will add the ability to label each row. Labeling the rows is a little tricky because you want all the row labels to be aligned, so you will need to determine which label is the longest and pad the shorter rows with spaces. This will be easier if you also define a helper function that can create a **String** containing a specified number of spaces.

## Listing 19.2 Labeling the rows

```
func padding(amount: Int) -> String {
    var paddingString = ""
    for _ in 0 ..< amount {
        paddingString += " "
    }
    return paddingString
}

func printTable(data: [[Int]]) {(rowLabels: [String], data: [[Int]]) {
    for row in data {
        // Create an empty string
        var out = ""

        // Create an array of the width of each row label
        let rowLabelWidths = rowLabels.map { $0.characters.count }

        // Determine length of longest row label
        guard let maxRowLabelWidth = rowLabelWidths.maxElement() else {
            return
        }

        for (i, row) in data.enumerate() {
            // Pad the row label out so they are all the same length
            let paddingAmount = maxRowLabelWidth - rowLabelWidths[i]
            var out = rowLabels[i] + padding(paddingAmount) + " |"

            // Append each item in this row to our string
            for item in row {
                out += " \(item) |"
            }

            // Done - print it!
            print(out)
        }
}

let rowLabels = ["Joe", "Karen", "Fred"]
let data = [
    [30, 6],
    [40, 18],
    [50, 20],
]

printTable(rowLabels, data: data)
```

You need to determine the width of the longest row label in order to align all the rows correctly. First, you use rowLabels.map to create a new array containing the width of each label. Next, you use a guard statement to safely unwrap the optional returned by rowLabelWidths.maxElement(), storing the result into maxRowLabelWidth. (If rowLabelWidths.maxElement() returns nil, **printTable(_:data:)** will immediately return because there are no rows to print anyway.) Then, when you iterate over each row of the data, you insert some padding to rows that are shorter than the maximum width. The paddingAmount instance holds the amount of padding needed for a row, and **padding(paddingAmount)** creates a string containing paddingAmount spaces.

The end result, in your debug area, is a nicely aligned table with labeled rows:

```
Joe   | 30 | 6  |
Karen | 40 | 18 |
Fred  | 50 | 20 |
```

Finally, add the ability to label each column. Labeling columns is trickier still. You want all the columns to line up vertically, which may require padding all of the data items. You will have to keep track of the width of each column label and pad all the items in that column out to that length.

## Listing 19.3  Labeling the columns

```swift
func printTable(rowLabels: [String], columnLabels: [String], data: [[Int]]) {
    // Create an array of the width of each row label
    let rowLabelWidths = rowLabels.map { $0.characters.count }

    // Determine length of longest row label
    guard let maxRowLabelWidth = rowLabelWidths.maxElement() else {
        return
    }

    // Create first row containing column headers
    var firstRow: String = padding(maxRowLabelWidth) + " |"

    // Also keep track of the width of each column
    var columnWidths = [Int]()

    for columnLabel in columnLabels {
        let columnHeader = " \(columnLabel) |"
        firstRow += columnHeader
        columnWidths.append(columnHeader.characters.count)
    }
    print(firstRow)

    for (i, row) in data.enumerate() {
        // Pad the row label out so they are all the same length
        let paddingAmount = maxRowLabelWidth - rowLabelWidths[i]
        var out = rowLabels[i] + padding(paddingAmount) + " |"

        // Append each item in this row to our string
        for item in row {
            out += " \(item) |"
        for (j, item) in row.enumerate() {
            let itemString = " \(item) |"
            let paddingAmount = columnWidths[j] - itemString.characters.count
            out += padding(paddingAmount) + itemString
        }

        // Done - print it!
        print(out)
    }
}

let rowLabels = ["Joe", "Karen", "Fred"]
let columnLabels = ["Age", "Years of Experience"]
let data = [
    [30, 6],
    [40, 18],
    [50, 20],
]

printTable(rowLabels, columnLabels: columnLabels, data: data)
```

You create and print firstRow, which contains all of the column headers. As you are constructing the first row, you also record the width of each column header in the columnWidths array. Then, when you append each data item to the output row, you use the columnWidths array and **padding(paddingAmount)** to pad each item so that it is the same width as its column header.

Check your debug area again. You now have a well-formatted table of data.

```
      | Age | Years of Experience |
Joe   | 30  |                   6 |
Karen | 40  |                  18 |
Fred  | 50  |                  20 |
```

However, there is at least one major problem with the **printTable(_:columnLabels:data:)** function: it is very difficult to use! You have to have separate arrays for row labels, column labels, and the data, and you have to manually make sure the number of row labels and column labels matches the number of elements in the data array.

You are much more likely to want to represent information like this using structures and classes. Replace the part of the code where you call **printTable(_:columnLabels:data:)** with some *model objects*, which are types that represent the data your app works with.

## Listing 19.4  Using model objects

```
...
let rowLabels = ["Joe", "Karen", "Fred"]
let columnLabels = ["Age", "Years of Experience"]
let data = [
    [30, 6],
    [40, 18],
    [50, 20],
]

printTable(rowLabels, columnLabels: columnLabels, data: data)
struct Person {
    let name: String
    let age: Int
    let yearsOfExperience: Int
}

struct Department {
    let name: String
    var people = [Person]()

    init(name: String) {
        self.name = name
    }

    mutating func addPerson(person: Person) {
        people.append(person)
    }
}

var department = Department(name: "Engineering")
department.addPerson(Person(name: "Joe", age: 30, yearsOfExperience: 6))
department.addPerson(Person(name: "Karen", age: 40, yearsOfExperience: 18))
department.addPerson(Person(name: "Fred", age: 50, yearsOfExperience: 20))
```

You now have a **Department**, and you would like to be able to print out the details of its people using the **printTable(_:columnLabels:data:)** function. You could modify the function to take a **Department** instead of the three arguments it takes now. However, the current implementation of **printTable(_:columnLabels:data:)** could be used to print any kind of tabular data, and it would be nice to keep that feature. A protocol can help to preserve this functionality.

# Protocols

A *protocol* allows you to define the interface you want a type to satisfy. A type that satisfies a protocol is said to *conform* to the protocol.

Define a protocol that specifies the interface you need for the **printTable(_:columnLabels:data:)** function. The **printTable(_:columnLabels:data:)** function needs to know how many rows and columns there are, what the label for each row and column is, and what the item of data to display in each cell should be. It does not matter to the Swift compiler where in your playground file you put this protocol. But it probably makes the most sense to put it at the top of the file, just before **printTable(_:columnLabels:data:)**, because you are going to use the protocol in the function.

Listing 19.5  Defining a protocol

```
protocol TabularDataSource {
    var numberOfRows: Int { get }
    var numberOfColumns: Int { get }

    func labelForRow(row: Int) -> String
    func labelForColumn(column: Int) -> String

    func itemForRow(row: Int, column: Int) -> Int
}
...
```

The syntax for a protocol should look familiar to you. It is very similar to defining a structure or a class, except that all the computed property and function definitions are omitted. The **TabularDataSource** protocol states that any conforming type must have two properties: numberOfRows and numberOfColumns. The syntax { get } signifies that these properties can be read. If the property were intended to be read/write, you would use { get set }. Note that marking a protocol property with { get } does not exclude the possibility that a conforming type might have a property that is read/write. It only indicates that the protocol requires it to be readable. Finally, **TabularDataSource** specifies that a conforming type must have the three methods listed with the exact types that are listed.

A protocol defines the minimum set of properties and methods a type must have. The type can have more than what the protocol lists – extra properties and methods are fine as long as all the requirements of the protocol are present.

Make **Department** conform to the **TabularDataSource** protocol. Begin by declaring that it conforms.

Listing 19.6  Declaring that **Department** conforms to **TabularDataSource**

```
...
struct Department: TabularDataSource {
...
}
```

The syntax for conforming to a protocol is to add : ProtocolName after the name of the type. (This looks similar to how you declare a superclass. We will cover how protocols and superclasses can be used together later.)

Your playground file now has an error. Open up the debug area to see the details. You have claimed that **Department** conforms to **TabularDataSource**, but **Department** is missing all the properties and methods that **TabularDataSource** requires. Add implementations of them all.

## Listing 19.7  Adding required properties and methods

```
...
struct Department: TabularDataSource {
    let name: String
    var people = [Person]()

    init(name: String) {
        self.name = name
    }

    mutating func addPerson(person: Person) {
        people.append(person)
    }

    var numberOfRows: Int {
        return people.count
    }

    var numberOfColumns: Int {
        return 2
    }

    func labelForRow(row: Int) -> String {
        return people[row].name
    }

    func labelForColumn(column: Int) -> String {
        switch column {
        case 0: return "Age"
        case 1: return "Years of Experience"
        default: fatalError("Invalid column!")
        }
    }

    func itemForRow(row: Int, column: Int) -> Int {
        let person = people[row]
        switch column {
        case 0: return person.age
        case 1: return person.yearsOfExperience
        default: fatalError("Invalid column!")
        }
    }
}
...
```

A **Department** has a row for each person, so its numberOfRows property returns the number of people in the department. Each person has two properties that should be displayed, so numberOfColumns returns two. The label of each row is the name of the person to be shown on that row. **labelForColumn(_:)** and **itemForRow(_:)** are a little more interesting: you use a switch statement to return one of the two column headers. (Why is there a default case? Refer back to Chapter 5 if you are unsure.)

The error in your playground is gone now that **Department** conforms to **TabularDataSource**. However, you still need to go back and modify **printTable(_:columnLabels:data:)** to accept and work with a **TabularDataSource**, because now you do not have any way of calling **printTable(_:columnLabels:data:)** with your department. Protocols do not just define the properties and methods a conforming type must supply. They can also be used as types themselves:

you can have variables, function arguments, and return values that have the type of a protocol. Change **printTable(_:)** to take a data source of type **TabularDataSource**, now that the protocol provides all the same data as the old arguments did (including all the column and row headers and the amount of data available).

## Listing 19.8 Making **printTable(_:)** take a **TabularDataSource**

```
func printTable(rowLabels: [String], columnLabels: [String], data: [[Int]]) {
func printTable(dataSource: TabularDataSource) {
    // Create arrays of the row and column labels
    let rowLabels = (0 ..< dataSource.numberOfRows).map { dataSource.labelForRow($0) }
    let columnLabels = (0 ..< dataSource.numberOfColumns).map {
        dataSource.labelForColumn($0)
    }

    // Create an array of the width of each row label
    let rowLabelWidths = rowLabels.map { $0.characters.count }

    // Determine length of longest row label
    guard let maxRowLabelWidth = rowLabelWidths.maxElement() else {
        return
    }

    // Create first row containing column headers
    var firstRow: String = padding(maxRowLabelWidth) + " |"

    // Also keep track of the width of each column
    var columnWidths = [Int]()

    for columnLabel in columnLabels {
        let columnHeader = " \(columnLabel) |"
        firstRow += columnHeader
        columnWidths.append(columnHeader.characters.count)
    }
    print(firstRow)

    for (i, row) in data.enumerate() {
    for i in 0 ..< dataSource.numberOfRows {
        // Pad the row label out so they are all the same length
        let paddingAmount = maxRowLabelWidth - rowLabelWidths[i]
        var out = rowLabels[i] + padding(paddingAmount) + " |"

        // Append each item in this row to our string
        for (j, item) in row.enumerate() {
        for j in 0 ..< dataSource.numberOfColumns {
            let item = dataSource.itemForRow(i, column: j)
            let itemString = " \(item) |"
            let paddingAmount = columnWidths[j] - itemString.characters.count
            out += padding(paddingAmount) + itemString
        }

        // Done - print it!
        print(out)
    }
}
...
```

You have seen the **map(_:)** method on arrays, but here you call it on two ranges of numbers. It functions exactly the same way: an array is returned that contains the result of calling the closure you provided on each of the numbers in the range in order. Under the hood, the `map(_:)` available on arrays and the `map(_:)` available on ranges is actually the same method. You will learn more about this in Chapter 23.

The `Department` type now conforms to `TabularDataSource`, and `printTable(_:)` has been modified to accept a `TabularDataSource`. Therefore, you can print your department. Add a call to `printTable(_:)`.

### Listing 19.9  Printing **Department**

```
...
var department = Department(name: "Engineering")
department.addPerson(Person(name: "Joe", age: 30, yearsOfExperience: 6))
department.addPerson(Person(name: "Karen", age: 40, yearsOfExperience: 18))
department.addPerson(Person(name: "Fred", age: 50, yearsOfExperience: 20))

printTable(department)
```

Confirm in the debug area that the output still reflects the `department` you created:

```
      | Age | Years of Experience |
Joe   | 30  |                   6 |
Karen | 40  |                  18 |
Fred  | 50  |                  20 |
```

# Protocol Conformance

As noted earlier, the syntax for protocol conformance looks exactly the same as the syntax you use to declare a class's superclass, as seen in Chapter 15. This brings up a few questions:

1. What types can conform to protocols?

2. Can a type conform to multiple protocols?

3. Can a class have a superclass and still conform to protocols?

All types can conform to protocols. You made a structure (`Department`) conform to a protocol. Enums and classes can also conform to protocols. The syntax for declaring that an enum conforms to a protocol is exactly the same as it is for a struct: a colon and the protocol name follow the declaration of the type. (Classes can be a little more complicated. We will get to them in a moment.)

It is also possible for a type to conform to multiple protocols. One of the protocols defined by Swift is named `CustomStringConvertible`, which types can implement when they want to control how their instances are converted into string representations. Other functions, like `print()`, will check to see if the values being printed conform to `CustomStringConvertible` when deciding how to display them. `CustomStringConvertible` has a single requirement: the type must have a gettable property named `description` that returns a `String`. Modify `Department` so that it conforms to both `TabularDataSource` and `CustomStringConvertible`, using a comma to separate the protocols.

### Listing 19.10  Conforming to **CustomStringConvertible**

```
...
struct Department: TabularDataSource, CustomStringConvertible {
    let name: String
    var people = [Person]()

    var description: String {
        return "Department (\(name))"
    }
...
}
```

Here, you implement `description` as a read-only, computed property. You can now see the name of your department when you print it.

### Listing 19.11  Printing the department's name

```
...
printTable(department)
print(department)
```

Finally, classes can also conform to protocols. If the class does not have a superclass, the syntax is the same as for structs and enums:

```
class ClassName: ProtocolOne, ProtocolTwo {
    // ...
}
```

If the class does have a superclass, the name of the superclass comes first, followed by the protocol (or protocols).

```
class ClassName: SuperClass, ProtocolOne, ProtocolTwo {
    // ...
}
```

# Protocol Inheritance

Swift supports *protocol inheritance*. A protocol that inherits from another protocol requires conforming types to provide implementations for all the properties and methods required by both itself and the protocol it inherits from. This is different from class inheritance, which defines a close relationship between the superclass and subclass. Protocol inheritance merely adds any requirements from the parent protocol to the child protocol. For example, modify **TabularDataSource** so that it inherits from the **CustomStringConvertible** protocol.

### Listing 19.12  Making **TabularDataSource** inherit from **CustomStringConvertible**

```
protocol TabularDataSource: CustomStringConvertible {
    var numberOfRows: Int { get }
    var numberOfColumns: Int { get }

    func labelForRow(row: Int) -> String
    func labelForColumn(column: Int) -> String

    func itemForRow(row: Int, column: Int) -> Int
}
...
```

Now, any type that conforms to **TabularDataSource** must also conform to **CustomStringConvertible**, meaning it has to supply all the properties and methods listed in **TabularDataSource** as well as the description property required by **CustomStringConvertible**. Make use of this in **printTable(_:)** to print a heading on the table. You will no longer need the call to **print()** you added in Listing 19.11, so delete it.

### Listing 19.13  Printing table heading

```
...
func printTable(dataSource: TabularDataSource) {
    print("Table: \(dataSource.description)")
    ...
}
...
printTable(department)
~~print(department)~~
```

Now the printout in your debug area includes a description of the table.

```
Table: Department (Engineering)
      | Age | Years of Experience |
Joe   | 30  |                   6 |
Karen | 40  |                  18 |
Fred  | 50  |                  20 |
```

Protocols are allowed to inherit from multiple other protocols, just as types can conform to multiple protocols. The syntax for multiple protocol inheritance is what you probably expect – separate additional parent protocols with commas, like so:

```
protocol MyProtocol: MyOtherProtocol, CustomStringConvertible {
    // ... requirements of MyProtocol
}
```

# Protocol Composition

Protocol inheritance is a powerful tool that lets you easily create a new protocol that adds requirements to an existing protocol or set of protocols. Nevertheless, using protocol inheritance can potentially lead you to make poor decisions in creating your types.

In fact, that is exactly what has happened with **TabularDataSource**. You made **TabularDataSource** inherit from **CustomStringConvertible** because you wanted to be able to print a description of the data source. (In fairness, you did it because we told you to.) But there is not anything inherently **CustomStringConvertible** about a tabular data source. Go back and fix that misguided attempt to print data sources.

### Listing 19.14  **TabularDataSource** should not be **CustomStringConvertible**

```
protocol TabularDataSource~~: CustomStringConvertible~~ {
    ...
}
```

The compiler now rightfully complains when you try to get the description of the data source passed to **printTable(_:)**. You can use *protocol composition* to solve this problem without polluting **TabularDataSource** with the unrelated requirement that it be convertible to a string. Protocol composition allows you to state that a type must conform to multiple protocols.

## Listing 19.15 Making **printTable**'s argument conform to **CustomStringConvertible**

```
...
func printTable(dataSource: TabularDataSource
                protocol<TabularDataSource, CustomStringConvertible>) {
    print("Table: \(dataSource.description)")
    ...
}
```

The syntax for protocol composition uses the keyword protocol to signal to the compiler that you are combining multiple protocols into a single requirement. You can use protocol composition with more than two protocols by adding additional protocols, separated by commas, inside the angle brackets (<>). The example above requires that dataSource conform to both **TabularDataSource** and **CustomStringConvertible**.

Consider another possibility. You could create a new protocol that inherits from both **TabularDataSource** and **CustomStringConvertible**, like so:

```
protocol PrintableTabularDataSource: TabularDataSource, CustomStringConvertible {
}
```

You could then use that protocol as the type of the argument to **printTable(_:)**. Both **PrintableTabularDataSource** and **protocol<TabularDataSource, CustomStringConvertible>** require conforming types to implement all properties and methods required by **TabularDataSource** and **CustomStringConvertible**. What is the difference between them?

The difference is that **PrintableTabularDataSource** is a distinct type. To use it, you would have to modify **Department** to state that it conforms to **PrintableTabularDataSource** – even though it already fulfills all the requirements. On the other hand, **protocol<TabularDataSource, CustomStringConvertible>** does not create a new type. It only indicates that **printTable(_:)**'s argument conforms to both of the protocols listed. So you do not have to go back and annotate **Department**. It already conforms to both **TabularDataSource** and **CustomStringConvertible**, so it also conforms to **protocol<TabularDataSource, CustomStringConvertible>**.

# Mutating Methods

Recall from Chapter 14 and Chapter 15 that methods on value types (structs and enums) cannot modify self unless the method is marked as mutating. Methods in protocols default to nonmutating. In the **Lightbulb** enum from Chapter 14, the **toggle()** method was mutating.

```
enum Lightbulb {
    case On
    case Off

    mutating func toggle() {
        switch self {
        case .On:
            self = .Off

        case .Off:
            self = .On
        }
    }
}
```

Suppose you want to define in a protocol that an instance is "toggleable":

```
protocol Toggleable {
    func toggle()
}
```

Declaring that **Lightbulb** conforms to **Toggleable** would result in a compiler error. The message you get includes a note that explains the problem:

```
error: type 'Lightbulb' does not conform to protocol 'Toggleable'

note: candidate is marked 'mutating' but protocol does not allow it
mutating func toggle() {
              ^
```

The note points out that in **Lightbulb**, the **toggle** method is marked as mutating, but the **Toggleable** protocol expects a nonmutating function. You can fix this problem by marking **toggle** as mutating in the protocol definition:

```
protocol Toggleable {
    mutating func toggle()
}
```

A class that conforms to the **Toggleable** protocol would not need to mark its **toggle** method as mutating. Methods on classes are always allowed to change properties of self because they are reference types.

## Silver Challenge

The **printTable(_:)** function has a bug – it crashes if any of the data items are longer than the label of their column. Try changing Joe's age to 1000 to see this in action. Fix the bug. (For an easier version of this challenge, just make the function not crash. For a harder version, make sure all the rows and columns of the table are still aligned correctly.)

## Gold Challenge

Create a new type, **BookCollection**, that conforms to **TabularDataSource**. Calling **printTable(_:)** on a book collection should show a table of books with columns for titles, authors, and average reviews on Amazon. (Unless all the books you use have very short titles and author names, you will need to have completed the previous challenge!)

# 20
# Error Handling

How often has a piece of software you have been using crashed or done something it was not supposed to do? The majority of the time, these issues are caused by incorrect error handling. Error handling is one of the unsung heroes of software development: Nobody thinks of it as a priority, and if it is done correctly nobody notices. But it is absolutely critical – users of your software will certainly notice (and complain!) if it is done poorly. In this chapter you will explore the tools that Swift provides to catch and handle errors.

## Classes of Errors

There are two broad categories of error that can occur: *recoverable errors* and *nonrecoverable errors*.

Recoverable errors are typically events that can occur that you must be ready for and handle. Common examples of recoverable errors are:

- trying to open a file that does not exist

- trying to communicate with a server that is down

- trying to communicate when a device does not have an Internet connection

Swift provides you with a rich set of tools for dealing with recoverable errors. You have become accustomed to Swift enforcing safety rules at compile time, and handling errors is no different. When you call a function that might fail with a recoverable error, Swift will require you to acknowledge and deal with that possibility.

Nonrecoverable errors are really just a special kind of bug. You have already encountered one: force-unwrapping an optional that contains `nil`. Another example is trying to access an element past the end of an array. These nonrecoverable errors will cause your program to trap.

Recall from Chapter 4 that when your program traps, it immediately stops executing. A trap is a low-level command to the OS to immediately stop the currently executing program. If you are running the program from Xcode, it will stop in the debugger and show you where the error occurred. For a user running your program, however, a trap looks the same as a crash – the program immediately shuts down.

Why is Swift so heavy-handed with this class of error? The name gives a hint: these errors are not recoverable, meaning there is nothing your program could do to fix the problem. Think about unwrapping an optional, for example. When you force-unwrap an optional, you expect to get a value, and the rest of your code is written assuming there is a value to work with. If the optional is nil, there is no value. The only reasonable thing Swift can do is immediately stop the program. If your program did continue, either it would crash when it tried to access a nonexistent value or, worse, it could continue to run but produce incorrect results. (Both of these possibilities come up in less-safe languages like C.)

In this chapter, you will build a very simple two-phase compiler. In doing so, you will implement a function that can evaluate basic mathematical expressions. For example, you will provide the input string "10 + 3 + 5", and the function will return the integer 18. Along the way, you will make use of Swift's facilities for dealing with both recoverable and nonrecoverable errors.

# Lexing an Input String

The first phase of your expression-evaluating compiler is *lexing*. Lexing is the process of turning some input into a sequence of *tokens*. A token is something with meaning, like a number or a plus sign (the two tokens your compiler will recognize). Lexing is sometimes referred to as "tokenizing" because you are turning some meaningless-to-the-compiler input (like a string) into a sequence of meaningful tokens.

Create a new playground named ErrorHandling. Define an enumeration that has cases for the two kinds of token.

### Listing 20.1  Declaring the **Token** type

```
import Cocoa

enum Token {
    case Number(Int)
    case Plus
}
```

Next, start building your lexer. To lex an input string, you will need to access the individual characters in the input string one by one. You will need to keep track of your current position in the collection of characters as well. Create the **Lexer** class and give it these two properties.

### Listing 20.2  Creating **Lexer**

```
import Cocoa

enum Token {
    case Number(Int)
    case Plus
}

class Lexer {
    let input: String.CharacterView
    var position: String.CharacterView.Index

    init(input: String) {
        self.input = input.characters
        self.position = self.input.startIndex
    }
}
```

Recall from Chapter 7 that every string has a `characters` property, which is a collection of **Character**s. The type of the `characters` property is **String.CharacterView**. Every **String.CharacterView** has `startIndex` and `endIndex` properties that let you step through the characters. You initialize the `input` property to the input **String**'s `characters` property and initialize the `position` property to the beginning of that character view.

Lexing the input characters is a straightforward process. The steps you will implement are outlined in Figure 20.1.

## Figure 20.1  Lexing algorithm

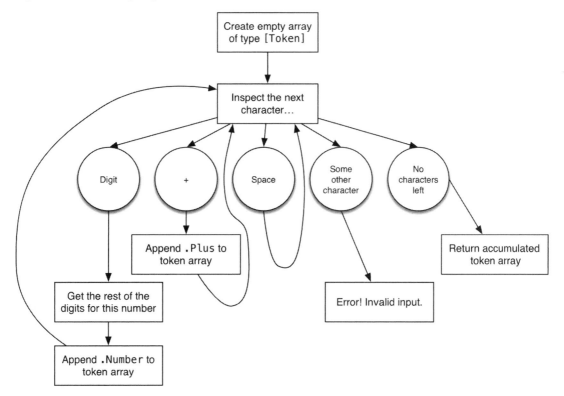

To implement this algorithm, **Lexer** will need two basic operations: a way to peek at the next character from the input and a way to advance the current position. Peeking at the next character requires a way to indicate that the lexer has reached the end of its input, so make it return an optional.

## Listing 20.3  Implementing **peek()**

```
...
class Lexer {
    let input: String.CharacterView
    var position: String.CharacterView.Index

    init(input: String) {
        self.input = input.characters
        self.position = self.input.startIndex
    }

    func peek() -> Character? {
        guard position < input.endIndex else {
            return nil
        }
        return input[position]
    }
}
```

You use a guard statement to ensure that you have not reached the end of the input, returning nil if you have. If there is still input remaining, you return the character at the current position.

Now that the lexer can peek at the current character, it also needs a way to advance to the next character. Advancing is actually very simple: just increment position.

## Listing 20.4  Implementing **advance()**

```
...
class Lexer {
    ...

    func peek() -> Character? {
        guard position < input.endIndex else {
            return nil
        }
        return input[position]
    }

    func advance() {
        ++position
    }
}
```

Before moving on, there is an opportunity here to introduce a check for a nonrecoverable error. As you implement the rest of **Lexer**, you will be calling **peek()** and **advance()**. **peek()** can be called any time, but **advance()** should only be called if you are not already at the end of the input. Add an *assertion* to **advance()** that checks for this condition.

## Listing 20.5  Adding an assertion to **advance()**

```
...
class Lexer {
    ...

    func advance() {
        assert(position < input.endIndex, "Cannot advance past the end!")
        ++position
    }
}
```

What does **assert(_:_:)** do? Its first argument is a condition to check. If the condition evaluates to true, nothing happens. If the condition evaluates to false, however, your program will trap in the debugger with the message you provide as the second argument.

Calls to the **assert(_:_:)** function will only be evaluated if your program is built in debug mode. Debug mode is the default when you are working in a playground or running a project in Xcode. Release mode is what Xcode uses when you build an app for submission to the App Store. Among other things, building in Release mode turns on a number of compiler optimizations and removes all calls to **assert(_:_:)**. If you want to keep your assertions around even in Release mode, you can use **precondition(_:_:)** instead. It takes the same arguments and has the same effect as **assert(_:_:)**, but it is not removed when your app is built for release.

Now that **Lexer** has the building blocks you need, it is time to start implementing the lexing algorithm. The output of lexing will be an array of **Token**s, but it is also possible for lexing to fail. To indicate that a function or method might emit an error, add the keyword throws after the parentheses containing the arguments. (This implementation of **lex()** is incomplete and will not compile, but you will finish it shortly.)

## Listing 20.6  Declaring the throwing **lex()** method

```
...
class Lexer {
    ...

    func advance() {
        assert(position < input.endIndex, "Cannot advance past the end!")
        ++position
    }

    func lex() throws -> [Token] {
        var tokens = [Token]()

        while let nextCharacter = peek() {
            switch nextCharacter {
            case "0" ... "9":
                // Start of a number - need to grab the rest

            case "+":
                tokens.append(.Plus)
                advance()

            case " ":
                // Just advance to ignore spaces
                advance()

            default:
                // Something unexpected - need to send back an error
            }
        }

        return tokens
    }
}
```

You have now implemented most of the lexing algorithm. You start by creating an array, tokens, that will hold every **Token** you lex. You use a while let condition to loop until you reach the end of the input. For each character you look at, you go into one of the four cases. You already implemented what to do if the character is a plus (append .Plus to tokens and then advance to the next character) or a space (ignore it and advance to the next character).

There are two cases left to implement. Let's start with the default case. If this case matches, then a character you were not expecting is next. That means you need to *throw* an error. In Swift, you use the throws keyword to send, or "throw," an error back to the caller.

What can you throw? You must throw an instance of a type that conforms to the **ErrorType** protocol. Most of the time, errors you want to throw will lend themselves to being defined as enumerations, and this is no exception.

Declare an enumeration nested inside the **Lexer** class that will let you express lexing errors.

### Listing 20.7  Declaring **Lexer.Error**

```
...
class Lexer {
    enum Error: ErrorType {
        case InvalidCharacter(Character)
    }

    let input: String.CharacterView
    var position: String.CharacterView.Index


    ...
}
```

If you Command-click on the **ErrorType** protocol, you will find that it is an empty protocol. That is, it does not require any properties or methods to be present. Any type you write can conform to **ErrorType** just by stating that it does, but enumerations are by far the most common **ErrorType**s.

Now that you have a throwable type, implement the **default** case in the **lex()** method to throw an instance of your new **Error** enum.

## Listing 20.8  Throwing an error

```
...
class Lexer {
    ...

    func lex() throws -> [Token] {
        var tokens = [Token]()

        while let nextCharacter = peek() {
            switch nextCharacter {
            case "0" ... "9":
                // Start of a number - need to grab the rest

            case "+":
                tokens.append(.Plus)
                advance()

            case " ":
                // Just advance to ignore spaces
                advance()

            default:
                // Something unexpected - need to send back an error
                throw Error.InvalidCharacter(nextCharacter)
            }
        }

        return tokens
    }
}
```

Like return, throw causes the function to immediately stop executing and go back to its caller.

Finally, the lexer needs to be able to extract integers from the input. Implement **getNumber()**, which builds up integers one digit at a time using the same **peek()** and **advance()** tools you are using in **lex()**. Next, update **lex()** by adding a call to **getNumber()** and appending the number to the array of tokens.

## Listing 20.9  Implementing **Lexer.getNumber()**

```
...
class Lexer {
    ...

    func getNumber() -> Int {
        var value = 0

        while let nextCharacter = peek() {
            switch nextCharacter {
            case "0" ... "9":
                // Another digit - add it into value
                let digitValue = Int(String(nextCharacter))!
                value = 10*value + digitValue
                advance()

            default:
                // A non-digit - go back to regular lexing
                return value
            }
        }

        return value
    }

    func lex() throws -> [Token] {
        var tokens = [Token]()

        while let nextCharacter = peek() {
            switch nextCharacter {
            case "0" ... "9":
                // Start of a number - need to grab the rest
                let value = getNumber()
                tokens.append(.Number(value))

            case "+":
                tokens.append(.Plus)
                advance()

            case " ":
                // Just advance to ignore spaces
                advance()

            default:
                throw Error.InvalidCharacter(nextCharacter)
            }
        }

        return tokens
    }
}
```

At this point, all your errors should be gone.

**getNumber()** loops over input characters, accumulating digits into a single integer value. Note that you do something we have cautioned against – force-unwrapping an optional – in `Int(String(nextCharacter))!`. However, it is perfectly safe in this case. Because you know `nextCharacter` contains a single digit, converting it to an **Int** will always succeed and never return nil. As soon as **getNumber()** encounters a character that is not a digit (or the end of the input), it stops and returns the accumulated value.

**Lexer** is complete! It is time to put it to the test. Write a new function that takes an input string and tries to lex it, and call it with a couple of trial inputs. (This function will not work quite yet – as you type it in, try to guess why.)

### Listing 20.10  Evaluating the lexer

```
...
func evaluate(input: String) {
    print("Evaluating: \(input)")
    let lexer = Lexer(input: input)
    let tokens = lexer.lex()
    print("Lexer output: \(tokens)")
}

evaluate("10 + 3 + 5")
evaluate("1 + 2 + abcdefg")
```

**evaluate(_:)** takes an input **String**, creates a **Lexer**, and lexes the input into **Token**s. But the compiler does not allow what you have entered. Note the error message on the line where you call **lex()**: `Call can throw, but it is not marked with 'try' and the error is not handled.` The compiler is telling you that because the **lex()** method is marked as `throws`, calls to **lex()** must be prepared to handle an error.

# Catching Errors

To handle errors, Swift uses a control construct you have not yet seen: `do` / `catch`, with at least one `try` statement inside of the do. We will explain in a moment. First, modify **evaluate(_:)** to use this control flow to handle errors coming from **lex()**.

### Listing 20.11  Error handling in **evaluate(_:)**

```
...
func evaluate(input: String) {
    print("Evaluating: \(input)")
    let lexer = Lexer(input: input)

    do {
        let tokens = try lexer.lex()
        print("Lexer output: \(tokens)")
    } catch {
        print("An error occurred: \(error)")
    }
}
```

What do all these new keywords mean? do introduces a new scope, much like an if statement. Inside of the do scope, you can write code as normal, like calling **print()**. In addition to that, you can call functions or methods that are marked as throws. Each such call must be indicated with the try keyword.

At the end of the do block, you write a catch block. If any of the try calls inside the do block throw an error, the catch block will run, with the thrown error value bound to the constant error.

You should now be seeing the output of running **evaluate(_:)**. (Make sure to show the debug area with Command-Shift-Y if it is not already open.)

```
Evaluating: 10 + 3 + 5
Lexer output: [Token.Number(10), Token.Plus,
               Token.Number(3), Token.Plus, Token.Number(5)]
Evaluating: 1 + 2 + abcdefg
An error occurred: Lexer.Error.InvalidCharacter("a")
```

The catch block you wrote above did not specify a particular kind of error, so it will catch any thrown **ErrorType**. You can add additional catch blocks to catch specific kinds of errors. In this case, you know that the lexer could throw a **Lexer.Error.InvalidCharacter** error, so add a catch block for it.

## Listing 20.12 Catching an **InvalidCharacter** error

```
...
func evaluate(input: String) {
    print("Evaluating: \(input)")
    let lexer = Lexer(input: input)

    do {
        let tokens = try lexer.lex()
        print("Lexer output: \(tokens)")
    } catch Lexer.Error.InvalidCharacter(let character) {
        print("Input contained an invalid character: \(character)")
    } catch {
        print("An error occurred: \(error)")
    }
}
```

You added a catch block that is specifically looking for the **Lexer.Error.InvalidCharacter** error. catch blocks support pattern matching, just like switch statements, so you were able to bind the invalid character to a constant for use within the catch block. You should see a more specific error message now:

```
Evaluating: 10 + 3 + 5
Lexer output: [Token.Number(10), Token.Plus,
               Token.Number(3), Token.Plus, Token.Number(5)]
Evaluating: 1 + 2 + abcdefg
Input contained an invalid character: a
```

Congratulations, the lexing phase of your compiler is complete! Before moving on to parsing, delete the call to **evaluate(_:)** that is causing an error.

## Listing 20.13 Removing bad input

```
...
evaluate("10 + 3 + 5")
evaluate("1 + 2 + abcdefg")
```

# Parsing the Token Array

Now that your lexer is complete, you can turn an input string into an array of **Token**s, each of which is either a **.Number** or a **.Plus**. The algorithm to parse this sequence of tokens is more restrictive than the algorithm you used for lexing, because the order in which the tokens appear is very important. The rules are:

- The first token must be a number.

- After parsing a number, either the parser must be at the end of input, or the next token must be **.Plus**.

- After parsing a **.Plus**, the next token must be a number.

The setup of your parser will be very similar to the lexer, although a bit simpler. The parser does not need separate **peek()** and **advance()** methods. They can be combined into one **getNextToken()** method that returns the next **Token** or nil if all tokens have been consumed.

Create the **Parser** class and implement **getNextToken()**.

### Listing 20.14  Beginning the implementation of **Parser**

```
...
class Lexer {
    ...
}

class Parser {
    let tokens: [Token]
    var position = 0

    init(tokens: [Token]) {
        self.tokens = tokens
    }

    func getNextToken() -> Token? {
        guard position < tokens.count else {
            return nil
        }
        return tokens[position++]
    }
}
...
```

A **Parser** is initialized with an array of tokens and begins with a position of 0. The **getNextToken()** uses guard to check that there are more tokens remaining, and if there are, returns the next one.

Two of the three rules for our parser used the phrase "must be a number." A good place to start implementing the parser is with a method to get a number. If the next token must be a number, there are two different error cases that need to be considered. The parser might be at the end of the token array, which means there is no number left. Or the next token might be a **.Plus** instead of a number. For example, someone may have fed the parser the input string "10 + + 5".

Define an error enumeration conforming to **ErrorType** for both of these cases.

## Listing 20.15  Defining possible **Parser** errors

```
...
class Parser {
    enum Error: ErrorType {
        case UnexpectedEndOfInput
        case InvalidToken(Token)
    }

    let tokens: [Token]
    var position = 0

    ...
}
...
```

Now that you can express the possible errors you might encounter when trying to get a number, add a method that gets the value of the next **.Number** token or throws an error if it cannot.

## Listing 20.16  Implementing **Parser.getNumber()**

```
...
class Parser {

    ...

    func getNextToken() -> Token? {
        guard position < tokens.count else {
            return nil
        }
        return tokens[position++]
    }

    func getNumber() throws -> Int {
        guard let token = getNextToken() else {
            throw Error.UnexpectedEndOfInput
        }

        switch token {
        case .Number(let value):
            return value
        case .Plus:
            throw Error.InvalidToken(token)
        }
    }
}
...
```

The **getNumber()** method has the signature throws -> Int, so you know it is a function that normally returns an **Int** but could throw an error. You use a guard statement to check that there is at least one more token available. Note that inside the else block of a guard, you can use throw instead of return: guard just requires that its else block causes the function to stop executing and return to its caller. After ensuring that you have a token, you use a switch statement to either extract the number's value (if the token is a **.Number**) or throw an **InvalidToken** error (if it is a **.Plus**).

Now that you have **getNumber()**, implementing the rest of the parsing algorithm is straightforward. Add a **parse()** method that does just that.

## Listing 20.17 Implementing **Parser.parse()**

```
...
class Parser {
    ...

    func parse() throws -> Int {
        // Require a number first
        var value = try getNumber()

        while let token = getNextToken() {
            switch token {

            // Getting a Plus after a Number is legal
            case .Plus:
                // After a plus, we must get another number
                let nextNumber = try getNumber()
                value += nextNumber

            // Getting a Number after a Number is not legal
            case .Number:
                throw Error.InvalidToken(token)
            }
        }

        return value
    }
}
...
```

Your implementation of **parse()** matches the algorithm outlined above for parsing. The input must start with a number (the initialization of value). After parsing a number, you enter a loop over the rest of the tokens. If the next token is **.Plus**, then you require that the *next* token is a **.Number**. Once you get to the end of the tokens, the while loop ends and you return value.

There is something new here, though. You mark the calls to **getNumber()** with the try keyword, which Swift requires because **getNumber()** is a throwing method. However, you do not use a do / catch block. Why does Swift allow you to use try outside of a do block?

Swift requires that any call marked with try "handles the error." It would be easy to assume that "handling the error" means catching the error, like you did in **evaluate(_:)**. But there is another perfectly reasonable way to handle an error: throw it again! That is what happens in this case. Because **parse()** is itself a throwing method, you are allowed to try calls within it outside of a do / catch. If any of the try calls fail, the error is "rethrown" out of **parse()**.

Your parser is now complete. Update **evaluate(_:)** to call the parser and to handle the specific errors that **Parser** might throw.

## Listing 20.18  Updating **evaluate(_:)** to use **Parser**

```
...
func evaluate(input: String) {
    print("Evaluating: \(input)")
    let lexer = Lexer(input: input)

    do {
        let tokens = try lexer.lex()
        print("Lexer output: \(tokens)")

        let parser = Parser(tokens: tokens)
        let result = try parser.parse()
        print("Parser output: \(result)")
    } catch Lexer.Error.InvalidCharacter(let character) {
        print("Input contained an invalid character: \(character)")
    } catch Parser.Error.UnexpectedEndOfInput {
        print("Unexpected end of input during parsing")
    } catch Parser.Error.InvalidToken(let token) {
        print("Invalid token during parsing: \(token)")
    } catch {
        print("An error occurred: \(error)")
    }
}
...
```

You should now see your two-phase compiler successfully evaluating the input expression:

```
Evaluating: 10 + 3 + 5
Lexer output: [Token.Number(10), Token.Plus,
               Token.Number(3), Token.Plus, Token.Number(5)]
Parser output: 18
```

Try changing the input. Add more or fewer numbers. Try some inputs that will pass your lexer (i.e., that only contain legal tokens) but should cause your parser to throw errors. A couple of simple examples are "10 + 3 5" and "10 + ".

# Handling Errors by Sticking Your Head in the Sand

You have seen that every call to a function that might throw an error must be marked with `try` and that any call with `try` must either be inside a do / catch block or inside a function that itself is marked with `throws`. These rules work together to make sure you are handling any potential errors. Try modifying your **evaluate(_:)** function to break one of these rules.

Listing 20.19  Modifying **evaluate(_:)** illegally

```
...
func evaluate(input: String) {
    print("Evaluating: \(input)")
    let lexer = Lexer(input: input)
    let tokens = try lexer.lex()

    do {
        let tokens = try lexer.lex()
        print("Lexer output: \(tokens)")

        let parser = Parser(tokens: tokens)
        let result = try parser.parse()
        print("Parser output: \(result)")
    } catch Lexer.Error.InvalidCharacter(let character) {
        print("Input contained an invalid character: \(character)")
    } catch Parser.Error.UnexpectedEndOfInput {
        print("Unexpected end of input during parsing")
    } catch Parser.Error.InvalidToken(let token) {
        print("Invalid token during parsing: \(token)")
    } catch {
        print("An error occurred: \(error)")
    }
}
...
```

You moved the `try lexer.lex()` call outside of the do block, so now the compiler is giving you an error. The compiler error says that "Errors thrown from here are not handled." It is possible to tell the Swift compiler that you do not want to handle potential errors. Change `try` to `try!` to see this in action.

Listing 20.20  Using `try!` in **evaluate(_:)**

```
...
func evaluate(input: String) {
    print("Evaluating: \(input)")
    let lexer = Lexer(input: input)
    let tokens = trytry! lexer.lex()

    ...
}
...
```

Your code now compiles, but you should be concerned. What is Swift going to do if an error is thrown by `lexer.lex()`? The exclamation mark at the end of the `try!` keyword should be a big hint. Just like force-unwrapping an optional, using the forceful keyword `try!` will cause your program to trap if an error is thrown.

Earlier, you had a call to **evaluate(_:)** that caused the lexer to throw an error. Add that call back in and see what happens.

## Listing 20.21 Lexing bad input with `try!`

```
...
evaluate("10 + 3 + 5")
evaluate("1 + 2 + abcdefg")
```

Instead of seeing the invalid token error message, your program now traps on the `try! lexer.lex()` line.

We recommended avoiding force-unwrapping optionals and implicitly unwrapped optionals. We even more strongly recommend avoiding `try!`. You should only use `try!` when there is no way for your program to handle an error and you really do want your program to trap (or crash, if it is running on a user's device) if an error occurs.

There is a third variant of `try` that lets you ignore the error without trapping if an error occurs. You can call a throwing function with `try?`, getting a return value that is an optional of whatever type the function usually returns. This means you need to use something like `guard` to check that the optional really contains a value.

Change your trapping `try!` into a combination of `guard` and `try?`.

## Listing 20.22 Using `try?` in **evaluate(_:)**

```
...
func evaluate(input: String) {
    print("Evaluating: \(input)")
    let lexer = Lexer(input: input)
    let tokens = try! lexer.lex()
    guard let tokens = try? lexer.lex() else {
        print("Lexing failed, but I don't know why")
        return
    }

    ...
}
...
```

`try?` is not as evil as `try!`, but we still recommend avoiding it most of the time. When you call a function with `try?`, you have to handle the possibility of getting back nil. You use a `guard` to return from **evaluate(_:)**. However, it is usually better to handle any errors in a `catch`, because you will have access to the error that the function threw.

`try?` will be most useful when you have a meaningful alternative to use when the function you are calling fails. **evaluate(_:)** does not have such an alternative, so restore it to its previous error-handling glory.

## Listing 20.23  Restoring **evaluate(_:)**

```
...
func evaluate(input: String) {
    print("Evaluating: \(input)")
    let lexer = Lexer(input: input)
    guard let tokens = try? lexer.lex() else {
        print("Lexing failed, but I don't know why")
        return
    }

    do {
        let tokens = try lexer.lex()
        print("Lexer output: \(tokens)")

        let parser = Parser(tokens: tokens)
        let result = try parser.parse()
        print("Parser output: \(result)")
    } catch Lexer.Error.InvalidCharacter(let character) {
        print("Input contained an invalid character: \(character)")
    } catch Parser.Error.UnexpectedEndOfInput {
        print("Unexpected end of input during parsing")
    } catch Parser.Error.InvalidToken(let token) {
        print("Invalid token during parsing: \(token)")
    } catch {
        print("An error occurred: \(error)")
    }
}
...
```

# Swift Error Handling Philosophy

Swift is designed to encourage safe, easy-to-read code, and its error-handling system is no different. Any function that could fail must be marked with throws. This makes it obvious from the type of a function whether or not you need to handle potential errors.

Swift also requires you to mark all calls to functions that might fail with try. This gives a great benefit to anyone reading Swift code. If a function call is annotated with try, you know it is a potential source of errors that must be handled. If a function call is not annotated with try, you know it will never emit errors that you need to handle.

If you have used C++ or Java, it is important to note the differences between Swift error handling and exception-based error handling. Even though Swift uses some of the same terminology, particularly try, catch, and throw, Swift does not implement error handling using exceptions. When you mark a function with throws, that effectively changes its return type from whatever type it normally returns to "either whatever type it normally returns or an instance of **ErrorType**."

Finally, there is one other important philosophical error-handling decision built into Swift. A function that throws does *not* state what kinds of errors it might throw. This has two practical impacts. First, you are always free to add more potential **ErrorType**s that a function might throw without changing the API of the function. Second, when you are handling errors with catch, you must always be prepared to handle an error of some unknown type.

The compiler enforces this second point. Try modifying **evaluate(_:)** by removing the final catch block.

## Listing 20.24  Avoid handling unknown **ErrorTypes** in **evaluate(_:)**

```
...
func evaluate(input: String) {
    print("Evaluating: \(input)")
    let lexer = Lexer(input: input)

    do {
        let tokens = try lexer.lex()
        print("Lexer output: \(tokens)")

        let parser = Parser(tokens: tokens)
        let result = try parser.parse()
        print("Parser output: \(result)")
    } catch Lexer.Error.InvalidCharacter(let character) {
        print("Input contained an invalid character: \(character)")
    } catch Parser.Error.UnexpectedEndOfInput {
        print("Unexpected end of input during parsing")
    } catch Parser.Error.InvalidToken(let token) {
        print("Invalid token during parsing: \(token)")
    } catch {
        print("An error occurred: \(error)")
    }
}
...
```

The compiler is now giving you errors on both lines in the do block where you made try calls. The error message should sound familiar: "Errors thrown from here are not handled because the enclosing catch is not exhaustive." As it does for switch statements, Swift performs exhaustiveness checks on your do / catch blocks, requiring you to handle any potential **ErrorType**.

Fix **evaluate(_:)** by restoring the catch block that will handle any error.

## Listing 20.25  Exhaustive error handling in **evaluate(_:)**

```
...
func evaluate(input: String) {
    print("Evaluating: \(input)")
    let lexer = Lexer(input: input)

    do {
        let tokens = try lexer.lex()
        print("Lexer output: \(tokens)")

        let parser = Parser(tokens: tokens)
        let result = try parser.parse()
        print("Parser output: \(result)")
    } catch Lexer.Error.InvalidCharacter(let character) {
        print("Input contained an invalid character: \(character)")
    } catch Parser.Error.UnexpectedEndOfInput {
        print("Unexpected end of input during parsing")
    } catch Parser.Error.InvalidToken(let token) {
        print("Invalid token during parsing: \(token)")
    } catch {
        print("An error occurred: \(error)")
    }
}
...
```

# Bronze Challenge

Your expression evaluator currently only supports addition. That is not very useful! Add support for subtraction. You should be able to call evaluate("10 + 5 - 3 - 1") and see it output 11.

# Silver Challenge

The error messages printed out by **evaluate(_:)** are useful, but not as useful as they could be. Here are a couple of erroneous inputs and the error messages they produce:

```
evaluate("1 + 3 + 7a + 8")
> Input contained an invalid character: a

evaluate("10 + 3 3 + 7")
> Invalid token during parsing: .Number(3)
```

Make these messages more helpful by including the character position where the error occurred. After completing this challenge, you should see error messages like this:

```
evaluate("1 + 3 + 7a + 8")
> Input contained an invalid character at index 9: a

evaluate("10 + 3 3 + 7")
> Invalid token during parsing at index 7: 3
```

Hint: Printing a **String.CharacterView.Index** will show the character position corresponding to that index. You will need to associate a **String.CharacterView.Index** with the error cases. You will also need to give the parser enough information for it to be able to report the index of a token.

# Gold Challenge

Time to step it up a notch. Add support for multiplication and division to your calculator. If you think this will be as easy as adding subtraction, think again! Your evaluator should give higher precedence to multiplication and division than it does for addition and subtraction. Here are some sample inputs and their expected output.

```
evaluate("10 * 3 + 5 * 3") // Should print 45
evaluate("10 + 3 * 5 + 3") // Should print 28
evaluate("10 + 3 * 5 * 3") // Should print 55
```

If you get stuck, try researching "recursive descent parsers." That is the kind of parser you have been implementing. Here is a hint to get you started: instead of parsing a single number and then expecting a .Plus or .Minus, try parsing a term computed from numbers and multiplication / division operators, and *then* expecting a .Plus or .Minus.

# 21

# Extensions

Imagine that you are developing an application that uses a particular type in the Swift standard library – say the **Double** type – quite frequently. It would make your development easier if the **Double** type supported some additional methods based on how you are using it in your app. Unfortunately, you do not have **Double**'s implementation available, so you cannot add functionality directly to it yourself. What can you do?

Swift provides a feature called *extensions* that is designed for just these cases. Extensions allow you to add functionality to an existing type. You can extend structs, enums, and classes.

You can use extensions to extend types with:

- computed properties

- new initializers

- protocol conformance

- new methods

- embedded types

In this chapter you will use extensions to add functionality to an existing type whose definition and implementation details are not available to you. You will also use extensions to add functionality to a custom type of your own creation. In both cases you will add functionality to these types in a modular fashion, meaning that you will group like functionality in a single extension.

## Extending an Existing Type

Create a new playground named Extensions.playground. You will be modeling the behavior of a car in this playground.

Velocity is an important characteristic of any vehicle. Because velocity can have decimal values, it is reasonable to represent it as a **Double**.

Given that you will be using the **Double** type frequently, it would be useful to refer to it in a way that is contextually relevant. Swift's typealias keyword provides a way to give another name to an existing type. Give the **Double** type an alternate name.

### Listing 21.1 Establishing a type alias

```
typealias Velocity = Double
```

The `typealias` keyword allows you to define **Velocity** as an alternative type name for **Double**. This interchangeability will help to contextualize **Double** in the extensions you will write in this chapter by making it more relevant to your use.

Now that you have a `typealias` set up, extend the type to support conversion between commonly used units for speed. Swift's extensions do not allow you to add stored properties to a type. You will use an extension to add two computed properties.

### Listing 21.2 Extending **Velocity** to support mph and kph

```
typealias Velocity = Double
extension Velocity {
    var kph: Velocity { return self * 1.60934 }
    var mph: Velocity { return self }
}
```

The `extension` keyword signifies that you are extending the **Velocity** type. You add two computed properties to **Velocity**: kph and mph. These properties on **Velocity** represent a vehicle's speed in kilometers per hour (kph) and miles per hour (mph). Note that the extension treats mph as the default unit: that computed property simply returns self, while kph performs the conversion.

While the interchangeability provided by a `typealias` can be a benefit, it can also be a bit tricky. You may encounter a case in this file where you will want to use the **Double** type and not the **Velocity** type. Because **Velocity** can be used interchangeably with **Double**, the extension you defined on **Velocity** is also available for the **Double** type. Adding the extension to **Double** using the **Velocity** typealias gives helpful context. It documents that the computed properties are only meaningful when used with the **Velocity** typealias, even though they are available to all **Double**s.

Recall that one of the goals of this chapter is to define the behavior of a vehicle. Protocols are one of Swift's most helpful features for defining the interface for a type. You can add protocol conformance to a type with an extension.

Create a new protocol called **VehicleType** to describe some of the basic characteristics of a vehicle.

### Listing 21.3 Adding protocol conformance with an extension

```
typealias Velocity = Double

extension Velocity {
    var kph: Velocity { return self * 1.60934 }
    var mph: Velocity { return self }
}
protocol VehicleType {
    var topSpeed: Velocity { get }
    var numberOfDoors: Int { get }
    var hasFlatbed: Bool { get }
}
```

**VehicleType** declares three properties: topSpeed, numberOfDoors, and hasFlatbed. Each property only requires the conforming type to implement a getter for the property. A type conforming to this protocol will be required to provide these properties, which describe some general characteristics of a vehicle.

# Extending Your Own Type

You will need to create a new type before you can add protocol conformance to it through an extension. Make a new struct to represent a **Car** type. You will later use an extension on **Car** to add conformance to the **VehicleType** protocol.

### Listing 21.4  A **Car** struct

```
typealias Velocity = Double

extension Velocity {
    var kph: Velocity { return self * 1.60934 }
    var mph: Velocity { return self }
}

protocol VehicleType {
    var topSpeed: Velocity { get }
    var numberOfDoors: Int { get }
    var hasFlatbed: Bool { get }
}
struct Car {
    let make: String
    let model: String
    let year: Int
    let color: String
    let nickname: String
    var gasLevel: Double {
        willSet {
            precondition(newValue <= 1.0 && newValue >= 0.0,
                         "New value must be between 0 and 1.")
        }
    }
}
```

Here you define a new struct called **Car**. The **Car** type defines a number of stored properties that will be specific to a given instance. All of the properties are constants, with one exception: gasLevel.

gasLevel is a mutable stored property with a property observer on it. The willSet observer will be called every time you are going to set a new value for gasLevel. You use a **precondition()** inside of this implementation to ensure that the newValue being assigned to the gasLevel property is between 0 and 1. These values indicate how full an instance's gas tank is in terms of percentage points.

## Use extensions to add protocol conformance

Extensions can provide a great mechanism to group related chunks of functionality. Grouping related pieces of functionality in a single extension can help to make your code more readable and maintainable. This pattern also helps a type keep its interface uncluttered.

Extend the **Car** type to conform to the **VehicleType** protocol.

## Listing 21.5  Extending **Car** to conform to **VehicleType**

```
...
struct Car {
    let make: String
    let model: String
    let year: Int
    let color: String
    let nickname: String
    var gasLevel: Double {
        willSet {
            precondition(newValue <= 1.0 && newValue > 0.0,
                         "New value must be between 0 and 1.")
        }
    }
}
extension Car: VehicleType {
    var topSpeed: Velocity { return 180 }
    var numberOfDoors: Int { return 4 }
    var hasFlatbed: Bool { return false }
}
```

Your new extension extends **Car** to conform to **VehicleType**. The syntax for conforming to a protocol is the same as you have seen before, but this time you use an extension to accomplish this protocol conformance: extension Car: VehicleType.

You implement the protocol's required properties inside of the extension's body. Each property is given a simple getter. For the sake of convenience, you simply return some default values for each of the protocol's properties.

# Adding an initializer with an extension

Recall that structs give you a free memberwise initializer if you do not provide your own. If you want to write a new initializer for your struct, but do not want to lose the memberwise initializer, you can add the initializer to your type with an extension. Add an initializer to **Car** in a new extension on the type.

## Listing 21.6  Extending **Car** with an initializer

```
...
extension Car: VehicleType {
    var topSpeed: Velocity { return 180 }
    var numberOfDoors: Int { return 4 }
    var hasFlatbed: Bool { return false }
}
extension Car {
    init(carMake: String, carModel: String, carYear: Int) {
        self.init(make: carMake,
            model: carModel,
            year: carYear,
            color: "Black",
            nickname: "N/A",
            gasLevel: 1.0)
    }
}
```

The new extension on the **Car** type adds an initializer that accepts arguments only for an instance's make, model, and year. This new initializer's arguments are passed into the free memberwise initializer on the **Car** struct, and you also provide default values for the missing arguments. The combination of these two initializers ensures that an instance of the **Car** type will have values for all of its properties.

The memberwise initializer is preserved on **Car** because the new initializer is defined and implemented on an extension. This pattern can be quite helpful.

To see the new initializer defined in the extension work, create an instance of **Car**.

Listing 21.7  An instance of **Car**

```
...
extension Car {
    init(carMake: String, carModel: String, carYear: Int) {
        self.init(make: carMake,
            model: carModel,
            year: carYear,
            color: "Black",
            nickname: "N/A",
            gasLevel: 1.0)
    }
}
var c = Car(carMake: "Ford", carModel: "Fusion", carYear: 2013)
```

The code above creates a new instance c. This instance is created with the initializer defined in an extension on **Car**. Take a look in the results sidebar. You should see that c's properties have the values you gave to the new initializer. The default values you gave to the memberwise initializer should be visible as well.

## Nested types and extensions

Swift's extensions can also add nested types to an existing type. Say, for example, that you want to add an enumeration to your **Car** struct to help classify the kind of car an instance might be. Create a new extension on the **Car** type to add a nested type.

Listing 21.8  Creating an extension with a nested type

```
...
var c = Car(carMake: "Ford", carModel: "Fusion", carYear: 2013)
extension Car {
    enum CarKind: CustomStringConvertible {
        case Coupe, Sedan
        var description: String {
            switch self {
            case .Coupe:
                return "Coupe"

            case .Sedan:
                return "Sedan"
            }
        }
    }
    var kind: CarKind {
        if numberOfDoors == 2 {
            return .Coupe
        } else {
            return .Sedan
        }
    }
}
```

This new extension on **Car** adds a nested type called **CarKind**. **CarKind** is an enumeration that has two cases: one for a Coupe and one for a Sedan. The extension also adds a computed property on **Car** called kind, which will represent the kind of car. The nested type also conforms to the **CustomStringConvertible** protocol to facilitate logging information.

kind returns values of the nested enumeration based on how many doors the instance has: if the instance has two doors, then it is a coupe; otherwise, it is a sedan.

Exercise the new nested type in the extension by accessing the computed property kind on the instance you created before.

## Listing 21.9 Accessing kind

```
...
extension Car {
    enum CarKind: CustomStringConvertible {
        case Coupe, Sedan
        var description: String {
            switch self {
            case .Coupe:
                return "Coupe"

            case .Sedan:
                return "Sedan"
            }
        }
    }
    var kind: CarKind {
        if numberOfDoors == 2 {
            return .Coupe
        } else {
            return .Sedan
        }
    }
}
c.kind.description
```

You should see "Sedan" logged to the results sidebar.

# Extensions with functions

You can use an extension to give an existing type a function. For example, you may have noticed that **Car** does not have a function to fill its gas. Make an extension to add this functionality to **Car**.

Listing 21.10  Using an extension to add functions

```
...
c.kind.description
extension Car {
    mutating func emptyGas(amount: Double) {
        precondition(amount <= 1 && amount > 0,
                    "Amount to remove must be between 0 and 1.")
        gasLevel -= amount
    }

    mutating func fillGas() {
        gasLevel = 1.0
    }
}
```

Your new extension adds two functions to the **Car** type: **emptyGas()** and **fillGas()**. Note that both functions are marked with the mutating keyword. Why? Remember that the **Car** type is a struct. If a function wants to change the value of any of the struct's properties, then it must be declared with the mutating keyword.

The **emptyGas()** function takes one argument: the amount of gas to remove from the tank. You use a **precondition** inside of the **emptyGas()** function to ensure that the amount removed from the tank is between 0 and 1. The implementation of the **fillGas()** function simply sets the gasLevel property on the **Car** to be full, or 1.0.

Exercise these new functions on your existing type.

Listing 21.11  Lowering and filling the gas tank

```
extension Car {
    mutating func emptyGas(amount: Double) {
        precondition(amount <= 1 && amount > 0,
                    "Amount to remove must be between 0 and 1.")
        gasLevel -= amount
    }

    mutating func fillGas() {
        gasLevel = 1.0
    }
}
c.emptyGas(0.3)
c.gasLevel
c.fillGas()
c.gasLevel
```

After you use the **emptyGas()** function, you should see that the gas level is 0.7 in the sidebar. After you fill the gas level, you see that the gas level is now 1.0.

# Bronze Challenge

Extend the **Int** type to have a `timesFive` computed property. The computed property should return the result of multiplying the integer by 5. You should be able to use it like so:

```
5.timesFive // 25
```

# Bronze Challenge

Sometimes you write code that looks and feels right at the time, but in using it later find that something is not quite right. This is the case with the `extension` you used to make **Car** conform to **VehicleType**.

When you made **Car** conform to the **VehicleType** protocol, you added a `numberOfDoors` computed property that always returns 4. This effectively makes `numberOfDoors` a constant on **Car**. As a consequence, the if/else condition in `kind` will always return `.Sedan`. There is no other possibility due to how **Car** conforms to **VehicleType**.

Refactor **Car** to have a constant stored property named `numberOfDoors`. Note: this change will mean that you need to make other changes. Use the new compiler errors to guide your solution.

# Silver Challenge

The **emptyGas()** method has some bugs. For example, if the current `gasLevel` is less than the amount to remove, then the new value for this property will be negative. A negative value does not make sense, and will actually stop the program from running (recall the **precondition()** in `gasLevel`'s property observer). Revise **emptyGas()**'s implementation to ensure that `gasLevel` is not decremented to be a negative value.

# 22

# Generics

So far, all the properties and functions you have written have worked on concrete types like **Int**, **String**, and **Monster**. You may have noticed, however, that Swift allows you to create arrays that contain any type at all. You can create arrays of built-in Swift types, like **[Int]** and **[Double]**, as well as arrays of types you create, like **[Monster]** and **[Person]**. How is **Array** implemented? How can you write code that can work with a variety of types in the same way? The answer to both of these questions is "generics."

Swift *generics* allow you to write types and functions that make use of types that are not yet known to you or the compiler. Many of the built-in types you have used throughout this book, including optionals, arrays, and dictionaries, are implemented using generics. In this chapter, you will investigate how to write generic types (much like an array). You will also see how you can use generics to write flexible functions and how generics are related to protocols.

## Generic Data Structures

You are going to create a generic *stack*, which is a venerable data structure in computer science. A stack is a last-in, first-out (LIFO) data structure. It supports two basic operations. You can *push* an item onto the stack, which adds the item to the stack, and you can *pop* to remove the most recently pushed item off of the stack.

To begin, create a new playground called `Generics.playground` and make a **Stack** structure that only stores integers.

Listing 22.1  Setting up a **Stack**

```
struct Stack {
    var items = [Int]()

    mutating func push(newItem: Int) {
        items.append(newItem)
    }

    mutating func pop() -> Int? {
        guard !items.isEmpty else {
            return nil
        }
        return items.removeLast()
    }
}
```

This struct has three elements of interest. The items stored property is an array you are using to hold on to the items currently in a stack. The **push(_:)** method pushes a new item onto the stack by appending it to the end of the items array. Finally, the **pop()** method pops the top item off of the stack by calling the **removeLast()** method of an array, which simultaneously removes the last item and returns it. Note that **pop()** returns an optional **Int** because the stack might be empty (in which case there is nothing to pop).

Create a **Stack** instance to see it in action.

## Listing 22.2  Creating an instance of **Stack**

```
...
var intStack = Stack()
intStack.push(1)
intStack.push(2)

print(intStack.pop()) // Prints Optional(2)
print(intStack.pop()) // Prints Optional(1)
print(intStack.pop()) // Prints nil
```

You create a new **Stack** instance, push two values on, then try to pop three values off. As expected, the **pop** calls return the integers you pushed in reverse order, and **pop** returns nil when the stack no longer has any items left.

Now, modify **Stack** to be a generic data structure that can hold any type, not just **Int**:

## Listing 22.3  Making **Stack** generic

```
struct Stack<Element> {
    var items = [Int]()[Element]()

    mutating func push(newItem: IntElement) {
        items.append(newItem)
    }

    mutating func pop() -> Int?Element? {
        guard !items.isEmpty else {
            return nil
        }
        return items.removeLast()
    }
}
...
```

You add a *placeholder type*, named **Element**, to the declaration of **Stack**. Swift's syntax for declaring a generic uses angle brackets (<>) and immediately follows the name of the type. The name between the angle brackets represents the placeholder type: <Element>. The placeholder type Element can be used inside the **Stack** structure anywhere a concrete type could be used. You can see this usage as you replaced all of the occurrences of **Int** with **Element**, including in a property declaration, the type of the argument in **push(_:)**, and the type of the return value of **pop()**.

There is now a compiler error where you create a **Stack** because you have not specified what type should be substituted for the placeholder type **Element**. The process of the compiler substituting a concrete type for a placeholder is called *specialization*. Fix the error by specifying that intStack should be an instance of **Stack** specialized for **Int**. You will use the same angle bracket syntax to do this.

### Listing 22.4  Specializing intStack

```
...
var intStack = Stack<Int>()
...
```

This resolves the compiler error.

You can now create **Stack**s of any kind of type. Create a **Stack** of **String**s.

### Listing 22.5  Creating a **Stack** of strings

```
...
print(intStack.pop()) // Prints Optional(1)
print(intStack.pop()) // Prints nil

var stringStack = Stack<String>()
stringStack.push("this is a string")
stringStack.push("another string")

print(stringStack.pop()) // Prints Optional("another string")
```

It is important to note that even though intStack and stringStack are both **Stack** instances, they do not have the same type. intStack is a **Stack<Int>**; it would be a compile-time error to pass anything other than an **Int** to **intStack.push(_:)**. Likewise, stringStack is a **Stack<String>**, which is distinct from **Stack<Int>**.

Generic data structures are both common and extremely useful. Classes and enumerations can also be made generic using the same syntax as you used here for structures. In addition, types are not the only element of Swift that can be generic. Functions and methods can also be generic.

## Generic Functions and Methods

Remember the **map(_:)** method defined on **Array** from Chapter 13? **map(_:)** applies a closure to each element in the array and returns an array of the results. Given what you just learned about generics, you can now implement a version of this function yourself. Add the following code to your playground.

### Listing 22.6  Your own map function

```
...
func myMap<T,U>(items: [T], f: (T) -> (U)) -> [U] {
    var result = [U]()
    for item in items {
        result.append(f(item))
    }
    return result
}
```

The declaration of `myMap(_:f:)` may look pretty ugly if you have not been exposed to generics in other languages. Instead of the concrete types you are familiar with, it just has **T** and **U**, and there are more symbol and punctuation characters than letters! But the only new thing is that it declares two placeholder types, **T** and **U**, not just one. Figure 22.1 shows a breakdown of that line:

## Figure 22.1 myMap declaration

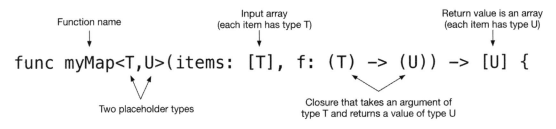

`myMap(_:f:)` can be used the same way `map(_:)` is used. Create an array of strings, then map it to an array of their character view's lengths.

## Listing 22.7 Mapping arrays

```
...
func myMap<T,U>(items: [T], f: (T) -> (U)) -> [U] {
    ...
}

let strings = ["one", "two", "three"]
let stringLengths = myMap(strings) { $0.characters.count }
print(stringLengths) // Prints [3, 3, 5]
```

The closure passed to `myMap(_:f:)` must take a single argument that matches the type contained in the `items` array, but the type of its return value can be anything. In this call to `myMap(_:f:)`, **T** is replaced by **String** and **U** is replaced by **Int**. (Note that in real projects there is no need to declare your own mapping function – just use the built-in `map(_:)`.)

Methods can also be generic, even inside of types that are already themselves generic. The **myMap(_:f:)** function you wrote only works on arrays, but it seems reasonable to want to map a **Stack**. Create a **map(_:)** method on **Stack**.

## Listing 22.8 Mapping on a **Stack**

```
struct Stack<Element> {
    var items = [Element]()

    mutating func push(newItem: Element) {
        items.append(newItem)
    }

    mutating func pop() -> Element? {
        guard !items.isEmpty else {
            return nil
        }
        return items.removeLast()
    }

    func map<U>(f: Element -> U) -> Stack<U> {
        var mappedItems = [U]()
        for item in items {
            mappedItems.append(f(item))
        }
        return Stack<U>(items: mappedItems)
    }
}
...
```

The **map(_:)** method only declares one placeholder type, **U**, but it uses both **Element** and **U**. The **Element** type is available because **map(_:)** is inside of the **Stack** structure, which makes the placeholder type **Element** available. The body of **map(_:)** is almost identical to **myMap(_:f:)**, differing only in that it returns a new **Stack** instead of an array. Try out your new method:

## Listing 22.9 Using **map**

```
...
var intStack = Stack<Int>()
intStack.push(1)
intStack.push(2)
var doubledStack = intStack.map({ 2 * $0 })

print(intStack.pop()) // Prints Optional(2)
print(intStack.pop()) // Prints Optional(1)
print(intStack.pop()) // Prints nil

print(doubledStack.pop()) // Prints Optional(4)
print(doubledStack.pop()) // Prints Optional(2)
```

# Type Constraints

One of the most important things to keep in mind when writing generic functions and data types is that, by default, you do not know anything about the concrete type that is going to be used. You created stacks of **Int** and **String**, but you could also create stacks of any other type at all. The practical impact of this lack of knowledge is that there is very little you can do with the value of a placeholder type. For example, you cannot check if two of them are equal; this code would not compile:

```
func checkIfEqual<T>(first: T, _ second: T) -> Bool {
    return first == second
}
```

This function could be called with any type at all, including types for which equality does not make sense, such as closures. (It is hard to describe what it would mean for two closures to be "equal." Swift does not allow the comparison.)

Generic functions would be relatively uncommon if you were never able to assume anything about the placeholder types. To solve this problem, Swift allows the use of *type constraints*, which place restrictions on the concrete types that can be passed to generic functions. There are two kinds of type constraints: a constraint that a type be a subclass of a given class, or a constraint that a type conform to a protocol (or a protocol composition). The **Equatable** protocol is a Swift-provided protocol that states that two values can be checked for equality. To see how this works, write a **checkIfEqual(_:_:)** function including a constraint that **T** must be **Equatable**.

## Listing 22.10  Using a type constraint to allow checking for equality

```
...
func checkIfEqual<T: Equatable>(first: T, _ second: T) -> Bool {
    return first == second
}

print(checkIfEqual(1, 1))
print(checkIfEqual("a string", "a string"))
print(checkIfEqual("a string", "a different string"))
```

Every placeholder type can have a type constraint. For example, write a function that checks if two **CustomStringConvertible** values have the same description.

## Listing 22.11  Using a type constraint to check **CustomStringConvertible** values

```
...
func checkIfDescriptionsMatch<T: CustomStringConvertible, U: CustomStringConvertible>(
        first: T, _ second: U) -> Bool {
    return first.description == second.description
}

print(checkIfDescriptionsMatch(Int(1), UInt(1)))
print(checkIfDescriptionsMatch(1, 1.0))
print(checkIfDescriptionsMatch(Float(1.0), Double(1.0)))
```

The constraint that both **T** and **U** are **CustomStringConvertible** guarantees that both first and second have a property named description that returns a **String**. Even though the two arguments may have different types, you can still compare their descriptions.

# Associated Type Protocols

Now that you know that types, functions, and methods can be made generic, it is natural to ask whether protocols can be made generic as well. The answer is "no." However, protocols support a similar and related feature: *associated types*.

Let's explore protocols with associated types by examining a couple of protocols defined by the Swift standard library. First, the **GeneratorType** protocol:

```
protocol GeneratorType {
    typealias Element

    mutating func next() -> Element?
}
```

The **GeneratorType** protocol requires a single mutating method, **next()**, which returns a value of type **Element?**. The purpose of **GeneratorType** is that you can call **next** repeatedly and it generates new values each time. If the generator is no longer able to generate new values, **next** returns nil. The new syntax present in this protocol is typealias Element.

You saw the typealias keyword in Chapter 21. In its typical use, typealias allows you to give another name to an existing type. Inside a protocol, however, you can create a typealias without specifying the existing type. A type that conforms to **GeneratorType** must provide an associated, concrete type to be used as the **Element** type. At the top of your playground, create a new struct called **StackGenerator** that conforms to **GeneratorType**.

## Listing 22.12 Creating **StackGenerator**

```
struct StackGenerator<T>: GeneratorType {
    typealias Element = T

    var stack: Stack<T>

    mutating func next() -> Element? {
        return stack.pop()
    }
}

struct Stack<Element> {
    ...
}
```

**StackGenerator** wraps up a **Stack** and generates values by popping items off of the stack. The type of the **Element** that **next** returns is **T**, so you set the typealias appropriately. Create a new stack, add some items, then create a generator and loop over its values to see **StackGenerator** in action.

## Listing 22.13 Using **StackGenerator**

```
...
var myStack = Stack<Int>()
myStack.push(10)
myStack.push(20)
myStack.push(30)

var myStackGenerator = StackGenerator(stack: myStack)
while let value = myStackGenerator.next() {
    print("got \(value)")
}
```

**StackGenerator** is a little more verbose than it needs to be. Swift can infer the type of a protocol's associated types, so you can remove the explicit typealias by indicating that **next** returns a **T?**.

## Listing 22.14  Tightening up **StackGenerator**

```
struct StackGenerator<T>: GeneratorType {
    typealias Element = T

    var stack: Stack<T>

    mutating func next() -> Element? T? {
        return stack.pop()
    }
}
...
```

The next associated type protocol you will examine is **SequenceType**. The definition of **SequenceType** is:

```
protocol SequenceType {
    typealias Generator: GeneratorType
    func generate() -> Generator
}
```

**SequenceType** has an associated type named **Generator**. The `: GeneratorType` syntax is a type constraint on the associated type. It has the same meaning as type constraints on generics: for a type to conform to **SequenceType**, it must have an associated type **Generator** that conforms to the protocol **GeneratorType**. **SequenceType** also requires conforming types to implement a single method, **generate()**, which returns a value of the associated type **GeneratorType**. Because you already have a suitable generator for stacks, modify **Stack** to conform to **SequenceType**.

## Listing 22.15  Making **Stack** conform to **SequenceType**

```
...
struct Stack<Element>: SequenceType {
    var items = [Element]()

    mutating func push(newItem: Element) {
        items.append(newItem)
    }

    mutating func pop() -> Element? {
        guard !items.isEmpty else {
            return nil
        }
        return items.removeLast()
    }

    func map<U>(f: Element -> U) -> Stack<U> {
        var mappedItems = [U]()
        for item in items {
            mappedItems.append(f(item))
        }
        return Stack<U>(items: mappedItems)
    }

    func generate() -> StackGenerator<Element> {
        return StackGenerator(stack: self)
    }
}
...
```

You again make use of Swift's type inference to avoid having to explicitly state typealias Generator = StackGenerator<Element>, although it would not be an error to do so.

The **SequenceType** protocol is what Swift uses internally for its for ... in loops. Now that **Stack** conforms to **SequenceType**, you can loop over its contents.

## Listing 22.16  Looping through myStack

```
...
var myStackGenerator = StackGenerator(stack: myStack)
while let value = myStackGenerator.next() {
    print("got \(value)")
}

for value in myStack {
    print("for-in loop: got \(value)")
}
```

**StackGenerator** pops values off of its stack every time **next()** is called, which is a fairly destructive operation. When a **StackGenerator** returns nil from **next()**, its stack property is empty. However, you were able to create a generator by hand from myStack, and then use myStack again in a for ... in loop. This reuse is possible because **Stack** is a value type, which means every time a **StackGenerator** is created, it gets a copy of the stack, leaving the original untouched.

A final note: if a protocol has an associated type, you cannot use that protocol as a concrete type. For example, you cannot declare a variable with the type **GeneratorType** or declare a function that accepts an argument of type **GeneratorType**, because **GeneratorType** has an associated type. However, protocols with associated types are fundamental to using *where clauses* in generic declarations.

# Type Constraint where Clauses

Write a new function that takes every element of an array and pushes it onto a stack.

## Listing 22.17  Pushing items from an array onto a stack

```
...
func pushItemsOntoStack<Element>(inout stack: Stack<Element>,
                                      fromArray array: [Element]) {
    for item in array {
        stack.push(item)
    }
}

pushItemsOntoStack(&myStack, fromArray: [1, 2, 3])
for value in myStack {
    print("after pushing: got \(value)")
}
```

**pushItemsOntoStack(_:fromArray:)** takes its first argument, a **Stack**, as an inout argument so that it can call the mutating method **push(_:)**. This function is useful, but it is not as general as it could be. You now know that any type that conforms to **SequenceType** can be used in a for ... in loop, so why should this function require an array? It should be able to accept any kind of sequence – even another **Stack**, now that **Stack** conforms to **SequenceType**.

However, a first attempt at this will produce a compiler error.

## Listing 22.18  Close, but no cigar

```
...
func pushItemsOntoStack<Element>(inout stack: Stack<Element>,
                                      fromArray array: [Element]) {
func pushItemsOntoStack<Element, S: SequenceType>(
        inout stack: Stack<Element>, fromSequence sequence: S) {
    for item in array sequence {
        stack.push(item)
    }
}

pushItemsOntoStack(&myStack, fromArrayfromSequence: [1, 2, 3])
for value in myStack {
    print("after pushing: got \(value)")
}
```

You made **pushItemsOntoStack(_:fromArray:)** generic with two placeholder types: **Element**, which is the type of the stack's elements, and **S**, which is some type that conforms to the **SequenceType** protocol. The constraint on **S** guarantees that you can loop over it with the for ... in syntax. However, this is not sufficient. In order to push the items you get from sequence onto the stack, you need to guarantee that the type of the items coming from the sequence matches the type of the stack's elements. That is, you need to add an additional constraint that the elements produced by **S** are themselves of type **Element**.

Swift supports constraints of this kind using a where clause.

## Listing 22.19  Using a where clause to guarantee type

```
...
func pushItemsOntoStack<Element, S: SequenceType
        where S.Generator.Element == Element>
        (inout stack: Stack<Element>, fromSequence sequence: S) {
    for item in sequence {
        stack.push(item)
    }
}
...
```

**pushItemsOntoStack(_:fromSequence:)** is a generic function with two placeholder types. The first placeholder type, **Element**, has no constraints – it can be anything. The second placeholder type, **S**, has a constraint that the concrete type used must conform to the **SequenceType** protocol.

Following the placeholder types, the where clause imposes further restrictions. S.Generator.Element refers to the **Element** type associated to the **Generator** type associated to **S**. The constraint S.Generator.Element == Element requires that the concrete type used for the **Element** associated type must match the concrete type used for your **Element** placeholder.

The syntax for generic where clauses can be difficult to read at first glance, but an example should make it clearer. If you pass a stack of **Int**s as the first argument to **pushItemsOntoStack(_:fromSequence:)**, the second argument must be a sequence that produces **Int**s. Two types you already know that are **Int**-producing sequences are **Stack<Int>** and **[Int]**. Try them out:

## Listing 22.20  Pushing items to the stack

```
...
var myOtherStack = Stack<Int>()
pushItemsOntoStack(&myOtherStack, fromSequence: [1, 2, 3])
pushItemsOntoStack(&myStack, fromSequence: myOtherStack)
for value in myStack {
    print("after pushing items onto stack, got \(value)")
}
```

You created a new, empty stack of integers: myOtherStack. Next, you pushed all the integers from an array onto myOtherStack. Finally, you pushed all the integers from myOtherStack onto myStack. You were able to use the same generic function in both cases because arrays and stacks both conform to **SequenceType**.

Generics are an extremely powerful feature of Swift. If generics have not sunk in, do not fret – they are a simultaneously complex and abstract concept. Take your time, go back over the **Stack** class you wrote throughout this chapter, and try your hand at the challenges.

# Bronze Challenge

Add a **filter(_:)** method to your **Stack** structure. It should take a single argument, a closure that takes an **Element** and returns a **Bool**, and return a new **Stack<Element>** that contains any elements for which the closure returns true.

# Silver Challenge

Write a generic function called **findAll(_:_:)** that takes an array of any type **T** that conforms to the **Equatable** protocol and a single element (also of type **T**). **findAll(_:_:)** should return an array of integers corresponding to every location where the element was found in the array. For example, findAll([5,3,7,3,9], 3) should return [1,3] because the item 3 exists at indices 1 and 3 in the array. Try your function with both integers and strings.

# Gold Challenge

Modify the **findAll(_:_:)** function you wrote for the silver challenge to accept a generic **CollectionType** instead of an array. Hint: you will need to change the return type from **[Int]** to an array of an associated type of the **CollectionType** protocol.

# For the More Curious: Understanding Optionals

Optionals are a mainstay of all nontrivial Swift programs, and the language has a lot of features that make it relatively easy to work with them. Under the hood, however, there is nothing particularly special about the **Optional** type. It is a generic enum with two cases:

```
enum Optional<T> {
    case None
    case Some(T)
}
```

As you probably expect, the None case corresponds to an optional that is currently nil, and the Some case corresponds to an optional that has a value of type T. Because the Some case is generic, you are able to create optional versions of any type at all.

Most of your interactions with optionals will make use of optional binding and optional chaining, but you can also treat them like any other enumeration. For example, if maybeAnInt is an **Int?**, you could switch over its two cases:

```
switch maybeAnInt {
case .None:
    print("maybeAnInt is nil")

case let .Some(value):
    print("maybeAnInt has the value \(value)")
}
```

This is not usually necessary, but it is nice to know that optionals are not magic. They are built on top of the same Swift features that are available to you.

# For the More Curious: Parametric Polymorphism

In Chapter 15, you learned about class inheritance. Any function that expects an argument of a class can also accept arguments that are subclasses of that class. This ability to accept either a class or any subclass of it is often referred to as *polymorphism*, but is more accurately known as *runtime polymorphism* or *subclass polymorphism*. Polymorphism, meaning "many forms," means you have written a single function that can accept different types.

Runtime polymorphism is a very powerful tool, and the frameworks Apple provides for iOS and Mac OS X development use it very frequently. Unfortunately, it has drawbacks. Classes that are related by inheritance are tied together tightly: it can be difficult to change one without affecting the others. There is also a small but observable performance penalty to runtime polymorphism due to how the compiler must implement functions that accept class arguments.

Swift's ability to add constraints to generics allows you to use another form of polymorphism: *compile-time polymorphism*, also known as *parametric polymorphism*. Generic functions with constraints are still true to the definition of polymorphism: you can write a single function that accepts different types. Compile-time polymorphic functions address both of the issues listed above that plague runtime polymorphism. Many different types can conform to a protocol, allowing them to be used in any generic function that requires a type conforming to that protocol – but the types can be otherwise unrelated, making it easy to change any one of them without affecting the others. Additionally, compile-time polymorphism generally does not have a performance penalty. In the playground, you called **pushItemsOntoStack** once with an array and once with a stack. The compiler actually produced two different versions of **pushItemsOntoStack** in the executable, meaning the function itself does not have to do anything at runtime to handle the different argument types.

Swift is entering into a programming community that has traditionally used class inheritance and runtime polymorphism extensively. Generics and compile-time polymorphism are starting to play a large role, however. The next time you start to write a class hierarchy, consider whether the problem you are trying to solve might be better served with a solution featuring protocols and generics. Chapter 23 will discuss even more tools for protocol-based designs.

# 23

# Protocol Extensions

The dominant software design philosophy of the past few decades has been object-oriented programming (OOP). OOP is powerful and well known; people have an intuition for what this style means for code. Traditionally, OOP uses classes to model data and methods to modify the properties on instances of those classes and to communicate with instances of other classes. Swift supports OOP, though its approach is often not idiomatic in that enums and structs can replace many typical uses of classes in OOP.

Swift also addresses some of OOP's flaws. In OOP, inheritance, in particular, has to be used with great care. It is easy to end up with a code base full of difficult-to-understand classes due to a deep inheritance hierarchy. Swift introduces a new opportunity for designing reusable and composable types: instead of using classes and inheritance, you can use protocols and generics. Protocols allow patterns that solve the same problems inheritance solves in OOP, even when using value types. One of the most powerful tools to enable this kind of design is the *protocol extension*.

## Modeling Exercise

Before you can begin exploring protocol extensions, you need a protocol and some conforming types to experiment with. You will write some very basic code that will let you track exercises.

Create a new playground called `ProtocolExtensions.playground`. Begin with an **ExerciseType** protocol.

### Listing 23.1  The **ExerciseType** protocol

```
import Cocoa

protocol ExerciseType {
    var name: String { get }
    var caloriesBurned: Double { get }
    var minutes: Double { get }
}
```

The **ExerciseType** protocol has three readable properties for the exercise's name, the number of calories burned, and the minutes spent performing the exercise. You are following the convention set by the Swift standard library, where protocol names end with one of the suffixes "-Type," "-able," or "-ible." You have already seen several other protocols that follow this convention, including **SequenceType**, **GeneratorType**, and **CustomStringConvertible**. You use the –Type suffix because the **ExerciseType** protocol defines the behavior of a type, as opposed to a protocol that defines how an element is able to do something.

Create two structs to track workouts: one for using an elliptical trainer and a second for running.

## Listing 23.2 **EllipticalTrainer** and **Treadmill** exercises

```
protocol ExerciseType {
    var name: String { get }
    var caloriesBurned: Double { get }
    var minutes: Double { get }
}

struct EllipticalTrainer: ExerciseType {
    let name = "Elliptical Machine"
    let caloriesBurned: Double
    let minutes: Double
}

struct Treadmill: ExerciseType {
    let name = "Treadmill"
    let caloriesBurned: Double
    let minutes: Double
    let distanceInMiles: Double
}
```

You define two new structs that both conform to **ExerciseType**. Each has a name that is constant for all instances. Each has caloriesBurned and minutes properties which will be set when the instance is created. **Treadmill** also has a distanceInMiles property to keep track of how far you ran. distanceInMiles is not required to conform to **ExerciseType**, but recall from Chapter 19 that extra properties or methods are perfectly acceptable.

Create an instance of each of these new types.

## Listing 23.3 Instances of **EllipticalTrainer** and **Treadmill**

```
...
struct EllipticalTrainer: ExerciseType {
    let name = "Elliptical Machine"
    let caloriesBurned: Double
    let minutes: Double
}

let ellipticalWorkout = EllipticalTrainer(caloriesBurned: 335, minutes: 30)

struct Treadmill: ExerciseType {
    let name = "Treadmill"
    let caloriesBurned: Double
    let minutes: Double
    let distanceInMiles: Double
}

let runningWorkout = Treadmill(caloriesBurned: 350, minutes: 25, distanceInMiles: 4.2)
```

# Extending ExerciseType

A natural question to ask about an instance of **ExerciseType** is how many calories were burned per minute of exercise. You can use your knowledge of generics and where clauses to write a function that will perform that calculation.

Listing 23.4  Computing calories burned per minute, generically

```
...
func caloriesBurnedPerMinute<Exercise: ExerciseType>(exercise: Exercise) -> Double {
    return exercise.caloriesBurned / exercise.minutes
}

print(caloriesBurnedPerMinute(ellipticalWorkout))
print(caloriesBurnedPerMinute(runningWorkout))
```

**caloriesBurnedPerMinute(_:)** is a generic function whose placeholder type is required to be a type that conforms to the **ExerciseType** protocol. The body of the function uses two of **ExerciseType**'s properties to compute the calories burned per minute.

There is nothing wrong with **caloriesBurnedPerMinute(_:)**, per se. But if you have an instance of **ExerciseType**, you have to remember that the **caloriesBurnedPerMinute(_:)** function exists. It would be more natural if every **ExerciseType** had a caloriesBurnedPerMinute property – but you do not want to have to copy and paste the same implementation into both **EllipticalTrainer** and **Treadmill** (and any new **ExerciseType**s you might create).

Instead, write an extension on the **ExerciseType** protocol to add this new property.

Listing 23.5  Adding caloriesBurnedPerMinute to **ExerciseType**

```
...
func caloriesBurnedPerMinute<Exercise: ExerciseType>(exercise: Exercise) -> Double {
    return exercise.caloriesBurned / exercise.minutes
}
extension ExerciseType {
    var caloriesBurnedPerMinute: Double {
        return caloriesBurned / minutes
    }
}
...
```

Protocol extensions use the same extension keyword as extensions on nonprotocol types. Protocol extensions can add new properties and methods that have implementations, but they cannot add new requirements to the protocol. Much like the restrictions when you wrote generic functions, the implementations inside a protocol extension can only access other properties and methods that are guaranteed to exist, as caloriesBurned and minutes are in this case. Properties and methods added in a protocol extension become available on all types that conform to the protocol.

You deleted the **caloriesBurnedPerMinute(_:)** function, so your playground is now showing an error. Replace the call to this function with an access of the new caloriesBurnedPerMinute property.

### Listing 23.6  Accessing caloriesBurnedPerMinute

```
...
print(caloriesBurnedPerMinute(ellipticalWorkout))
print(caloriesBurnedPerMinute(runningWorkout))
print(ellipticalWorkout.caloriesBurnedPerMinute)
print(runningWorkout.caloriesBurnedPerMinute)
```

The results are the same.

# Protocol Extension where Clauses

Extensions allow you to add new methods and properties to any type, not just types you have defined. Likewise, protocol extensions allow you to add new methods and properties to any protocol. However, as we said earlier, the properties and methods you add in a protocol extension can only make use of other properties and methods that are guaranteed to exist.

Do you remember the built-in protocol **SequenceType** from Chapter 22? It has a typealias named Generator, which must itself conform to **GeneratorType**. And **GeneratorType** has a typealias named Element that indicates the type of elements produced by the generator. When writing a protocol extension on **SequenceType**, there are not very many properties and methods that would be useful. You can use a where clause to restrict the protocol extension to only **SequenceType**s whose Element is a particular type.

Write a protocol extension on **SequenceType** that contains elements that are of type **ExerciseType**.

### Listing 23.7  Extending **SequenceType**s containing **ExerciseType**s

```
...

extension SequenceType where Generator.Element == ExerciseType {
    func totalCaloriesBurned() -> Double {
        var total: Double = 0
        for exercise in self {
            total += exercise.caloriesBurned
        }
        return total
    }
}
```

The where clause syntax for protocol extensions is the same as the where clause syntax for generics. You add a **totalCaloriesBurned()** method to compute the total number of calories burned in all exercises contained in the sequence. In the implementation, you loop over every exercise in self, which is allowed because self is some kind of **SequenceType**. You then access the caloriesBurned property of each element, which is allowed because the where clause restricts this method to sequences whose elements are **ExerciseType**.

Create an array of **ExerciseType**s. **Array** conforms to **SequenceType**, so you can call your new **totalCaloriesBurned()** method.

### Listing 23.8  Calling **totalCaloriesBurned()** on an array of **ExerciseType**s

```
...
extension SequenceType where Generator.Element == ExerciseType {
    func totalCaloriesBurned() -> Double {
        var total: Double = 0
        for exercise in self {
            total += exercise.caloriesBurned
        }
        return total
    }
}

let mondayWorkout: [ExerciseType] = [ellipticalWorkout, runningWorkout]
print(mondayWorkout.totalCaloriesBurned())
```

The **totalCaloriesBurned()** method is available on this array because it is of type **[ExerciseType]**, so you get the result 685.0. If you were to create an array of type **[Int]**, for example, the **totalCaloriesBurned()** method would not be available. It would not show up in Xcode's autocompletion, and if you were to type it in manually your program would not compile.

# Default Implementations with Protocol Extensions

Both of the protocol extensions you have written so far add new properties or methods to protocols. You can also use protocol extensions to provide default implementations for the protocol's own requirements.

Recall from Chapter 19 that the **CustomStringConvertible** protocol has a single requirement: a readable **String** property named description. Change **ExerciseType** to inherit from **CustomStringConvertible**, meaning it also requires the description property.

### Listing 23.9  Making **ExerciseType** inherit from **CustomStringConvertible**

```
protocol ExerciseType: CustomStringConvertible {
    var name: String { get }
    var caloriesBurned: Double { get }
    var minutes: Double { get }
}
...
```

Your playground now has two errors because neither **EllipticalTrainer** nor **Treadmill** has the required description property.

You could go back and modify both types to add a description, but that seems silly when **ExerciseType** already has enough properties to provide a reasonable **String** representation. Use a protocol extension to add a default implementation of description to all types that conform to **ExerciseType**.

## Listing 23.10  Adding a default implementation of description to **ExerciseType**

```
protocol ExerciseType: CustomStringConvertible {
    var name: String { get }
    var caloriesBurned: Double { get }
    var minutes: Double { get }
}

extension ExerciseType {
    var description: String {
        return "Exercise(\(name), burned \(caloriesBurned) calories
                in \(minutes) minutes)"
    }
}
...
```

The playground no longer has any errors. Your extension provides a default implementation of description, so types that conform to **ExerciseType** do not have to provide it themselves.

Print out both of your **ExerciseType** instances.

## Listing 23.11  Seeing the default description implementation

```
...
print(ellipticalWorkout.caloriesBurnedPerMinute)
print(runningWorkout.caloriesBurnedPerMinute)

print(ellipticalWorkout)
print(runningWorkout)
...
```

Open the debug area of your playground and you should see the following output; it is exactly as you would expect from your implementation of description.

```
Exercise(Elliptical Machine, burned 335.0 calories in 30.0 minutes)
Exercise(Treadmill, burned 350.0 calories in 25.0 minutes)
```

When a protocol provides default implementations for some (or all) of its properties or methods, conforming types are not required to implement them. But they can choose to implement them if the default implementation is not suitable.

Your **Treadmill** type also knows how many miles were run, but that information is not included in the description. Implement the `description` property on **Treadmill**, which will take precedence over the default implementation supplied by your extension on **ExerciseType**. Stylistically, it is cleaner to separate this property from the core functionality of **Treadmill** by placing it in an extension.

## Listing 23.12  Overriding a protocol's default implementation

```
...
struct Treadmill: ExerciseType {
    let name = "Treadmill"
    let caloriesBurned: Double
    let minutes: Double
    let distanceInMiles: Double
}

extension Treadmill {
    var description: String {
        return "Treadmill(\(caloriesBurned) calories and
                \(distanceInMiles) miles in \(minutes) minutes)"
    }
}
...
```

Now that **Treadmill** implements `description` itself, you should see in the output that the default implementation is only used when printing `ellipticalWorkout`.

```
Exercise(Elliptical Machine, burned 335.0 calories in 30.0 minutes)
Treadmill(350.0 calories and 4.2 miles in 25.0 minutes)
```

# Naming Things: A Cautionary Tale

There is an edge case with protocol extensions that may prove to be a great source of frustration if you are not careful. In the previous section, you added `description` to the requirements of **ExerciseType**, added a default implementation, and added a specific implementation to **Treadmill** that took precedence over the default implementation. This worked correctly because `description` was required by the **ExerciseType** protocol. What happens, though, if you write a protocol extension to add a property or method, then add the same property or method (with a different implementation) to a conforming type?

The answer is that it depends on how the instance is being accessed – does the compiler know its specific type, or does it only know that it is an instance of the protocol? If this sounds confusing, that is okay – this is a little confusing! Let's look at an example.

Use a protocol extension to implement a `title` property on **ExerciseType**. Print out the titles of all the workouts in `mondayWorkout`.

Listing 23.13  Extending **ExerciseType** to add a `title`

```
...

extension ExerciseType {
    var title: String {
        return "\(name) – \(minutes) minutes"
    }
}

for exercise in mondayWorkout {
    print(exercise.title)
}
```

You add an implementation of `title` that includes the **ExerciseType**'s name and duration. You should see the following output.

```
Elliptical Machine – 30.0 minutes
Treadmill – 25.0 minutes
```

Now go back and implement a `title` property on **EllipticalTrainer**. The title of **EllipticalTrainer** instances will be the brand name of the elliptical machine used in the workout.

Listing 23.14  Adding a `title` to **EllipticalTrainer**

```
...
struct EllipticalTrainer: ExerciseType {
    let name = "Elliptical Machine"
    let title = "Go Fast Elliptical Machine 3000"
    let caloriesBurned: Double
    let minutes: Double
}
...
```

Check the output of your for loop.

```
Elliptical Machine – 30.0 minutes
Treadmill – 25.0 minutes
```

Nothing changed. To make sure you did not mistype something, try printing out `ellipticalWorkout`'s title directly.

## Listing 23.15 Printing `ellipticalWorkout`'s title

```
...
for exercise in mondayWorkout {
    print(exercise.title)
}

print(ellipticalWorkout.title)
```

You should see the following output.

```
Elliptical Machine - 30.0 minutes
Treadmill - 25.0 minutes
Go Fast Elliptical Machine 3000
```

Yikes! The same value of `ellipticalWorkout` is giving two different values for `title`. Why is the implementation provided by **EllipticalTrainer** not taking precedence over the implementation in the extension on **ExerciseType**? Because `title` is not required by the **ExerciseType** protocol.

When the compiler sees `ellipticalWorkout.title`, it knows `ellipticalWorkout` is an instance of **EllipticalTrainer**, so it uses the `title` you defined in the struct. Inside the `for` loop, on the other hand, the compiler only knows that `exercise` is an instance of some type that conforms to **ExerciseType**. When you access `exercise.title`, the compiler does not check to see if the underlying type *also* provides a `title` property, because it is not part of the protocol. The compiler jumps straight to the implementation provided by your extension on **ExerciseType**.

At the risk of being repetitive, it is okay if this is confusing. Here is what is most important to understand: be careful when you are considering writing a protocol extension that adds properties or methods that are not default implementations for requirements of the protocol. The runtime behavior may not be what you expect if conforming types also implement those same properties and methods.

# Bronze Challenge

Clean up the messiness introduced with the `title` properties. Add `title` to the **ExerciseType** protocol and make sure you see the output you expect.

# Gold Challenge

This challenge is unique in that it does not have a specific problem or solution. Instead, it is an encouragement to spend some time reading interfaces written by the Swift team at Apple.

You first encountered the `map(_:)` method in Chapter 13, where you called it on arrays. Then in Chapter 19, you called `map(_:)` on a range constructed with the `..<` operator. Both of these were actually calling `map(_:)` methods defined in protocol extensions by the Swift standard library.

The Swift standard library contains a large number of properties and methods provided by protocol extensions. Many of them also include `where` clauses that restrict their use based on various criteria.

Remember that you can Command-click on a type, function, method, or even operator to jump to a view in Xcode that shows you how the element is declared. The Swift standard library makes use of many of the advanced features you have learned about. It may be difficult to read, especially at first, and especially if Swift is your first exposure to programming or generics. It is worth investing some time, though, in looking at how the library is organized. Try Command-clicking on **SequenceType** in your playground and skimming through some of the extensions defined there. See if you can figure out what some of the `where` clauses mean. Do some experiments and explore!

# 24

# Memory Management and ARC

All computer programs use memory. Most computer programs use memory dynamically: as a program runs, it allocates and deallocates memory as needed. Swift's stance on memory management is relatively unique. Most memory issues are handled for you automatically, but Swift does not use a garbage collector (a common tool for automatic memory management in programming languages). Instead, Swift uses a system of reference counting. In this chapter, you will investigate how that system works and learn what you need to be aware of to avoid memory leaks.

## Memory Allocation

The memory allocation and management for value types – enumerations and structures – is very simple. When you create a new instance of a value type, an appropriate amount of memory is automatically set aside for your instance. Anything you do to pass the instance around, including passing it to a function and storing it in a property, creates a copy of the instance. Swift reclaims the memory when the instance no longer exists. You do not have to do anything to manage the memory of value types.

This chapter is about managing the memory for reference types – specifically, class instances. When you create a new class instance, memory is allocated for the instance to use, just as it is for value types. However, the difference is in what happens when you pass the class instance around. Passing a class instance to a function or storing it in a property creates an additional reference to the same memory, rather than copying the instance itself. Having multiple references to the same memory means that when any one of them changes the class instance, that change is apparent to all of the references.

Swift does not require you to manually manage memory, as languages like C do. Instead, every class instance has a *reference count*, which is the number of references to the memory making up the class instance. The instance remains alive as long as the reference count is greater than 0. Once the reference count becomes 0, the instance is deallocated and your `deinit` method will run.

In the not-too-distant past, apps that were developed for iOS and Mac OS X in Objective-C used manual reference counting. Manual reference counting required you, the programmer, to manage the reference counts of all your class instances. Every class had a method to *retain* the object (incrementing its reference count) and a method to *release* the instance (decrementing its reference count). As you can probably imagine, manual reference counting was the source of many bugs: if you retained an instance too many times, it would never get deallocated (causing what is called a memory leak), but if you released an instance too many times, a crash would usually result.

In 2011, Apple introduced *Automatic Reference Counting* (ARC) for Objective-C. Under ARC, the compiler is responsible for analyzing your code and inserting retain and release calls in all of the appropriate places. Swift is also built on top of ARC. You do not have to do anything to manage the reference count of class instances – the compiler does that for you. However, it is still important for you to understand how the system works. There are some common mistakes that can cause memory management problems.

# Strong Reference Cycles

Create a new command-line tool named CyclicalAssets. Add a new file to your project named Person.swift and insert the following definition of the **Person** class.

Listing 24.1  Defining the **Person** class (Person.swift)

```
import Foundation

class Person: CustomStringConvertible {
    let name: String

    var description: String {
        return "Person(\(name))"
    }

    init(name: String) {
        self.name = name
    }

    deinit {
        print("\(self) is being deallocated")
    }
}
```

The **Person** class has a single property that you set in its initializer. It conforms to the **CustomStringConvertible** protocol by implementing the description computed property. You add an implementation of **deinit** so you can see when a person is being deallocated – i.e., when its memory is being reclaimed because the reference count has dropped to 0.

Now, modify main.swift to create an optional **Person**.

Listing 24.2  Creating an optional **Person** (main.swift)

```
import Foundation

print("Hello, world!")
var bob: Person? = Person(name: "Bob")
print("created \(bob)")

bob = nil
print("the bob variable is now \(bob)")
```

Here, you create a new **Person?**, print out its name, then set it to nil. (You make this an optional so that you can set it to nil and therefore see the **deinit** execute.) Build and run your program. You should see the following output:

```
created Optional(Person(Bob))
Person(Bob) is being deallocated
the bob variable is now nil
```

The bob variable is an optional that contains a class instance – a reference type. By default, all references that you create are *strong references*, which means they increment the reference count of the instance they refer to. Therefore, the **Person** whose name is Bob has a reference count of 1 after it is created and assigned to the bob variable. When you set bob to nil, Bob's reference count is decremented. You then see the Person Bob is being deallocated message, because the reference count has dropped to 0.

Next, create a new Swift file called Asset.swift and insert an **Asset** class.

## Listing 24.3  Defining the **Asset** class (Asset.swift)

```
import Foundation

class Asset: CustomStringConvertible {
    let name: String
    let value: Double
    var owner: Person?

    var description: String {
        if let actualOwner = owner {
            return "Asset(\(name), worth \(value), owned by \(actualOwner))"
        } else {
            return "Asset(\(name), worth \(value), not owned by anyone)"
        }
    }

    init(name: String, value: Double) {
        self.name = name
        self.value = value
    }

    deinit {
        print("\(self) is being deallocated")
    }
}
```

The **Asset** class is very similar to the **Person** class. **Asset** has name and value properties, conforms to **CustomStringConvertible**, and prints a message when it is deallocated. It also has a variable stored property, owner, which will refer to the **Person** who owns the asset. owner is optional because it is reasonable for an asset to exist without someone owning it.

Create a few assets in main.swift.

## Listing 24.4  Creating assets (main.swift)

```
import Foundation

var bob: Person? = Person(name: "Bob")
print("created \(bob)")

var laptop: Asset? = Asset(name: "Shiny Laptop", value: 1500.0)
var hat: Asset? = Asset(name: "Cowboy Hat", value: 175.0)
var backpack: Asset? = Asset(name: "Blue Backpack", value: 45.0)

bob = nil
print("the bob variable is now \(bob)")

laptop = nil
hat = nil
backpack = nil
```

You again use optionals so that you can set the instances to be nil, which fires off the **deinit** methods. As expected, all of the assets are deallocated and do not have owners:

```
created Optional(Person(Bob))
Person(Bob) is being deallocated
the bob variable is now nil
Asset(Shiny Laptop, worth 1500.0, not owned by anyone) is being deallocated
Asset(Cowboy Hat, worth 175.0, not owned by anyone) is being deallocated
Asset(Blue Backpack, worth 45.0, not owned by anyone) is being deallocated
```

People can own things; your **Person** class will model this quality by having a property for assets. Go back to Person.swift and add a property and method for people to gain assets.

## Listing 24.5  Letting a **Person** own assets (Person.swift)

```
import Foundation

class Person: CustomStringConvertible {
    let name: String
    var assets = [Asset]()

    var description: String {
        return "Person(\(name))"
    }

    init(name: String) {
        self.name = name
    }

    deinit {
        print("\(self) is being deallocated")
    }

    func takeOwnershipOfAsset(asset: Asset) {
        asset.owner = self
        assets.append(asset)
    }
}
```

You add **assets**, an array of **Asset**s that the person owns, and **takeOwnershipOfAsset(_:)**, a method to give an asset to a person. Taking ownership of an asset means the person adds it to their **assets** array and sets the asset's owner property to refer back to this person. In main.swift, give Bob ownership of a couple of assets.

## Listing 24.6  Bob is taking ownership (main.swift)

```
...
var laptop: Asset? = Asset(name: "Shiny Laptop")
var hat: Asset? = Asset(name: "Cowboy Hat")
var backpack: Asset? = Asset(name: "Blue Backpack")

bob?.takeOwnershipOfAsset(laptop!)
bob?.takeOwnershipOfAsset(hat!)

bob = nil
...
```

Build and run again. The output may be surprising:

```
created Optional(Person(Bob))
the bob variable is now nil
Asset(Blue Backpack, worth 45.0, not owned by anyone) is being deallocated
```

The only instance being deallocated now is the backpack – its reference count dropped to 0 when you set `backpack = nil`. The laptop, hat, and Bob himself are no longer being deallocated. Why not? Take a look at Figure 24.1, which shows who has a reference to whom before any of the variables are set to nil in `main.swift`:

## Figure 24.1 CyclicalAssets before

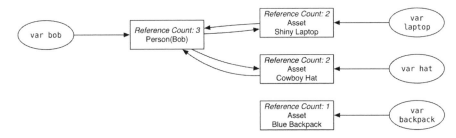

Each instance is labeled with its current reference count. The reference count is exactly the number of arrows pointing to the instance; i.e., the number of references to the instance. After you set all the variables in `main.swift` to nil, those references go away, leaving what you see in Figure 24.2:

## Figure 24.2 CyclicalAssets after

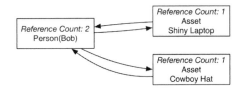

You have created two *strong reference cycles*, which is the term for when two instances have strong references to each other. Bob has a reference to the laptop (via his `assets` property), and the laptop has a reference to Bob (via its `owner` property). Same for Bob and the hat. The memory for these instances is no longer reachable – all the variables pointing to them are gone – but the memory will never be reclaimed because each instance has a reference count greater than 0.

Strong reference cycles are one kind of *memory leak*. Your application allocated the memory necessary to store Bob and his two assets, but it did not return that memory to the system even after your program no longer needed it.

Do not worry about causing problems with your computer: when a program like CyclicalAssets stops running, all memory (including any leaked memory) is reclaimed by the OS. However, memory leaks are still serious, especially in iOS. iOS keeps track of how much memory apps use, and it can kill apps that use too much. When an app leaks memory, that memory still counts as part of the app's total memory usage, even though it is no longer needed or useful.

The solution to a strong reference cycle is to break the cycle. You could break the cycle in **Person**'s **deinit** method by looping over each asset and setting its owner to nil. However, Swift provides a keyword to get the same effect automatically. Modify **Asset** to make the owner property a *weak reference* instead of a strong reference.

## Listing 24.7  Making the owner property a weak reference (Asset.swift)

```
class Asset: CustomStringConvertible {
    let name: String
    let value: Double
    weak var owner: Person?
    ...
}
```

A weak reference is a reference that does not increase the reference count of the instance it refers to. In this case, making owner a weak reference means that when you assign Bob as the owner of the laptop and the hat, Bob's reference count does not increase. The only strong reference to Bob is the bob variable in main.swift.

Now, when you set the bob variable to nil, the reference count on Bob drops to 0, so it is deallocated. When Bob is deallocated, he no longer holds a strong reference to his assets, so their reference counts drop to 0 as well. Running your program again confirms that all the objects are deallocated.

```
created Optional(Person(Bob))
Person(Bob) is being deallocated
the bob variable is now nil
Asset(Shiny Laptop, worth 1500.0, not owned by anyone) is being deallocated
Asset(Cowboy Hat, worth 175.0, not owned by anyone) is being deallocated
Asset(Blue Backpack, worth 45.0, not owned by anyone) is being deallocated
```

What happens to a weak reference if the instance it is referring to is deallocated? The weak reference is set to nil. You can see this in action by editing main.swift.

## Listing 24.8  Who owns the hat? (main.swift)

```
...
bob?.takeOwnershipOfAsset(laptop!)
bob?.takeOwnershipOfAsset(hat!)

print("While Bob is alive, hat's owner is \(hat!.owner)")
bob = nil
print("the bob variable is now \(bob)")
print("After Bob is deallocated, hat's owner is \(hat!.owner)")
...
```

Running your program again demonstrates weak variables in action:

```
created Optional(Person(Bob))
While Bob is alive, hat's owner is Optional(Person(Bob))
Person(Bob) is being deallocated
the bob variable is now nil
After Bob is deallocated, hat's owner is nil
Asset(Shiny Laptop, worth 1500.0, not owned by anyone) is being deallocated
Asset(Cowboy Hat, worth 175.0, not owned by anyone) is being deallocated
Asset(Blue Backpack, worth 45.0, not owned by anyone) is being deallocated
```

There are two requirements for weak references:

- Weak references must always be declared as var, not let.

- Weak references must always be declared as optional.

Both of these requirements are the result of weak references being changed to nil if the instance they point to is deallocated. The only types that can become nil are optionals, so weak references must be optional. And instances declared with let cannot change, so weak references must be declared with var.

In most cases, strong reference cycles like the one you just resolved are easy to avoid. **Person** is a class that owns assets, so it makes sense that it would keep strong references to the assets. **Asset** is a class that is owned by a **Person**. If it wants a reference to its owner, that reference should be weak. After all, a person owns an asset – an asset does not own a person!

There is another way to create reference cycles that is much more subtle: capturing self in a closure.

# Reference Cycles in Closures

Time to add an accountant class that will keep track of a **Person**'s net worth. Create a new Swift file called Accountant.swift and define your new class.

### Listing 24.9  Defining an **Accountant** (Accountant.swift)

```
import Foundation

class Accountant {
    typealias NetWorthChanged = (Double) -> ()

    var netWorthChangedHandler: NetWorthChanged? = nil
    var netWorth: Double = 0.0 {
        didSet {
            netWorthChangedHandler?(netWorth)
        }
    }

    func gainedNewAsset(asset: Asset) {
        netWorth += asset.value
    }
}
```

**Accountant** defines a typealias, **NetWorthChanged**, which is a closure that takes a **Double** (the new net worth value) and returns nothing. It has two properties: netWorthChangedHandler, which is an optional closure to call when the net worth changes, and netWorth, the current net worth of a person. netWorth has a didSet property observer that calls the netWorthChangedHandler closure if it is non-nil. Finally, the **gainedNewAsset(_:)** function should be called to tell the accountant that the value of a new asset should be added to the net worth value.

Update `Person.swift` to have an accountant to track a **Person**'s net worth.

## Listing 24.10  Adding an **Accountant** to the **Person** class (`Person.swift`)

```
import Foundation

class Person: CustomStringConvertible {
    let name: String
    let acccountant = Accountant()
    var assets = [Asset]()

    var description: String {
        return "Person(\(name))"
    }

    init(name: String) {
        self.name = name

        accountant.netWorthChangedHandler = {
            netWorth in

            self.netWorthDidChange(netWorth)
            return
        }
    }

    deinit {
        print("\(self) is being deallocated")
    }

    func takeOwnershipOfAsset(asset: Asset) {
        asset.owner = self
        assets.append(asset)
        accountant.gainedNewAsset(asset)
    }

    func netWorthDidChange(netWorth: Double) {
        print("The net worth of \(self) is now \(netWorth)")
    }
}
```

You add an accountant property that has a default value of a new **Accountant**. **Person** has a strong reference to its **Accountant**, which is perfectly reasonable. In **init()**, you set the netWorthChangedHandler on the accountant to call your new **netWorthDidChange(_:)** method, which logs the person's new net worth. Finally, you update **takeOwnershipOfAsset(_:)** to notify the accountant of new assets. Build and run your program. You should see the following:

```
created Optional(Person(Bob))
The net worth of Person(Bob) is now 1500.0
The net worth of Person(Bob) is now 1675.0
While Bob is alive, hat's owner is Optional(Person(Bob))
the bob variable is now nil
After Bob is deallocated, hat's owner is Optional(Person(Bob))
Asset(Blue Backpack, worth 45.0, not owned by anyone) is being deallocated
```

You get the log messages of the net worth changing, so all of the accountant code you added appears to be working correctly. However, the memory leak is back: Bob, the laptop, and the hat are not being deallocated. Why aren't these instances being removed from memory?

Your new code includes a not-so-obvious strong reference cycle. **Person** has a strong reference to **Accountant**, but **Accountant** does not have a strong reference back to **Person**, at least at first glance. To get a hint about what is going on, try modifying the **init()** method of **Person** (this will cause a compiler error).

### Listing 24.11  Modifying **init()** (Person.swift)

```
...
    init(name: String) {
        self.name = name

        accountant.netWorthChangedHandler = {
            netWorth in

            self.netWorthDidChange(netWorth)
            return
        }
    }
}
```

Try to build your program now. The error message you receive states `Call to method 'netWorthDidChange' in closure requires explicit 'self.' to make capture semantics explicit`. What are the "capture semantics" of a closure?

A closure has its own scope within its definition. By default, a closure takes a strong reference to any variables that it uses inside the scope. **netWorthDidChange(_:)** is a method on self, so calling it would give the closure a strong reference to self. This explains why you are leaking memory: **Accountant** actually *does* have a strong reference back to **Person**! **Accountant**'s netWorthChangedHandler is holding a strong reference to its owning **Person** via that **Person**'s self, as shown in Figure 24.3.

### Figure 24.3 **Person** to **Accountant** to **Person** strong reference cycle

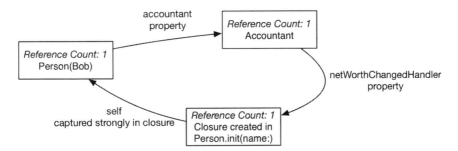

Take another look at the error message: "to make capture semantics explicit." Swift could allow you to use self implicitly in closures, but doing so would make it very easy to accidentally create strong reference cycles, as you have done here. Instead, the language requires you to be *explicit* about your use of self, forcing you to consider whether a reference cycle is a possibility.

To change the capture semantics of a closure to capture references weakly, you can use a *capture list*. Modify Person.swift to use a capture list when creating the closure.

### Listing 24.12  Using a capture list (`Person.swift`)

```
init(name: String) {
    self.name = name

    accountant.netWorthChangedHandler = {
        [weak self] netWorth in

        self?.netWorthDidChange(netWorth)
        return
    }
}
```

The capture list syntax is a list of variables inside square brackets ([]) immediately before the list of the closure arguments. The capture list you wrote here tells Swift to capture self weakly instead of strongly. Now that the **Accountant**'s closure no longer strongly references the **Person**, the strong reference cycle is broken.

Note the use of self? in the body of the closure. Because self is captured weakly and all weak instances must be optional, self inside the closure is optional.

Run your program again and confirm that all the instances are being deallocated appropriately:

```
created Optional(Person(Bob))
The net worth of Person(Bob) is now 1500.0
The net worth of Person(Bob) is now 1675.0
While Bob is alive, hat's owner is Optional(Person(Bob))
Person(Bob) is being deallocated
the bob variable is now nil
After Bob is deallocated, hat's owner is nil
Asset(Shiny Laptop, worth 1500.0, not owned by anyone) is being deallocated
Asset(Cowboy Hat, worth 175.0, not owned by anyone) is being deallocated
Asset(Blue Backpack, worth 45.0, not owned by anyone) is being deallocated
```

# Bronze Challenge

The idea of asset ownership by a **Person** is incomplete. **Person** has a way to take ownership of an asset, but no way to give up ownership of an asset. Update **Person** so that an instance can relinquish an asset. (Hint: you will probably need to update **Accountant**, too, if you want a valid net worth value.)

# Silver Challenge

Create another **Person** in main.swift. Immediately after you give Bob ownership of the laptop, try giving your new **Person** ownership of the same laptop. Now both people own the laptop! Fix this bug.

# For the More Curious: Can I Retrieve the Reference Count of an Instance?

Unfortunately, Swift does not give you access to the actual reference count of any instances.

Even if you could ask an instance what its reference count is, the answer you get might not be what you expect. Throughout this chapter, we said things like, "At this point, the reference count is 2." That was a white lie.

Conceptually, it is perfectly reasonable for you to think of reference counts the way we described. Under the hood, the compiler is free to insert additional calls to retain (increment the reference count) and release (decrement the reference count). As long as it does its job correctly, there is no harm to your program. If you could ask what the actual reference count of an instance is, the answer would depend on what sort of analysis the compiler had done at that point. Additionally, there are some classes in the Mac and iOS system libraries that behave in strange ways when it comes to reference counting (the details of which are beyond the scope of this book).

The important things for you to remember are how to recognize the potential for strong reference cycles and how to use weak to break them.

# 25

# Equatable and Comparable

Much of programming depends on comparing values. It is important to know whether two values are equal or, if not, *how* one value compares to another: is this value less than or greater than that value?

It is good practice to have your custom value types know how to compare themselves to other instances. In fact, you have been doing this with Swift's basic types throughout the book. Does this string equal another string? Is this integer smaller than that integer? All of Swift's basic types know how to compare themselves to other instances of the same type. Why?

The answer is closely related to the purpose of value types. Instances of these types represent specific *values*. There is an intrinsic expectation here that values can and should be comparable. We intuitively want to know how one integer compares to another integer.

Swift provides two protocols for testing equality and comparability: `Equatable` and `Comparable`. This chapter will show you how you can make a custom type conform to these protocols. This will involve implementing a few functions that will teach instances of your type how to compare themselves to other instances of the same type. Create a new playground called `Comparison.playground` to begin.

## Conforming to Equatable

Create a new type that does not yet conform to the `Equatable` protocol.

Listing 25.1 Defining **Point**

```
struct Point {
    let x: Int
    let y: Int
}
```

The struct above defines a `Point` type. `Point` uses its x and y properties to describe a location on a two-dimensional plane.

At the moment, `Point` does not know how to determine whether an instance is equal to another instance. Create two instances of this type to see what happens when you check whether the two are equal.

Listing 25.2 Creating two **Points**

```
struct Point {
    let x: Int
    let y: Int
}
let a = Point(x: 3, y: 4)
let b = Point(x: 3, y: 4)
```

You create two new points, a and b, using the free memberwise initializer provided by the compiler. You give both points the same values for their x and y properties. Now try to use the == operator to test for equality between these two points.

## Listing 25.3  Is a the same as b?

```
struct Point {
    let x: Int
    let y: Int
}

let a = Point(x: 3, y: 4)
let b = Point(x: 3, y: 4)
let abEqual = (a == b)
```

You should see in the timeline that this check for equality does not work. In fact, it generates an error from the compiler. This error stems from the fact that you have not yet taught your **Point** struct how to test for equality between two instances.

Teaching this to your struct will involve making **Point** conform to the **Equatable** protocol. Add the following code to your struct's declaration.

## Listing 25.4  Adding a protocol conformance declaration

```
struct Point: Equatable {
    let x: Int
    let y: Int
}

let a = Point(x: 3, y: 4)
let b = Point(x: 3, y: 4)

let abEqual = (a == b)
```

Now you have a new error. This time, the error is on the line where you declare the **Point** struct. The error will say something about **Point** not conforming to the **Equatable** protocol. In short, this means that the compiler does not know how to check if a and b are equal.

To figure out how to conform to the **Equatable** protocol, open the documentation. Option-click on **Equatable** and, in the pop-up, click on the link at the bottom to the "Equatable Protocol Reference" to bring up the full reference.

The documentation tells you that you are required to implement the == operator. This implementation must be done at global scope in order to conform to this protocol. Recall that a function, for example, defined at global scope is not defined on any particular type so you need to write an implementation of == outside of the definition of your **Point** type.

But == already has a definition; several, in fact. You can use == to compare strings, double, integers, dictionaries, and so on. Because **Point** is a type that you have created yourself, you need to provide another implementation of == so that Swift knows how to compare two instances of that type.

In Swift, *overloading* refers to providing multiple definitions for a function or method with the same name. Each definition of the function will have its own implementation, meaning that the different definitions will do different things. For the compiler to know which function you want to call, the overloaded functions or methods need to differ in terms of their parameters (the number of parameters and/or the types the parameters expect).

Why do you have to conform at global scope? If you think about it, this requirement makes sense because == is not a method that you call on a specific type. Instead, == appears between and operates on two targets at once: it checks to see whether the value on the lefthand side is equal to the value on the righthand side. Operators that work on two targets like this are called *infix operators*.

You can now write an implementation of == that compares two instances of the **Point** type and tests for their equality. Your implementation of == will be defined at global scope; that is, it will not be defined on the **Point** struct. It will test for equality by checking to see if two instances of **Point** have the same values in both the x and y properties.

## Listing 25.5 Changing the implementation of ==

```
struct Point: Equatable {
    let x: Int
    let y: Int
}

func ==(lhs: Point, rhs: Point) -> Bool {
    return (lhs.x == rhs.x) && (lhs.y == rhs.y)
}

let a = Point(x: 3, y: 4)
let b = Point(x: 3, y: 4)

let abEqual = (a == b)
```

You now have a new implementation of the == operator. (Note that an operator is a just a function with a special name.) This definition has two arguments: an lhs argument for the lefthand side and an rhs for the righthand side of the equality check. Both of these arguments are expected to be of type **Point**.

The function's implementation is straightforward. It compares the x and y values for both instances of the **Point** type that are passed into the function's arguments. Then it returns a **Bool** indicating whether the instances are equal.

Take a look at your playground's results sidebar. You should see that the errors are gone and that your test for equality between a and b succeeds. The two points are equal because both of their x and y values are the same. (Try changing just the x values so that they do not match. You should see that the two points are no longer equal. Make sure to change the values back to their previous values before proceeding.)

Your **Point** struct now conforms to **Equatable**, so you can test **Point**s for equality. And there is more. Swift's standard library provides a default implementation of the != function that depends on the definition of ==. This feature means that if your type conforms to **Equatable** by implementing its own version of ==, then it also has a working implementation of the != function.

Try it out by adding the following test.

## Listing 25.6 Is a not the same as b?

```
struct Point: Equatable {
    let x: Int
    let y: Int
}

func ==(lhs: Point, rhs: Point) -> Bool {
    return (lhs.x == rhs.x) && (lhs.y == rhs.y)
}

let a = Point(x: 3, y: 4)
let b = Point(x: 3, y: 4)

let abEqual = (a == b)
let abNotEqual = (a != b)
```

The results sidebar should update to show that this test for inequality yields `false`. In other words, the two points *are* equal, which means that they are *not* unequal.

# Conforming to Comparable

Now that your **Point** type conforms to the **Equatable** protocol, you may be interested in more nuanced forms of comparison. For example, perhaps you want to know if a point is less than another point. You accomplish this functionality by conforming to the **Comparable** protocol.

Open the documentation for **Comparable**. Because you have not entered **Comparable** yet (so cannot Option-click on its name), click on the Help menu and select Documentation and API Reference. Search for "Comparable" to determine what is needed. You will find that you need to overload one operator: the < infix operator. Add the following code to your struct to make it conform to **Comparable**.

## Listing 25.7 Conforming to **Comparable**

```
struct Point: Equatable, Comparable {
    let x: Int
    let y: Int
}

func ==(lhs: Point, rhs: Point) -> Bool {
    return (lhs.x == rhs.x) && (lhs.y == rhs.y)
}

func <(lhs: Point, rhs: Point) -> Bool {
    return (lhs.x < rhs.x) && (lhs.y < rhs.y)
}

let a = Point(x: 3, y: 4)
let b = Point(x: 3, y: 4)

let abEqual = (a == b)
let abNotEqual = (a != b)
```

You have added a new declaration to your **Point** that says that it conforms to the **Comparable** protocol. You also added a global implementation of the < operator. This implementation works similarly to your implementation of ==. It checks whether the point passed in on the lefthand side is less than the point passed in on the righthand side. If the x and y values for the point on the lefthand side are both smaller than the values on the righthand side, the function will return true. Otherwise, the function will return false, indicating that the point on the lefthand side is not less than the righthand side.

Create two new points to test this function.

## Listing 25.8  Testing the < function

```
struct Point: Equatable, Comparable {
    let x: Int
    let y: Int
}

func ==(lhs: Point, rhs: Point) -> Bool {
    return (lhs.x == rhs.x) && (lhs.y == rhs.y)
}

func <(lhs: Point, rhs: Point) -> Bool {
    return (lhs.x < rhs.x) && (lhs.y < rhs.y)
}

let a = Point(x: 3, y: 4)
let b = Point(x: 3, y: 4)

let abEqual = (a == b)
let abNotEqual = (a != b)
let c = Point(x: 2, y: 6)
let d = Point(x: 3, y: 7)

let cdEqual = (c == d)
let cLessThanD = (c < d)
```

You create two new points with different values for x and y. You check to see whether c and d are equal, which returns false: the two points are not the same. Last, you exercise your overload of the < operator to determine whether c is less than d. In this case, the comparison evaluates to true. The point c is less than the point d because both its x and y values are smaller than d's.

As with conforming to the **Equatable** protocol, implementing one function can give you much more functionality. The Swift standard library defines the >, >=, and <= operators in terms of the < and == operators. This is why **Comparable** only requires that you overload the < operator. If your type conforms to **Comparable**, then it will get implementations of these operators for free.

Test this functionality by adding a series of new comparisons.

## Listing 25.9  Exercising comparisons

```
struct Point: Equatable, Comparable {
    let x: Int
    let y: Int
}

func ==(lhs: Point, rhs: Point) -> Bool {
    return (lhs.x == rhs.x) && (lhs.y == rhs.y)
}

func <(lhs: Point, rhs: Point) -> Bool {
    return (lhs.x < rhs.x) && (lhs.y < rhs.y)
}

let a = Point(x: 3, y: 4)
let b = Point(x: 3, y: 4)

let abEqual = (a == b)
let abNotEqual = (a != b)
let c = Point(x: 2, y: 6)
let d = Point(x: 3, y: 7)

let cdEqual = (c == b)
let cLessThanD = (c < d)

let cLessThanEqualD = (c <= d)
let cGreaterThanD = (c > d)
let cGreaterThanEqualD = (c >= d)
```

These last three comparisons check whether:

- c is less than or equal to d

- c is greater than d

- c is greater than or equal to d

As anticipated, these comparisons evaluate to true, false, and false, respectively.

# Comparable's Inheritance

`Comparable` actually inherits from `Equatable`. You may be able to guess what the implication of this inheritance is. In order to conform to the `Comparable` protocol, you must also conform to the `Equatable` protocol by supplying an implementation of the `==` operator. This relationship also means that a type does not have to explicitly declare conformance to `Equatable` if it declares conformance to `Comparable`. Remove the explicit declaration of conformance to `Equatable` from your `Point` struct.

Listing 25.10  Removing the unnecessary conformance declaration

```
struct Point: Equatable, Comparable {
    let x: Int
    let y: Int
}

func ==(lhs: Point, rhs: Point) -> Bool {
    return (lhs.x == rhs.x) && (lhs.y == rhs.y)
}

func <(lhs: Point, rhs: Point) -> Bool {
    return (lhs.x < rhs.x) && (lhs.y < rhs.y)
}

...
```

You should see that the playground works just as it did before.

One final note on style. While it is not wrong to explicitly declare conformance to both `Equatable` and `Comparable`, it is unnecessary. If your type conforms to `Comparable`, then it must conform to `Equatable` as well. This point is a detail listed in the documentation, which makes it an expected consequence of conforming to `Comparable`. Adding the explicit conformance to `Equatable` does not add that much more information.

On the other hand, it may make sense to have a type explicitly conform to all protocols involved when conforming to a custom protocol that inherits from another protocol. Although it is still unnecessary, it may make your code more readable and easier to maintain, because your custom protocol is not listed in the official documentation.

# Bronze Challenge

Make it possible to add two points together. The addition of two points should return a new `Point` that adds the given points' x values and y values. You will need to overload the `+` operator for the `Point` struct.

# Gold Challenge

Create a new `Person` class with two properties: `name` and `age`. For convenience, create an initializer that provides arguments for both of these properties.

Next, create two new instances of the `Person` class. Assign those instances to two constants named `p1` and `p2`. Also create an array named `people` to hold these instances and then put them inside the array.

You will occasionally need to find the index of an instance of a custom type within an array. Call the `indexOf(_:)` method on your array to do so. The argument takes the value of some element in the collection whose index you would like to find. Use the method to find the index of p1 inside of the people array.

You will get an error. Take some time to understand the error, and then resolve it. You should be able to assign the result of the **indexOf** to a constant named p1Index. Its value should be 0.

# Platinum Challenge

**Point**'s current conformance to **Comparable** yields some confusing results.

```
let c = Point(x: 3, y: 4)
let d = Point(x: 2, y: 5)

let cGreaterThanD = (c > d) // false
let cLessThanD = (c < d)    // false
let cEqualToD = (c == d)    // false
```

As the above example demonstrates, the trouble arises in comparing two points when one point's x and y properties are not both larger than the other point's. In actuality, it is not reasonable to compare two points in this manner.

Fix this problem by changing **Point**'s conformance to **Comparable**. Calculate each point's Euclidean distance from the origin instead of comparing x and y values. This implementation should return true for a < b when a is closer to the origin than b.

Use the formula shown in Figure 25.1 to calculate a point's Euclidean distance:

Figure 25.1  Euclidean distance

$$distance(a, b) = \sqrt{(a_x - b_x)^2 + (a_y - b_y)^2}$$

# For the More Curious: Custom Operators

Swift allows developers to create custom operators. This feature means that you can create your own operator to signify that one instance of the **Person** type has married another instance. Say, for example, you want to create the +++ to marry one instance to another.

Create a new **Person** class like so:

Listing 25.11  Setting up a **Person** class

```
...
class Person: Equatable {
    var name: String
    weak var spouse: Person?

    init(name: String, spouse: Person?) {
        self.name = name
        self.spouse = spouse
    }
}
```

The class has two properties: one for a name and another for a spouse. It also has an initializer that will give values to those properties. Note that the `spouse` property is an optional to indicate that a person may not have a spouse.

Next, create two instances of this class.

## Listing 25.12  Creating two instances of person

```
...
class Person: Equatable {
    var name: String
    weak var spouse: Person?

    init(name: String, spouse: Person?) {
        self.name = name
        self.spouse = spouse
    }
}

let matt = Person(name: "Matt", spouse: nil)
let drew = Person(name: "Drew", spouse: nil)
```

Now, declare your new infix operator. It has to be declared at global scope. Also, define how the new operator function will work.

## Listing 25.13  Declaring a custom operator

```
...
class Person: Equatable {
    var name: String
    weak var spouse: Person?

    init(name: String, spouse: Person?) {
        self.name = name
        self.spouse = spouse
    }
}

let matt = Person(name: "Matt", spouse: nil)
let drew = Person(name: "Drew", spouse: nil)

infix operator +++ {}

func +++(lhs: Person, rhs: Person) {
    lhs.spouse = rhs
    rhs.spouse = lhs
}
```

The new operator, **+++**, will be used to marry two instances of the **Person** class. As an infix operator, it will be used between two instances. The implementation of **+++** will assign each instance to the other's `spouse` property.

Exercise this new operator like so:

## Listing 25.14  Using the custom operator

```
...
class Person: Equatable {
    var name: String
    weak var spouse: Person?

    init(name: String, spouse: Person?) {
        self.name = name
        self.spouse = spouse
    }
}

let matt = Person(name: "Matt", spouse: nil)
let drew = Person(name: "Drew", spouse: nil)

infix operator +++ {}

func +++(lhs: Person, rhs: Person) {
    lhs.spouse = rhs
    rhs.spouse = lhs
}

matt +++ drew
matt.spouse?.name
drew.spouse?.name
```

The code `matt +++ drew` serves to marry the two instances. Check that this process worked by examining the playground's results sidebar.

While this operator works, and it is not too difficult to determine what is going on by looking at it, we generally recommend that you avoid declaring custom operators. It is good practice to only create custom operators for your own types when the operator will be recognizable to anyone who may read your code. That typically means restricting your custom operators to the realm of well-known mathematical operators. (In fact, Swift only allows you to use a well-defined collection of mathematical symbols to create custom operators. For example, you cannot refactor the **+++** operator to be the emoji "face throwing a kiss" (i.e., U+1F61A).

Someone reviewing your code in the future may not know exactly what you meant by **+++**. (You might even forget, yourself.) After all, it is fairly ambiguous in this case.

Moreover, it is not as though this custom operator accomplishes something more elegantly or efficiently than a **marry(_:)** method would. For example, a **marry(_:)** method might look like this:

```
func marry(spouse: Person) {
    self.spouse = spouse
    spouse.spouse = self
}
```

This code is far more readable, and it is quite clear what the code is doing. These qualities will make it easier to maintain in the future.

# Part VI
## Event-Driven Applications

In this part of the book, you will apply your knowledge of Swift to develop your first Mac and iOS applications. Along the way, you will see the basics of interoperating between Swift and Objective-C, Apple's precursor to Swift.

# 26

# Your First Cocoa Application

One of Swift's most compelling features is its ability to interact with Objective-C, the language in which Mac and iOS apps have traditionally been written. We are not going to cover the full story of how the two languages live side by side in one app, but the next three chapters will give you a taste. Swift makes it possible to use Objective-C libraries like Cocoa, the native API for developing desktop Mac apps.

Swift is able to talk to Cocoa (and other Objective-C frameworks) using techniques broadly described as *bridging*. Bridging is the process by which a function or instance in one language can be called from or given to the other language. The bridging goes in both directions: Swift can call Objective-C functions, and Objective-C can call Swift functions (with some restrictions). Most of the time, the compiler handles all the details of bridging for you, but occasionally it needs you to step in and give it some help. You will see some examples of that shortly.

In this chapter, you are going to create VocalTextEdit, a desktop application for Mac. VocalTextEdit is a very simple text editor that has the bonus feature of being able to read your document aloud to you. This application is very simple; it will give you only a taste of how Cocoa development works. For a much more thorough exploration of Cocoa, see the most recent edition of *Cocoa Programming for OS X: The Big Nerd Ranch Guide*.

VocalTextEdit will be a *document-based application*. This allows users to have multiple windows open at the same time, each representing a different file. When you are done, your application will look like Figure 26.1.

## Figure 26.1  Complete VocalTextEdit application

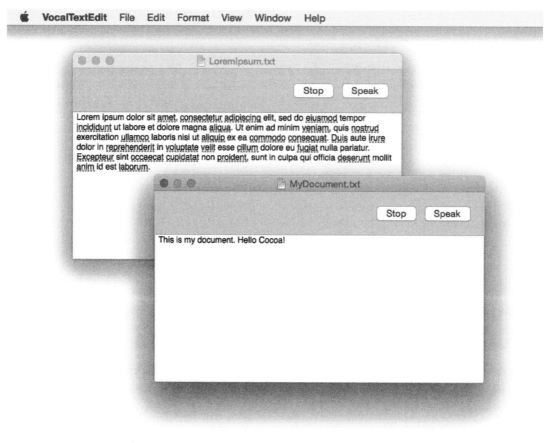

The bottom portion of each VocalTextEdit document window should look familiar: it is a simple text editor. The Speak button at the top allows the user to have the computer speak the contents of the text document. The Stop button stops any active speaking. VocalTextEdit, as a user would expect from a document-based application, also supports the normal save and open operations as well as autosaving.

Please note that this chapter uses OS X Storyboards, which requires you to be running OS X 10.10 (Yosemite) or later.

# Getting Started with VocalTextEdit

In Xcode, choose File → New → Project... (or, from the Welcome screen, Create a new Xcode project). Select Application under the OS X section (not iOS). Select the Cocoa Application template and click Next (Figure 26.2).

Figure 26.2  Choosing the Cocoa Application template

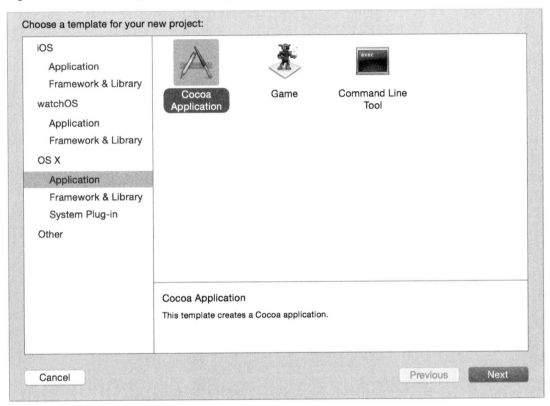

In the next window, name the project VocalTextEdit (Figure 26.3). Make sure the selected language is Swift. Check both the Use Storyboards and Create Document-Based Application boxes. Enter **txt** as the Document Extension (VocalTextEdit is ultimately just a text editor, and it will save text files).

Figure 26.3  Configuring VocalTextEdit

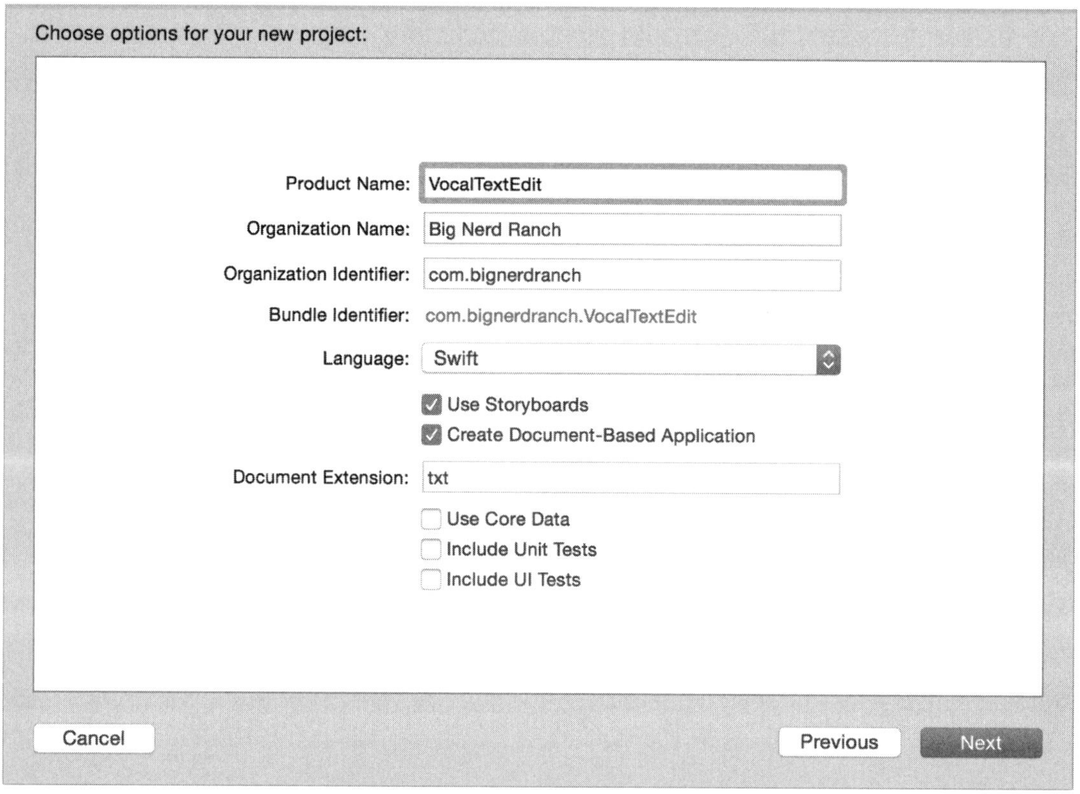

Click Next and finish creating your project by saving it to the location of your choice.

Before diving into your app, let's briefly look at a core pattern that is used by both Cocoa and iOS applications.

# Model-View-Controller

*Model-View-Controller*, or MVC, is a design pattern that is based on the idea that any class that you create should fall into one of three job categories: model, view, or controller. Here is a breakdown of the division of labor:

- *Models* are responsible for storing data and making it available to other objects. Models have no knowledge of the user interface or how to draw themselves on the screen. Their sole purpose is holding and managing data. For example, an application that tracks attendance for a school would define a model object for **Student**. A **Student** would "model" all of the attributes a real student would have, such as a name and a grade. Swift types like **String** and **Array** are traditional building blocks of model objects. In VocalTextEdit, the **Document** class will act as the model object for each of the user's text files.

- *Views* are the visual elements of an application. Views know how to draw themselves on the screen and how to respond to user input. Views have no knowledge of the actual data that they display or how it is structured and stored. A simple rule of thumb is: if you can see it, it is a view. In VocalTextEdit, your view objects will include instances of **NSTextView** and **NSButton**.

- *Controllers* perform the logic necessary to connect your views and models. They process events, often from the user of the application, and relay information from your views down to your models and back again. Controllers are the real workhorses of any application, as they are the mediators between models and views. In VocalTextEdit, the **ViewController** class will coordinate between the appropriate **Document** and the views that are visible on the screen.

Figure 26.4 shows the flow of control between objects in response to a user event, like a button click. Notice that models and views do not talk to each other directly – controllers sit squarely in the middle of everything, receiving messages from some objects and dispatching instructions to others.

Figure 26.4  MVC flow with user input

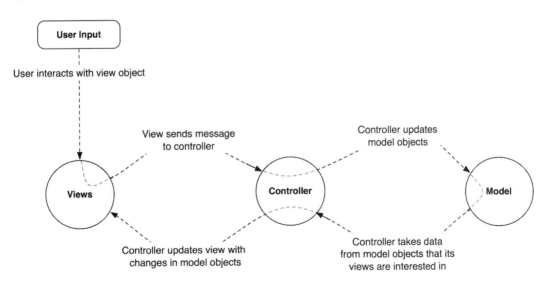

# Setting Up the View Controller

The template creates a few Swift files and a file called Main.storyboard, which you will get to momentarily. First, open ViewController.swift. Begin by removing the overridden functions the template provided for you, as you will not need them for this app.

Listing 26.1  Cleaning out template code (ViewController.swift)

```
class ViewController: NSViewController {

    override func viewDidLoad() {
        super.viewDidLoad()

        // Do any additional setup after loading the view.
    }

    override var representedObject: AnyObject? {
        didSet {
        // Update the view, if already loaded.
        }
    }

}
```

Note that the **ViewController** class is a subclass of **NSViewController**. As the name suggests, a view controller manages the user interface and responds to actions by the user.

Add one new property and two instance methods. Some of this code will look unfamiliar; we will explain it after you have typed it in.

Listing 26.2  Adding a property and two instance methods (ViewController.swift)

```
class ViewController: NSViewController {

    @IBOutlet var textView: NSTextView!

    @IBAction func speakButtonClicked(sender: NSButton) {
        print("The speak button was clicked")
    }

    @IBAction func stopButtonClicked(sender: NSButton) {
        print("The stop button was clicked")
    }

}
```

Ignore @IBOutlet and @IBAction for just a moment and examine the rest of what you typed. You declared an implicitly unwrapped optional property, textView, and two functions that take **NSButton** arguments and return nothing. The textView property will be your handle to the portion of the document window that displays editable text. On Mac, the class that Cocoa gives you to provide this functionality is **NSTextView**.

Look at the documentation for **NSTextView** by Option-clicking its name. In the pop-up, click on the NSTextView Class Reference link at the bottom to bring up the full reference documentation for **NSTextView** (Figure 26.5).

## Figure 26.5 **NSTextView** reference documentation

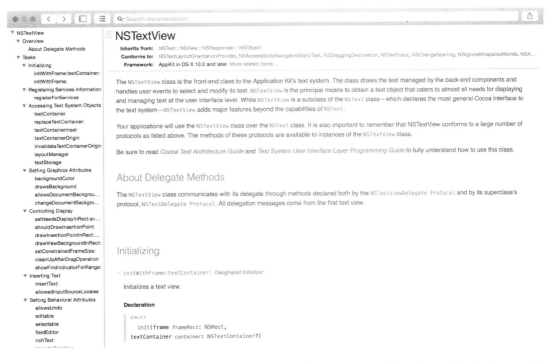

**NSTextView** has many properties and methods, but the only one you need for this application is actually provided by **NSTextView**'s superclass, **NSText**. You can jump to **NSText**'s reference documentation by clicking on the **NSText** link at the very top, in **NSTextView**'s Inherits from: section. **NSText** supplies the string property, which will allow you to get and set the contents of the text view as a **String**.

The IB in @IBOutlet and @IBAction stands for "Interface Builder." A long time ago (by software standards), Apple provided two different tools for developing apps: Xcode, used for source code, and Interface Builder, used for laying out the user interface. Interface Builder was merged into Xcode, but iOS and Cocoa programmers and Apple still often refer to the "user interface layout" parts of Xcode as Interface Builder.

@IBOutlet and @IBAction are attributes. The @IBOutlet and @IBAction here do not change the code in any meaningful way. Instead, they let Xcode know that the attributed properties and methods are involved with Interface Builder. @IBOutlet tells Xcode that the textView property can be assigned in Interface Builder. @IBAction advertises the method to Interface Builder as one that can be called when a user interacts with a view, such as by clicking on a button.

# Setting Up Views in Interface Builder

Time to set up your views. In the project navigator on the lefthand side of Xcode, select the
Main.storyboard file. A storyboard file allows you to visually lay out the windows and views of your
application using Interface Builder. Large applications may use many storyboards. You are only going
to use Main.storyboard for VocalTextEdit. Main.storyboard starts out looking like Figure 26.6.

Figure 26.6  Initial Main.storyboard contents

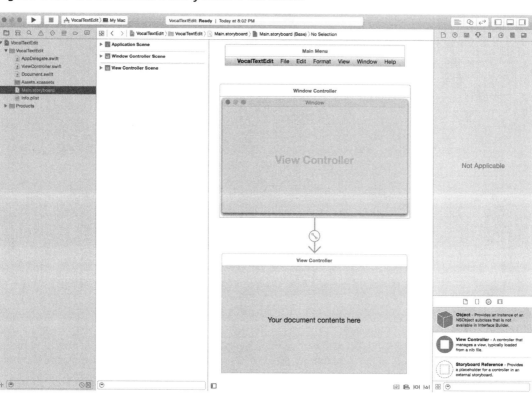

The pane just to the left of the user interface in Figure 26.6 is the *document outline*. The document
outline presents a tree showing how each object contains its children. If the document outline is not
visible, click the Show Document Outline button at the bottom of Interface Builder (Figure 26.7).

Figure 26.7  Show the document outline

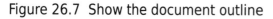

There are currently three top-level *scenes* in `Main.storyboard`. From top to bottom, you are seeing the application's main menu, a window controller scene, and a view controller scene. You will only be working with the view controller scene. Right now, the view controller scene contains a single line of text contained in an **NSTextField**. You do not need that, so remove it by clicking on the Your document contents here text and pressing Delete on your keyboard.

Now that you have prepared a blank canvas for your application, you are going to lay out the views for VocalTextEdit. If the utilities area is not already visible, click the button in the far top-right corner of Xcode to make it visible, as shown in Figure 26.8.

## Figure 26.8  Showing Xcode's utilities

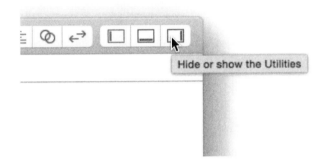

The bottom half of the utilities area is the *library*. The library is divided into tabs, identified by icons. Select the ⊚ icon to reveal the *object library*. The object library presents the different object types that you can drag and drop on the layout grid to build your user interface.

## Adding the Speak and Stop buttons

At the bottom of the object library is a search field. Search for "button." The item at the top of the object library, Push Button, represents an instance of the **NSButton** class.

To add an instance of a push button to your view controller's user interface, drag the button from the object library onto the view controller scene. As you drag the button toward the top-right corner of the view, you will see dashed blue lines and the button will snap into place, as shown in Figure 26.9. The dashed lines are from Apple's *Human Interface Guidelines*, or HIGs. The HIGs represent Apple's standards for designing user interfaces for the Mac. There are also HIGs for iOS devices, and you can find all the HIGs in the developer documentation.

## Figure 26.9  Dragging from object library to storyboard

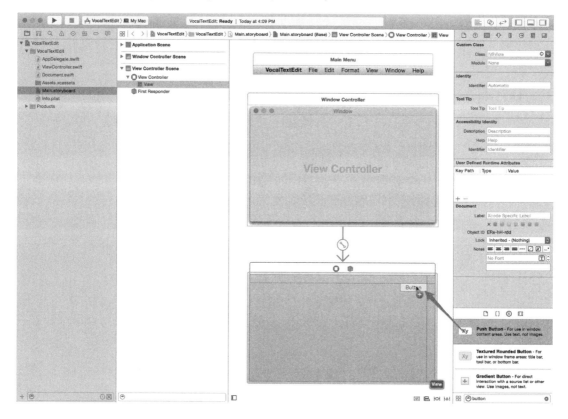

Now that the button is in the view controller scene, you need to change its title. Double-click on the button's text and type in **Speak**. Because "Speak" is slightly shorter than "Button," this may nudge the button out of place. Drag it back into the corner until it snaps back to the dashed blue lines. (We will cover a way to fix this a little later in the chapter.)

VocalTextEdit needs both a Speak and a Stop button. Drag another push button onto your view controller. Rename this second button Stop and drag it until it snaps into place just to the left of the Speak button. Your view controller layout should look like Figure 26.10.

Figure 26.10  VocalTextEdit layout: two buttons

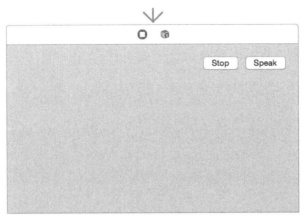

## Adding the text view

VocalTextEdit is predominantly a text editor, so you need to add a place for the user to enter text. Back in the search field for the object library, type in "textview." Drag a text view object onto your view controller layout and place it in the middle of the empty area below the buttons, as in Figure 26.11.

Figure 26.11  VocalTextEdit layout: adding a text view

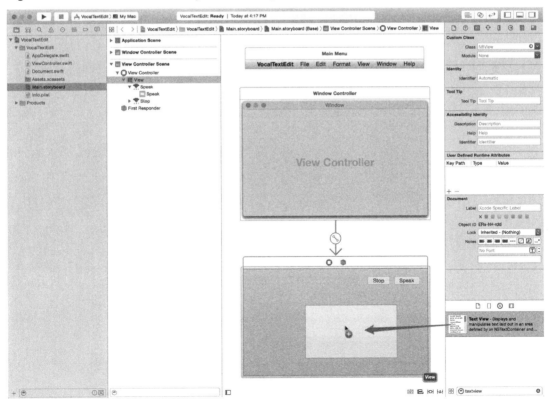

In addition to being able to select items by clicking on them in the layout, you can select them by clicking them in the document outline. Select the Bordered Scroll View - Text View item in the document outline, as shown in Figure 26.12.

Figure 26.12  Selecting a text view in the document outline

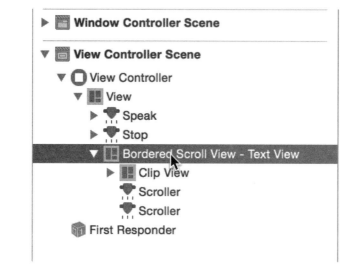

Notice that the text view is now selected both in the document outline (where it is highlighted in blue) and in the view controller scene (where it has square grab-points at its corners and on each side). Use the squares around the edges of the text view in the layout to resize it. Drag the left, right, and bottom edges until they are even with the view controller's edges, and drag the top until it snaps into place beneath the two buttons you have already added. At this point, your layout should look like Figure 26.13.

Figure 26.13  VocalTextEdit: layout

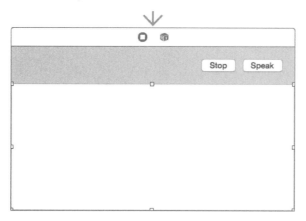

Build and run your app. After VocalTextEdit starts, you can create documents using Command-N (or File → New). You can also type into the text view. Unsurprisingly, the Speak and Stop buttons do nothing. Also, you may see error pop-ups about failures to autosave. You will fix both of these problems by the end of this chapter.

There is another problem that is not obvious. Try resizing your document window to give yourself more room to see your document. You may be surprised to find that your interface does not behave well (Figure 26.14).

Figure 26.14 Resizing failure

This resizing (mis)behavior is clearly undesirable. You will fix it next.

## Auto Layout

Cocoa and iOS provide a system called Auto Layout that allows you to set up constraints that define how views interact with each other during layout calculations. Full coverage of Auto Layout is outside the scope of this book, but you can set up some basic constraints that will allow you to get reasonable behavior when you resize a VocalTextEdit document.

Begin by creating constraints that will force the Speak button to stay in the top-right corner of the document window. Hold down the Control key, click on the Speak button, and drag to the upper right until the view controller's view is highlighted, as in Figure 26.15. (This is called "Control-dragging.")

Figure 26.15  Auto Layout: Speak

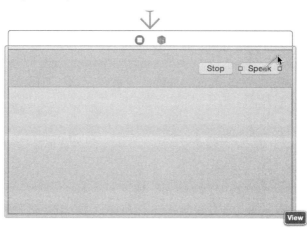

When you let go of the mouse, a contextual menu will pop up. You want to constrain the right and top edges of the button, so hold down the Shift key and click on both Trailing Space to Container and Top Space to Container (Figure 26.16).

Figure 26.16  Auto Layout: Speak button constraints

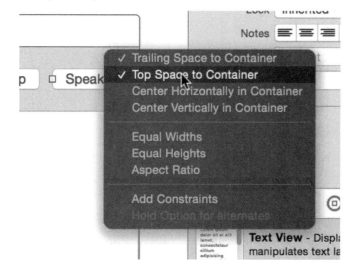

Press Return, and you will see a blue *I-beam* line connecting the top of the Speak button to the top of the view controller's view and another connecting the right edges. Run VocalTextEdit again and try resizing the window. You will see the Speak button stay in the correct place – the top-right corner – as you resize the window.

The Stop button and the text view still do not behave correctly; you need to add constraints to them. The Stop button is straightforward. You could add the same kinds of constraints to the Stop button as you did to the Speak button, pinning its top and right edges to the view controller's view. But that does not express the real layout relationship. You do not really care where the Stop button is relative to the view controller's view. What you want is for it to always be just to the left of the Speak button.

To create constraints between the Stop and Speak buttons, Control-drag from the Stop button to the Speak button. When the pop-up menu appears, hold down Shift and select both Horizontal Spacing and Baseline (Figure 26.17), then press Return.

Figure 26.17  Auto Layout: Stop button constraints

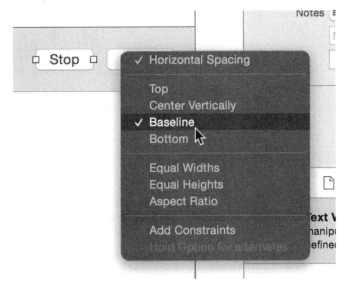

The horizontal spacing constraint ensures that the horizontal distance between the buttons stays fixed. The baseline constraint ensures that the two buttons are vertically aligned, using the baseline of the text within the buttons. Run VocalTextEdit again, resize the window, and confirm that the Stop button always stays in the correct place.

Creating constraints for the text view is a bit more complicated. You want the text view to stay the same size as the window, minus the space at the top for the two buttons. Remember how you can select items in the document outline? You can also create constraints in the document outline. Control-drag from Bordered Scroll View - Text View to its parent, View, as shown in Figure 26.18.

## Figure 26.18  Auto Layout: text view to view controller view

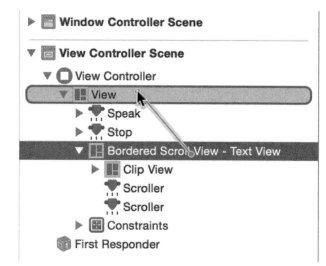

In the pop-up menu, hold down Shift and select three constraints: Leading Space to Container, Trailing Space to Container, and Bottom Space to Container. These constraints will pin the left, right, and bottom edges to always stick to the window's edges.

You still need to constrain the top edge. Back in the layout area, Control-drag from the text view to the Speak button. Select Vertical Spacing from the pop-up. This will maintain the spacing between the button and the text view.

Run VocalTextEdit again and resize your windows. Now all of the interface elements properly resize with the window.

# Making Connections

Creating views and laying out your user interface is not the only purpose of Interface Builder. You can also use Interface Builder to wire up connections between your views and your Swift code.

## Setting target-action pairs for VocalTextEdit's buttons

When you run your application and `Main.storyboard` is loaded, the Cocoa runtime will create an instance of your **ViewController** class, configure its views, and set up any outlets and actions you have configured. For VocalTextEdit, you want the **speakButtonClicked(_:)** method to be called on the instance of **ViewController** that is managing the current document. Control-drag from the Speak button to the icon representing the **ViewController**, as in Figure 26.19.

Figure 26.19  Connecting the Speak button

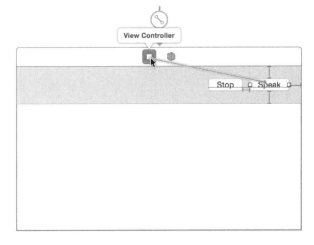

You will see a pop-up menu when you let go of the mouse. This menu shows you all the possible actions to take when the Speak button is clicked. Select the speakButtonClicked(_:) action from the Received Actions section of the pop-up.

You just created a *target-action pair*. A target-action pair associates an action (e.g., a method) to be called on a target (e.g., an instance of some type), usually in response to an action by a user (e.g., clicking on a button). When the user clicks on the Speak button, the **speakButtonClicked(_:)** method will be called on your **ViewController**.

Repeat the process to create a target-action pair for the Stop button. Control-drag from the Stop button to the **ViewController** icon. Select the stopButtonClicked(_:) action from the pop-up menu.

Build and run the application. Try clicking on the buttons. Back in Xcode, you will see log messages being printed whenever you click either button. Those are the result of the **print()** calls you put into the **speakButtonClicked(_:)** and **stopButtonClicked(_:)** methods back at the beginning of this chapter.

## Connecting the text view outlet

You have now connected both buttons, and your methods are called whenever the user clicks them. However, you still cannot get the text the user has entered into the text view. To do that, you need to connect the @IBOutlet you created for the text view.

To connect an outlet, Control-drag from the View Controller icon down to the text view, as in Figure 26.20. Note that this is the opposite of how you connected the button actions.

Figure 26.20  Connecting the text view outlet

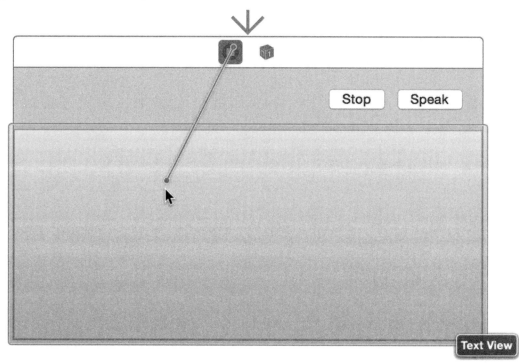

From the pop-up that appears, select textView, which matches the name of the @IBOutlet property you created.

You can build and run your application now, but nothing will behave any differently. Your @IBActions fire whenever the user clicks a button, but connecting an @IBOutlet does not by itself affect your program. Now that you have an outlet to the text view, open ViewController.swift and modify your **speakButtonClicked(_:)** method to log the current contents of the text view.

Listing 26.3  Making the Speak button log the contents of the text view
(ViewController.swift)

```
class ViewController: NSViewController {

    @IBOutlet var textView: NSTextView!

    @IBAction func speakButtonClicked(sender: NSButton) {
        print(~~"The speak button was clicked"~~ "I should speak \(textView.string)")
    }

    @IBAction func stopButtonClicked(sender: NSButton) {
        print("The stop button was clicked")
    }

}
```

Build and run your application. Type some text into the text view and click the Speak button. The text you typed is logged via your **print()** call, with a note that the string property of an **NSTextView** is optional:

```
I should speak Optional("Hello, world!")
```

# Making VocalTextEdit... Vocal

Logging the text is nice, but the real goal of VocalTextEdit is that the computer will read your users' text to them. Cocoa provides a class for synthesizing speech, suitably named **NSSpeechSynthesizer**. Begin by adding a property to your **ViewController** that is an instance of **NSSpeechSynthesizer**.

Listing 26.4  Adding an instance of **NSSpeechSynthesizer**
(ViewController.swift)

```
class ViewController: NSViewController {

    let speechSynthesizer = NSSpeechSynthesizer()

    @IBOutlet var textView: NSTextView!

    @IBAction func speakButtonClicked(sender: NSButton) {
        print("I should speak \(textView.string)")
    }

    @IBAction func stopButtonClicked(sender: NSButton) {
        print("The stop button was clicked")
    }

}
```

The default initializer of **NSSpeechSynthesizer** creates a speech synthesizer that uses a default voice. Now that you have a speech synthesizer, modify your **speakButtonClicked(_:)** method to actually synthesize the contents of textView. Use **NSSpeechSynthesizer**'s method **startSpeakingString(_:)**, which expects a **String**.

### Listing 26.5  Activating the speech synthesizer (ViewController.swift)

```
class ViewController: NSViewController {

    let speechSynthesizer = NSSpeechSynthesizer()

    @IBOutlet var textView: NSTextView!

    @IBAction func speakButtonClicked(sender: NSButton) {
        print("I should speak \(textView.string)")
        if let contents = textView.string {
            speechSynthesizer.startSpeakingString(contents)
        } else {
            speechSynthesizer.startSpeakingString("The document is empty.")
        }
    }

    @IBAction func stopButtonClicked(sender: NSButton) {
        print("The stop button was clicked")
    }

}
```

You use optional binding to get the contents of the text view, if there are any, and then speak them. If **textView.string** is nil, **speechSynthesizer** will speak the sentence "The document is empty."

Build and run your application. Type in some text – perhaps "Hello, world!" – and click the Speak button. You should hear your computer read your text back to you! (Make sure your sound is not muted.)

Now try deleting all the text and clicking Speak. Nothing happens! Why didn't the computer synthesize "The document is empty"?

There are actually two different ways the contents of a text view can be "empty." The string property could be nil, which would be handled by the code you already wrote. The other possibility is that the string property is not nil, but the **String** it contains is "", the empty string. Modify **speakButtonClicked(_:)** to handle this case.

### Listing 26.6  Handling both types of empty string (ViewController.swift)

```
...
    @IBAction func speakButtonClicked(sender: NSButton) {
        if let contents = textView.string where !contents.isEmpty {
            speechSynthesizer.startSpeakingString(contents)
        } else {
            speechSynthesizer.startSpeakingString("The document is empty.")
        }
    }
...
```

Build and run the application again. Leaving the text view empty, click the Speak button. Now you should hear the synthesized comment that the document is empty.

Now that VocalTextEdit can read your documents back to you, it would be nice to be able to stop the speaking. You already have a Stop button. The only thing you have to do is change the **stopButtonClicked(_:)** method to actually do something instead of calling **print()**. **NSSpeechSynthesizer** provides a convenient method to do exactly what you want:

## Listing 26.7 Stop! (`ViewController.swift`)

```
...
    @IBAction func stopButtonClicked(sender: NSButton) {
        print("The stop button was clicked")
        speechSynthesizer.stopSpeaking()
    }
...
```

Now, if VocalTextEdit is speaking, the Stop button will immediately stop the vocalization. There is no harm in calling **speechSynthesizer.stopSpeaking()** when VocalTextEdit is not speaking, so you do not need to guard against that possibility.

Build and run VocalTextEdit. Type some text – something long enough that it will take a while for the computer to vocalize it – and click the Speak button. Then, while the text is being read, click the Stop button. The vocalization should stop immediately.

## Saving and Loading Documents

VocalTextEdit is starting to come together! You can enter text and hear it spoken back to you. Unfortunately, there is a pretty major feature missing: the files cannot be saved. You might have seen a notification that your documents cannot be autosaved, as in Figure 26.21.

Figure 26.21  VocalTextEdit autosave failure

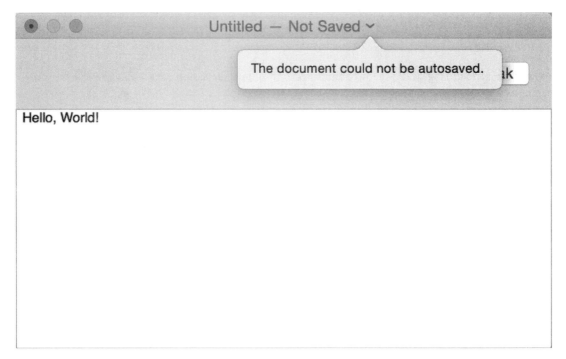

Even worse, if you try to save a document, you get a pretty nasty error message, as shown in Figure 26.22.

Figure 26.22  VocalTextEdit save failure

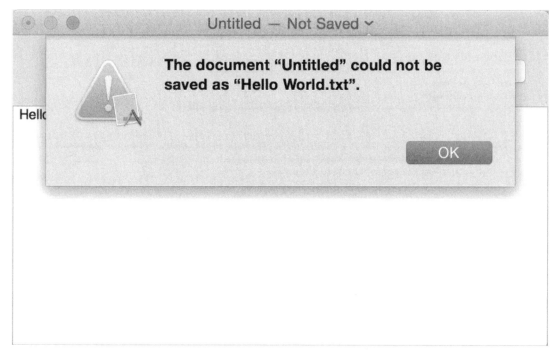

This might be a little surprising, because VocalTextEdit just works with text documents. The problem is that although you and your users know VocalTextEdit is working with text documents, Cocoa does not know that. You have to fill in some methods that allow Cocoa to save and load your documents.

To begin, open up `Document.swift` and delete some of the boilerplate that you do not need.

## Listing 26.8  Clearing the decks (`Document.swift`)

```
class Document: NSDocument {

    override init() {
        super.init()
        // Add your subclass-specific initialization here.
    }

    override func windowControllerDidLoadNib(aController: NSWindowController) {
        super.windowControllerDidLoadNib(aController)
        // Add any code here that needs to be
        // executed once the windowController has ...
    }

    override class func autosavesInPlace() -> Bool {
        return true
    }

    override func makeWindowControllers() {
        // Returns the Storyboard that contains your Document window.
        let storyboard = NSStoryboard(name: "Main", bundle: nil)
        let windowController =
            storyboard.instantiateControllerWithIdentifier(
              "Document Window Controller"
            ) as! NSWindowController

        self.addWindowController(windowController)
    }

    override func dataOfType(typeName: String) throws -> NSData {
        // Insert code here to write your document to data of the specified type. ...
        throw NSError(domain: NSOSStatusErrorDomain, code: unimpErr, userInfo: nil)
    }

    override func readFromData(data: NSData, ofType typeName: String) throws {
        // Insert code here to read your document
        // from the given data of the specified type. ...
        throw NSError(domain: NSOSStatusErrorDomain, code: unimpErr, userInfo: nil)
    }

}
```

Let's walk through the remaining methods.

**autosavesInPlace()** is a class-level method on **NSDocument**. If **autosavesInPlace()** returns `true`, that means the document class supports autosaving files right where they are whenever the user makes changes. The default implementation returns `false`, so the Xcode template helpfully inserts an override to return `true`, and it is up to you to make sure autosaving works correctly. (This will not be difficult for VocalTextEdit.)

The next method, **makeWindowControllers()**, is called when a new document is created or an old document is open and is responsible for setting up the **NSWindowController** that will manage the document's window. Because you are using a storyboard, setting up the window controller is pretty easy: it needs to be loaded from the storyboard (the first two lines) and then added to the document (the final line).

There is one feature on the second line of **makeWindowControllers()**'s implementation that you have not seen before. The **as!** operator is one of Swift's *type casting* operators.

# Type casting

Type casting allows you to tell the compiler, "This object, which you think is of type X, is actually of type Y." In pure Swift code, type casting should usually be avoided, as other tools like inheritance and generics can often solve the same problems. However, type casting comes up quite frequently when dealing with Mac and iOS libraries that were written in Objective-C.

The **as!** operator acts similarly to unwrapping an optional. If you try to type cast to a type that does not match the actual type, you will get a trap. (If you do not remember what a trap is, refer back to Chapter 20.) There are two other variants of this type-casting operator: **as?** attempts to perform a type cast and returns **nil** if the type you request does not match the actual type, and **as** performs type casts that the Swift compiler can guarantee will succeed, such as from **NSString** to **String**.

Option-click on the **instantiateControllerWithIdentifier(_:)** method call in the second line of **makeWindowControllers()**'s implementation. Note that its return type is **AnyObject**. **AnyObject** is a Swift protocol that has no methods or properties: the only thing you know is that it is an instance of some class. **instantiateControllerWithIdentifier(_:)** returns an **AnyObject** because storyboards can contain controllers of many different types. In order to make use of the returned controller, you need to cast it to its actual type: **NSWindowController**. When you create a storyboard-based application, Xcode assigns the Document Window Controller identifier to the **NSWindowController** it creates, and inserts the same identifier for you on this line.

# Saving documents

The final two methods in Document.swift support saving and loading. The **dataOfType(_:)** method is called whenever a document needs to be saved. It typically returns an instance of **NSData**. You can think of **NSData** as something akin to an array of bytes. If you are able to save the document, **dataOfType(_:)** returns the bytes that should be saved to disk. If you cannot save the document for any reason, it throws an error.

The associated method to implement loading a document is **readFromData(_:ofType:)**. Its first parameter is an instance of **NSData**, and **readFromData(_:ofType)** loads the document from those bytes. If the loading is unsuccessful, it throws an error.

At the moment, both **dataOfType(_:)** and **readFromData(_:ofType)** always fail, which explains why you see autosave failures. Note that the project has comments in these methods indicating that you will need to do something: // Insert code here to write your document to data of the specified type. …. You are going to fix them. Begin by implementing **dataOfType(_:)** to be able to save VocalTextEdit's text files.

To save the document, you need to convert the contents of the text view into an **NSData**. The first step is to get the **ViewController** associated with this **Document**.

## Listing 26.9  Getting the associated **ViewController** (Document.swift)

```
...
    override func dataOfType(typeName: String) throws -> NSData {
        // Insert code here to write your document to data of the specified type. ...
        throw NSError(domain: NSOSStatusErrorDomain, code: unimpErr, userInfo: nil)
        let windowController = windowControllers[0]
        let viewController = windowController.contentViewController as! ViewController
    }
...
```

In general, an **NSDocument** may have multiple window controllers. In this case, you only created one (in **makeWindowControllers()**), so windowControllers[0] gives you that sole window controller.

An **NSWindowController** may or may not have a view controller for its content – the Mac platform has had window controllers much longer than it has had view controllers. Option-click on contentViewController to see its type, and you will see **NSViewController?**. windowController may not have a content view controller, in which case the property is nil. If windowController does have a content view controller, the compiler knows it will be an **NSViewController** or some subclass of **NSViewController**.

In this application, you only have one **ViewController** type, but in a large application, you might have many. You used the as! type casting operator to tell the compiler, "I know that the view controller for **Document**'s window controllers are of type **ViewController**."

Now that you have a handle to the view controller, you can implement the rest of **dataOfType(_:)**.

## Listing 26.10  Implementing **dataOfType(_:)** for saving (Document.swift)

```
...
    override func dataOfType(typeName: String) throws -> NSData {
        let windowController = windowControllers[0]
        let viewController = windowController.contentViewController as! ViewController

        let contents = viewController.textView.string ?? ""

        if let data = contents.dataUsingEncoding(NSUTF8StringEncoding) {
            return data
        } else {
            let userInfo = [
                NSLocalizedRecoverySuggestionErrorKey:
                "File cannot be encoded in UTF-8."
            ]
            throw NSError(
                domain: "com.bignerdranch.VocalTextEdit", code: 0, userInfo: userInfo)
        }
    }
...
```

Let's break this down line by line.

```
        let contents = viewController.textView.string ?? ""
```

First, you attempt to get the contents of the text view via the string property, the same way you did inside **ViewController** to get the text to synthesize. If string is nil, you use the nil-coalescing operator that you saw in Chapter 8 to use a default of "", the empty string.

```
        if let data = contents.dataUsingEncoding(NSUTF8StringEncoding) {
            return data
```

Next, you use **dataUsingEncoding(_:)** on a string to attempt to convert contents into an **NSData**. The **dataUsingEncoding(_:)** method requires you to specify a string encoding – that is, how to convert the text inside contents into bytes. NSUTF8StringEncoding is a constant that specifies UTF8, a common Unicode encoding.

```
    } else {
        let userInfo = [
            NSLocalizedRecoverySuggestionErrorKey:
            "File cannot be encoded in UTF-8."
        ]
        throw NSError(
            domain: "com.bignerdranch.VocalTextEdit", code: 0, userInfo: userInfo)
    }
```

Finally, you have to handle the error case: what do you do if the string cannot be encoded in UTF8? You could define an enumeration that conforms to **ErrorType** and throw an instance of that as you did in Chapter 20. In this case, though, Cocoa will do some extra work for you if you throw an instance of **NSError**. If file-saving fails, an alert will pop up to the user. If you used an **ErrorType** enum, the alert would contain a generic failure message as you saw in Figure 26.22. By supplying an **NSError**, you can supply an additional error message that will be displayed in the alert.

**NSError** was the standard mechanism for handling errors in Objective-C. It is much more cumbersome to use than defining **ErrorType** enumerations, as you see here, but it still useful. You create an **NSError** by supplying three pieces of information:

- a domain, which is a string

- a code, which is an integer

- userInfo, which is a dictionary that can contain multiple keys and values describing the error

In small applications, it is common to use a single custom error domain. The code can help you differentiate error cases. In this app, there are not many opportunities for error, so you are not going to supply codes. Finally, the userInfo dictionary allows you to give detail. Arguably the most important key to include is NSLocalizedRecoverySuggestionErrorKey, whose value should be a (localized) string giving the user information about how they could fix the problem. You cheated a little bit by using an English string, but localization is outside the scope of this book.

Build and run your application. Type some text into a document, then save it. Success! Well, almost. Close the document you saved, and try to open it via File → Open.

No dice. You can save documents, but you still need to implement **readFromData(_:ofType)** to load them.

## Loading documents

When you saved the document, you got the contents from the view controller's text view, converted the string to an **NSData**, and returned the data. To load a document, it would make sense to perform the inverse: you are given an **NSData**, so you need to convert it to a string and then put the contents into the view controller's text view. Try the following, which might look correct at first glance, but actually has a major problem.

**Listing 26.11  Loading a document – the wrong way (`Document.swift`)**

```
...
    override func readFromData(data: NSData, ofType typeName: String) throws {
        // Insert code here to read your document
        // from the given data of the specified type...
        throw NSError(domain: NSOSStatusErrorDomain, code: unimpErr, userInfo: nil)
        if let contents = NSString(data: data, encoding: NSUTF8StringEncoding)
             as? String {
            // WARNING: BIG PROBLEM HERE
            let windowController = windowControllers[0]
            let viewController = windowController.contentViewController
              as! ViewController
            viewController.textView.string = contents
            return true
        } else {
            let userInfo = [
                NSLocalizedRecoverySuggestionErrorKey: "File is not valid UTF-8."
            ]
            throw NSError(
                domain: "com.bignerdranch.VocalTextEdit", code: 0, userInfo: userInfo)
        }
    }
}
```

Build and run your application. Close all the windows, then try to open the document you saved a few minutes ago. Uh-oh: your application crashed on the line where you try to assign the contents to the view controller. You get the following error message:

```
fatal error: Array index out of range
```

"Array index out of range" is telling you that when you tried to get element 0 from the **windowControllers** array, it did not exist. Why doesn't it exist? Cocoa calls **readFromData(_:ofType)** *before* it creates the window and its associated controllers, so the document does not yet have a window controller or a view controller.

So that implementation, while logical on the surface, does not work. Instead, you can save off the string and then update the view controller's contents once it is loaded from the storyboard. Start by creating a new property to hold the contents that will be filled in when the view controller is available.

**Listing 26.12  Loading a document a better way – creating a `contents` property (`Document.swift`)**

```
class Document: NSDocument {

    var contents: String = ""

    override class func autosavesInPlace() -> Bool {
        return true
    }

    ...
}
```

You can default the contents to an empty string, because that is the correct value for brand-new Documents that are not the result of opening a file. Next, modify **readFromData(_:ofType:)** to store into this property instead of attempting to update a view controller that does not exist.

### Listing 26.13  Loading a document a better way – storing the contents property (Document.swift)

```
...
    override func readFromData(data: NSData, ofType typeName: String) throws {
        if let contents = NSString(data: data, encoding: NSUTF8StringEncoding)
            as? String {
            // WARNING: BIG PROBLEM HERE
            let windowController = windowControllers[0]
            let viewController = windowController.contentViewController
                as! ViewController
            viewController.textView.string = contents
            self.contents = contents
            return true
        } else {
            let userInfo = [
                NSLocalizedRecoverySuggestionErrorKey: "File is not valid UTF-8."
            ]
            throw NSError(
                domain: "com.bignerdranch.VocalTextEdit", code: 0, userInfo: userInfo)
        }
    }
```

Finally, you need to forward the document contents on to the view controller when it is created. Update **makeWindowControllers()** to do just that.

### Listing 26.14  Loading a document a better way – forwarding document contents to view controller (Document.swift)

```
...
    override func makeWindowControllers() {
        // Returns the Storyboard that contains your Document window.
        let storyboard = NSStoryboard(name: "Main", bundle: nil)
        let windowController =
            storyboard.instantiateControllerWithIdentifier(
                "Document Window Controller"
                ) as! NSWindowController

        let viewController = windowController.contentViewController as! ViewController
        viewController.textView.string = contents

        self.addWindowController(windowController)
    }
...
```

Build and run the application. Now you can successfully open files! VocalTextEdit is nearly complete.

# MVC cleanup

VocalTextEdit is now feature-complete: it can save and load documents, and it can read them back to you. But before you say it is completely finished, think back to something we said about MVC: "Models have no knowledge of the user interface." You are using **Document** as a model class, but it reaches out and touches a text view in a couple of different places. A text view is definitely part of the user interface!

The **ViewController** should be the class coordinating between the user interface (the text view) and the model (the document). For the sake of good programming, clean up VocalTextEdit's layers. Start by opening up ViewController.swift and creating a new property for the contents of the text view.

## Listing 26.15 Creating a new property for the text view's contents (`ViewController.swift`)

```
class ViewController: NSViewController {

    let speechSynthesizer = NSSpeechSynthesizer()

    @IBOutlet var textView: NSTextView!

    var contents: String? {
        get {
            return textView.string
        }
        set {
            textView.string = newValue
        }
    }

    ...

}
```

Here, you create a new computed property, contents, whose getter and setter read from and write to textView's string property.

Now, back in `Document.swift`, replace both of the references to the view controller's text view with this new property.

## Listing 26.16  Replacing text view references with `contents` (`Document.swift`)

```
...
    override func makeWindowControllers() {
        // Returns the Storyboard that contains your Document window.
        let storyboard = NSStoryboard(name: "Main", bundle: nil)
        let windowController =
            storyboard.instantiateControllerWithIdentifier(
              "Document Window Controller"
            ) as! NSWindowController

        viewController = windowController.contentViewController as! ViewController
        viewController.textView.string = contentscontents = contents

        self.addWindowController(windowController)
    }

    override func dataOfType(typeName: String) throws -> NSData {
        let windowController = windowControllers[0]
        let viewController = windowController.contentViewController as! ViewController

        let contents = viewController.textView.stringcontents ?? ""

        if let data = contents.dataUsingEncoding(NSUTF8StringEncoding) {
            return data
        } else {
            let userInfo = [
                NSLocalizedRecoverySuggestionErrorKey:
                "File cannot be encoded in UTF-8."
            ]
            throw NSError(
                domain: "com.bignerdranch.VocalTextEdit", code: 0, userInfo: userInfo)
        }
    }
...
```

Build and run VocalTextEdit and confirm that you can still save and load files as expected.

The refactoring of the code you just did may seem small, but it is an important change. **Document** does not, and should not, care how the string is going to be displayed. The **ViewController** class is responsible for managing the user interface (so it knows about the text view) and for communicating with the document (so it exposes what the document needs: a **contents** property).

This change has a couple of benefits aside from good programming practice. One is that **Document** is more readable now, because the code more directly expresses your intention. To save a document, get the contents from the view controller and save them. To load a document, put the contents into a property and give them to a view controller as soon as you can.

The second extra benefit is that the refactored code makes **Document** more robust to potential future changes in the view controller. You might decide to add a second text view for users to type in a document title, for example, or you might decide to use a different view than a text view. Changes of that nature are less likely to impact the readability and correctness of **Document** now that you have clarified its interactions with **ViewController**.

Congratulations – you have written an app for the Mac! It may not be the most impressive app, but that is not the point. You have applied your knowledge of Swift and made use of some of the Cocoa libraries provided by Apple. And you have made a fully functional, well-designed app. Bravo!

As you worked through this chapter, your programmer Spidey-sense may have tingled a little bit at some of the techniques you used. Implicitly unwrapped optionals can be dangerous. The as! operator can be dangerous. You made frequent use of both of these.

Unfortunately, the purity and safety of Swift is not always available when you start working with tools and frameworks that were designed with Objective-C in mind. Some concessions have to be made, particularly when working with the systems built up around Interface Builder. Take heart, however: in a larger application, the parts of your code that feel a little shaky will be well offset by the safety and security you get from using Swift throughout the rest of the app.

# Silver Challenge

Right now, users of VocalTextEdit can click the Speak or Stop buttons at any time. That is not ideal: clicking Speak while VocalTextEdit is currently synthesizing will abruptly restart the vocalization, for example. Modify VocalTextEdit so that users can only click on Speak if the application is not currently synthesizing, and only click Stop when it is.

To complete this challenge, you will need a way to set the enabled property of the two buttons. You will also need a way to know when speaking ends. (You already know when it starts.) Investigate the documentation for the **NSSpeechSynthesizerDelegate** protocol to find out how to do these things.

# Gold Challenge

If you have not already completed the silver challenge, do that first!

Now that your buttons react when the app starts or stops speaking, give the user a way to know how long speaking will continue. Add an **NSProgressIndicator** to your interface and update it to show a rough estimate of how much speaking has been completed. For bonus points, make the progress indicator visible only when the app is speaking.

# 27

# Your First iOS Application

In this chapter, you are going to create iTahDoodle, an iOS application for iPhone. iTahDoodle will allow users to create to-do lists. Like VocalTextEdit, iTahDoodle is a relatively simple app, and building it will give you only a taste of what iOS development is all about.

When you are done, iTahDoodle will look like Figure 27.1.

Figure 27.1  Completed iTahDoodle application

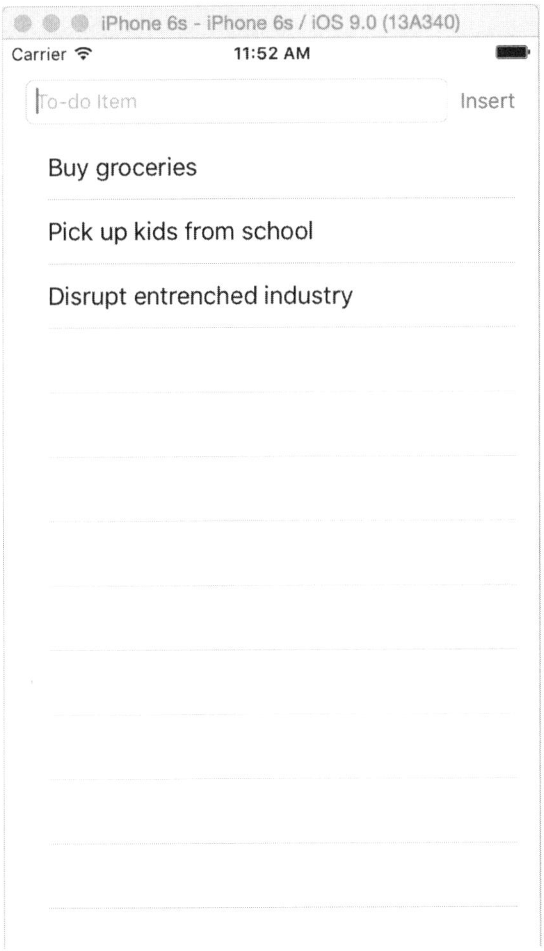

Users can add an item to the to-do list by typing in the text field at the top and tapping Insert. You will persist the to-do list so that users will not lose their list if they close the application.

# Getting Started with iTahDoodle

In Xcode, choose File → New → Project.... Select Application under the iOS section. Select the Single View Application template (Figure 27.2) and click Next.

Figure 27.2  Choosing the iOS Single View Application template

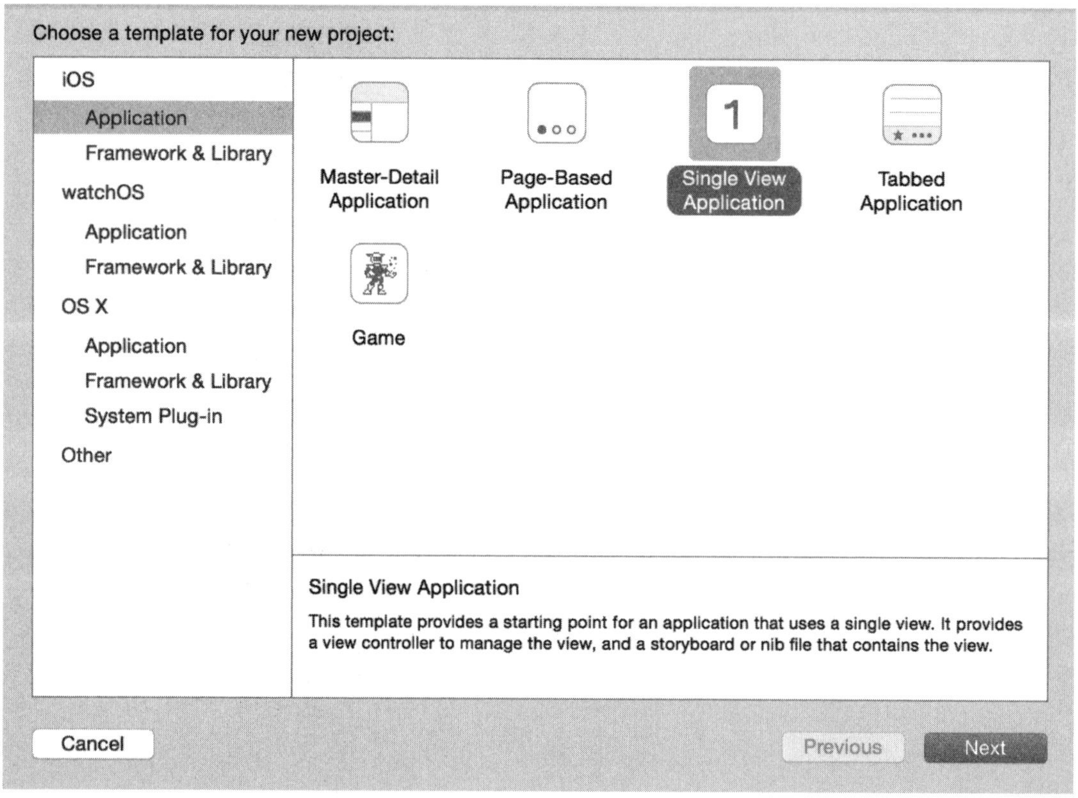

In the project options window, name the project iTahDoodle, as in Figure 27.3. Make sure the selected language is Swift and the device is set to iPhone. Leave the Use Core Data, Include Unit Tests, and Include UI Tests boxes unchecked.

Figure 27.3  Configuring iTahDoodle

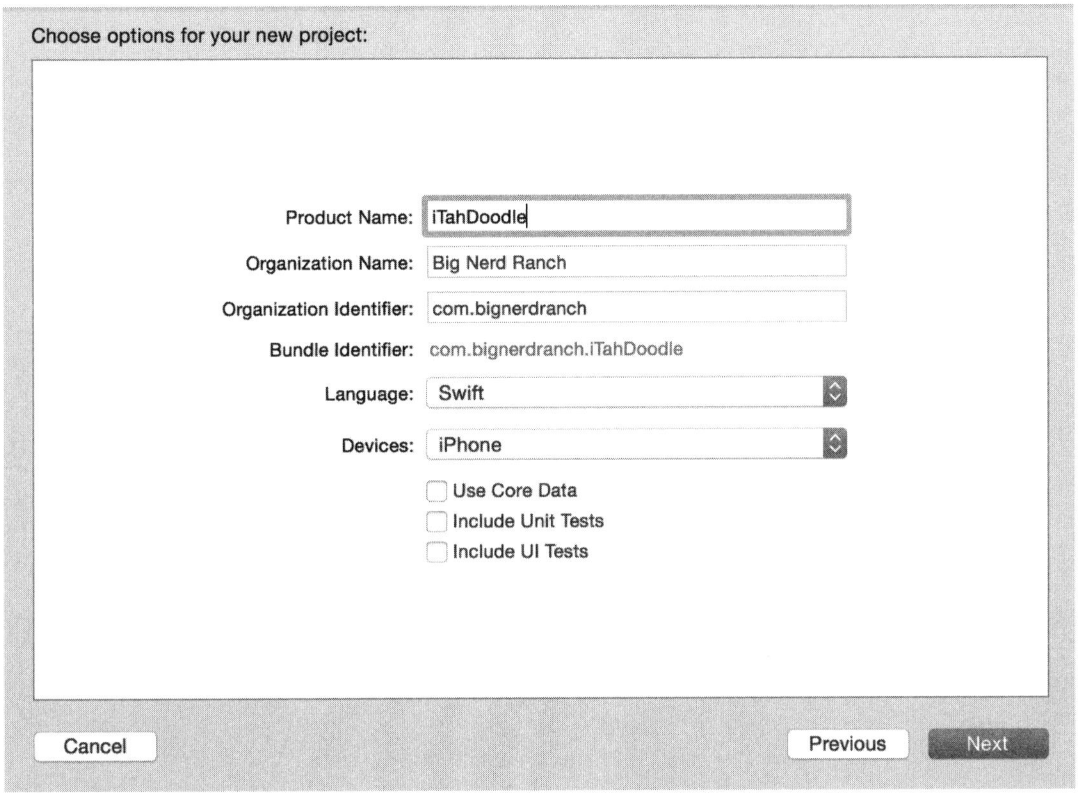

Click Next and finish creating your project saving it to the location of your choice.

# Laying Out the User Interface

Select Main.storyboard from the project navigator. The iOS single view application template is much simpler than the Cocoa storyboard you used in the previous chapter. Your storyboard currently contains only a single, empty view controller.

Add a button to your view controller. In the object library (at the bottom of the utilities pane), search for "button." Drag a Button onto your view controller canvas and drop it in the top-right corner where it will snap into place against the dashed blue guidelines. Finally, change the title of the button to "Insert" in the *attributes inspector*. The attributes inspector is one tab of the utilities pane, and it allows you to configure properties of views. Your view controller should look like Figure 27.4.

## Figure 27.4  iTahDoodle with Insert button

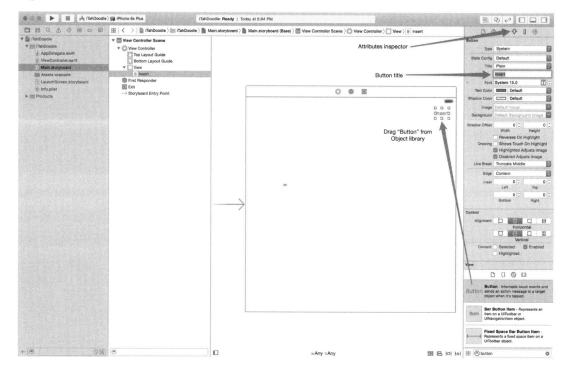

Next, add the text field where users will type in their to-do items. Search for "text field" in the object library. Drag a Text Field into the top-left corner of your view controller canvas. Resize the text field using the square resize anchor so that its right edge is adjacent to the button you added. Use the attributes inspector to set the text field's placeholder text to "To-do Item" (Figure 27.5).

## Figure 27.5 iTahDoodle with a text field

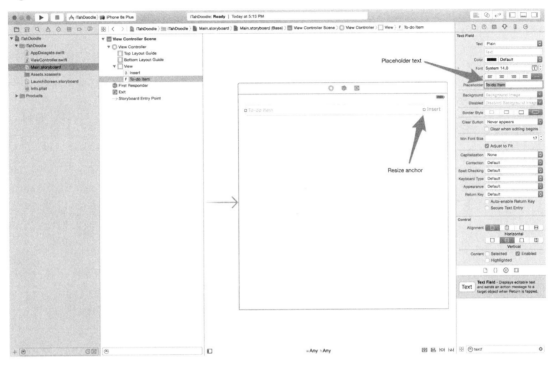

In the previous chapter, you used Auto Layout to make sure your interface would look correct when the user resized the window. Currently, users cannot resize the windows of iOS applications, but there is a comparable problem. You want your app to look correct on a variety of screen sizes. Specifying iPhone as the target device (as you did when you set up iTahDoodle) is not enough, as iPhone 5, iPhone 6, and iPhone 6 Plus all have different screen sizes. However, you can use the same Auto Layout system to ensure that your interface adjusts to fit correctly on each screen size.

In the document outline, Control-drag from Insert to its parent, View. In the pop-up menu, Shift-click on both Trailing Space to Container Margin and Vertical Spacing to Top Layout Guide (Figure 27.6).

Figure 27.6  Auto Layout constraints for Insert button

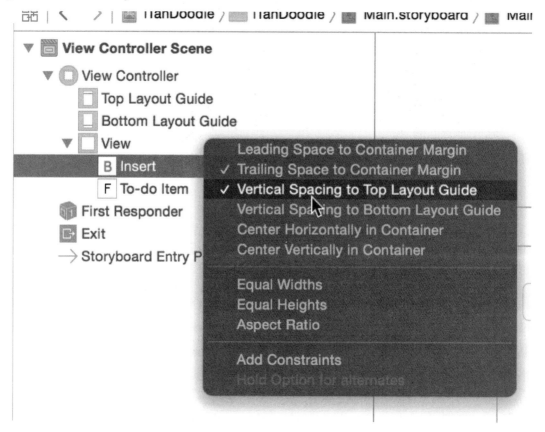

These constraints will ensure that the button stays pinned to the top-right corner of the view.

Next, create constraints between the text field and the button. Control-drag from the text field to the button. In the pop-up menu, Shift-click on both Horizontal Spacing and Baseline (Figure 27.7). (You may notice a yellow icon indicating a warning in Interface Builder – you will address it momentarily.)

Figure 27.7  Auto Layout constraints between text field and button

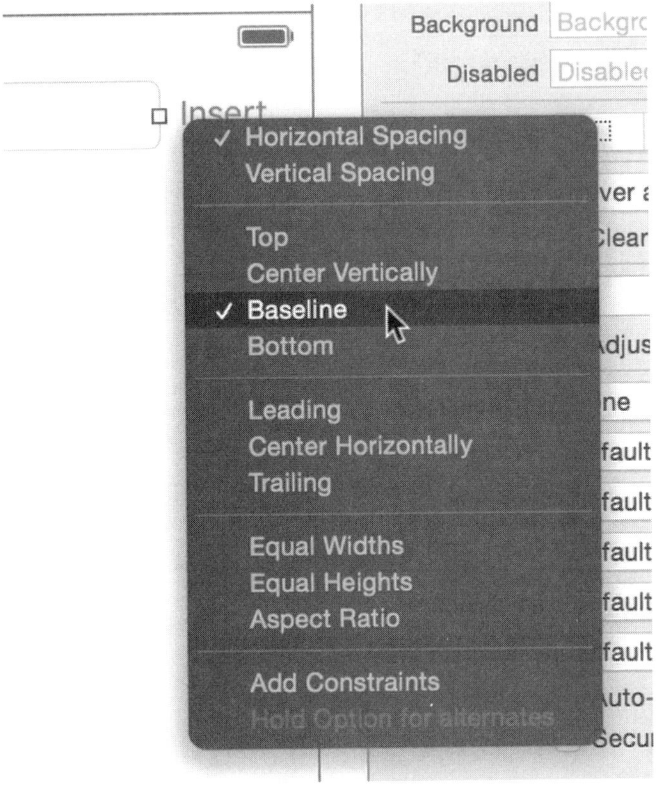

These constraints will ensure that the right side of the text field stays next to the button and that the text in the text field will be vertically aligned with the button's text.

The final constraint to add is to pin the left edge of the text field to the left edge of the view. In the document outline, Control-drag from the text field to its parent view and select Leading Space to Container Margin from the pop-up (Figure 27.8).

Figure 27.8  Auto Layout constraint between text field and superview

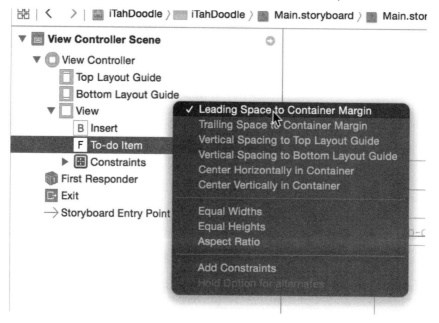

You may notice that Interface Builder still has a warning. Press Command-4 to open the issue navigator, where you will see "2 views are horizontally ambiguous." The problem is that you have constrained the text field and button together to fill up the entire horizontal space, but Auto Layout does not know how to divide the space. According to the constraints you have added, Auto Layout could make the button skinny and the text field wide or vice versa (or anything in between). To fix this problem, select the button, open up its size inspector in the utilities pane, and set its Horizontal Content Hugging Priority to be 251 instead of 250 (Figure 27.9).

## Figure 27.9  Insert button horizontal content hugging priority

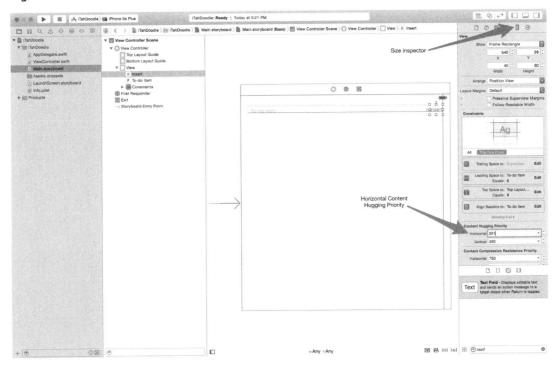

The content hugging priority determines how strongly Auto Layout should attempt to keep an element from expanding. You bumped the button's content hugging priority up to 251, higher than the text field's default of 250. When Auto Layout tries to determine how to fill the entire horizontal space, it will see that the button does not want to expand horizontally. Therefore, the text field will grow to fill the available space, leaving the button the same size.

The final UI element you need is a way to display the list of to-do items. iOS provides a perfect class for this purpose: the **UITableView**. Search for "table" in the object library and drag a Table View onto your view controller (make sure you grab the Table View, not the Table View Controller), as in Figure 27.10.

## Figure 27.10  Adding a table view

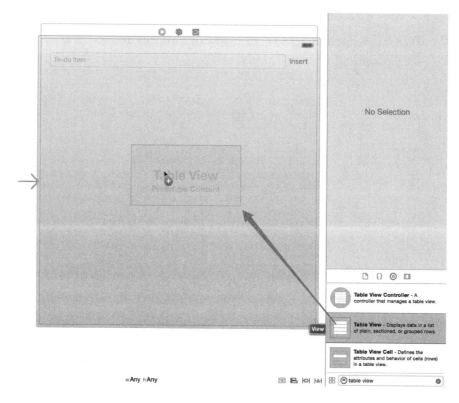

Resize the table view until it snaps into place around the edges (Figure 27.11).

Figure 27.11  Resize table view to fill view controller

You need to add Auto Layout constraints to make sure the table view always fills the available screen space. In the document outline, Control-drag from table view to its parent, view. In the pop-up menu, Shift-click on Leading Space to Container Margin, Trailing Space to Container Margin, and Vertical Spacing to Bottom Layout Guide (Figure 27.12).

Figure 27.12  Auto Layout constraints between table view and superview

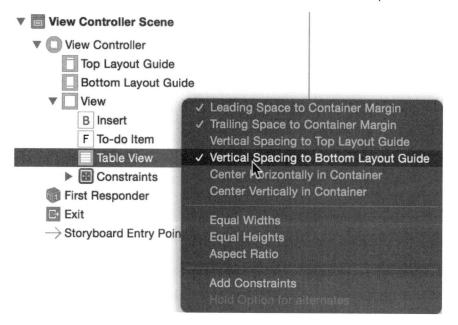

Finally, add a constraint to fix the spacing between the table view and the text field just above it. Control-drag from the table view to the text field and select Vertical Spacing from the pop-up menu (Figure 27.13).

Figure 27.13  Auto Layout constraints between table view and text field

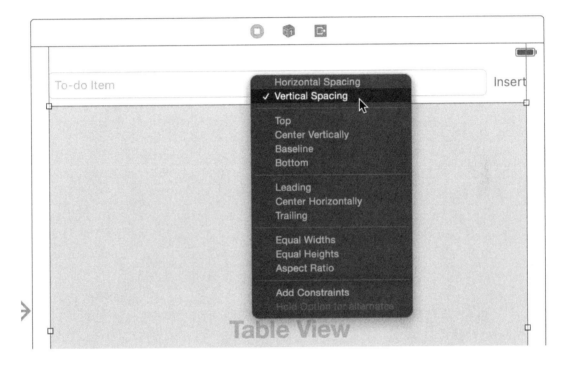

Build and run your application by clicking on the triangular play button in Xcode's toolbar. (You can also use the keyboard shortcut Command-R.) This will open iTahDoodle in Xcode's iOS simulator, as shown in Figure 27.14. It does not do anything yet, but you should see the user interface you designed.

Figure 27.14  iTahDoodle user interface

## Wiring up your interface

Now that you have an interface, it is time to create outlets and actions so that you can start to make your app interactive. Open `ViewController.swift` and add properties for your UI elements and an action method to call when the user taps the Insert button.

## Listing 27.1  Adding UI element properties and a button action method (ViewController.swift)

```swift
class ViewController: UIViewController {

    @IBOutlet var itemTextField: UITextField!
    @IBOutlet var tableView: UITableView!

    override func viewDidLoad() {
        super.viewDidLoad()
        // Do any additional setup after loading the view, typically from a nib.
    }

    override func didReceiveMemoryWarning() {
        super.didReceiveMemoryWarning()
        // Dispose of any resources that can be recreated.
    }

    @IBAction func addButtonPressed(sender: UIButton) {
        print("Add to-do item: \(itemTextField.text)")
    }
}
```

Next, go back to Main.storyboard and create connections to the items you just added. Control-drag from the view controller to the text field, selecting itemTextField from the pop-up menu (Figure 27.15).

## Figure 27.15  Connecting text field to view controller **@IBOutlet**

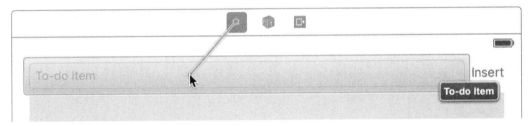

Repeat the same process to connect the table view. Control-drag from the view controller to the table view and select tableView from the pop-up menu.

Remember from Chapter 26 that to connect an action you Control-drag in the opposite direction? Control-drag from the Insert button to the view controller and select addButtonPressed: underneath Sent Events in the pop-up menu (Figure 27.16).

## Figure 27.16  Connecting Insert button to view controller **@IBAction**

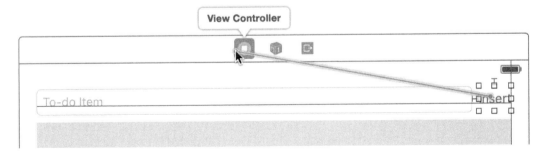

Build and run your application again. Try typing in the text field and tapping the Insert button. Your text logs in Xcode:

```
Add to-do item: Buy groceries
Add to-do item: Walk the dog
```

## Modeling a To-Do List

Recall from Chapter 26 that iOS and Mac applications usually follow a Model-View-Controller architecture. You have already created a view (your storyboard and UI elements) and a controller (your **ViewController** class). At this point, however, you do not have a model. Create a Cocoa Touch class by selecting File → New → File.... Select Source under iOS, then select Cocoa Touch Class (Figure 27.17).

### Figure 27.17  Creating a new Cocoa Touch class

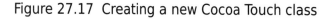

Choose a template for your new file:

| | | |
|---|---|---|
| **iOS** | | |
| Source | Cocoa Touch Class | UI Test Case Class | Unit Test Case Class | Playground |
| User Interface | | |
| Core Data | Swift File | Objective-C File | Header File | C File |
| Apple Watch | | |
| Resource | | |
| Other | C++ File | Metal File | |
| **watchOS** | | |
| Source | | |
| User Interface | | |
| Core Data | | |
| Resource | | |
| Other | | |
| **OS X** | | |
| Source | | |
| User Interface | | |
| Core Data | | |
| Resource | | |

Cocoa Touch Class
A Cocoa Touch class.

Cancel                    Previous    Next

On the next screen, name your class **TodoList**, make it a subclass of **NSObject**, and make sure the language is set to Swift (Figure 27.18).

## Figure 27.18  Creating the **TodoList** class

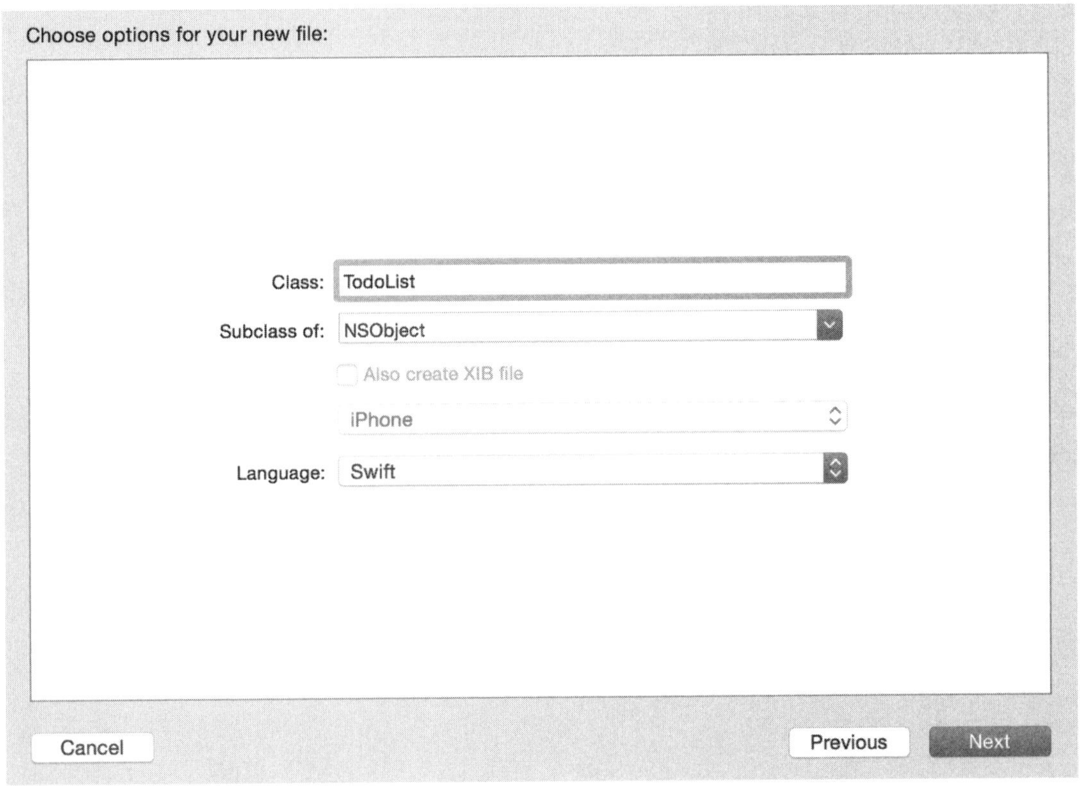

Choose options for your new file:

Class:          TodoList

Subclass of:    NSObject

○ Also create XIB file

iPhone

Language:       Swift

Cancel          Previous    Next

Click Next, then Create.

Xcode creates and opens your new class:

```
class TodoList: NSObject {

}
```

What is **NSObject**? In Swift, you can create classes that do not have a superclass. In Objective-C, all classes are required to have a superclass. **NSObject** is called a *root class*: it provides some basic Objective-C runtime support.

You need **TodoList** to inherit from **NSObject** because you are going to use it to interact with Cocoa Touch classes that expect to receive Objective-C objects. (The relationship between Swift and Objective-C is the subject of Chapter 28.)

At its most basic, a to-do list is just a list of strings with the capability to add new things to the list. Add a property and a method to **TodoList** to meet those requirements.

## Listing 27.2  Adding basic list functionality (TodoList.swift)

```
class TodoList: NSObject {
    private var items: [String] = []

    func addItem(item: String) {
        items.append(item)
    }
}
```

Earlier you placed a **UITableView** into your interface to display your to-do list. Every **UITableView** has a property named dataSource that provides the content for its cells. To act as a table view's data source, **TodoList** must conform to the **UITableViewDataSource** protocol. As you learned in Chapter 21, you can add protocol conformance in an extension to keep related chunks of functionality grouped together. Add an extension on **TodoList** declaring that it conforms to **UITableViewDataSource**.

## Listing 27.3  Adding protocol conformance in an extension (TodoList.swift)

```
class TodoList: NSObject {
    private var items: [String] = []

    func addItem(item: String) {
        items.append(item)
    }
}

extension TodoList: UITableViewDataSource {
}
```

If you were to try to build your project now, you would get an error that **TodoList** does not conform to **UITableViewDataSource**. Open the documentation for **UITableViewDataSource** (Figure 27.19). (Recall from Chapter 26 that you Option-click on **UITableViewDataSource** to bring up the quick reference, then click on the UITableViewDataSource Protocol Reference link to bring up the full documentation.)

### Figure 27.19 **UITableViewDataSource** protocol reference

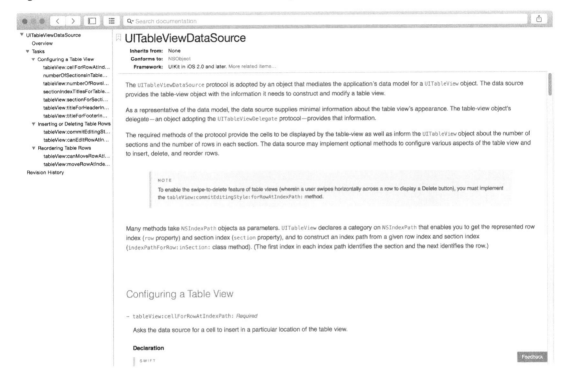

There are a lot of methods in the **UITableViewDataSource** protocol! However, only two of them are required: **tableView(_:cellForRowAtIndexPath:)**, which configures and returns cells (the rows of your table view), and **tableView(_:numberOfRowsInSection:)**, which tells the table view how many rows there are going to be. Begin by implementing **tableView(_:numberOfRowsInSection:)**.

### Listing 27.4 Adding **tableView(_:numberOfRowsInSection:)** (TodoList.swift)

```
...
extension TodoList : UITableViewDataSource {
    func tableView(tableView: UITableView,
                   numberOfRowsInSection section: Int) -> Int {
        return items.count
    }
}
```

**UITableView** supports a table having multiple sections, each of which can have 0 or more rows. For iTahDoodle, you are only going to use a single section, so in the method above, you ignore the section argument. You return `items.count`, telling the table view that there will be one row for each to-do list item.

Next, implement `tableView(_:cellForRowAtIndexPath:)`.

## Listing 27.5  Adding `tableView(_:cellForRowAtIndexPath:)` (TodoList.swift)

```
...
extension TodoList : UITableViewDataSource {
    func tableView(tableView: UITableView,
                   numberOfRowsInSection section: Int) -> Int {
        return items.count
    }

    func tableView(tableView: UITableView,
                   cellForRowAtIndexPath indexPath: NSIndexPath)
        -> UITableViewCell {
        let cell = tableView.dequeueReusableCellWithIdentifier("Cell",
            forIndexPath: indexPath)
        let item = items[indexPath.row]

        cell.textLabel!.text = item

        return cell
    }
}
```

Here is a line-by-line walk-through of what this method does:

```
let cell = tableView.dequeueReusableCellWithIdentifier("Cell",
    forIndexPath: indexPath)
```

This line asks the table view to dequeue a reusable cell with the identifier "Cell" and the given index path.

What does *reusable cell* mean? In order to achieve good scrolling performance on mobile devices, **UITableView** makes use of a *reuse pool* of cells. When cells are no longer needed by the system, such as when the user scrolls and cells "fall off" the screen, the table view puts that cell into its reuse pool. If the table view has a cell in the reuse pool, it will give that one to you, dequeueing it from the pool. Otherwise, it will create a new one. Either way, you are guaranteed to get an instance back.

Keep the `"Cell"` identifier and the cast to **UITableViewCell** in the back of your mind. We will revisit them shortly.

```
let item = items[indexPath.row]
```

The `tableView(_:cellForRowAtIndexPath:)` method is called every time the table view needs the data source to configure a cell that will be displayed to the user. The `indexPath` argument indicates which row the table view needs to display. It contains properties for both a `section` and a `row`. As mentioned above, the iTahDoodle table view only has one section, so you can ignore the section and just look up which item to display based on the `row`.

```
cell.textLabel!.text = item
```

Now that you have both a **UITableViewCell** and the to-do list item you want to display, this line sets the text property of the cell's textLabel to be equal to the to-do list item. You are force-unwrapping textLabel; not all **UITableViewCell**s are guaranteed to have a **textLabel**, but the one you are using does.

```
return cell
```

Finally, the method returns the fully configured cell.

Your **TodoList** is now ready to act as a data source for a **UITableView**. Build your application to make sure you implemented all the methods correctly. You will not see any new behavior yet, because you still need to set up the table view. But you should not see any errors.

## Setting Up the UITableView

Your model class is now ready. Return to your controller in ViewController.swift. Add an instance of **TodoList** as a new property and change **addButtonPressed(_:)** to add items to todoList instead of printing them.

### Listing 27.6 Adding the model class to the controller as a property (ViewController.swift)

```
class ViewController: UIViewController {

    @IBOutlet var itemTextField: UITextField!
    @IBOutlet var tableView: UITableView!

    let todoList = TodoList()

    override func viewDidLoad() {
        super.viewDidLoad()
        // Do any additional setup after loading the view, typically from a nib.
    }

    override func didReceiveMemoryWarning() {
        super.didReceiveMemoryWarning()
        // Dispose of any resources that can be recreated.
    }

    @IBAction func addButtonPressed(sender: UIButton) {
        print("Add to do item: \(itemTextField.text)")
        guard let text = itemTextField.text else {
            return
        }
        todoList.addItem(text)
    }
}
```

You used a guard statement to check that itemTextField.text is not nil, storing the string into text for use in the rest of the method. If itemTextField.text is nil, you just return – there is nothing to add to the to-do list.

Next, you need to configure the table view. The Xcode template that you used to create your project includes a comment directing you where to "do any additional setup after loading the view": inside **viewDidLoad()**. (The "nib" that the comment refers to is the format your storyboard is compiled into when you build your application.) Add two lines to configure your table view.

### Listing 27.7  Configuring the table view (`ViewController.swift`)

```
class ViewController: UIViewController {

    @IBOutlet var itemTextField: UITextField!
    @IBOutlet var tableView: UITableView!

    let todoList = TodoList()

    override func viewDidLoad() {
        super.viewDidLoad()
        // Do any additional setup after loading the view, typically from a nib.
        tableView.registerClass(UITableViewCell.self, forCellReuseIdentifier: "Cell")
        tableView.dataSource = todoList
    }

    override func didReceiveMemoryWarning() {
        super.didReceiveMemoryWarning()
        // Dispose of any resources that can be recreated.
    }

    @IBAction func addButtonPressed(sender: UIButton) {
        guard let text = itemTextField.text else {
            return
        }
        todoList.addItem(text)
    }
}
```

The first line you added tells the table view what to do when the data source tries to dequeue a reusable cell with the identifier "Cell" (which is the identifier you used in **TodoList**). Specifically, it registers the class **UITableViewCell**, which tells the table view to create instances of **UITableViewCell**. The second line tells the table view that the todoList is its data source.

There is one more step to finish the controller. Whenever the data source changes, the table view needs to be notified. In **addButtonPressed(_:)**, tell the table view to reload its data after you add the new item to the to-do list:

## Listing 27.8 Notifying the view to reload data (`ViewController.swift`)

```swift
class ViewController: UIViewController {

    @IBOutlet var itemTextField: UITextField!
    @IBOutlet var tableView: UITableView!

    let todoList = TodoList()

    override func viewDidLoad() {
        super.viewDidLoad()
        // Do any additional setup after loading the view, typically from a nib.
        tableView.registerClass(UITableViewCell.self, forCellReuseIdentifier: "Cell")
        tableView.dataSource = todoList
    }

    override func didReceiveMemoryWarning() {
        super.didReceiveMemoryWarning()
        // Dispose of any resources that can be recreated.
    }

    @IBAction func addButtonPressed(sender: UIButton) {
        guard let text = itemTextField.text else {
            return
        }
        todoList.addItem(text)
        tableView.reloadData()
    }
}
```

Build and run your application. Type in your text field and tap Insert. You should see items populate the table view below.

# Saving and Loading TodoList

iTahDoodle is now functional. Unfortunately, it forgets the to-do list every time the app is launched. You need to add the ability for **TodoList** to save and load its state.

## Saving TodoList

In Chapter 26, you implemented document saving and loading by taking advantage of features of the **NSDocument** class. Document-based Mac apps follow patterns (both in the code and the user interface) that have existed for years in Mac OS X. Most iOS apps, on the other hand, do not operate on documents. iTahDoodle definitely does not – there is a single to-do list, and the user will expect it to stick around.

All iOS applications live inside of an application sandbox. This means that your app cannot see files created by other applications, and vice versa. Another side effect of the sandbox is that the directories you should use to store files can change. Because you want to save a file containing the contents of the to-do list, the first thing you need is to ask iOS where you should store files. Add a new property, computed from a closure, to **TodoList**.

## Listing 27.9  Asking iOS where to store files (TodoList.swift)

```
import UIKit

class TodoList: NSObject {
    private let fileURL: NSURL = {
        let documentDirectoryURLs = NSFileManager.defaultManager().URLsForDirectory(
            .DocumentDirectory, inDomains: .UserDomainMask)
        let documentDirectoryURL = documentDirectoryURLs.first!
        return documentDirectoryURL.URLByAppendingPathComponent("todolist.items")
    }()

    private var items: [String] = []

    func addItem(item: String) {
        items.append(item)
    }
}
...
```

The first line of the closure asks the default **NSFileManager** (a class that lets you interact with iOS's filesystem) to give you an array of URLs containing the user's document directories. The next line gets the first element out of the returned array, making use of force-unwrapping because iOS will always return the app's documents directory in the array. Finally, you return a new URL that contains the filename todolist.items appended to the user's documents directory.

Next, add a method to actually save the to-do list items.

## Listing 27.10  Saving the to-do list (TodoList.swift)

```
class TodoList: NSObject {
    private let fileURL: NSURL = {
        let documentDirectoryURLs = NSFileManager.defaultManager().URLsForDirectory(
            .DocumentDirectory, inDomains: .UserDomainMask)
        let documentDirectoryURL = documentDirectoryURLs.first!
        return documentDirectoryURL.URLByAppendingPathComponent("todolist.items")
    }()

    private var items: [String] = []

    func saveItems() {
        let itemsArray = items as NSArray

        print("Saving items to \(fileURL)")
        if !itemsArray.writeToURL(fileURL, atomically: true) {
            print("Could not save to-do list")
        }
    }

    func addItem(item: String) {
        items.append(item)
        saveItems()
    }
}
...
```

The **saveItems()** method first gets the URL using the function you just wrote. Next, you cast the items array into an **NSArray**. This is so you can call a method that exists on **NSArray**s but not Swift arrays. You then call that method – **writeToURL(_:atomically:)** – on **NSArray**.

**writeToURL(_:atomically:)** attempts to save the contents of the array to the given URL, and it returns a **Bool** indicating whether it succeeded.

You also add a call to **saveItems()** in **addItem(_:)**. Saving the full item list every time you add a new item is not ideal. It would be better to only save the items when the app is about to close, but for the purposes of iTahDoodle, saving after every addition is fine.

Build and run your application. Add some items to the to-do list. You should see a logged message after each addition documenting that the to-do list has been saved.

## Loading TodoList

Loading saved to-do lists uses many of the same features as saving them. Add a **loadItems()** method to **TodoList**.

Listing 27.11  Loading a saved to-do list (`TodoList.swift`)

```
class TodoList: NSObject {
    private let fileURL: NSURL = {
        let documentDirectoryURLs = NSFileManager.defaultManager().URLsForDirectory(
            .DocumentDirectory, inDomains: .UserDomainMask)
        let documentDirectoryURL = documentDirectoryURLs.first!
        return documentDirectoryURL.URLByAppendingPathComponent("todolist.items")
    }()

    private var items: [String] = []

    func saveItems() {
        let itemsArray = items as NSArray

        print("Saving items to \(fileURL)")
        if !itemsArray.writeToURL(fileURL, atomically: true) {
            print("Could not save to-do list")
        }
    }

    func loadItems() {
        if let itemsArray = NSArray(contentsOfURL: fileURL) as? [String] {
            items = itemsArray
        }
    }

    func addItem(item: String) {
        items.append(item)
        saveItems()
    }
}
...
```

The **loadItems()** method first grabs the same file URL that you saved the items to in **saveItems()**. Next, you attempt to construct an **NSArray** using its initializer, which expects a URL from which the array should be loaded. If the array can be constructed and you can cast the array to **[String]**, you store it in **TodoList**'s items property.

You can now load the saved to-do list, but when should you do so? The simplest answer is to attempt to load the saved items when you first create a **TodoList**. So far, you have been taking advantage of the no-argument initializer provided automatically, but now you need to write an explicit initializer.

## Listing 27.12  Adding an explicit initializer (`TodoList.swift`)

```
class TodoList: NSObject {
    private let fileURL: NSURL = {
        let documentDirectoryURLs = NSFileManager.defaultManager().URLsForDirectory(
            .DocumentDirectory, inDomains: .UserDomainMask)
        let documentDirectoryURL = documentDirectoryURLs.first!
        return documentDirectoryURL.URLByAppendingPathComponent("todolist.items")
    }()

    private var items: [String] = []

    override init() {
        super.init()
        loadItems()
    }

    ...
}
...
```

You add a new **init()** method that overrides **NSObject**'s initializer. In the implementation, you call the superclass initializer, which you are required to do before you access self in any way (for example, by calling methods). Finally, you attempt to load the saved items. If loading fails, the **TodoList** will be created with an empty items array.

And with that, you are now the proud author of your first iOS application! There is much more to learn about iOS development. This chapter has just been a small taste of what awaits you.

# Bronze Challenge

There are a couple of small – but annoying – bugs in iTahDoodle. First, when you add a new item to the to-do list, the text field is not cleared: it keeps the text you just added to the list. Second, you are able to add empty rows to the to-do list by tapping Insert when the text field is empty. Fix both of these bugs.

# Silver Challenge

Your **ViewController** class is currently taking on a little too much responsibility. When it is setting up the table view, the view controller is registering the cell class and reuse identifier, but **TodoList** is the class that actually wants to use the created cells. Fix this problem by coming up with a way for **ViewController** to successfully set up the table view without having to know the details of what kind of cells **TodoList** is going to want.

# Gold Challenge

There is a pretty glaring omission in iTahDoodle: the user cannot remove items! Make it possible for users to remove an item by tapping on it. You already know enough to update **TodoList**. Here is a hint about how to detect when the user taps on a row: make your view controller the table view's delegate. This will require conforming to the **UITableViewDelegate** protocol. **UITableViewDelegate** has a method that will be very useful for this challenge: tapping on a row results in *selection* of that row.

# 28

# Interoperability

Because Swift is a very new language, it will be common in your Mac and iOS development career to work on an existing project implemented in Objective-C. After all, there are many years of Mac and iOS development behind us at this point. If you want to continue development using Swift on projects originally developed in Objective-C, you will need to learn how to make the two languages work together.

This chapter will show you exactly that. If you are not familiar with Objective-C, just follow along and type in the code. Not knowing Objective-C will not stop you from understanding the basic mechanics of interoperability. If you would like to learn more about Objective-C, check out the latest edition of *Objective-C Programming: The Big Nerd Ranch Guide*.

In addition to adding Swift code to an existing Objective-C project, you may need to use the two languages together if you have a Swift project that needs to either interact with the Cocoa or Cocoa Touch SDKs or take advantage of Objective-C.

As you saw in Chapter 26 and Chapter 27, all Mac and iOS apps will need to interact with the Cocoa or Cocoa Touch frameworks. These frameworks provide the basic building blocks for developing Mac and iOS apps, and are mostly written in Objective-C. So using them means interoperating with Objective-C, which affects how you write Swift code.

To see how this works, you will start by writing a small application in Objective-C. Next, you will add a Swift file to that project to define a Swift class and use it in an Objective-C file. Finally, you will create another Objective-C class and use that class in your Swift code.

## An Objective-C Project

To illustrate interoperability, you are going to create a simple version of the iOS Contacts application. The project will begin in Objective-C, and later you will incorporate some new Swift code.

Create a new Xcode project. Choose the Single View Application template under the iOS label (Figure 28.1).

## Figure 28.1  The Single View Application template

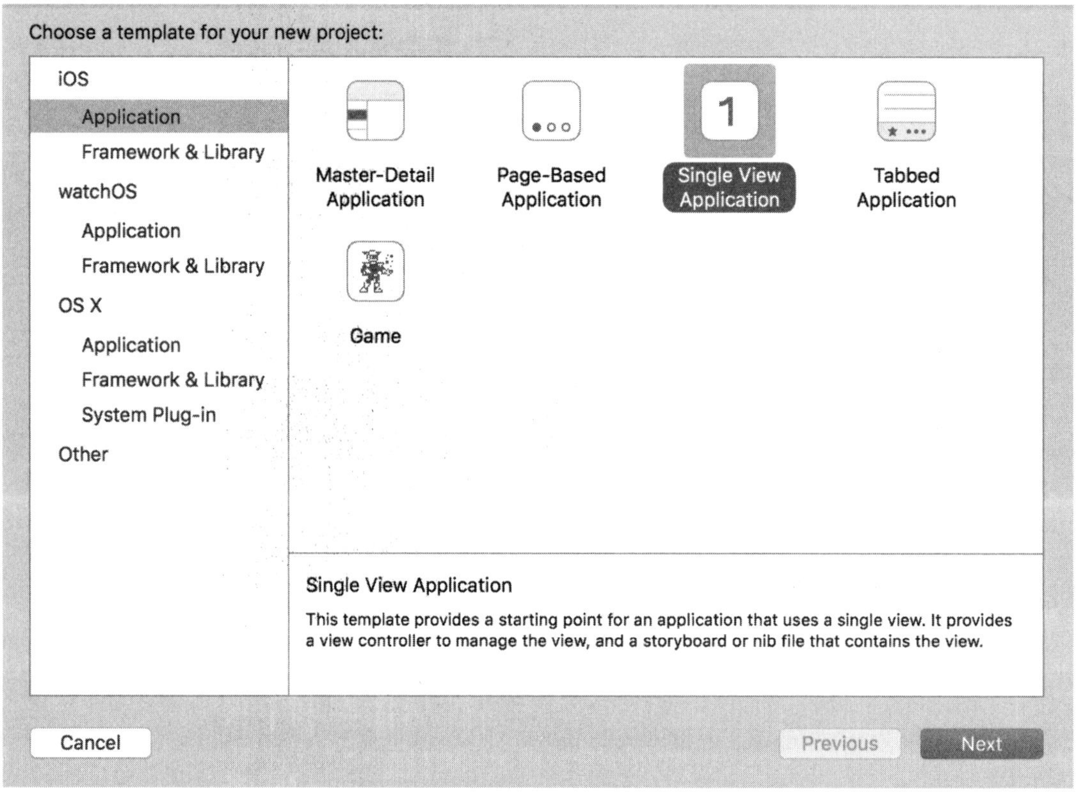

Name the project Contacts and make sure that the language selection is Objective-C (Figure 28.2).

## Figure 28.2 Setting project options

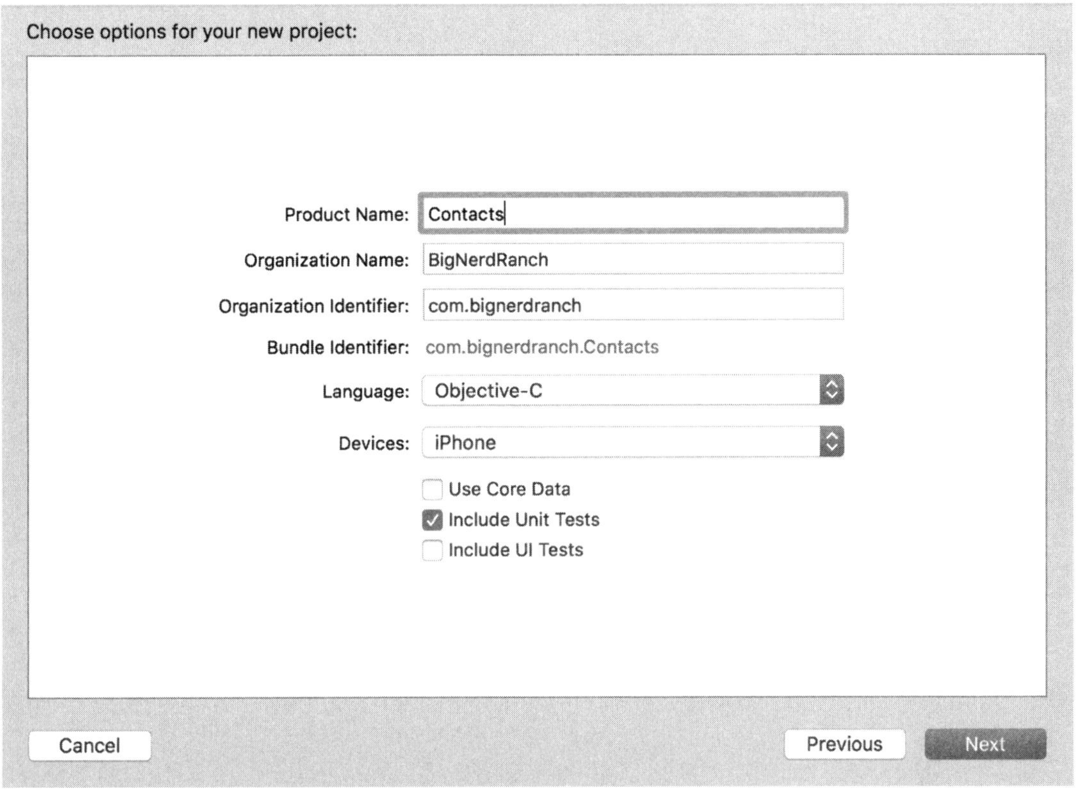

Click Next, choose a location to save your project, and click Create.

# Creating a contacts app

Begin your simple contacts organizer application by adding a table to your main view in the storyboard. This table will hold a list of hardcoded contacts. Remember, a storyboard is an interface provided by Xcode that allows you to manage your views and their relationships.

Open Main.storyboard. Your first step is to delete the view controller that came with the template, as you will not be using it. Select the view controller in the document outline (Figure 28.3).

## Figure 28.3  Deleting a view controller scene

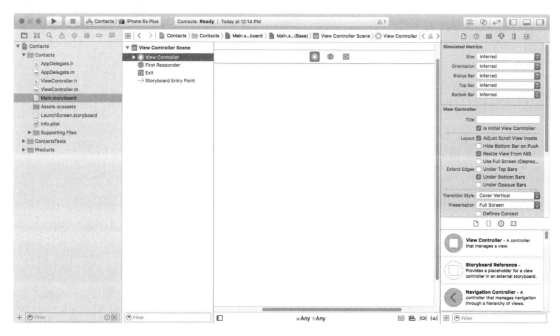

With the view controller selected, press Delete.

Deleting this scene was a necessary step, but it introduced a problem. The scene that you deleted was the application's point of entry upon launch. Therefore, your app no longer has an initial view to display.

In fact, if you try to build and run your application now, you will see the following message log to the console: "Failed to instantiate the default view controller for UIMainStoryboardFile 'Main' – perhaps the designated entry point is not set?" Fix this problem by adding a new default view controller.

Open the object library and search for "table." Drag a Table View Controller onto your storyboard's canvas.

You have now added a new view controller to your storyboard, but you have not yet made it the default. Select the table view controller and open the attributes inspector. Check the box to make the table view controller the Initial View Controller (Figure 28.4).

## Figure 28.4  The attribute inspector

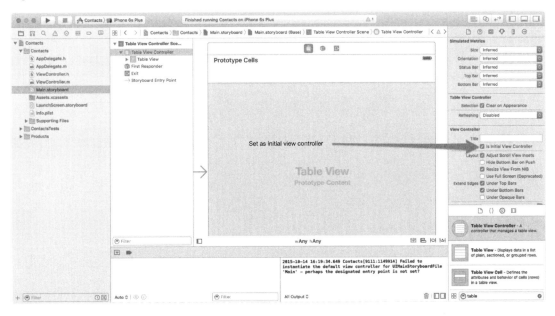

Try running your app now: no error, just an empty table view. To display data in this table view, you need to give the table view a data source, as you saw in Chapter 27.

The first step is to associate the table view controller scene with the **ViewController** class that the template provided. This class was originally associated with the scene that you deleted. Because this relationship was broken when you deleted the view controller's scene, you need to associate this class with the **UITableViewController** in the storyboard. (You could create a brand-new view controller class, but it is simpler to adapt the one that was provided by the template.)

Your first step in adapting the class will be to change its name from the overly generic **ViewController** to **ContactsViewController**. This name more concretely describes its purpose. Click on ViewController.h in the project navigator. Its contents should look like this:

```
#import <UIKit/UIKit.h>

@interface ViewController : UIViewController

@end
```

To rename the class, right-click on `ViewController` and select Refactor → Rename... from the pop-up. In the sheet that pops up, change **ViewController** to **ContactsViewController**, as shown in Figure 28.5.

## Figure 28.5  Renaming **ViewController**

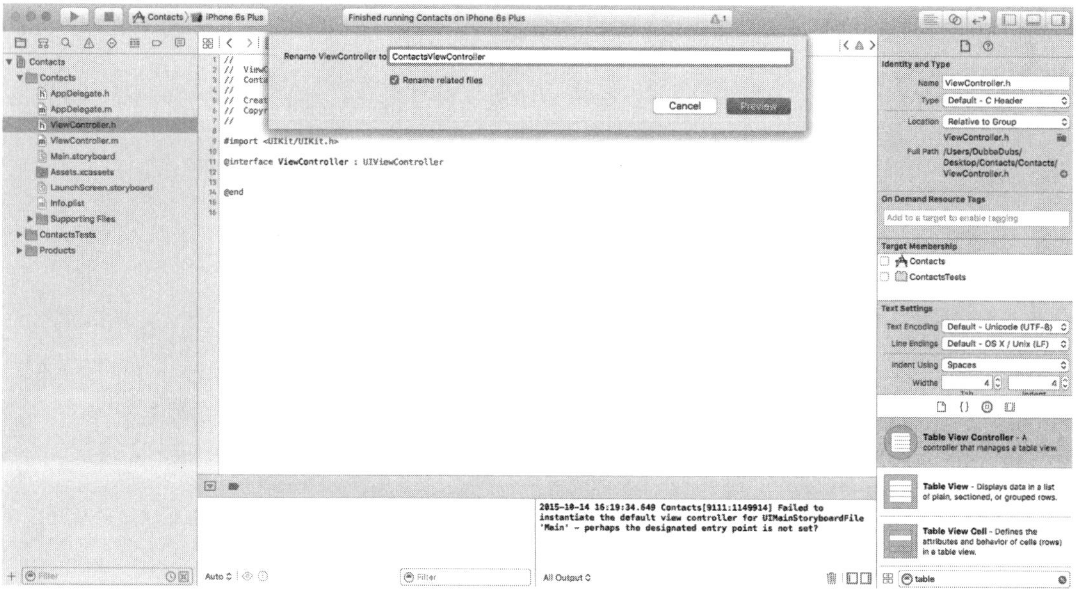

Click Preview, and the sheet will expand to display the changes that will be made. Click Save. (If Xcode asks you if you would like to enable snapshotting, click Enable to proceed.)

Now that your class has a more specific name, the next step is to change its superclass to be **UITableViewController**, the kind of controller you added to your storyboard.

## Listing 28.1  Changing the superclass (`ContactsViewController.h`)

```
#import <UIKit/UIKit.h>

@interface ContactsViewController : UIViewController UITableViewController

@end
```

Now that you have adapted this view controller, you can put it to work. It will be responsible for populating the app's table view with contacts. Your class **ContactsViewController** inherits from **UITableViewController**, which makes it ideal for displaying lists. In this case, you want to display a list of contact names.

To make contact names display in the table view, the table view controller will need to know what contacts should be displayed and it will need to serve as the table view's data source.

**UITableViewController** conforms to the **UITableViewDataSource** protocol. Conformance requires that you implement two methods, but before you do this you will create an array containing some hardcoded strings for contact names. Switch to ContactsViewController.m to add a property for this array in the class extension. Give this array some data in **initWithCoder:**.

## Listing 28.2 Hardcoding contact names (ContactsViewController.m)

```
#import "ContactsViewController.h"

@interface ContactsViewController ()

@property (nonatomic, readonly, strong) NSMutableArray *contacts;

@end

@implementation ContactsViewController

- (id)initWithCoder:(NSCoder *)aDecoder {
    self = [super initWithCoder:aDecoder];
    if (self) {
        NSArray *contactArray = @[@"Johnny Appleseed",
                                  @"Paul Bunyan",
                                  @"Calamity Jane"];
        _contacts = [NSMutableArray arrayWithArray:contactArray];
    }
    return self;
}

- (void)viewDidLoad {
    [super viewDidLoad];
    // Do any additional setup after loading the view, typically from a nib.
}

- (void)didReceiveMemoryWarning {
    [super didReceiveMemoryWarning];
    // Dispose of any resources that can be recreated.
}

@end
```

This mutable array, named contacts, contains a small list of strings for contacts that you will display on the table view. In order to get these names in the table, you will need to implement the required methods in the **UITableViewDataSource** protocol. Add the following method implementations to populate the table with data.

## Listing 28.3  Implementing required methods for protocol conformance (ContactsViewController.m)

```
...

- (void)viewDidLoad {
    [super viewDidLoad];
    // Do any additional setup after loading the view, typically from a nib.
    [self.tableView registerClass:[UITableViewCell class]
           forCellReuseIdentifier:@"UITableViewCell"];
}

- (void)didReceiveMemoryWarning {
    [super didReceiveMemoryWarning];
    // Dispose of any resources that can be recreated.
}

- (NSInteger)tableView:(UITableView *)tableView
 numberOfRowsInSection:(NSInteger)section
{
    return self.contacts.count;
}

- (UITableViewCell *)tableView:(UITableView *)tableView
         cellForRowAtIndexPath:(NSIndexPath *)indexPath
{
    UITableViewCell *cell = [tableView
                             dequeueReusableCellWithIdentifier:@"UITableViewCell"
                                          forIndexPath:indexPath];

    NSString *contact = self.contacts[indexPath.row];

    cell.textLabel.text = contact;

    return cell;
}
```

Here, you register the **UITableViewCell** class with the table view controller's tableView property so the table view knows how to create new cells and reuse existing ones. Next, you use the contacts property to determine the number of rows the table view needs to provide in **tableView:numberOfRowsInSection:**. You also ask the table view for an instance of **UITableViewCell**, if necessary, in **tableView:cellForRowAtIndexPath:**. In this data source method, you use the current indexPath to put the appropriate contact name in the cell instance. Finally, you return the cell to display it in the table view.

Build and run the application. Your contact names are not displayed on the table. You made **ContactsViewController** the table view's data source and gave it contacts data. What is the problem? One thing is missing: you have not yet associated the table view controller scene in the storyboard with the class that contains the data source code.

You can make this association in the Main.storyboard file. Open the storyboard and click on the table view controller scene. Make sure to have the utilities area displayed. In the inspector pane, click on the identity inspector icon, which is third from the left.

Find the section labeled Custom Class. This section provides a Class field to identify the custom class that should be associated with the scene. Currently, that class is defaulting to **UITableViewController**, which is why your table view is not displaying your contact names.

Change the value of this field to be **ContactsViewController**. Your storyboard should now look like Figure 28.6.

Figure 28.6  Table view controller scene's custom class

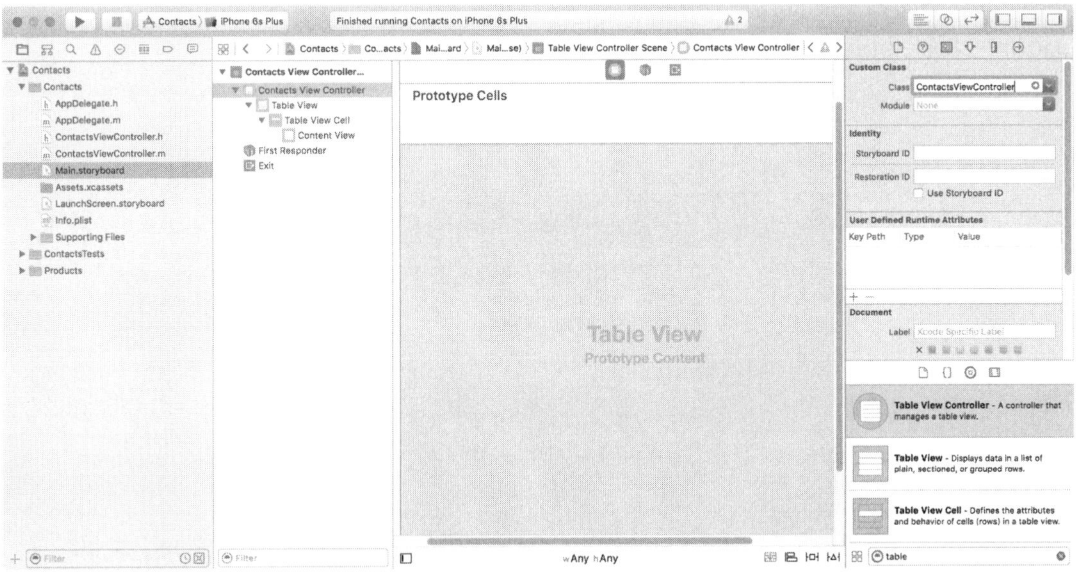

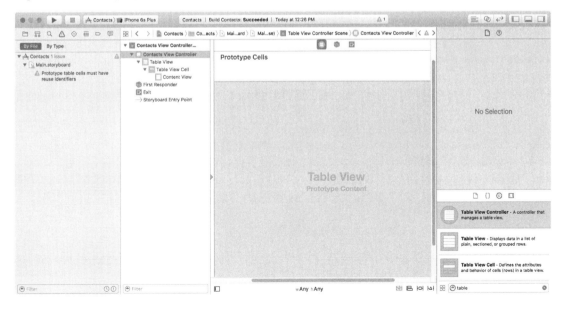

While you are here, you can take care of the warning coming from the storyboard. At the top of the project navigator, choose the issue navigator icon, which is fourth from the left (Figure 28.7). This navigator displays your project's current warnings and errors.

Figure 28.7  Displaying issues in the issue navigator

The issue navigator shows a warning from Main.storyboard that you need to give your prototype table cells a reuse identifier. Because you are not using the prototype cells feature on the storyboard, you can resolve this issue by telling the table view that it will not use prototype cells. In Main.storyboard, make sure that the document outline is displayed. Expand the Contacts View Controller so that you can see its hierarchy, as in Figure 28.8.

Figure 28.8  Table view outline in storyboard

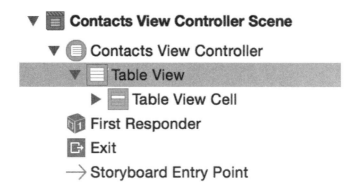

Select the table view and make sure that the utilities area is displayed. In the inspector pane, select the attributes inspector. Find the field for Prototype Cells and change the number to 0 (Figure 28.9).

Figure 28.9  Changing the prototype cells in storyboard

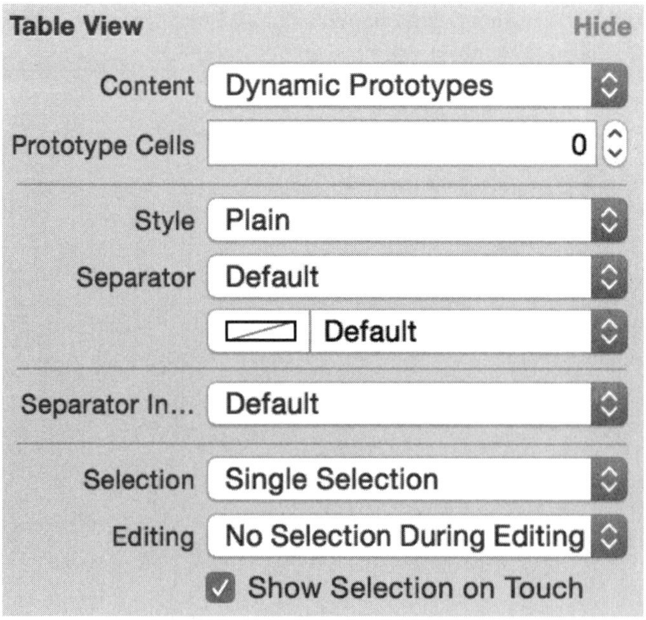

Build and run the application, and you should see the warning disappear and data populate the table view, as in Figure 28.10.

Figure 28.10 Displaying the contacts

# Adding Swift to an Objective-C Project

Now that you have a small Objective-C project working, it is time to add some Swift files. Imagine, for example, that you have an epiphany: it would be far better not to hardcode your contacts as strings in an array. Instead, you could create a **Contact** type and then display the contacts' names in the table. You decide to use Swift for your new type because you heard how safe its initialization process is, and you want to take advantage of it.

Add a new Swift file to your project. Click File → New → File.... In the window that pops up, select Swift File and click Next (Figure 28.11).

Figure 28.11  Adding a new Swift file

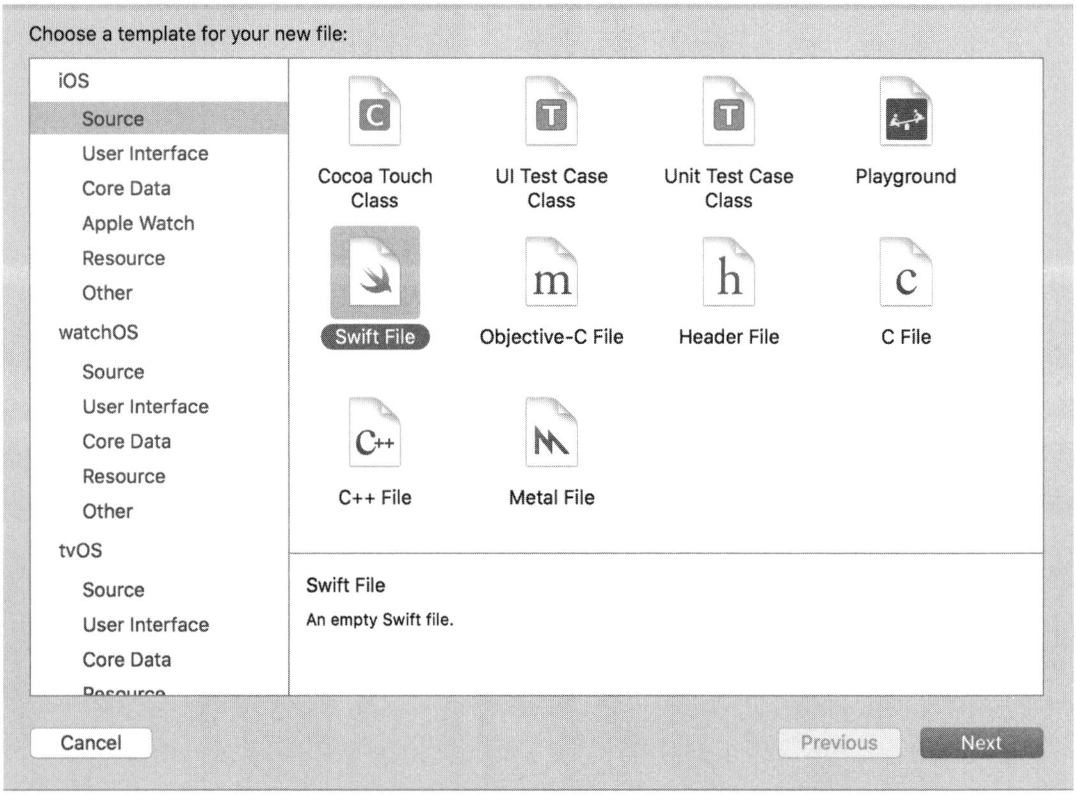

In the next window, name the file Contact.swift. Also, make sure the box at the bottom that adds the new file to the Contacts target is checked. Click Create.

Because you are now adding a Swift file to your Objective-C project, Xcode asks if you would like to add a *bridging header* (Figure 28.12).

Figure 28.12  Would you like to configure an Objective-C bridging header?

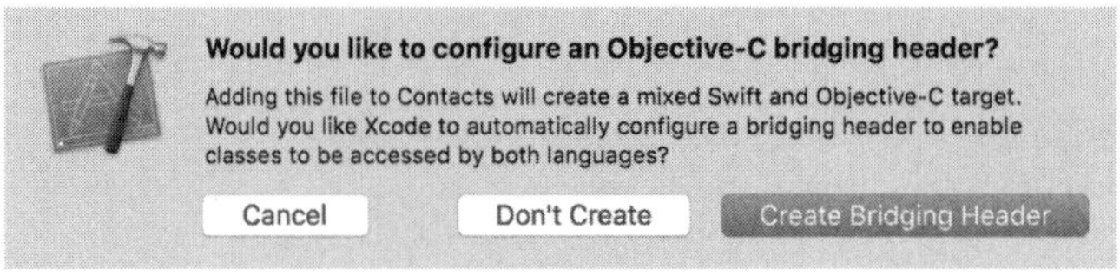

Click Create Bridging Header. Xcode will create your new Swift file, `Contact.swift`, as well as the Objective-C *bridging header*, `Contacts-Bridging-Header.h`. The bridging header is used to bridge from Objective-C code to Swift code.

Find and select the `Contacts-Bridging-Header.h` file in the project navigator. You will see that it is empty except for the following comments.

### Listing 28.4 Looking at `Contacts-Bridging-Header.h`

```
//
//  Use this file to import your target's public headers
//  that you would like to expose to Swift.
//
```

As you can see, nothing is entered to this file for you. Later in this chapter, you will add an import of the header file of a class written in Objective-C that you would like to expose to Swift. That is the role of the bridging header.

But that comes later. Now, it is time to create your **Contact** class. Switch to the `Contact.swift` file and add the following code.

### Listing 28.5 Creating the **Contact** class (Contact.swift)

```
import Foundation

class Contact: NSObject {
    let name: String
    init(contactName: String) {
        name = contactName
    }
}
```

Your new class inherits from **NSObject**, which allows it to be exposed to the Objective-C portion of the application. Subclassing from an Objective-C class is necessary to call Swift code from Objective-C. In this example, you subclass from **NSObject**, which is the base class in Objective-C. **Contact**'s simple implementation includes a `name` property for instances of this class and an initializer with a `contactName` parameter to help prepare the instance.

If this project were written solely in Swift, you would probably want to make **Contact** a struct. However, this would not work for your mixed Objective-C/Swift project, because Swift's structs are not visible to Objective-C.

Now that you have written the class, you are ready to use it in your Objective-C code. You are going to change **ContactsViewController** to maintain an array of **Contact** objects rather than an array of **String**s.

First, you need to import an Xcode-generated header file into `ContactsViewController.m`. This will allow you to use your new Swift **Contact** class in the table view controller.

## Listing 28.6  Importing the `Contacts-Swift.h` header file (`ContactsViewController.m`)

```
#import "ContactsViewController.h"
#import "Contacts-Swift.h"

@interface ContactsViewController ()

@property (nonatomic, strong) NSMutableArray *contacts;

@end

...
```

This header file, `Contacts-Swift.h`, exposes your Swift code to the file that imports it. It contains interfaces for your Swift code to share with the Objective-C component of your application.

The naming convention for these header files is: `ProductModuleName-Swift.h`. Here, the product name is `Contacts` – as is the module name, because this application has a single target. Thus, the name for your generated header is `Contacts-Swift.h`.

Now that the **Contact** class is visible in `ContactsViewController.m`, change the `contacts` array to hold instances of the **Contact** class instead of hardcoded strings. Also, be sure to use `contact`'s name in the data source method, **`tableView:cellForRowAtIndexPath:`**.

## Listing 28.7  Updating the contacts array (`ContactsViewController.m`)

```objc
#import "ContactsViewController.h"
#import "Contacts-Swift.h"

@interface ContactsViewController ()

@property (nonatomic, strong) NSMutableArray *contacts;

@end

@implementation ContactsViewController

- (id)initWithCoder:(NSCoder *)aDecoder {
    self = [super initWithCoder:aDecoder];
    if (self) {
        NSArray *contactArray = @[@"Johnny Appleseed",
                                  @"Paul Bunyan",
                                  @"Calamity Jane"];
        Contact *c1 = [[Contact alloc] initWithContactName: @"Johnny Appleseed"];
        Contact *c2 = [[Contact alloc] initWithContactName: @"Paul Bunyan"];
        Contact *c3 = [[Contact alloc] initWithContactName: @"Calamity Jane"];
        _contacts = [NSMutableArray arrayWithArray:contactArray @[c1, c2, c3]];
    }
    return self;
}

- (void)viewDidLoad {
    [super viewDidLoad];
    // Do any additional setup after loading the view, typically from a nib.
    [self.tableView registerClass:[UITableViewCell class]
            forCellReuseIdentifier:@"UITableViewCell"];
}

- (void)didReceiveMemoryWarning {
    [super didReceiveMemoryWarning];
    // Dispose of any resources that can be recreated.
}

- (NSInteger)tableView:(UITableView *)tableView
 numberOfRowsInSection:(NSInteger)section
{
    return self.contacts.count;
}

- (UITableViewCell *)tableView:(UITableView *)tableView
        cellForRowAtIndexPath:(NSIndexPath *)indexPath
{
    UITableViewCell *cell = [tableView
                        dequeueReusableCellWithIdentifier:@"UITableViewCell"
                                             forIndexPath:indexPath];

    NSString Contact *contact = self.contacts[indexPath.row];

    cell.textLabel.text = contact.name;

    return cell;
}
```

Build and run the application. You should see the same results on the simulator.

# Adding contacts

You are now using your new Swift type, but you are still hardcoding the contacts' names. This practice is obviously unsustainable – what if a user wants to add a contact? Your application needs a mechanism to add new contacts.

Begin by removing your hardcoded contacts. Instead, initialize an empty `contacts` array to be filled with data later.

### Listing 28.8  Replacing hardcoded contact names with an array (`ContactsViewController.m`)

```
...

- (id)initWithCoder:(NSCoder *)aDecoder {
    self = [super initWithCoder:aDecoder];
    if (self) {
        Contact *c1 = [[Contact alloc] initWithContactName: @"Johnny Appleseed"];
        Contact *c2 = [[Contact alloc] initWithContactName: @"Paul Bunyan"];
        Contact *c3 = [[Contact alloc] initWithContactName: @"Calamity Jane"];
        _contacts = [NSMutableArray arrayWithArray: @[c1, c2, c3];
        _contacts = [NSMutableArray array];
    }
    return self;
}

...
```

Next, create a new file that will be a new view controller to handle contact creation.

When you are asked to choose a template for the new file, select Source under the iOS section, then Cocoa Touch Class. You are going to subclass a class available in UIKit, which is only available for iOS projects. Name this new file NewContactViewController, and make it a subclass of **UIViewController**. Also, make sure to choose Swift as the language (Figure 28.13).

## Figure 28.13  Subclassing **UIViewController**

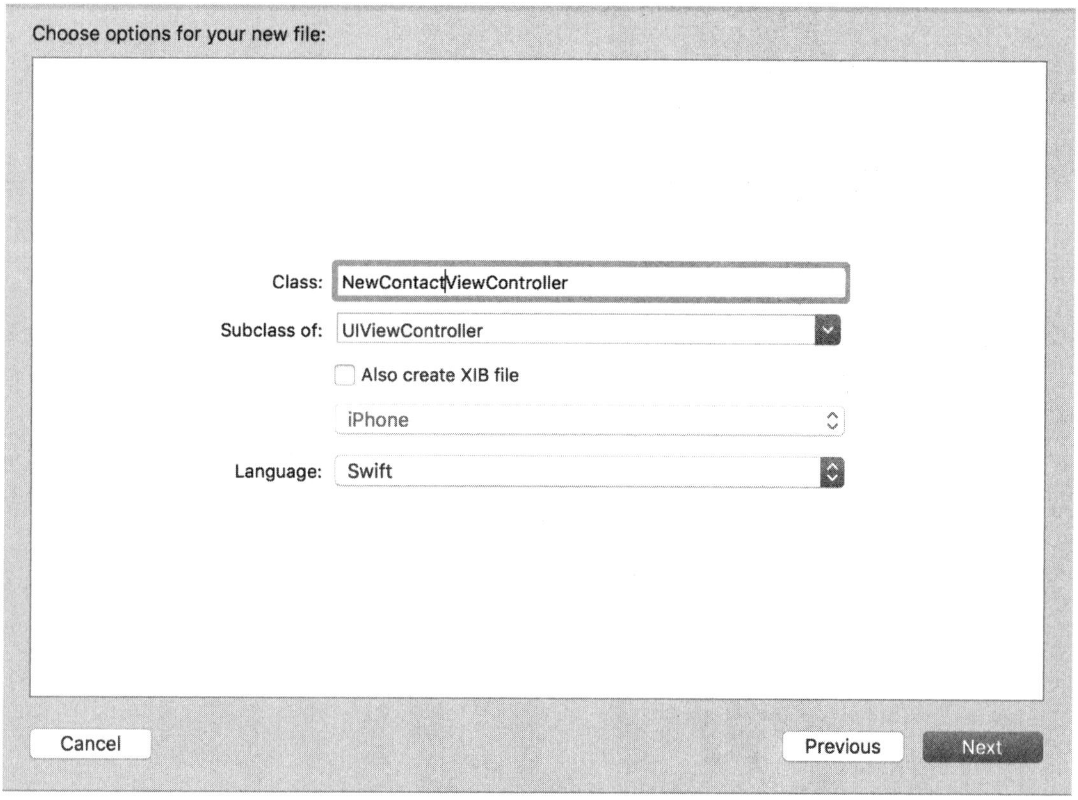

Choose options for your new file:

| | |
|---|---|
| Class: | NewContact|ViewController |
| Subclass of: | UIViewController |
| | ☐ Also create XIB file |
| | iPhone |
| Language: | Swift |

Cancel   Previous   Next

Click Next and make sure to create the file with the project's target selected.

You are going to fill in the details of this new class, **NewContactViewController**, in just a bit. For now, switch to the Main.storyboard file and select the contacts view controller. You need to add something to the view that a user can select to add a new contact. You will add a navigation bar to the top of the view with a button to launch **NewContactViewController**.

The simplest way to do this is to add a **UINavigationController** as the initial view controller of the storyboard. Search for a navigation controller in the object library. Drag one of these onto the storyboard canvas.

Dropping a **UINavigationController** object onto the storyboard gives you a navigation controller with an empty root view controller scene. You do not really need this extra scene. In fact, you have already created a root view controller – contacts view controller. Delete the root view controller scene.

Next, make the navigation controller the initial view controller. In the document outline, expand the Navigation Controller Scene and select the Navigation Controller. Open the attributes inspector and check the Is Initial View Controller box.

Note that this change means that the app currently has no way to display the contacts view controller scene. Fix this by creating a *relationship segue* between the navigation controller and the contacts view controller. Select the navigation controller scene and Control-drag from the navigation controller to the contacts view controller. In the pop-up, choose the root view controller option from the relationship segue section (Figure 28.14).

## Figure 28.14  Setting the root view controller

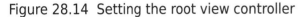

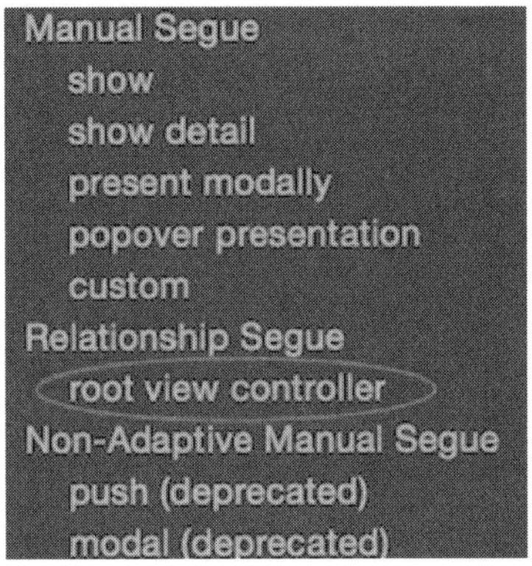

Your app is now living inside of a navigation controller. This means that every view controller inside of the navigation controller will have a configurable **UINavigationItem**, which gives access to a `title` property that can be set in the storyboard. Click on the contacts view controller scene and select the navigation item. Find the field in the attributes inspector for the item's `title`. Enter **Contacts** into this field.

If you build and run the application, you will see the same empty table view, but it will now be included in a navigation controller and will have a navigation item with Contacts as the title.

Next, add a button to the navigation bar. Search for a **UIBarButtonItem** in the object library. Drag an instance of this type onto the righthand side of the contacts view controller scene's navigation item (Figure 28.15).

Figure 28.15  Adding a bar button item to the navigation item

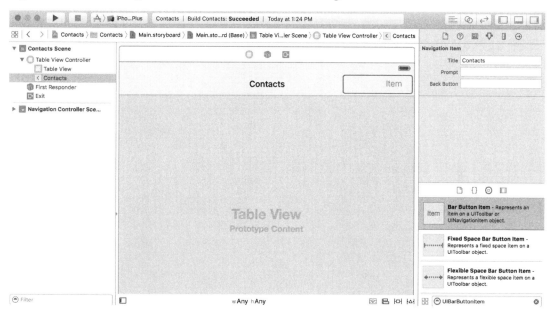

Select the new **UIBarButtonItem** and change its appearance. In the attributes inspector, change the button's identifier from Custom to Add. The button changes to a graphic plus symbol.

You want this bar button item to launch a new view that is dedicated to creating a new contact. Drag a new view controller from the object library onto the storyboard. Associate the new view controller with your new Swift class, **NewContactViewController**, by clicking on the view controller and changing its class name in the identity inspector to **NewContactViewController**. In the document outline, the view controller scene is renamed New Contact View Controller Scene.

Now you need to add some labels and text fields to the new contact view controller so that users can add a new contact. Drag two instances of **UILabel** and two **UITextField**s from the object library onto the storyboard. Set the view up as shown in Figure 28.16.

### Figure 28.16  New contact view controller

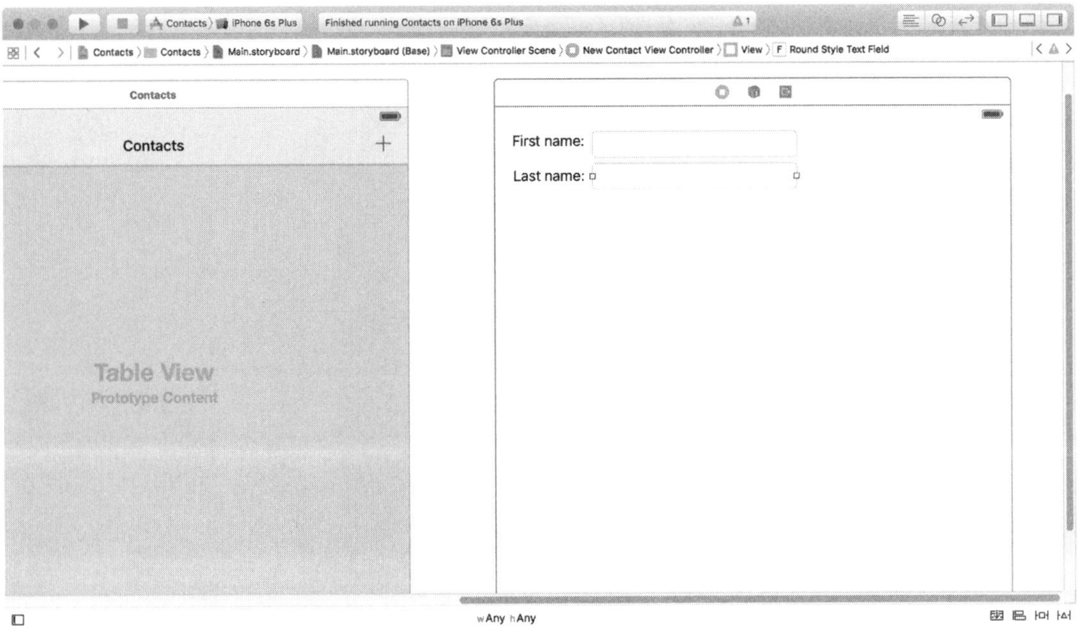

Next, you need to connect a segue between the **UIBarButtonItem** on the table view controller's navigation bar and **NewContactViewController**. Control-drag from the plus button to the new contact view controller scene. Release the mouse, and a menu pops up asking what sort of Action Segue you want to create. Select Present Modally.

Build and run the application. Click the plus button, and you will find that the **NewContactViewController**'s view is presented modally.

So far, so good. But you are not finished. There is no way to dismiss the view once the user has entered the new contact's information. And there is no way for the user to save the new contact. The next step is to give the user a way to save the new contact and dismiss the view controller.

You could just add a button to the view controller to let the user save the entered contact information and dismiss the **NewContactViewController**. But it would look clunky in combination with the navigation bar button you already have. Instead, you are going to embed the **NewContactViewController** inside a navigation controller. Then you can add a button to the new contact view controller's navigation item. Actually, you are going to add two buttons to the navigation item: one to save the new contact and one to cancel the process.

Drag a new **UINavigationController** from the object library and drop it on the canvas in Main.storyboard. As before, you will need to replace this navigation controller's root view controller with the existing New Contact View Controller. Delete the existing root view controller, Control-drag from the navigation controller to the **NewContactViewController**, and select the root view controller relationship segue.

Now that **NewContactViewController** is embedded within a **UINavigationController**, you can set its navigation item's title as you did for **ContactsViewController** earlier. Select **NewContactViewController**'s naviation item and change its title to "Contact."

Though you have made the new contact view controller the root view controller of your new navigation controller, if you run the app now the new contact view controller will not be displayed inside a navigation controller. The contacts view controller does not know about the new navigation controller. To fix that, you are going to replace the **ContactViewController**'s plus button's segue with one whose destination is the new navigation controller.

Control-click on **ContactsViewController**'s plus button and click the small x button next to present modally, as in Figure 28.17. This deletes the segue.

## Figure 28.17  Deleting a connected segue

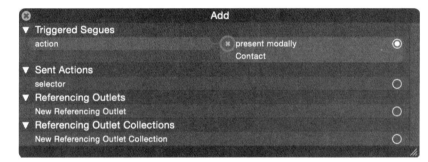

Next, add a segue to display the **UINavigationController**. Control-drag from the plus button to the **UINavigationController**. Choose the option to present the navigation controller modally.

Now you are ready to add two instances of **UIBarButtonItem** to **NewContactViewController**'s navigation bar. Drag them from the object library and place one on the left side of the navigation bar and one on the right. Select the button on the left and, in the attributes inspector, change its title to **Cancel**. Change the title of the button on the right to **Save**. Your storyboard's layout should look like Figure 28.18.

## Figure 28.18  New storyboard layout

Before you set these two buttons' actions, you are going to create two outlets on **NewContactViewController** for the first name and last name text fields. These outlets will allow you to access their text, which you will use to build a new instance of the **Contact** type when the Save button is pressed. Open NewContactViewController.swift and add the following properties for the text fields.

## Listing 28.9  Adding outlets for text fields (NewContactViewController.swift)

```swift
import UIKit

class NewContactViewController: UIViewController {
    @IBOutlet var firstNameTextField: UITextField!
    @IBOutlet var lastNameTextField: UITextField!
    override func viewDidLoad() {
        super.viewDidLoad()

        // Do any additional setup after loading the view.
    }

    override func didReceiveMemoryWarning() {
        super.didReceiveMemoryWarning()
        // Dispose of any resources that can be recreated.
    }

}
```

Now that you have added IBOutlet properties for these text fields, you will connect them in the storyboard. Open Main.storyboard and connect the outlets in the contact scene. Control-dragging from the contact view controller to each text field will allow you to select the appropriate IBOutlet, as you saw in Chapter 26.

With your properties connected to their corresponding **UITextField**s, you are ready to give the two buttons actions so that they can either create a contact or cancel. You will take advantage of a feature of **UIStoryboard** called an *unwind segue*. An unwind segue allows you to define a relationship between a view controller and the view controller that precedes it in the navigation flow. You can think of unwind segues as a mechanism for creating *backwards navigation*. This feature of storyboards is quite handy, as you want to use these buttons to pop back to the user's list of contacts.

To take advantage of unwind segues, you must first write an unwind method programmatically on the view controller you want to unwind to. In this case, you want to unwind to the contacts view controller when the user cancels the creation of a new contact, so you will add the method to **ContactsViewController**.

Open ContactsViewController.m and add the new method.

## Listing 28.10  Adding a method for canceling (ContactsViewController.m)

```
...
- (UITableViewCell *)tableView:(UITableView *)tableView
        cellForRowAtIndexPath:(NSIndexPath *)indexPath
{
    ...
}

- (IBAction)cancelToContactsViewController:(UIStoryboardSegue *)segue
{
    // No action to take if user cancels
}

@end
```

Your new method, **cancelToContactsViewController:**, takes an instance of **UIStoryboardSegue**. Notice, also, that you have exposed this method to the storyboard via the IBAction return type. The segue argument carries with it a lot of useful information, which you will use to capture the new contact's first and last name.

You need to connect the unwind segue to the contact view controller in `Main.storyboard`. Open the storyboard and select the view controller. Notice the Exit icon at the top of the contact scene (Figure 28.19)? You will use this element to connect your new segue to the unwinding action and dismiss the **NewContactViewController**.

## Figure 28.19  Exiting from a scene

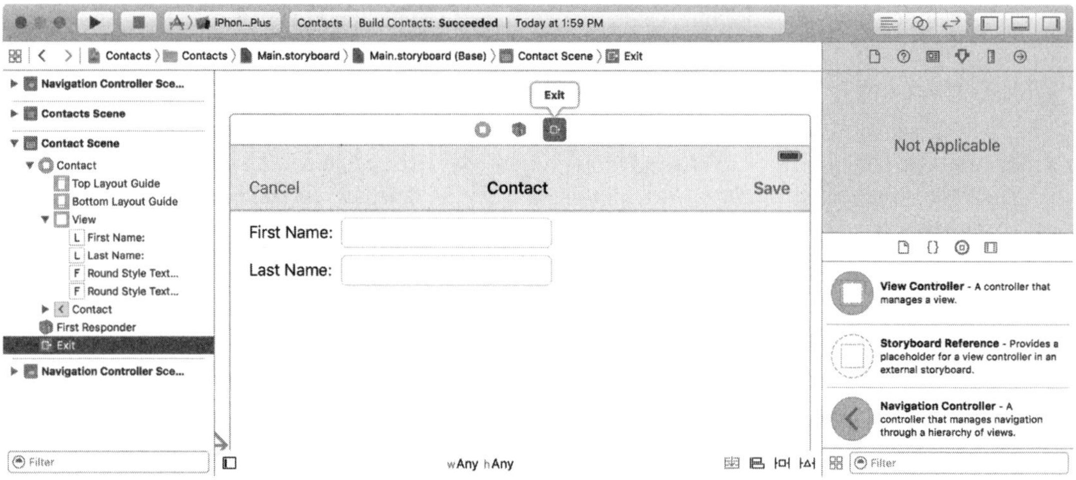

Control-drag from the Cancel bar button item to the Exit icon. Release, and you will see an option to connect the button's action to **cancelToContactsViewController:**. Select this method.

Run your application, tap the button to add a new contact, then tap Cancel. You will unwind back to the table's list of the user's contacts.

Your next step is to wire up the Save bar button to save the new contact's information and also unwind back to the list of contacts. Also, the list of contacts should be updated to display the new contact. You will follow the same strategy as with the Cancel button, but this time you will create an unwind action that makes use of the information sent along with the **UIStoryboardSegue** instance.

Open `ContactsViewController.m` and add a new unwind action. You will use this method when the user clicks the Save button in the contacts scene.

## Listing 28.11  Adding **createNewContact:** (ContactsViewController.m)

```
...

- (UITableViewCell *)tableView:(UITableView *)tableView
        cellForRowAtIndexPath:(NSIndexPath *)indexPath
{
    UITableViewCell *cell = [tableView
                            dequeueReusableCellWithIdentifier:@"UITableViewCell"
                                                forIndexPath:indexPath];

    Contact *contact = self.contacts[indexPath.row];

    cell.textLabel.text = contact.name;

    return cell;
}

- (IBAction)cancelToContactsViewController:(UIStoryboardSegue *)segue
{
    // No action to take if user cancels
}

- (IBAction)createNewContact:(UIStoryboardSegue *)segue
{
    NewContactViewController *newContactVC = segue.sourceViewController;
    NSString *firstName = newContactVC.firstNameTextField.text;
    NSString *lastName = newContactVC.lastNameTextField.text;
    if (firstName.length != 0 || lastName.length != 0) {
        NSString *contactName = [NSString stringWithFormat:@"%@ %@",
                                 firstName, lastName];
        Contact *newContact = [[Contact alloc] initWithContactName:contactName];
        [self.contacts addObject:newContact];
        [self.tableView reloadData];
    }
}

@end
```

Here, you define a new unwind action. This action uses the segue parameter passed into the method's argument to get the sourceViewController that originated the unwind action. After you get the sourceViewController from the segue, you can then grab the text from the **UITextField** property outlets on **NewContactViewController**.

Next, you check to make sure at least one of the strings is not empty. If they contain any text, you create a new instance of the **Contact** type and add it to the contacts property. Last, you reload the tableView to display the new contact's name.

You can now use this method as the unwind action when the user taps the Save button to create a new contact. Switch back to Main.storyboard and select the new contact view controller. Control-drag from the Save button to the Exit icon, and choose **createNewContact:**.

Run the application. Add a new contact and tap Save. You should be transferred back to your list of contacts, and you should see the newly added contact.

# Adding an Objective-C Class

Now that you have interoperated from Objective-C to Swift, your next task is to interoperate from Swift to Objective-C. You will create a new Objective-C class to make a default image for new contacts. Your Swift class **NewContactViewController** will use this new Objective-C class. This simulates a fairly common reality: an existing Mac or iOS project will often have a number of Objective-C classes that are needed in the Swift components of the project.

Create a new Objective-C file that is a Cocoa Touch Class and call it `DefaultImage`. Its job will be to create a new contact's default image. Make this new class a subclass of **NSObject**. Be sure to select Objective-C as the language for this class.

Before you begin to add new code to this class, you need to add a **UIImageView** to the contact scene in `Main.storyboard`. This image view will display the default image for the new contact. Drag an Image View from the object library onto the contact scene. Make the image view 240 points wide and 240 points tall, and place it in the center of the view.

Add Auto Layout constraints to ensure that the view for **NewContactViewController** displays its subviews correctly.

Center the image view in the view with vertical and horizontal constraints. Select the **UIImageView**, and open the Auto Layout Align menu in the bottom righthand corner of the storyboard. Check the options for Horizontal Center in Container and Vertical Center in Container in the menu that appears, as in Figure 28.20. Select the button that says Add 2 constraints.

## Figure 28.20 Centering the image view

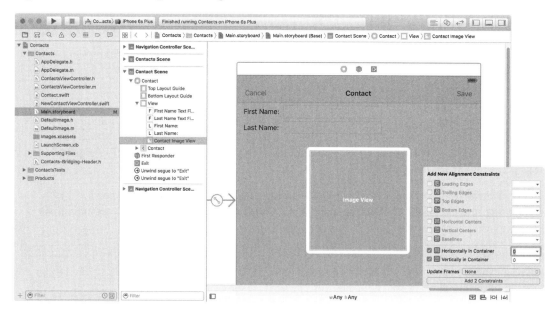

Next, set a width and height constraint for the image view. With the image view still selected, open the Auto Layout Pin menu in the bottom righthand corner of the storyboard. Check the boxes for Width and

Height, leaving the values as they appear (Figure 28.21). Add the two constraints to pin the image view to this width and height.

## Figure 28.21  Width and height constraints for the image view

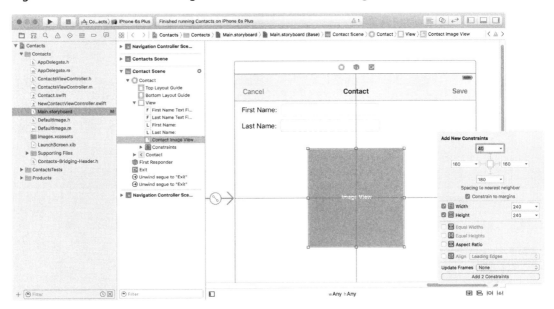

When you are done, your Contact scene should look like Figure 28.22.

## Figure 28.22  New contact view Auto Layout

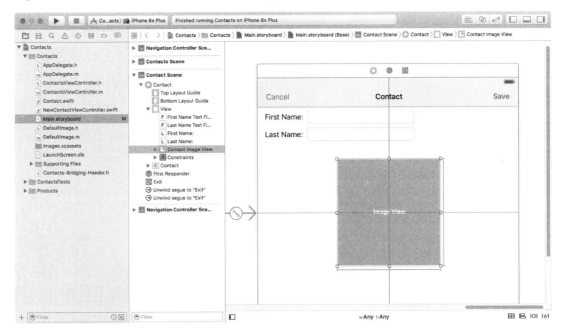

These simple constraints will work fine in portrait mode on the simulator for iPhone 6 or 6 Plus. If you change to a different device or orientation, then the layout will be disturbed.

Now that you have an image view on the contact scene, you need to add a new IBOutlet for the image view to **NewContactViewController**. Add an **UIImageView** property to **NewContactViewController** so that you can set the image that will be displayed. Last, make sure to connect this property to the image view in Main.storyboard.

### Listing 28.12  Adding an IBOutlet to the image view (NewContactViewController.swift)

```
class NewContactViewController: UIViewController {

    @IBOutlet var firstNametext field: UITextField!
    @IBOutlet var lastNametext field: UITextField!
    @IBOutlet var contactImageView: UIImageView!

    override func viewDidLoad() {
        super.viewDidLoad()
    }

    override func didReceiveMemoryWarning() {
        super.didReceiveMemoryWarning()
        // Dispose of any resources that can be recreated.
    }
}
```

Time to implement your **DefaultImage** class. Switch to DefaultImage.h, and add a **generateDefaultImageOfSize** method as shown below. Make sure that you import UIKit at the top of the file.

### Listing 28.13  Implementing **DefaultImage** (DefaultImage.h)

```
#import <UIKit/UIKit.h>

@interface DefaultImage : NSObject

+ (UIImage *)generateDefaultImageOfSize:(CGSize)size;

@end
```

This new method will be the public interface for the **DefaultImage** class. It will use the size argument to do some drawing in an offscreen context. Open DefaultImage.m and enter the drawing code. It is a sizeable block of code – take your time.

## Listing 28.14 Drawing the default image (`DefaultImage.m`)

```objc
#import "DefaultImage.h"

@implementation DefaultImage

+ (UIImage *)generateDefaultImageOfSize:(CGSize)size
{
    // Make frame
    CGRect frame = CGRectMake(0, 0, size.width, size.height);

    // Get image context
    UIGraphicsBeginImageContext(size);

    // Get context reference
    CGContextRef context = UIGraphicsGetCurrentContext();

    // Draw white background to avoid default black
    CGColorRef white = [[UIColor whiteColor] CGColor];
    CGContextSetFillColorWithColor(context, white);
    CGContextFillRect(context, frame);

    // Make yellow circle
    CGColorRef yellow = [[UIColor yellowColor] CGColor];
    CGContextSetFillColorWithColor(context, yellow);
    CGContextFillEllipseInRect(context, frame);

    // Center of circle
    CGFloat x = frame.origin.x + size.width / 2;
    CGFloat y = frame.origin.y + size.height / 2;
    CGPoint center = CGPointMake(x, y);

    // Draw eyes
    CGColorRef black = [[UIColor blackColor] CGColor];
    CGRect leftEyeRect = CGRectMake(center.x - 50, center.y - 50, 20, 20);
    CGRect rightEyeRect = CGRectMake(center.x + 30, center.y - 50, 20, 20);
    CGContextSetFillColorWithColor(context, black);
    CGContextFillEllipseInRect(context, leftEyeRect);
    CGContextFillEllipseInRect(context, rightEyeRect);

    // Draw smile
    CGContextSetLineWidth(context, 5.0);
    CGContextBeginPath(context);
    CGContextMoveToPoint(context, center.x - 50, center.y + 35);
    CGContextAddCurveToPoint(context,
        center.x - 25, center.y + 50,
        center.x + 25, center.y + 50,
        center.x + 50, center.y + 35);
    CGContextStrokePath(context);

    UIImage *image = UIGraphicsGetImageFromCurrentImageContext();
    UIGraphicsEndImageContext();
    return image;
}
@end
```

The drawing code may look pretty gnarly, but do not worry too much about it. The framework you are using here is called Core Graphics, and its details are outside the scope of this book. Apple's documentation on Core Graphics is very thorough if you are curious about what all those functions are doing. The end result is a yellow smiley face, which you are going to use as a contact's default image.

**generateDefaultImageOfSize**'s main job is to create an instance of **UIImage**. To do so, you begin a new graphics context of the appropriate size. You next grab a reference to that context so that you can use various Core Graphics drawing functions. You use **UIGraphicsGetImageFromCurrentImageContext()** to create an image from the current context. Because you created a new context, you had to end it to clean up your drawing environment. Last, you returned the image you created.

When you are interoperating with Objective-C in Swift, it is a good idea to consider how these two languages will communicate with each other in your project. For example, the **generateDefaultImageOfSize:** method provides a simple interface for the Swift code to generate the default image.

Before you can use your Objective-C class in the Swift portions of your project, you need to import the class in the project's bridging header file. Open `Contacts-Bridging-Header.h` and import the header file for **DefaultImage** there. Doing so will ensure that this Objective-C class is available to your Swift code.

## Listing 28.15  Importing the Objective-C class's header in the bridging header file (`Contacts-Bridging-Header.h`)

```
//
//  Use this file to import your target's public headers
//  that you would like to expose to Swift.
//
#import "DefaultImage.h"
```

With the **DefaultImage** class visible to Swift, it is time to use it. Create an instance of **DefaultImage** in **NewContactViewController**'s **viewDidLoad** method.

## Listing 28.16  Using the Objective-C **DefaultImage** class in **NewContactViewController** (`NewContactViewController.swift`)

```
class NewContactViewController: UIViewController {

    @IBOutlet var firstNametext field: UITextField!
    @IBOutlet var lastNametext field: UITextField!
    @IBOutlet var contactImageView: UIImageView!

    override func viewDidLoad() {
        super.viewDidLoad()
        contactImageView.image =
            DefaultImage.generateDefaultImageOfSize(contactImageView.frame.size)
    }

    override func didReceiveMemoryWarning() {
        super.didReceiveMemoryWarning()
        // Dispose of any resources that can be recreated.
    }
}
```

Adding `DefaultImage.h` to the `Contacts-Bridging-Header.h` means that this file will be automatically visible to any Swift file within the same target. You can use the **DefaultImage** class as if it were written in Swift, as you can see in the above implementation of **viewDidLoad**.

Besides importing `DefaultImage.h` into the bridging header, you do not have to do any additional work to use your **DefaultImage** Objective-C class from your Swift code. You simply call **DefaultImage**'s class method just as if it were on a Swift class. Doing so triggers the drawing code in **DefaultImage** and returns an image. The resulting image is given to the `contactImageView`'s image property.

Run the application to see the product of your work. Click the plus button at the upper-right corner of the app to create a new contact. **NewContactViewController** will be displayed with the default image below the text fields (Figure 28.23).

Figure 28.23  A default image for a new contact

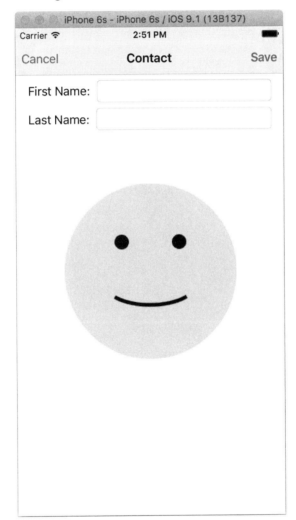

In this chapter, you developed an app that simulates a common real-world programming situation. Many apps that were developed prior to the release of Swift will likely require a mixed-language approach for the near future: older parts will remain in Objective-C, and newer parts will be developed in Swift. The code you wrote for Contacts in Objective-C is like the "older," pre-existing parts of the application. You added "newer" parts in Swift to see the process of organizing an application that needs to take advantage of interoperability.

You will most frequently be interoperating with the Cocoa and Foundation frameworks when you write a Mac or iOS application. This form of interoperation is seamless and is handled for you automatically. Things become more complicated, as you have seen, when you want to interoperate between Objective-C and Swift code that you have written.

# Silver Challenge

Add functionality to the app to allow a user to view a contact's information. A user should be able to tap on a row in **ContactsViewController**, and that should push a new **UIViewController** onto the current **UINavigationController**'s stack. Call this new view controller **ExistingContactViewController** and implement it in Swift.

# Gold Challenge

Users should be able to edit an existing contact's information. Add this functionality to **ExistingContactViewController**. Make sure that the changes made in this view controller are reflected in the **ContactsViewController**.

# 29
# Conclusion

Congratulations, you have made it to the end of this introduction to the Swift programming language. Thank you for sticking with us.

Along the way, you covered quite a bit of material, from the basic features of Swift like `let` and `var` to more advanced features like generics and interoperability. You also saw how to put these pieces together to write pure Swift programs and applied your understanding of Swift to write some simple Mac OS X and iOS applications. You are now a Swift developer.

## Where to Go from Here?

After all your hard work, what should you expect for your Swift development? The truth is that your journey is just beginning. Swift is a rich language, and there is ample opportunity to learn more every day. Furthermore, Swift truly begins to show its power in its interaction with the various Apple frameworks used to develop Mac and iOS applications. That is where you should focus your work.

## Shameless Plugs

Matt and John are both on Twitter. You can follow Matt with `@matthewDmathias`, and you can follow John with `@nerdyjkg`. We occasionally tweet useful information on Swift programming in between our usual photos of cats.

If you enjoyed this book, please take a look at other Big Nerd Ranch texts at `http://www.bignerdranch.com/books`. We have references on Mac OS X and iOS programming and offer weeklong training bootcamps for both that will help you learn these platforms more deeply. Visit `http://www.bignerdranch.com/we-teach` for more details.

## An Invitation

Your knowledge of Swift will continue to grow with practice. Take the time to begin a project; make something new. If you do not have a project available or in mind, visit `https://developer.apple.com`. This website provides a good overview of the resources available to Mac and iOS developers and also provides some examples that may inspire your creativity.

Another recommendation is to find the Meetup groups for Mac and iOS development in your area. Most major cities have such groups, and they host regular talks. Going to these meetings will help you learn, practice, and get to know your peers.

So, come join us. We're out here making things, and we would love to see what you can create.

# Index

## Symbols

! (force-unwrap operator), 66
! (implicitly unwrapped optionals), 69, 201
! (not operator), 21
!= operator, 303
$0 (argument reference), 116
% operator, 109
%= operator, 30
&& operator, 23
&+ operator, 31
*= operator, 30
+ operator, 7
++ operator, 30
+= operator, 7, 30, 81
-- operator, 30
-= operator, 30
. syntax, 154
... syntax, 104
// (code comment), 6
/= operator, 30
: for protocol conformance, 229
< operator, 20, 304
<> syntax, 87, 266
= operator, 7, 11
== operator, 33, 83, 218, 302, 303
=== operator, 218
>= operator, 23
? (failable initializers), 201
? (optional), 65
@IBAction, 331
@IBOutlet, 331
[:] (Dictionary literal syntax), 88
[] (Array literal syntax), 76
\() (string interpolation), 15
\u{} syntax, 60
_ (as parameter name), 206
_ (wildcard), 44
|| operator, 21

## A

a ? b : c statements, 22
access control, 180-183
action segues, 390
addition assignment operator (+=), 7, 30, 81
addition operator (+), 7
advancedBy(_:) function, 62
and operator (&&), 21
append(_:) function, 77
appendContentsOf(_:) method, 71
Application Programming Interfaces (APIs), 6
application sandbox, 367
applications, document-based, 313
ARC (Automatic Reference Counting), 289
arguments
    (see also parameters)
    functions as, 118-120
    shorthand names for, 116
Array index out of range error, 340
Array literals, 76
Array() syntax, 93
arrays
    about, 75
    appending items, 77
    changing items, 79
    checking equality of, 83, 84
    combining, 81, 82
    converting dictionaries to, 93
    copying, 216, 217
    counting items, 78
    creating sets from, 96
    declaring, 75, 76
    filtering, 125
    immutable, 84, 85
    initializing, 76
    inserting items, 82
    looping over, 80, 81
    mapping contents, 124
    NSArray, 368
    reducing, 126
    removing items, 78, 80
    sets vs., 95
    sorting, 113-117
    subscripting, 79, 80
as! operator, 337
assert(_:_:) function, 241
assertions, 241
assignment operator (=), 7, 11
associated types, 271-274
associated values, 138-140
associativity, 29
attributes, 319
attributes inspector, 348, 374